# Land into Water—
# Water into Land

D1089307

UNIVERSITY PRESS OF FLORIDA

Florida A&M University, Tallahassee
Florida Atlantic University, Boca Raton
Florida Gulf Coast University, Ft. Myers
Florida International University, Miami
Florida State University, Tallahassee
New College of Florida, Sarasota
University of Central Florida, Orlando
University of Florida, Gainesville
University of North Florida, Jacksonville
University of South Florida, Tampa
University of West Florida, Pensacola

# Land into Water—
# Water into Land

A History of Water Management in Florida

Nelson Manfred Blake

With Contributions by
Christopher F. Meindl, Steven Noll, and David Tegeder

University Press of Florida
Gainesville/Tallahassee/Tampa/Boca Raton
Pensacola/Orlando/Miami/Jacksonville/Ft. Myers/Sarasota

Copyright 1980 by Nelson M. Blake
Additional content copyright 2010 by Christopher F. Meindl, Steven Noll, and David Tegeder
Printed in the United States of America on acid-free paper
All rights reserved

15  14  13  12  11  10      6  5  4  3  2  1

Library of Congress Cataloging-in-Publication Data
The University Press of Florida is the scholarly publishing agency for the State University System
of Florida, comprising Florida A&M University, Florida Atlantic University, Florida Gulf Coast
University, Florida International University, Florida State University, New College of Florida, University of Central Florida, University of Florida, University of North Florida, University of South
Florida, and University of West Florida.

University Press of Florida
15 Northwest 15th Street
Gainesville, FL 32611-2079
www.upf.com

To Anne

# Contents

# Introduction

Half-remembering some high school encounter with "The Ancient Mariner," the visitor flying into Florida may murmur, "Water, water everywhere..." as the plane follows the east coast down to Daytona Beach or Palm Beach or Fort Lauderdale or Miami. Far below him, the glittering coastline stretches out to the south as far as the eye can see. The Atlantic Ocean spreads out to the eastern horizon with its water, now blue, now green, sparkling in the brilliant sunlight. Sailboats and fishing yachts, like toys in a bathtub, bob in and out of sight. The coast has its own unusual character. Mile after mile of sandy beaches hug the shoreline, but beyond the beaches one sees a narrow ribbon of blue where the intracoastal waterway runs parallel to the shore for hundreds of miles. From the air it is obvious that this is where the population of eastern Florida is concentrated. Along the beaches and waterways and for a few miles inland there are evidences of heavy habitation—high-rise buildings, neat tracts of closely built houses, sprawling shopping centers, and congested highways. But beyond this the newcomer sees a great deal of nothing, stretches of brown and green, reminders that much of Florida's interior is still sparsely settled, a region of sandy wastes, ranch lands, and scattered farms.

If the visitor flies into Tampa, he may have a somewhat different impression since his trip will take him over more of the interior of northern and central Florida and less over the seacoast. The land that stretches below him will be lusher and greener, with thousands of acres of citrus groves dotting the rolling countryside. Here and there he will catch glimpses of glistening water—meandering rivers and scores of lakes, most of them small, but a few impressively large. And as he descends into the airport, he will catch his breath at still another lovely scene of gracious bays, arching bridges, long causeways, and clustering buildings.

The casual observer is conscious only of the great natural beauty of Florida with its juxtaposition of land and water, but the visitor who looks more closely begins to notice something else. Much of the landscape has an oddly unnatural pattern, long stretches of water running in geometrically straight lines. These are the places where the engineers have left their mark, digging mile after mile of canal and ditch. The farther south the traveler flies the more geometrical the scene below him becomes, and he suddenly realizes that very little of this country has been left in its natural state. Not only does the water flow meekly through man-made channels, but the cultivated fields have the sharp angles and the rectangular and triangular shapes imposed by drainage ditches and irrigation canals. In this region obviously man has not so much adapted to nature as he has reordered nature to serve his own ends.

As the plane makes its descent into Fort Lauderdale or Miami, the traveler is even more aware of the artificial character of the scene. He sees not just the usual gridwork of urban streets and avenues but another gridwork of waterways—scores of canals leading off from the intracoastal waterway, thus creating hundreds of waterfront properties, each with its own private dock or mooring place.

The motorist is similarly impressed by the degree to which Florida water has been brought under human control. He almost always finds a drainage ditch running parallel to the road, sometimes on one side, sometimes on both. To build almost any Florida highway or railroad the obvious precondition has been to divert the water into an artificial channel. With herons and egrets wading in the water or hovering on the banks, these drainage ditches are sometimes a delight to the traveler, but at other times when the ditches are putrescent with scum or choked with vegetation they are eyesores. Driving along the Florida turnpike or one of the interstates, the motorist is forever crossing a bridge, and the water beneath him often flows in the straight line characteristic of the great drainage canals that carry the excess water of interior Florida off to the Atlantic Ocean and the Gulf of Mexico. And the traveler soon observes still more evidence that the engineers have been at work: frequent dikes and levees keep the water under control, their great gates either holding it back or permitting it to flow through the canals.

The tourist who visits Lake Okeechobee witnesses an extreme example of this human command over nature. Although this body of water covers almost 700 square miles, an area exceeded by only a few

Everglades in Broward County. The geometrical pattern of the landscape emphasizes man's reordering of nature with drainage canals, ditches, roads, and fields. SPA.

American lakes, it is almost impossible to get a glimpse of it from nearby highways. Surrounded by a huge wall of earth and masonry, the vast expanse of water can be viewed only by driving to the top of this barrier. The principal source of the lake is the Kissimmee River, now rigidly straightened and controlled by gates; the principal outlets are the great artificial waterways that slice straight through the countryside to the Gulf and the Atlantic Ocean. Beside the drainage canals lie vast rectangular fields of sugarcane intercepted by a network of lateral canals and irrigation ditches.

But if the prison-like walls around Lake Okeechobee and the spoke-like canals bespeak the engineers' disciplining of the water on behalf of agriculture, the intracoastal waterway testifies to their beneficence toward the state's other major economic interests, tourism and recreation. When the motorist leaves the north-south expressways and turns east for a view of the Atlantic Ocean, he inevitably finds himself crossing the intracoastal waterway. Glancing right and left as he crosses this canal, he sees that its rigidly straight banks are confined within sturdy bulkheads and generally lined with high-rise apartment houses and condominiums. Frequently he will be delayed as a drawbridge is raised to let through some high-masted sailboat or fancy yacht with towering superstructure. Almost always the passing boat will be a pleasure craft; almost never will it be carrying a cargo. An occasional dredge will be almost the only working vessel to be seen on this aquatic avenue.

To the speeding motorist each Florida community appears to be a tank town. Water towers stand hulking over the one-story commercial buildings and the one-story dwellings that predominate except where high-rises soar along the ocean front and the intracoastal waterway. The larger cities have clusters of them. This ubiquitous structure reminds the visitor that almost every Florida community draws its drinking water from underground sources. Upon the wells, pumps, and tanks, the life of cities and villages depends.

Water is everywhere necessary for human habitation, but in Florida the conservation and management of water gains unusual importance from a number of geological and historical circumstances. The state has a heavy annual rainfall. Over a thirty-year period from 1941 to 1970 Florida's annual precipitation, as measured at Miami, averaged almost 60 inches—more than that of any other state. But the rainfall is highly seasonal, drenching the region with unwanted downpours in the months from May through October and parching it the other six months of the year.

Before the canals and drainage ditches were dug, nature took care of the excess water of the wet season in its own prodigal way. The higher lands were located in the northern and central parts of the state; from these watersheds substantial rivers like the St. Marys, the St. Johns, the Apalachicola, and the Suwannee ran out to the Atlantic Ocean and the Gulf of Mexico. But a much more diffuse flow of water drained most of southern Florida. Gathering up water from the swampy interior, the meandering Kissimmee River discharged its swollen burden into the vast shallow basin of Lake Okeechobee, which in turn regularly overflowed its banks during the rainy season. Some of this water eventually found channels to the Atlantic Ocean through such rivers as the St. Lucie, the New, and the Miami, and to the Gulf through the Caloosahatchee. But a major portion of it simply flowed sluggishly through the Everglades southward and westward until it eventually ran out into Florida Bay. As far as the eye could see in this flooded wilderness there was only sawgrass waving in the wind with here and there a slightly elevated tree-covered hammock. The "River of Grass," as one writer called it, was a region some 30 miles wide and 120 miles long. Not only the Everglades but extensive regions of northern and central Florida were too swampy for cultivation in their original condition. In these parts of the state, nature had provided an ideal environment for birds and alligators, but one scarcely inviting to human beings. For the restless Americans who began to settle the state after the annexation

The Everglades, around 1906. Before drainage the Everglades were flooded much of the year, but during the dry months drivers might venture into the region with horse and buggy. SPA.

treaty of 1819, the desire to make "improvements" in nature's arrangements was overwhelming.

But the lakes, rivers, and swamps visible to the settlers did not contain all the water important to their welfare. Wherever they sank their wells, they tapped water not far below the surface. These vital supplies still flow through subterranean channels peculiar to the state's geological structure. Beneath the state's thin layer of sandy soil lie deep strata of limestone deposited when the ocean covered most of the peninsula during periods between the glaciers. Surplus water accumulated during Florida's wet season soaks through the soil and into this highly permeable limestone. Thence it replenishes

the vast underground reservoirs or aquifers on which Florida cities
and towns depend for their water supplies. Fortunately, the principal engineering works—the dams, levees, drainage canals, and irrigation ditches—have so far interfered mostly with the flow of surface
water and left largely undisturbed the subterranean streams on
which the health of the urban population depends. But the aquifers
are by no means unthreatened. Excessive growth of population with
the resulting heavy use of water for drinking, washing, sanitizing,
air-conditioning, and lawn sprinkling creates such demands on the
underground supplies as to lower the water table near the coasts and
allow salt water to invade the aquifers. Runaway growth also
threatens to pollute the aquifers with inadequately treated sewage
and industrial wastes. An even greater threat, recently warded off,
was the cross-Florida barge canal that would have bisected the
peninsula, disrupting the vital southward flow of surface water and
endangering the underground flow with leakages of oil and other
contaminants.

Bitter controversy over the barge canal dramatized the fact that
there are two levels of politics in Florida. The first concerns parties
and personalities, Democrats and Republicans, and competing factions within each party. The second and ultimately more important
struggle is that between competing interest groups: real estate
promoters and construction workers pushing for rapid growth and
development; sugar growers, citrus grove owners, ranchers, and
vegetable growers resisting urban sprawl and seeking to open new
acreage to agriculture; city dwellers trying to protect and enhance
the pleasures of urban life with flowering shrubs, green lawns, and
swimming pools; hunters and fishermen yearning to preserve conditions that have long made Florida a sportsman's paradise; bird-
watchers and nature lovers seeking to protect the wilderness. For all
these competing groups water is a primary concern. Each feels its
interest threatened by the water demands of the others. Too much
drainage and diversion of water ruins the fishing; too much water or
too little water in the drainage canals injures the croplands; too much
consumption of water for irrigation threatens both the wildlife of the
Everglades and the water supplies of the cities; too much development of new urban areas creates water shortages in the older sections. Somewhat unwillingly, state and federal agencies have become deeply involved in the problems of water management and
find themselves pushed this way and that by the conflicting interest
groups.

How did Florida get this way? Why and when were the waterways, the canals, and the ditches dug? Why and when were the swamplands drained? What visions of progress danced before the eyes of the settlers and influenced the early politicians? What dreams of profit impelled succeeding generations of businessmen to

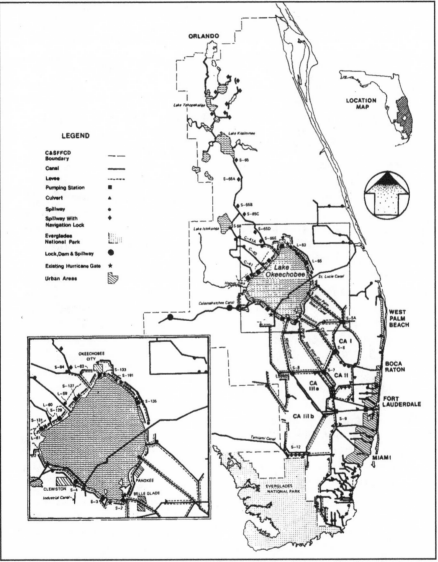

Works of the Central and Southern Florida flood control project. Canals and locks control the inlets and outlets of Lake Okeechobee. From Florida Division of State Planning, *Final Report on the Special Project to Prevent Eutrophication of Lake Okeechobee.*

concoct vast schemes for cutting up the landscape? Why did the shifting goals of the populace—private aggrandizement, agricultural expansion, reclamation, flood control, conservation, environmentalism—favor a certain public policy at one time and quite different ones during later periods? It is to answer such questions as these that this book is written.

The story of man and water in Florida might have been carried back into remote times. Archaeological discoveries have suggested that some of the early Indian tribes built villages upon the islands off the Florida coast and sometimes dug canals to support their culture. But to keep this account within manageable bounds we begin with the raising of the American flag over the territory in 1821. Settlers making their way to this new frontier needed communications and at once began to agitate for better harbors and artificial waterways. The powerful American passion for "internal improvements" has been continuously at work in Florida history. Without this motivation the state would never have developed as a supplier of citrus crops, sugar, vegetables, and cattle, a year-round home for thousands of pensioners, and a vacation spot for hordes of tourists. From the beginning the boosters yearned to do things with Florida water—to prevent shipwrecks by building sheltered waterways along the coasts, to save sailing time by digging a canal across the peninsula, to facilitate the building of roads and railroads by digging drainage ditches, to create new farmlands by draining the swamps. During the nineteenth century the engineers began to rearrange the water of Florida; during the twentieth century they carried out their most ambitious projects. At first it was only an occasional eccentric who questioned the desirability of all these improvements and asked whether the digging and damming might be carried too far. But in recent years a much more broadly based environmental movement has developed, asking ever more insistently whether excessive interference with nature might not jeopardize not only the beauty of the wilderness but the health and well-being of the people.

The story of man and water in Florida history is in some respects unique because of the state's special conditions of climate and terrain. But it is nevertheless relevant to the larger problems of American, indeed of world, civilization. Everywhere the same questions arise: Must the growth of population and the advance of technology inevitably cause such waste of resources and pollution of the air and water that human life will be increasingly threatened? Or can men before it is too late learn to analyze their problems, perceive their alternatives, make their choices, and persist in the policies that these choices require?

# 1 The Watery Eden

With the ratification of the Adams-Onis Treaty in February 1821 the United States finally came into legal possession of the Florida peninsula. Although a few Americans—naturalists, ship-wrecked sailors, adventurous traders, General Andrew Jackson and his troops—had visited Spanish Florida or squatted on its soil, the great majority knew very little about this remote region except that it had been a hideout for marauding Indians and runaway slaves. But in the early years after annexation an increasing number of soldiers and settlers had an opportunity to see the newly acquired territory for themselves. Most of them were enthusiastic.

Lt. George A. McCall, a recent graduate of West Point, exulted in the "glorious clime" of the army base at Pensacola. In January 1823 when most of the United States was in the icy grip of winter, north-western Florida was balmy. Except for a few small fleecy clouds the sky was "clear and serene, unruffled and undisturbed by the breath of a zephyr." McCall described the air as "light and elastic, and of that happy temperature which, inducing a calm repose of the physical faculties, and leading the mind to indulge in a dreamy tranquillity, causes the mere consciousness of existence to become an unspeakable delight."[1]* The young officer continued to love his Florida assignment. The Indians were quiet; military duties were minimal; the fishing and hunting were exhilarating. Transferred to a fort near Tampa, McCall was even happier. On 1 December 1827, he wrote: "Here we have the most charming weather imaginable; I should say, unparalleled in any part of our country, if, indeed, it is surpassed in any part of the world. Since the third day of October not a drop of rain has fallen, and not twice in a month has a cloud as big as a blanket appeared in the bright canopy above us. . . . It is a paradise for those who love to live in the open air."[2]

Florida cast a similar enchantment over other early visitors. The

*Note section begins on page 303.

9

sober Quaker naturalist William Bartram, exploring the St. Johns River in 1774, described an Edenic grove: "How happily situated is this retired spot of earth! What an elisium it is! Where the wandering Seminole, the naked red warrior, roams at large, and after the vigorous chase retires from the scorching heat of the meridian sun. Here he reclines and reposes under the odoriferous shades of Zanthoxilon, his verdant couch guarded by the Deity, Liberty, and the Muses, inspiring him with wisdom and valour, whilst the balmy zephyrs fan him to sleep."[3]

Northern Florida, the only part visited by most of these earliest travelers, was a region of many rivers, lakes, and springs. Unroiled by man, these languid streams and placid bodies of water possessed extraordinary clarity. William Bartram described the Suwannee River as "the cleanest and purest of any river" he ever saw; the water was "almost as transparent as the air we breathe"; he could see the sharp outlines of fish darting about and even resting on the bottom.[4]

To the hopeful eyes of early settlers northern Florida's rivers offered special promise. Enthusiasts envisioned flourishing farms and plantations along the valleys and heavily laden ships and rafts moving over the waterways. In a message to the Florida legislative council assembled at Tallahassee for the first time in 1825, Gov. William P. Duvall pronounced the lands along the Apalachicola to be as fertile as the banks of the Mississippi with a climate better adapted to the production of sugar cane and sea island cotton. "The bold and navigable rivers which run through our territory," he said, "will be of more value than mines of gold."[5]

These rivers ran in and out of singularly beautiful ponds and lakes. Dr. William Hayne Simmons, who moved from Charleston, South Carolina, to St. Augustine in 1821, described central Florida as "a land of lakes and innumerable sheets of water." The territory's noblest stream, the St. Johns River, was a continuous range of such lakes. "The number of these pieces of water, which gleam upon the traveller's eye...," he said, "is scarcely credible, and presents a singularity that, I believe, is not to be met with in the topography of any other region of the world."[6] Simmons was impressed both by the extraordinary depth of some of these lakes and by the mysterious rise and fall in the level of the water. He reported local conjecture that "a subterraneous intercommunication" existed among the various bodies of water.[7]

Florida's many springs provided more intriguing evidence that great streams of water were moving through limestone channels deep below the surface of the land. William Bartram described one such spring near the St. Johns River as an "enchanting and amazing crystal fountain, which incessantly threw up, from dark, rocky caverns below, tons of water every minute, forming a bason, capacious enough for large shallops to ride in, and a creek four or five feet depth of water, and near twenty yards over, which meanders six miles through green meadows, pouring its limpid water into the great Lake George, where they seem to remain pure and unmixed."[8] Near the Gulf of Mexico Bartram visited Manatee Springs, where he found "the ebullition" to be "astonishing and continual, though its greatest force intermits, regularly, for the space of thirty seconds of time." Despite this churning of the water there was a remarkable clarity: "it is amazing and almost incredible, what troops and bands of fish, and other watery inhabitants are now in sight, all peaceable, and in what variety of gay colours and forms, continually ascending and descending, roving and figuring amongst one another. . . ."[9]

Even more beautiful were the Silver Springs in central Florida, near present-day Ocala. Lieutenant McCall rode horseback to this tranquil spot in July 1823. With two companions he paddled a canoe into the center of the little lake. "Think," he wrote to his brother, "of a body of water coming from under a limestone bluff of rugged front, in volumes of almost incalculable bulk, and filling a deep rocky cup of oval form, whose surface was one hundred and fifty yards in length by one hundred in width, and so pellucid that looking into it is like looking into the air, and you may form some faint idea of the scene in which we became, as it were, actors as well as spectators." One of McCall's companions cut a button from his shirt and dropped it into the pool. The three men watched it fall slowly through the water. When it came to rest on the brown sandy bottom they could even make out its tiny holes. "This, at the distance of forty feet under water," he wrote, "will no doubt appear to you incredible, but it is nevertheless a *downright fact*; and is, as you are doubtless aware, attributable to the high refractive power of the lime-stone water, as well as its limpidness."[10]

Riding through the countryside north of Silver Springs in 1828, Lieutenant McCall came unexpectedly upon "one of the strange features of this strange land." This was one of Florida's many "sinks," yawning holes in the earth where the subsurface limestone has given way. "The opening in the rock," he wrote, "was elliptical or nearly circular, of six feet in diameter. It was eighteen feet deep, as I subsequently ascertained, and the walls almost as regular as they might have been had they been built by the hands of an unskilful stone mason."[11] McCall meant eighteen feet to the surface of the water; when

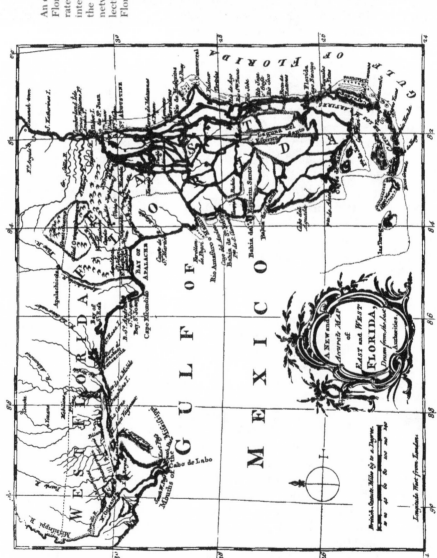

An early conception of Florida, 1760. Lacking accurate information about the interior of southern Florida, the mapmaker conjectured a network of rivers. Map Collection, Strozier Library, Florida State University.

he dropped a weighted line thirty-six feet long into this natural pool he failed to touch bottom. Some of the sinks were much larger than this; in 1830 a party of horsemen hunting at night fled in terror when they heard a deafening roar in the earth just behind them. Investigating by daylight, residents discovered that on a spot where a heavy growth of timber had previously stood there was now a cavity half an acre in extent. Its nearly perpendicular sides dropped forty or fifty feet to the surface of a new crystal-pure lake of unknown depth.[12]

Despite the enthusiasm of many early Florida visitors, not all Americans felt the enchantment of the new acquisition. Congressman John Randolph of Virginia opposed an early appropriation bill with the comment that "he would not give up an eligible position in hell for all Florida."[13] One of Randolph's many enemies observed that the cantankerous Virginian was a greater expert on hell than on Florida, which he had never seen. However, actually to see the territory was not necessarily to love it.

Long before annexation American sailors were all too familiar with its seemingly interminable coastline. To get from the eastern cities to New Orleans or Mobile, ships had to sail south four hundred miles along the Atlantic coast of Florida and then north and west some six hundred miles more along the Gulf coast. These seas were unpredictable; most days they were calm enough for the smallest boat to navigate with safety. But at other times, especially in the late summer and early fall, sudden storms, some of them hurricanes, blew out of the Caribbean, beating vessels to pieces on the coral reefs. In 1822 *Niles Weekly Register* called navigation along the Florida coast "the most dangerous in the world." Seven vessels had been lost during recent summer storms, "some of which were never again heard of."[14] Over seventy ships are known to have been wrecked in these waters during the decade preceding annexation and at least thirty-five in the first decade under American rule.[15] And ships continued to go down throughout most of the nineteenth century. In November 1835, *Niles* reported that property to the amount of $200,000 had recently been lost off the Florida coasts. "The shores are strewn with wrecks. Several vessels have been sunk with every soul on board."[16]

Sailors and passengers might survive these disasters and still not see home again. Some were killed or enslaved by the Indians; some were fatally injured in encounters with sharks, alligators, or rattlesnakes; some died from thirst and starvation. Emulating Robinson Crusoe, a few kept themselves alive until they could make their way to some outpost of civilization.

The ships that broke up along the Florida coasts provided welcome spoils for whoever found them. Indians pried open the barrels and chests that washed up on the shores, decked themselves in silks and brocades, and feasted on exotic wines and provisions. White beachcombers roamed the lonely coasts, building shanties from planks and spars and filling their larders from the stores of the wrecked ships. One notorious gang lived on Biscayne Bay near present-day Coconut Grove. They built fires to lure ships onto the reefs, attacked the stranded vessels, killed the crews, and kidnapped the women. Other wreckers haunted the Florida Keys, where they bribed local pilots to wreck ships deliberately. Crooked ship captains sometimes conspired with the wreckers. After the United States established a naval base at Key West in 1822, many wreckers validated their salvage claims in the local court. The territory's first salvage law was so lenient that wreckers were sometimes awarded as much as 95 percent of what they collected instead of the maximum 50 percent historically allowed by British and American admiralty courts.[17] In response to pleas from shipowners and insurance companies, Congress established a new Superior Court in Key West in 1828. A hard-nosed judge soon imposed a measure of order by allowing only court-approved vessels to engage in the wrecking business and by refusing to recognize salvage claims where there was evidence of collusion between the wreckers and the pilots or the owners. Legalized wrecking became a thriving business, reaching a peak of activity during the 1850s when five hundred vessels valued at $16 million were salvaged. But in regions so sparsely settled, the rule of law had only a shaky foundation, and in the early days ruffians continued to operate in defiance of the courts, swooping down on the broken ships and hiding their plunder. Indeed there had always been a great deal of outright piracy during the Spanish period, and enough persisted during the early days of American rule to require hunt and destroy missions by the army and navy.[18]

Compelled to keep a nervous eye out for tempests and pirates, American sailors jumped to the conclusion that Florida was almost worthless. Bored by the flat and uninteresting appearance of its shores, they reported that "the whole country was little better than a dreary succession of sands, marshes, and lagoons, fit for few others than reptiles or beasts of prey." And sailors were not the only skeptics. As early as 1827 a cynical observer noted that the people most eager to depict the territory as a terrestrial paradise were "landjobbers and others interested in the sale of property."[19] Although northern and central Florida had lovely rivers, lakes, and springs, it had vast swamps and mosquito-plagued lagoons as well. In 1872 a disillusioned newcomer wrote: "From what I have observed, I should think Florida was nine-tenths water, and the other tenth swamp."[20]

To many of these early visitors Florida seemed to possess a dangerous superfluity—too much water, too much summer heat, too many strange creatures. There were huge snakes and such clouds of mosquitoes that travelers sometimes feared for their lives. Even more terrifying were the alligators and crocodiles. During his 1775 exploration of the upper St. Johns River, William Bartram encountered alligators "in such incredible numbers, and so close together from shore to shore, that it would have been easy to have walked across on their heads, had the animals been harmless."[21] But harmless they were not, Bartram had concluded, after two of the beasts attacked his boat and forced him to retreat to shore.[22]

There seemed indeed to be two Floridas, northern Florida, an inviting region of gently rolling land, pine forests, and sparkling lakes and rivers, and southern Florida, a menacing country of barren coasts, scrubby pines and palmettos, and swamps—a fit home only for "varmints." In a report presented to Congress in 1826, Col. James Gadsden pronounced the southern third of Florida to be almost worthless for agriculture with the only fertile soil lying along the margins of rivers and inlets. Summarizing his findings, *Niles Weekly Register* concluded that the St. Lucie River was "beyond the ultimate limits of population on the Atlantic border."[23]

Gradually Americans began to learn of a remote and mysterious region stretching across most of southern Florida. In a travel account published in 1823, Charles Vignoles said: "The Glade, or as it is emphatically termed the *Never Glade*, appears to occupy almost the whole interior from about the parallel of Jupiter inlet to cape Florida, thence round to cape Sable to which point it approaches very near, and northwardly as far as the Delaware river discharging into Charlotte bay: its general appearance is a flat sandy surface mixed in the large stones and rocks, with from six inches to two feet of water lying upon it, in which is a growth of saw, and other water grasses, so thick as to impede the passage of boats where there is no current."[24] Comparing Vignoles's findings with other early reports, Dr. Simmons of St. Augustine concluded that almost all of Florida south of the St. Johns River was a "watery desart."[25] At first Lake Okeechobee was almost unknown, and the Everglades were thought to extend much farther north than they actually did. In 1837 John Lee Williams described the part of the peninsula lying south of the twenty-eighth parallel, approximately the location of Tampa, as shaped like a dish with the coast forming the rim. "This vast basin," Williams wrote, "is filled with marshes, wet savannas, intersected by extensive lakes and lagoons, forming a labyrinth which taken together, is called the Everglades." He described the region as "an unexplored grassy lake to which you can discover no bounds."[26]

After a remnant of the Seminoles rejected President Jackson's policy of relocating them west of the Mississippi and fled into southern Florida, a writer in the *North American Review* described their sanctuary as one "which seemed to invite no molestation." It was a place of "half deluged plains, deep morasses, and almost inaccessible forests," which "appeared to offer a home or a shelter only for beasts, or for men little elevated above beasts as to wants."[27] But land-hungry frontiersmen were unwilling to concede even this wasteland to the Indians, and the United States army became involved in the Seminole War (1835–42), a long-drawn-out conflict almost as exasperating as a later generation's Vietnam War.

Unable to enjoy the luxury of compaigning only in Florida's dry winters, the soldiers had to march and fight during the long hot summers when heavy showers were likely to fall almost daily. Once again there was superfluity. When the rains came, they were drenching downpours, "realizing," a contemporary writer complained, "the seemingly extreme exaggeration of Shakespeare who says of a shower, 'it could not choose but fall by pailsful.' "[28] Often there was no place for the rainwater to go. Central and southern Florida was so flat that the land might be submerged for days or weeks. "In riding from the St. John's to St. Augustine, a distance of eighteen miles," wrote Maj. Henry Whiting, "the road will be found, after a moderate rain, one half or two thirds under water, which is carried off more by evaporation than by subsistence; and this is a sample of the country in general."[29] Farther south the situation became still worse. According to the *North American Review*, marches had sometimes been made "for the principal part of a day through these shallow seas, with only a faint hope of finding dry ground of suitable extent for an encampment."[30]

In their desperation the Indians resorted to bloodier deeds and withdrew still deeper into the Big Cypress Swamp and the Everglades, and the United States army had to push its punitive expeditions ever further into this unknown terrain. Lt. Col. William Harney used Indian canoes to carry out a mission of vengeance deep in the Everglades. "No country that I have ever heard of bears any resemblance to it," a member of the expedition wrote. "It seems like a vast sea filled with grass and green trees, and expressly intended as a retreat for the rascally Indian."[31]

George M. McCall, who as a young officer had taken such delight in his Florida tour of duty, was sent back to share in the painful assignments of the Seminole War. In December 1840 and January 1841 he ws slogging through the Big Cypress Swamp with his men. He described the experience in these words: "The campaign lasted fifty-two days, during which period we made seven explorations of its depth, or, as they were called 'scouts,' averaging seven days each;

A Florida swamp. Typical of the desolate region in which U.S. soldiers had to campaign during the Seminole wars. SPA.

in other words, we were marching through water from six inches to three feet deep, forty-eight days. . . . On the seventh scout, no more than two hundred men of the eight hundred could be mustered for duty; fevers, diarrhoeas, and swollen feet and ankles—the latter attributed by the surgeons to constant marching in the water—having laid up in the hospital three-fourths of the command."[32]

In 1842 an unsatisfactory war came to an inconclusive ending. By then many of the most troublesome Indians had been killed or hanged; still others had accepted resettlement; a defiant remainder eluded capture and continued to hide out in remote settlements in the Everglades and the Big Cypress. But the red man's Florida grew steadily smaller and the white man's Florida inexorably greater. Despite the hardships of the recent campaigns many officers and soldiers discovered the delights of life in the subtropics. In 1836 the army established Fort Dallas at the mouth of the Miami River. Once the danger of Indian attack subsided, the men assigned to duty there found it a true paradise—blue skies, bright sunlight, cooling breezes, sparkling ocean and river. Five years later the demands of the Seminole War led to the construction of Fort Myers at the mouth of the Caloosahatchee River on the Gulf of Mexico, another delightful spot. Less attractive were the army posts built in the interior regions, but they served to open up new sections of Florida. Wartime needs also led to opening up new paths of trade. Steamboats from Charleston and Savannah carried armies and supplies 150 miles up the St. Johns River to Lake Harney. Once occupied by the Spanish but largely abandoned at the time of annexation, east central Florida appealed to army men as an ideal region for settlement once the Indian threat had been removed. According to Major Whiting, "Invalids have long looked to Florida as a refuge from the northern winter, and during the disturbances of the last few years, St. Augustine has necessarily been the only place of resort. But when peace shall be established, and the St. John's reoccupied, that river will present many places of great attraction to the infirm and pulmonic."[33]

Thus by 1842 Americans were gaining more vivid impressions of the territory that they had annexed from Spain. Still a remote region reached usually after a long and dangerous voyage, Florida offered the blessings of a warm climate and sparklingly clear rivers and lakes. To sickly people it provided a ray of hope, to planters of cotton and sugarcane an inviting frontier. But this Florida of promise was northern Florida. Except for a few oases, southern Florida was regarded as a water-soaked wasteland, suitable only for alligators, snakes, and Indians.

# 2 Early Boosters

I n the early nineteenth century, Americans displayed a passionate faith in "improvements." As the national boundaries steadily expanded, the need for transportation became urgent. Farmers, merchants, and manufacturers had to move themselves and their goods about the country. They wanted to have the oceans charted, lighthouses built, and ports equipped with wharves and breakwaters. They wanted rivers to be deepened and straightened and connecting canals to be built. They wanted the construction of highways and railroads. Assured by political philosophers that they were the more valuable class in society, farmers sought to acquire new fertile acres through drainage. Who was to pay for all these benefits? Whenever the cost was not excessive and the hope of return was great enough, private businessmen were eager to make the venture. It was an age of turnpike companies, canal companies, water companies, manufacturing companies, and banking companies. But many improvements cost too much, the benefits to be gained were too far in the future, and the probable profits were too small to be attractive to private capital. So demands for government spending were insistent. Everybody professed a belief in economical government, but everyone had his own favorite project for building roads, harbors, canals, or railroads. Some might need appropriations; others might need only land grants, and land was a resource that federal and state governments then owned in abundance.

Politicians came to differ on many aspects of the "internal improvements" issue. They set forth contrasting constitutional theories concerning the powers of the national government and state sovereignty. But the legislators usually reserved their constitutional scruples and budgetary fears for proposals involving other politicians' constituencies. Whether Federalist, Republican, Democrat, or Whig, the officeholder usually became a vigorous supporter of projects that would benefit his own part of the country.

This booster spirit was particularly characteristic of frontier Florida. The pioneers who moved into the new territory loved the warm sun, the clear air, and the sparkling springs and streams, but they deplored the widely scattered settlements, the long distances from markets, and the water-soaked soil. They wanted safer coasts for their ships and boats; they wanted to have their rivers and harbors dredged; they wanted highways, canals, and railroads; they wanted drainage ditches and levees to turn swamps into farmland. Lacking private capital, the frontier boosters clamored for government support. And until Florida was admitted to statehood in 1845, these supplicants converged on Washington. Both the economic and the political facts of life dictated this strategy. The Florida government was too poor to finance its own improvements, and the constitutional arguments against federal projects within the states did not apply to those benefiting the territories—in theory, the common property of all the states.

Once the Spanish flag was lowered and the Stars and Stripes raised over Florida, American patriots never doubted that a glorious future was assured for the region. In 1825 a writer in *Niles Weekly Register* boasted: "Florida has had a greater accession of population and made more progress in improvement during the few years it has belonged to the United States than would have happened in 100 years, had it remained under the dominion of dull and gloomy Spain."[1] Acting out their nationalist impulses, the early American settlers scorned the Spanish towns and built their new capital city Tallahassee in the forests of the Panhandle, on the site of an Indian village almost equidistant from St. Augustine and Pensacola.

After a few acrimonious months in office Gen. Andrew Jackson, the first American governor of the territory, resigned, and Judge William P. Duvall succeeded him. Born near Richmond, Virginia, Duvall had been shaped by his early life on the Kentucky frontier. He had studied law and gained admission to the bar, commanded a company of volunteers in the War of 1812, and represented Kentucky for one term in Congress. His first Florida assignment was as U.S. judge of the East Florida district; his elevation to the governorship soon followed. Short and rotund, ruddy in complexion, "radiant with good nature and humor, with a drolling voice and rather a blustering manner,"[2] Duval was well equipped for the post he held for the twelve years from 1822 to 1834. He maintained a precarious peace with the Indians, guided the legislative council in its initial lawmaking, and pointed out the need for improvements.

During the years that Governor Duvall was preaching progress at Tallahassee, Florida's representatives to Congress, Gen. Richard K. Call and Col. Joseph W. White, were conveying the frontiersmen's requests to Washington. Call, born in Virginia and raised in Tennessee, prided himself on his close friendship with Andrew Jackson. He had held important commands in Jackson's campaigns and shared in his glorious victories. Brought to Florida by Jackson, Call practiced law, invested in land and slaves, and commanded the territorial militia. Imperious in manner, he inevitably made enemies and served only two terms as territorial representative before losing out to his perennial rival, Col. Joseph White. The latter was a genial man, a shrewd country lawyer, and a successful vote-getter. In the later political evolution of the region White was destined to become the leader of the Democrats, while Call, despite his veneration of Jackson, was the natural leader of the Whigs.

Both General Call and Colonel White championed a project for cutting a waterway across the Florida peninsula. Schemes of this kind to protect ships sailing from the Gulf of Mexico to the Atlantic Ocean from the danger of wrecks were much discussed during the 1820s. In *Sketches, Historical and Topographical, of the Floridas* (1821), Col. James Grant Forbes touched on the matter. He described "Lake Mayaco," a large lake known only to the Indians, from which rivers descended eastward to the Atlantic and westward to the Gulf and suggested that this was destined "to form the grand central source of communication between the Atlantic and the Mexican Sea."[3] Lake Mayaco was obviously the body of water soon to be known as Lake Okeechobee. In *Notices of East Florida* (1822), Dr. William Hayne Simmons carried the idea a little further, describing "the Coolisihatchie," a river that fell into the Gulf of Mexico, as having its headwaters within twenty miles of the St. Johns with an open prairie lying between "so that a communication between the two streams might easily be formed." Simmons was also intrigued by "Lake Mayaco," which he thought either connected with the St. Johns or could be made to do so. This could provide the means by which "an extensive inland navigation may be opened throughout the peninsula."[4]

But Lake Okeechobee and the Caloosahatchee River were too far south to provide the most promising route for a cross-Florida waterway. Much more exciting was a route that would link the Suwannee

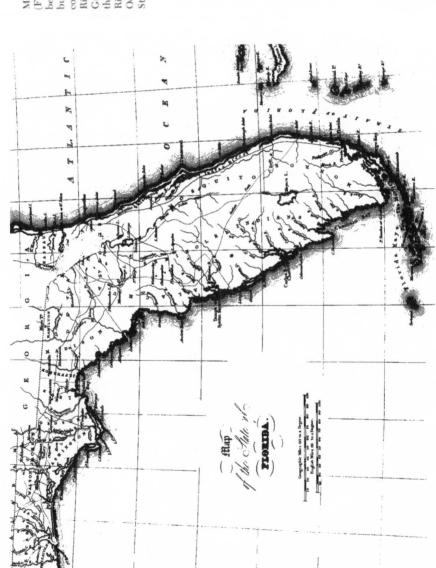

Map of Florida, 1823 (Fenner-Sears). Early boosters believed it would be easy to build a cross-Florida canal by connecting the Suwannee River, which flowed into the Gulf of Mexico, with either the St. Marys or St. Johns River flowing into the Atlantic Ocean. Map Collection, Strozier Library.

River, which began in the Okefenokee Swamp of southern Georgia and northern Florida and ran southwestward into the Gulf of Mexico, with either the St. Marys River or the St. Johns River running into the Atlantic Ocean. Charles Vignoles suggested such a canal in *Observations upon the Floridas* (1823): "Connecting the waters of Black creek and Santaffy rivers by a navigable canal of thirty or forty miles a route may be opened, that will afford many facilities for bringing the produce that comes down to Appalachie bay, to the Atlantic markets, and of conveying the returns: independent of the fruits of the plantations for many miles around the canal."[5] Black Creek, it should be explained, runs into the St. Johns River, while the Santaffy, or Santa Fe, has its outlet in the Suwannee.

In a memorial to Congress, adopted 28 December 1824, the legislative council proposed "the opening of a canal across the Peninsula of East Florida from the river Suwaney to St. Johns or between such other points as on examination may prove to be more eligible." In no part of the United States could an object of so much utility be promoted with less difficulty or expenditure, "the Peninsula being intersected at various points by water courses, the connexion of which would render the expense of this work an object of comparative insignificance."[6]

Diligently supporting this proposal, General Call wrote a strong communication to the House Committee on Roads and Canals. He estimated that a sheltered navigation from the Mississippi River to the Atlantic Ocean would be about 800 miles long but that almost 700 miles of this was already navigable by sea, river, and lake. Only about five miles of canal would be enough to open up 200 miles of sheltered waterway along the Gulf coast from Pensacola to St. Marks; the next stretch from St. Marks to the mouth of the Suwannee River would be more difficult and might have to be postponed since it would require 60 miles of canal; but the cross-peninsula connection between the Suwannee and St. Johns rivers would need only about 20 miles of digging. The proposed waterway would provide a route 1,000 miles shorter than that around the Florida capes and much safer. Stressing "the danger, the delays, and the difficulty, attendant on the navigation among the keys and shoals of Florida," Call argued that saving the annual cost of shipwrecks, estimated at $500,000, would provide "a sum nearly sufficient to complete the contemplated route."[7]

The political climate of the 1820s was highly favorable to canal projects. The famous Erie Canal across New York State was completed in 1825, and in other regions a score of waterways—some built by the states, some by private companies—were under construction. In these years just before the railroads became practicable the surest way to promote economic growth seemed to be the improvement of waterways. On the rivers steamboating was just entering its golden age; on the seas sailing vessels and steamboats were competing for the coasting trade. Exhilarated by the promised profits, merchants favored federal policies that would open new markets and make the sea lanes safer. In this atmosphere the Florida representative to Congress, though voteless, was in a position to mobilize support for his schemes. Hezekiah Niles, Baltimore spokesman for eastern mercantile interests, took up the Florida cause. In April 1825 he wrote: "Ever since the cession of this country, we have thought that the time was not far distant when the peninsula of Florida would be converted into an island, by means of a canal large enough for the passage of heavy ships." Niles believed that the distance across the peninsula was only about 90 miles and that a canal not more than 18 miles in length would be enough to link existing waterways.[8] In October 1825 he argued that a project costing only $90,000 would bring huge benefits, increasing the value of the public lands and giving "safety and expedition" to the nation's "immense trade in the Gulf of Mexico."[9]

In November the merchants became even more interested following the publication of an exchange of letters between Colonel White, Florida's new territorial representative, and Secretary of War James Barbour. White urged that army engineers be assigned to survey possible routes for a cross-Florida canal. Barbour replied that his department did not have the necessary funds, but suggested an appeal to Congress.[10]

Shortly after Congress convened in December, Congressman Daniel Webster of Massachusetts, spokesman for eastern commercial interests, offered a resolution recommending a federal survey to ascertain the feasibility of the suggested canal. Such a waterway, he said, would cut off 800 or 1,000 miles of "most dangerous navigation." It would benefit the states on the Ohio and Mississippi rivers and the Gulf of Mexico as well as those on the Atlantic seaboard. If the project were practicable, it would be "one of the greatest objects connected with general improvement, which could engage the attention of government."[11]

Before the House could consider Webster's resolution the Senate had seized the initiative in response to two new Florida documents. The first was a recent resolution of the Florida legislative council praising "the magnificent policy which the United States have adopted upon internal improvements" and asking for not only a survey across Florida but an extension of this westward to Mobile Bay.[12] The second was a memorial from James Gadsden and Edward R. Gibson, two of three commissioners appointed by the legislative council to study the feasibility of the canal. The commissioners urged a federal survey. If the engineers' report was favorable, they hoped that the federal government would build the canal. If Congress decided against this, the commissioners hoped for "a proportional pecuniary contribution to a joint stock company" as a means of encouragement for private investment in the project.[13]

On 11 January 1826 Sen. Josiah Johnston of Louisiana introduced a bill providing for an examination of all the country south of the St. Marys and Apalachicola rivers to ascertain the most eligible route through which to connect the Atlantic Ocean and the Gulf of Mexico. The Committee on Roads and Canals approved the bill but added an amendment extending the survey all the way from the Apalachicola River to the Mississippi. It was this amendment that led to a sharp Senate debate on 14 February. Virginia's John Randolph had such strict constitutional scruples that he opposed any federal survey at all. Almost all the other senators were willing to vote for the Florida survey, but many opposed the proposed extension across the Gulf states to the Mississippi. The issue was largely regional. Senators from the Atlantic seaboard favored the Florida survey, but opposed the extension; those from the frontier states bordering on the Ohio, the Mississippi, and the Gulf supported both the Florida survey and the extension. In the end the extension amendment was voted down 26 to 16, but the survey across Florida was approved without a roll call, and the House went along with this decision.[14] It was not love for Florida but hatred for its treacherous coastline that determined the issue. According to the *Register of Debates in Congress*, Sen. John Holmes of Maine claimed that he "would do almost anything to avoid the navigation round the capes, the keys, and reefs of Florida. It is the bane of sailors; it is a Golgotha—a grave yard. He should not think it much of a loss to the United States were the whole Peninsula of Florida sunk into the Gulf of Mexico. He believed it would be a blessing to this country if they could dig it down with shovels and sink it into the deepest place in the Gulf."[15]

The John Quincy Adams administration appointed Maj. P. H. Perrault of the Topographical Engineers to head a seven-man surveying party, and in August 1826 *Niles Register* reported that this team was "busily employed in surveying the route of a ship canal across the territory of Florida."[16] While the survey was in progress, Niles continued to boost the canal. In January 1827 his paper said that the importance of Florida was becoming more manifest every day. "We take it for granted, that a *ship canal* will be cut through it—the object is one of such overwhelming interest, that constitution, or law, or power, will be found somewhere or somehow to effect it." Not only would the canal aid the western states needing outlets for their products, it would benefit the whole union "deeply concerned with prompt and safe communication." Opened to commerce, Florida would soon supply the nation with large quantities of sugar and coffee, "and because of the heavy duties on these articles, the people, it is expected, will be friendly to the protective system."[17]

But the army engineers became increasingly skeptical of the feasibility of a canal. Writing to his superior, Brig. Gen. Simon Bernard, on 4 January 1827, Major Perrault reported that soundings of possible harbors on the Gulf coast had given unsatisfactory readings. Even at high tide there was a depth of only seven or eight feet over the sandbar at the mouth of the Suwannee River. The only possible terminal might be Tampa Bay. General Bernard ordered him to explore this region, but the results were still discouraging. On 13 November 1837, President Adams made the following entry in his diary: "General Bernard and Captain Poussain called, having lately returned from their surveys in Florida. Bernard says that the project of a ship-channel across the isthmus must be given up as impracticable: that a steamboat canal six feet deep is the utmost that could be effected; that there is not more than nineteen feet of water at the bar at the Bay of St. Joseph; but that a canal at no great expense may be made between the Bay of Mobile and Pensacola."[18]

In July 1828 Colonel White wrote to the Secretary of War urging that the engineers' report be released before the next session of Congress. Referring to an enclosed clipping from a New York newspaper, he said: "You will perceive that *here* a considerable interest is yet manifested & complaints uttered for the delay."[19] On 25 February 1829, just a week before he left office, President Adams finally transmitted the report of the Florida survey to Congress. General Bernard's doubts were reflected in his emphasis upon the shallowness of the Gulf coast harbors, the necessity of locks to traverse the highlands, and the uncertainty of the water sources. The engineers had explored two possible routes—a northern one using the St. Marys River and passing through the Okefenokee Swamp and one further south using the St. Johns River, Black Creek, and the Santa Fe and Suwannee rivers and terminating at St. Marks. "Respecting distance and expense of lockage," the report concluded, "the St. John's route has the advantage." Because of the elevation of the terrain and the difficulty of storing water for the locks, the engineers advised that a deep ship canal would not be practical, but that a shallow canal for steamboats might be possible. To estimate probable costs, further surveys would be necessary.[20]

Congress appropriated a small sum for continuing the work, and in 1832 a second engineers' report was made public. This dealt only with the capacity of the ponds that lay along the summit of the route. These were found adequate to operate the proposed locks, but the engineers still did not provide any estimate of costs.[21] Recognizing that Congress had lost interest in the idea of a canal, the Florida legislative council made a significant change in its plans. In a memorial to Congress dated 16 February 1834, it asked for aid in building a railroad from Jacksonville to St. Marks.[22] In 1837 John Lee Williams wrote: "Many of our projected canals will probably be superseded by rail roads. Where the elevation requires much lockage, rail roads will be far preferable, and less expensive. Stone for locks is scarce, the soil is light, and scarcely solid enough to support heavy dams, and they are very easily undermined by the water. Near the coast, where thorough cuts can be made, canals may answer, but in the rolling country, rail roads are both cheaper and more expeditious, besides, they are far more permanent."[23]

Although the dream of a cross-Florida canal faded for the time being, less ambitious projects to aid navigation were put in motion. In 1822 Lt. Comdr. Matthew C. Perry, later to make a memorable voyage to Japan, was sent to take possession of Key West. Reporting on his mission on 28 March 1822, Perry urged that lighthouses be built at five locations along the treacherous east coast and the southern reefs. Congress responded promptly by appropriating money in May 1822 for the construction of lighthouses at Cape Florida off Biscayne Bay and Dry Tortugas, the westernmost of the keys. A year later it voted funds for lighthouses at St. Augustine and Pensacola and in 1824 for lights at two other danger spots on the southern reefs, Careysfoot Reef and Sambo Keys.[24]

American diplomats cooperated in the efforts to reduce shipwrecks. In July 1824 the Monroe administration suggested that the British government might like to cede part of the Bahamian island of Abaco so that the United States could erect a lighthouse to guide shipping in the dangerous straits between the Bahamas and southern Florida. The British rejected the idea but expressed a willingness to build their own lighthouse on Abaco. On 15 November 1825 Secretary of State Henry Clay again raised the issue by notifying the British government that the United States planned to build lighthouses at Dry Tortugas, Sambo Keys, and Careysfoot Reef. "Other lights," Clay wrote, "are contemplated near cape Florida and cape Canaveral. When all these works shall be completed, there will be a chain of lights along the Florida coast, so that a vessel may almost constantly have one in view." The British did as they had promised, building lights on their side of the channel between the Bahamas and Florida.[25]

Clay's boast that his government would build a continuous string of lighthouses was by no means fulfilled. Except for the lighthouse at

Cape Florida Lighthouse. Originally built around 1825, gutted by fire during an Indian attack in 1836, subsequently rebuilt and heightened. SPA.

St. Augustine, the east coast was almost entirely unprotected: the lighthouse at Cape Canaveral was not built until 1848 and the one at Jupiter Inlet not until 1860. The principal effort was made along the southern reefs where four lighthouses or lightships were provided between 1824 and 1830 at Cape Florida, Careysfoot Reef, Sand Key, and Dry Tortugas. For many years the long Gulf coast had only two or three lights—one at Pensacola (1826), one at Cape St. George opposite Apalachicola (1833), and one at Egmont Key at the entrance to Tampa Bay (1848).[26]

These isolated beacons were not erected or maintained without

adventure and danger. Enroute to Careysfoot Reef in 1825 the light-
ship ran onto the rocks and was abandoned by its crew. Wreckers
took possession of the vessel, and its builders had to ransom it before
it could be repaired and anchored at its destination. In 1836 a band of
Indians attacked the Cape Florida lighthouse. They set fire to the
structure and shot to death the keeper's black helper. The keeper
received six musketshot wounds and was unable to climb down the
burned-out stairs. A passing ship finally rescued the wounded man
after sighting his flag of distress. In 1846 a new lighthouse had to be
built to replace the damaged one.[27]

But lighthouses, however comforting to mariners, were not
enough to prevent the sickening toll of ships lost off the treacherous
Florida coasts. Each decade witnessed more shipwrecks. During the
1840s the annual losses were estimated at about $1 million. In 1846, a
particularly disastrous year, at least 53 ships with cargoes valued at
$1.6 million were reported to have piled up on the Florida reefs.[28]

If a ship canal across Florida seemed too ambitious a project, less
costly local schemes had a better chance of adoption. The natural
terrain along hundreds of miles of the Florida coasts favored the development of waterways that would permit at least the smaller vessels to navigate behind sheltering island barriers. General Call had
pointed out one such possibility in 1825. Along the Gulf coast in the
Panhandle section there were a succession of great bays — Pensacola,
Choctawhatchee, St. Andrews, Apalachicola, Apalachee — and other
lakes and sounds. By connecting these bodies of water it would be
possible to provide a sheltered waterway, some 200 miles long, from
Pensacola to St. Marks. Only a little dredging and the building of a
few short canals would be required. Yet even these projects took
many years to achieve. Congress appropriated a few thousand dollars to improve navigation of rivers like the Apalachicola and the St.
Marks. Aside from this, it did no more than grant permission to the
territory to cut its own canals through some of the public lands,[29] and
since the territory had no money, it could only charter private canal
companies for this purpose. In 1832 the legislative council incorporated a company to build a canal between St. Andrews Bay and the
Apalachicola River.[30] Since similar projects were under discussion in
other parts of Florida, John Lee Williams was excited by the prospects: "Indeed, the whole of our extensive sea coast is lined by inland water courses that might, at the expense of a few miles cutting,
be rendered navigable for steamboats, and the whole danger from
our southern reefs, keys and currents be obviated."[31] But not enough
capital could be raised to put through these private ventures.

Along the east coast of Florida the possibilities of developing an inland waterway were even more intriguing. Flowing parallel to the coast and widening into bays and lagoons were a succession of rivers—the St. Marys, the St. Johns, the Matanzas, the Halifax, the Indian. Since the St. Marys River and other Georgia waterways provided a safe entrance into the territory, the first demand was for an improved waterway to connect the St. Marys and the St. Johns. Congress appropriated money for this purpose during the 1820s and 1830s, but it was many years before mariners were satisfied with the condition of the channel.[32] In 1837 Williams complained that an appropriation of $15,000 had been expended "to very little purpose."[33] In 1843 *Niles Weekly Register* reported that the mouth of the St. Johns was impeded by a large bar that extended almost all the way across its mouth.[34]

Despite these difficulties the St. Johns served as a gateway to much of eastern Florida. According to Dr. Simmons, it served "all the ends of the most judiciously contrived canals, running in a direction the best adapted to the purposes of internal trade."[35] At first this route brought most of its profits to the old Spanish port of Fernandina at the mouth of the St. Marys, but in 1822 the new port of Jacksonville was laid out some 24 miles up the St. Johns River. Jacksonville grew slowly and had only 200 inhabitants in 1843, but its use as a military depot during the Seminole War called attention to its magnificent potentialities.[36]

The St. Johns River provided a favorite route to St. Augustine. Travelers could go by ship to Picolata and then make a 20-mile trip by horseback or coach to the old Spanish city, thus avoiding the dangerous approach by the open sea and treacherous harbor. Early boosters urged construction of a canal to connect the St. Johns with the San Sebastian River, which ran past St. Augustine. In 1833 the legislative council chartered a company for this purpose.[37]

But this modest proposal was overshadowed by more grandiose schemes for an intracoastal waterway extending down the entire east coast. As early as 1825 Col. James Gadsden had claimed that it would be easy to open up such a sheltered passage. Commissioned to survey a possible route for a road between St. Augustine and Cape Florida, he reported that the southern part of the territory was attracting only cattle raisers and wreckers—"adventurous emigrants who attach little value to roads and would prefer in their neighborhood communications making use of those water channels provided by nature." He said that only nine miles of canals would be enough to connect the Matanzas River with the Indian River, providing more than 200 miles of protected waterways south of St. Augustine. With another ten miles of digging, the North River and the St. Johns could be linked, thereby opening up a passage all the way to Charleston, South Carolina.[38]

In 1837 the legislative council chartered the East and South Florida Canal Company with authority to issue $500,000 in capital stock and to construct a waterway from "Biscaino Bay" to St. Augustine and the St. Johns River.[39] The outbreak of the Seminole War ruined whatever chances this project may have had, but the idea of an intracoastal canal persisted. Doing a tour of duty in Florida, Maj. Henry Whiting wrote a persuasive argument for the waterway. There were, he explained, a succession of lagoons along the east coast. These long narrow bodies of water were separated from the sea by strips of land, generally not more than a mile or two in width. These strips were broken by occasional inlets linking the lagoons with the sea. But these inlets provided unreliable channels for navigation because they were constantly filling up at one point and opening up at another. Summarizing the situation, Whiting wrote: "These lagoons extend from above St. Augustine to Jupiter inlet, a stretch of three or more hundred miles, with but a few miles interrupted by land. Their common depth is several feet, though they are all transversed by shoals or bars, which reduce their navigable facility to about three feet. These shoals, however, could easily be made passable for useful purposes." By building a canal 10 to 15 miles long, the St. Johns River could be connected with the Matanzas River; another canal 20 to 30 miles long could link the Matanzas with the Halifax River; a cut only one-half mile long could link the Mosquito Lagoon at the mouth of the Halifax with the Indian River. "Such a project," wrote Whiting, "would open an interior navigation from Charleston to Jupiter inlet and below Cape Florida. It is well known that a practicable and sheltered channel runs around the peninsula, within the 'keys.' "[40]

The long waterway envisioned by these early boosters was not finally built until a half century later, but one small step was taken soon after the Seminole War. In moving supplies to the south, the army had found it a nuisance to have to use the "Haulover" portage, about one-half mile in length, between the Mosquito Lagoon and the Indian River (not far from the present-day Kennedy Space Center). In December 1843 Brig. Gen. William Worth asked permission to dig a canal through this barrier "thus effecting an uninterrupted batteaux navigation" from Mosquito Lagoon to Biscayne Bay.[41] In February 1844 the Florida legislative council petitioned Congress to appropriate funds not only for this canal but for two others, ten and one miles in length, that would benefit settlers in the Indian River, Jupiter Inlet, and Lake Worth regions. Congress went part way by appropriating $1,500 for the Haulover Canal.[42]

The Seminole War had terrified the frontier settlers and halted migration into the state, but the pacification of 1842 brought about a

Sand Key Light Station. Original stone structure, built in 1827, was destroyed by a hurricane and replaced by an iron structure in 1853. SPA.

dramatic reversal. Gloom about Florida's future dissipated, and a surge of optimism took its place. In November 1842 a report from St. Augustine predicted the speedy settlement of East Florida: "No part of the United States holds out such temptations to emigrants as this peninsula, whether we regard the fertility of its soil, the mildness of its climate, or the richness of its productions."[43] Above all, Florida offered health. In 1843 the *Savannah Georgian* reported that "a substantial settlement" was being made in the neighborhood of Fort Pierce, "that place being considered remarkably healthy as a military post during the Seminole war, the climate being delightful and the water excellent."[44] In 1846 hundreds of cures were attributed to drinking and bathing at various mineral springs on the upper St. Johns River. According to *Niles Weekly Register*, the spring waters acted "like a charm in cases of chronic rheumatism, paralysis, and diseases of the liver and kidneys, in diseases incident to the female constitution and upon all cutaneous afflictions."[45] Fort Dallas, the future Miami, although almost impossibly isolated during these years, enjoyed an unsurpassed reputation for salubrity. A correspondent to *De Bow's Review* in 1851 reported that a company of soldiers stationed there had suffered no cases of illness in eighteen months. "The inhabitants, some of whom have resided there for many years, are all grateful witnesses of the remarkable healthfulness of that vicinity; and although the summers are warm, the air, during the entire day, is fanned by the easterly winds prevailing in that season, and rendering it comfortable for the laborers to pursue their vocations at all times."[46]

During these buoyant years Florida graduated into statehood. Although sectional politics delayed her admission until 1845, when Congress could balance the slave state of Florida with the new free state of Iowa, hopeful delegates had drafted a state constitution as early as 1838. This document had proclaimed that "a liberal system of internal improvements" was essential to the country, and had imposed upon the legislature the duty of ascertaining "proper objects of improvement, in relation to roads, canals, and navigable streams" and making funds available for such projects.[47]

In December 1845 the new state legislature passed a highly significant resolution. Conceding that the Everglades had long been regarded as "wholly valueless," the legislators noted the rise of a contrary belief, "which is daily strengthening, that these opinions are without foundation, and, on the contrary, that at a comparatively small expense, the aforesaid region can be entirely reclaimed, thus opening to the habitation of man an immense and hitherto unexplored domain, perhaps not surpassed in fertility and every natural ability by any other on the globe." The legislature instructed the Florida delegation to ask Congress for the appointment of engineers to examine the Everglades with a view to reclamation.[48]

This audacious dream of pulling the plug and letting the water out of the Everglades had been taking form for at least ten years. In 1837 John Lee Williams asked whether the Everglades might not be drained "by deepening the natural outlets." If the level of waters could be lowered by ten feet, "what a field would it open for tropical productions!"[49] Perhaps, as Spanish tradition held, the mysterious Everglades would yield a treasure in pearls. In 1845 a writer in the *Key West Gazette* thought that "millions of acres" might be reclaimed. "If this be ever done, South Florida will indeed be the garden of our country; for, in addition to its adaptation to the culture of tropical fruits and hemp, this immense tract will afford unequalled advantages of soil, climate, and position for the sugar, cotton, rice, and tobacco planters."[50]

Carrying out the instruction of the legislature, Sen. James T. Westcott obtained the support of the Treasury Department for "a reconnaissance" of the Everglades. The assignment was given to Buckingham Smith, a respected St. Augustine lawyer. In 1848 Smith provided the Florida politicians with a persuasively argued case for draining the Everglades. With the skill of a painter, Smith described the region as it then looked. "Imagine," he wrote, "a vast lake of fresh water extending in every direction from shore to shore beyond the reach of human vision, ordinarily unruffled by a ripple on its surface, studded with thousands of islands of various sizes, from one-fourth of an acre to hundreds of acres in area, and which are generally covered with dense thickets of shrubbery and vines." He told about the pale green sawgrass rising through the surface of the limpid waters and gently bending in the breeze. He depicted the lilies and the vari-colored plants that floated on the water and the blooming flowers of the wild myrtle and honeysuckle covering the islands. "The profound and wild solitude of the place," he said, "the solemn silence that pervades it. . . add to awakened and excited curiosity bordering on awe."[51] Today's nature-lover might draw the conclusion that such exquisite beauty should not be disturbed but left forever wild and unspoiled. But the nineteenth-century booster sternly shook off his romantic mood and hurried on to the no-nonsense findings that his employers expected. To "a man of practical, utilitarian turn of thought," Smith reasoned, "the first and the abiding impression [of the region] is [its] utter worthlessness to civilized man, in its present condition, for any useful or practical object.... A solitary inducement can not now be offered to a decent white man to settle in the interior of the Everglades."[52] Left as it was, the region was suitable "only for the haunt of noxious vermin, or the resort of pestilent reptiles."[53]

Smith believed that it would be entirely feasible to lower the level of the waters and open up a vast expanse of fertile soil. He estimated that the Everglades were at least twelve feet above sea level; all that restrained the waters was a ridge of slightly higher ground a few miles inland from the coast. If this rim were cut through by deepening the Miami River and other streams running eastward into the Atlantic and westward into the Gulf, the excess water in Lake Okeechobee and the Glades would drain off, opening up the entire region to agriculture. Smith estimated the cost of the project at $500,000. He believed that the soil and climate of the reclaimed region would be suitable for a wide range of crops—tropical fruits, coffee, tobacco, and especially sugar. The new production would benefit the nation by lessening dependence on the West Indies. "In less than 10 years," Smith prophesied, "a new, independent State may be added to the Union, formed out of east and south Florida, dissevering that unnatural connection now existing between them and middle and west Florida...."[54] A new state based upon a plantation economy would of course become a slave state—a prospect sure to appeal to southern legislators in the political climate of the 1840s.

To support his findings, Buckingham Smith appended letters from military commanders who had served in Florida, either during the Seminole War or earlier. Gen. William S. Harney was sure that the Everglades could be drained and that within five years the reclaimed land would attract a population of 100,000 persons. Gen. James Gadsden and Gen. Thomas S. Jessup also believed that the reclamation scheme was both feasible and desirable.[55] The only dissenting voice was that of Stephen R. Mallory, collector of customs at Key West, later to become secretary of the navy in the Confederate government. He had, he said, been in the Glades. He had eaten its fish, drunk its waters, smelled its snakes and alligators, and waded through its mud, "besides possessing some little acquaintance with its mosquitoes and horseflies, both of which can be recommended." He thought that many regions within the Everglades were fully as low as the surrounding seas and could never be drained. Some lands around the margins might be reclaimed by draining or dyking, but, Mallory warned, "it will be found wholly out of the question to drain all the Everglades."[56]

Ignoring Mallory's sour comments, Senator Westcott promptly introduced a bill providing that the federal government should cede most of southern Florida directly to the state instead of following the usual policy of selling the land for the benefit of the federal treasury. The federal grant should be contingent on the state commencing within three years and completing within ten a system of drains and canals for lowering the level of water in Lake Okeechobee and the Everglades. If practicable, these canals connecting Lake Okeechobee with the Atlantic and the Gulf were to be developed into a waterway across the state.[57] Thus two dreams of the boosters — to build a cross-Florida canal and to drain the Everglades—were linked in the Westcott bill. Undoubtedly the senator hoped to gain the support of the merchants and shippers of other states. He sent copies of the Buckingham Smith report and the text of his bill, together with the latest statistics on shipwrecks, to such newspapers as the *Baltimore Patriot* and the *New York Journal of Commerce*. *Niles Register* and *De Bow's Review* gave friendly mention to the Westcott bill and also approved the senator's appeal for the federal government to provide new charts of the treacherous Florida coasts.[58]

However, the Westcott bill encountered stormy weather. Florida's other senator, David Levy Yulee, refused to support it. He believed that its provisions were unrealistic because a poor and sparsely populated state would be unable to carry through such a herculean project within the specified time limits.[59] Besides, as subsequent events revealed, Yulee was placing all his bets not on canals and drainage ditches but on railroads. With the Florida delegation thus divided, Congress took no action.

But a generous federal government did endow the new state with abundant potential resources. In 1845 it granted to Florida 500,000 acres of public land for "internal improvements." In 1850 Congress passed a law highly important for Florida's future. For the purpose of enabling Arkansas and other states "to reclaim the swamp and overflowed land therein," the federal government promised to turn over to them all unsold public land "wet and unfit for cultivation." The state legislatures were to have authority to dispose of the land, provided that the proceeds were "applied, exclusively, as far as necessary, to the purpose of reclaiming said lands by means of the levees and drains aforementioned."[60]

How would Florida convert several million acres into the engineering works needed to speed the growth of the state? In 1851 the legislature established a Board of Internal Improvement, but gave it no effective powers.[61] This feeble policy disappointed two leading politicians, U.S. Congressman Edward Carrington Cabell and Gov. Thomas Brown, both Whigs and ardent boosters for internal improvements. Responding on 29 April 1852 to a Treasury Department request for information about the commercial prospects of the various states, Cabell provided an extensive inventory of the state's needs. He revived every scheme for internal improvements that had been suggested during the past thirty years. He deplored the meagerness of federal expenditures for aiding navigation. Florida with its 1,200 miles of dangerous coast had fewer lighthouses than the approaches to New York or Boston; important harbors like Apalachicola still needed to be dredged; rivers running from Alabama and Georgia through Florida to the Gulf needed to be deepened. The intracoastal waterway along the upper Gulf coast was still not built. On the east coast things were as bad: sand bars still impeded the commerce of St. Augustine and Jacksonville; shipwrecks along the Florida reefs were costing $1 million a year—costs that might be largely saved by building an intracoastal waterway from the St. Marys River to Cape Sable. The entire expense of such a passage had been estimated at no more than $250,000. "But if it should be three or four times that sum," Cabell said, "it would not equal the value of the benefits resulting in a *national* point of view, and to other states besides Florida."[62] He also gave his blessing to the two major booster projects of earlier years, building a cross-Florida canal and draining the Everglades. Alluding to contemporary agitation for linking the Atlantic and Pacific oceans by a canal across the Isthmus of Tehuantepec or some other means, Cabell pointed out that, whatever was done, "a means of speedy and sure travel across Florida...will become imperatively necessary to enable the eastern and middle Atlantic states to participate in the benefits of such a route."[63] The drainage of the Everglades, he said, would serve a dual purpose. It would "reclaim vast quantities of rich sugar lands" and it would provide "the means of facile *interior* communication, and also between every part of the interior region and the sea coast."[64] Cabell also strongly urged the building of railroads.

Governor Brown transmitted Cabell's summary of state needs to the legislature along with his own strong recommendations for action.[65] In response, the legislature set up a new Board of Internal Improvements with the state engineer as its president. This agency was to recommend "plans for the reclamation of swamp lands" and other "local works of internal improvement."[66] Meanwhile, Florida boosters, seconded by commercial spokesmen from other sections, had succeeded in getting army engineers to make further studies of the possibilities for a cross-Florida canal. On 30 October 1852 the officer in charge reported that he had surveyed two routes, one using the St. Johns and Oklawaha rivers and terminating at Tampa Bay, the other a more southern route leaving the St. Johns about four miles south of Lake Monroe and also terminating at Tampa Bay. He estimated that a six-foot-deep waterway might be built for around $3.7 million. Of the two routes surveyed he preferred the Oklawaha, but he believed other alternatives should be studied.[67]

But canal proposals were destined to be postponed as the boosters turned all their attention to projects for building railroads—an enthusiasm that had been sweeping the country and was now spilling over into Florida. Overcoming local prejudice against corporations, the Florida legislature chartered a number of new railroad companies. Democrats now vied with Whigs in concocting schemes for extending state aid. The new Democratic governor, James E. Broome, not only commended the principle, but pointed out a promising source of funds. By 1854 the state had already piled up a sum of $228,000 from the sale of internal improvement lands. Further sales of this land and of the swamplands promised to bring in some $3 million. Why not, the governor asked, invest this money in the railroad projects?[68] Meanwhile, a committee appointed by the Board of Internal Improvements had been preparing important recommendations for the legislature. The committee was made up of U.S. Senator David Yulee, president of the Florida Railroad Company, and four other politicians and businessmen deeply involved in the railroad business. Predictably, they drafted a bill that promised huge benefits to the railroads and only minimal aid for canals and drainage works.[69]

As enacted into law on 6 January 1855, the Internal Improvement Act earmarked all unsold lands and unappropriated money received through the federal grants of 1845 and 1850 as an "Internal Improvement Fund" to be administered by a Board of Trustees composed of the governor, comptroller, state treasurer, attorney general, and register of state lands. The board was empowered to sell the land and invest the proceeds. The act specified the railroad routes to be developed and the means by which the companies were to be enabled to finance construction, principally through the issuance of $10,000 worth of bonds for each mile of track, with interest guaranteed by the

Internal Improvement Fund. Although the act dealt mostly with railroads, two sops were thrown to the advocates of drainage and canals. Section 16 authorized the trustees to "make such arrangement for the drainage of the swamp or overflowed lands, as in their judgment may be most advantageous to the Internal Improvement Fund." Section 17 authorized the trustees to construct a navigable canal connecting the St. Johns and Indian rivers at a cost per mile of not more than $4,000 plus 4,000 acres of land.[70]

Over the course of the next few years the trustees of the Internal Improvement Fund (IIF) and the railroad promoters worked together smoothly. The company executives took the necessary steps to begin construction; the trustees countersigned the company bonds, thus pledging IIF assets to guarantee the interest. But public aid did not stop here. Both the federal and the state governments made land grants, and Florida counties and municipalities bonded themselves to buy railroad stock. The IIF trustees invested a good portion of their assets in railroad securities, purchasing many of the very construction bonds that they had guaranteed. They also accepted railroad company stock in return for interest payments that became due while the roads were being built. The state had to provide more and more aid because of unanticipated delays: first the panic of 1857, then a quarrel between Gov. Madison S. Perry and Senator Yulee, and finally the onset of the Civil War slowed down construction and delayed the time when the railroads could be expected to be on their own. According to one student of these complicated finances, the IIF put up about $5.4 million in land, guarantees, and cash—more than five-sixths of the construction costs.[71]

Florida had at least gained some needed railroads. In 1855 the situation had been ludicrous. Only 20 miles of track between Tallahassee and St. Marks had been in operation, and mules provided the motive power on this rickety line; all the other early projects had failed. Eight years later the state had 368 miles of new railroads; passengers and freight could move from Fernandina on the Atlantic coast to Cedar Key on the Gulf and from Jacksonville on the east coast to Tallahassee and Quincy in the Panhandle.[72]

But by placing all their bets on railroads, the IIF trustees had shelved all the other booster projects for dredging rivers, digging canals, and draining swamps. This was made clear by the miscarriage of plans for linking the St. Johns and Indian rivers. The legislature had promised land grants and financial aid for such a waterway; the state engineer enthusiastically supported the idea, arguing that it would not only open up a great inland passage but would drain over three million acres of potentially valuable state land.[73] In 1857 the legislature established a board of commissioners with authority to issue $300,000 worth of bonds, with interest guaranteed by the IIF trustees, who were also directed to make a land grant of 52,000 acres. Even in this legislation, however, the state officials were admonished not to grant any money or land that would injure the interests of the railroad companies.[74]

Thus shackled, the canal project made only halting progress. Governor Broome, a railroad enthusiast, delayed the appointment of the commissioners; Governor Perry finally set up the board in 1858. Then the IIF trustees decided that all current funds were needed for payment of the interest on the railroad construction bonds. Not until 1860 did they give the commissioners the go-ahead. But the first solicitation for bids was unsuccessful, and the size of the proposed canal had to be reduced before any contractor would consider building it for the authorized $300,000. A New York firm was ready to sign a contract when the Civil War broke out. A South Carolina contractor was finally found and construction began, only to be interrupted by the Union blockade and invasion of the St. Johns River region. In 1862 a disgusted legislature halted the project completely. Some $17,500 had been wasted.[75]

A second demonstration of the stranglehold of the railroads was provided by the Apalachicola River affair. In 1860 the legislature directed that IIF funds be used to clean out the channel to make it safe for navigation.[76] Under this mandate the IIF trustees ordered a survey to see what needed to be done. But an investor who had purchased a $1,000 railroad construction bond appealed to the courts to prohibit this expenditure on the grounds that IIF assets were totally committed to guarantee the interest on the railroad bonds. In 1862 the Florida supreme court upheld the bondholder's contention. Dismissing the argument that the IIF assets consisted largely of swamplands granted to the state for reclamation, the court held that the legislature had been within its powers in directing how the IIF trustees should expend the proceeds from the fund. In 1855 the legislature had specified "only a few grand objects, vital to the whole state." Only after the first group of improvements—the specific railroads and the one canal—had been placed in successful operation would the legislature and the trustees be free to support other projects.[77]

By doing nothing for reclamation and everything for the railroads, the Florida authorities clearly violated the spirit of the federal Swamplands Act of 1850. If their policy had been successful, this flaunting of the law might have been defended on pragmatic grounds. If all had gone well, the railroads would soon have been able to pay their interest charges, thus relieving the IIF. Moreover, by opening up the interior of the state and bringing in settlers, the railroads might have helped the trustees to sell land and replenish the fund. Thus enriched, the trustees could have built canals, dug drainage ditches, and dredged rivers.

The Civil War made any such happy outcome impossible. Instead of being able to pay their own way, the railroads suffered one financial blow after another. For hauling soldiers and supplies they were paid in rapidly depreciating paper money. Northern armies destroyed their terminals and seized some of their rolling stock; Confederate authorities tore up some of their track and confiscated locomotives for use elsewhere in the South. By the time the great conflict was over, the railroad companies were hopelessly insolvent, with huge debts and devastated physical property. The Internal Improvement Fund was itself in deplorable condition. The trustees had invested in assets now largely worthless—railroad stocks and bonds and Confederate and state securities. To be sure, they had sold thousands of acres of land during the war. As paper currency, both state and Confederate, flooded the state, many investors sought to exchange this rapidly depreciating money for land. When salt-making from seawater became a booming wartime industry along the Gulf coast, speculators hurried to buy up the tidelands. Determined to combat this profiteering, the IIF trustees under the leadership of Gov. John Milton put strict restrictions on the sale of swamplands within two miles of the coast.[78] In August 1863 the trustees raised the price on all IIF swamplands from 75¢ to $2.50 an acre, payable only in gold, silver, or Florida treasury notes.[79] On 11 September 1863 they took the drastic step of withdrawing all IIF land from the market.[80] As the trustees retreated to wait out the storm, the IIF debt grew larger and larger because of defaulted interest on railroad construction bonds.

When the Confederate forces finally laid down their arms in the spring of 1865, the dreams of the early boosters looked more improbable than ever.

# 3 The Big Dealers

$\mathbf{F}$or three decades after the Civil War adventurous businessmen were placing their bets. It was the right moment because the rapidly growing nation needed everything—lumber, coal, oil, steel, railroads, electricity. Money, usually borrowed, staked the new ventures; and money, by the millions, rewarded the winners, men like Vanderbilt, Carnegie, and Rockefeller. But why did these enterprisers strike it rich, while hundreds of others gambled and lost? Sometimes the winners were shrewder than the losers and sometimes they were luckier, but often they won just because they had the right political connections. Only in theory was it an age of rugged individualism; in practice businessmen looked to government at all levels—municipal, state, federal—for contracts, franchises, charters, land grants, and subsidies. To succeed, one needed the right political friends, such as officeholders, legislators, and judges.

Businessmen in search of quick rewards found the Florida situation particularly inviting. The state needed railroads and canals to open up the interior and drainage to convert swampy acres into farmland. But there were problems as well as opportunities for the capitalists. The state had a population of only 140,000 in 1860, so where were the passengers and shippers to make railroads and canals profitable or the farmers to purchase reclaimed lands? Unless massive state aid was forthcoming, investors were not interested in Florida ventures. Bitter experience, however, had made the politicians somewhat cautious. Forced to default on government-guaranteed loans to banks and other enterprises during the early decades of statehood and saddled with heavy debts by the guaranteed railroad construction bonds of the 1850s, the state authorities would no longer buy the stock or guarantee the bonds of private corporations. But they did have one golden resource. Unlike other states where the federal government itself granted or sold most of the public land, Florida largely controlled its own land policy. By a liberal interpretation of the Swamplands Act, the national government eventually turned over about 58 percent of the land in Florida, about 22 million acres out of a total of 38 million, to the state's Internal Improvement Fund. To transform these soggy acres into arable fields, pasturelands, and residential subdivisions would require large expenditures, but there were huge short-run profits to be made by getting control of the public domain and stripping off the timber. Speculators were aided in their schemes by the state's shaky finances and the confused governmental situation. The IIF was administered by a highly political Board of Trustees composed of the governor and four other state officers. Land policy shifted from administration to administration as Democratic leadership of the state gave way to Republican and then to Democratic again. And if the Board of Trustees was vulnerable to the manipulations of the speculators, the Florida legislature was equally so. Charges of graft and bribery filled the political debates of the day, and it seems clear that the accusations were often true.

A persistent applicant for land grants was William H. Gleason. About thirty-six years old when he moved to the state, Gleason had spent most of his earlier years in Wisconsin. With vague credentials as a land surveyor and civil engineer, he had dabbled in frontier politics, land speculation, and small-town banking.[1] Early in 1866 he had traveled extensively in Florida investigating the possibility of establishing a colony to cultivate tropical fruit.[2] Making his way into some of the most remote regions of the state, he had taken particular delight in the Biscayne Bay country where only a few settlers, many of them from the Bahamas, were then living. Falling in love with this isolated paradise, Gleason not only moved his family there but began a series of maneuvers intended to bring all South Florida under his control.

In April 1866 Gleason proposed to the IIF trustees that he be permitted to drain any of the swamplands in a vast area lying east and south of the Everglades and also in one tier of townships south of the Caloosahatchee River. For each 50,000 cubic feet of ditch that he dug, he wanted the right to buy 640 acres (one square mile) of the reclaimed land at the price of $40—that is, 6.25 cents an acre instead of the established price of $1.25. The amount of ditching sounds impressive, but actually it was paltry. A ditch one mile long, three feet wide, and three feet deep would provide the specified 50,000 cubic feet. Yet the Democratic governor of the state, David Walker, and his fellow trustees readily agreed to give Gleason what he asked, a conditional grant of over six million acres of state land.[3]

Gleason's generous drainage contract was only one of the many benefits being showered on ambitious businessmen by the Democratic state administration. In May 1867 the IIF trustees promised to sell 250,000 acres of swampland at five cents an acre to the Florida Canal and Inland Transportation Company provided it built a waterway along the Atlantic coast from Fernandina to Jupiter Inlet.[4] In October 1867 the trustees promised to make extensive land grants to Hubbard L. Hart of Palatka on condition that he clear out the Oklawaha River and make it navigable.[5] Hart, who owned a profit-

William H. Gleason. After a tempestuous interval as lieutenant governor and claimant to the governor's office, Gleason devoted his energies to promoting a wide variety of drainage, land, and canal schemes. SPA.

able steamship line plying between Charleston and Savannah and the towns along the lower St. Johns River, carried out this project promptly. In February 1868 a dispatch from Palatka applauded the progress he was making: "It is believed that this is the best public enterprise undertaken for some years past."[6] As his reward, Hart received 33,000 acres of state land and began to profit by carrying steamboat passengers up the mysterious and beautiful Oklawaha River to Silver Springs, an excursion that proved to be one of the most popular tourist attractions of the 1870s.[7]

The new Reconstruction policy dictated by Congress overthrew Democratic control of Florida and instituted eight years of Republican rule. Elected lieutenant governor in June 1968, William H. Gleason was one of the new men coming to power. The political weather appeared to be excellent for his ventures because the Republican governor was another Wisconsin man, Harrison Reed. The new legislature, made up of whites and blacks, granted corporate charters freely. During its first session in 1868 it created no fewer than five new canal companies. Most of these were small local projects, but one, the Southern Inland Navigation and Improvement Company, embodied another of Gleason's wide-ranging schemes. Ignoring the grant to an earlier canal company, the legislature authorized this one to connect Biscayne Bay with the waters of the Indian River, Halifax River, Mosquito Lagoon, and St. Johns River and to dredge out the inside passage from Key West to Biscayne Bay and from the St. Johns to the St. Marys River, thus providing a steamboat navigation through protected waters from Key West to Fernandina. The IIF trustees were authorized to "make such concessions of land in aid in completion of said improvements as they may deem for the best interests of the state." Among the incorporators were Lieutenant Governor Gleason, his partner William H. Hunt, state senator from Dade County, and U.S. Sen. Thomas W. Osborn, reputed to be the most powerful Republican politician in the state.[8]

Although the carpetbaggers appeared to be in firm control of the state, they could not agree among themselves. Within a few months Governor Reed became engaged in a bitter fight with Senator Osborn and Lieutenant Governor Gleason. According to Reed, the trouble began when he refused to go along with the corrupt schemes of the other men. Whether or not this was true, Osborn and Gleason tried to drive Reed from the governorship. On 6 November 1868 a majority in the state house of representatives, nursing grievances of their own, appointed a committee to prepare impeachment charges. The lieutenant governor issued a proclamation declaring that Reed was suspended from office and naming himself acting governor. For about three weeks Florida had two governors, Reed holding on to his office in the state capitol and "Governor" Gleason doing business in Tallahassee's principal hotel. Gleason boasted of his possession of the state seal, but Reed had a much more important asset, firm control of the state supreme court, all of whose justices he had appointed. Not only did the court rule that Reed was still governor pending trial on the impeachment charges, but on 14 December the judges ousted Gleason from his office as lieutenant governor on the ground that he had not fulfilled the constitutional residence requirement.[9] One more act in the farce of the rival governors was played out after the legislature came back into session in January. Still claiming to be president of the senate, Gleason presided over the body during its early sessions. But the anti-Reed movement suddenly and rather mysteriously collapsed. On 9 January 1869 Gleason resigned as president of the senate, and on 26 January the house, by a vote of 43 to 5, cleared Reed of all charges.[10] All that remained to Gleason was the glory of having been lieutenant governor for half a year and "acting governor" for three weeks. However, in a southern climate where even businessmen found it useful to be called "colonel," "general," or "judge," it was no small advantage to the Miami promoter to be known for the rest of his life as "Governor Gleason."

Subsequent events suggest, moreover, that Governor Reed had made some kind of a deal with the Osborn-Gleason faction. On 23 January, three days before the crucial impeachment vote in the house, the IIF trustees had voted to strip Gleason of all his privileges under the drainage contract of 1866,[11] but once the governor's name was cleared he cooperated in a series of measures designed to advance Gleason's business interests. On 1 February Reed approved a bill liberalizing the charter of the Southern Inland Navigation and Improvement Company. Among the new incorporators was Dr. N. H. Moragne of Palatka, a physician, merchant, and member of the state house of representatives, who became president of the company with Gleason designated as chief engineer.[12] On 4 February Reed and the other IIF trustees voted new drainage contracts to Gleason and his partner, state senator William H. Hunt. Gleason received the right to dig ditches and reclaim land along the southeast coast from Jupiter Inlet to Fort Lauderdale; Hunt got the same authority for the region from Fort Lauderdale to the mouth of the Miami River. Both men were given the privilege of buying the reclaimed land for 6.25 cents an acre. The IIF trustees made still a third significant grant at this same meeting. Hubbard Hart, the Palatka steamboat magnate, was given the right to dig a series of canals connecting rivers and canals across the middle of the state. If carried to completion, this system of waterways would fulfill the old dream of a cross-Florida canal. Like Gleason and Hunt, Hart received permission to purchase reclaimed swampland for 6.25 cents an acre.[13]

On 13 February 1869 Governor Reed and his fellow trustees bestowed further benefits on Gleason's Southern Navigation Company. Arguing that the construction of the inland waterway would not only aid navigation but reclaim 3 million acres of swampland, enhancing its value to at least $2.50 an acre, spokesmen for the company requested the right to purchase about 1.5 million acres at $25 a section—less than 4 cents an acre, the land to be conveyed on a schedule as the work proceeded.[14] Not only did the Reed administration approve the contract, but it continued to help the Gleason group in a number of other ways.

In March 1869 Governor Reed addressed a memorial to Congress asking for the restitution of federal land grants to Florida withheld from the state because of secession. The land, he said, was necessary "to induce capitalists to enter again upon the work of completing Florida's internal improvement system." The governor listed four railroads that needed to be built and also urged canals to connect the St. Johns with the Indian River and the Indian River with Biscayne Bay. These two waterways would provide an inland navigation almost 1,000 miles in length extending from Savannah to New York. "The State," Reed explained, "has granted liberal franchises to these enterprises, and if the Federal Government will renew the former grants with the necessary additions, four years will complete the entire system of internal improvements in Florida."[15]

In the fall of 1869 Gleason made a survey of his proposed canal route between the St. Johns and Indian rivers. To pay his expenses, Governor Reed and his friend Milton S. Littlefield each advanced $500, later repaid.[16] In January 1870, by a vote of four to one, the IIF trustees doubled the earlier land grant to Gleason's company.[17] But northern contractors wanted cash, not land. In February the IIF trustees obligingly agreed that if the company would pay in advance the state would give a deed for the land, thereby enabling the company to mortgage it and issue bonds to pay construction costs.[18] It required delicate manipulation on Gleason's part to take advantage of this promise. On 26 March 1870 the Southern Inland Navigation Company signed a contract with Willis Gaylord of New York for construction of the canal. On 13 April Gleason was back in Tallahassee lobbying another resolution through the IIF Board of Trustees. This one would make the proposed construction bonds more attractive by providing for their conversion into land at the option of the holders. Proceeds from the bond sale were to be deposited in a New York bank and drawn upon for construction costs on orders requiring the signature of the state comptroller. The trustees divided 4 to 2, with one of the opposing votes cast by Col. Robert Gamble, the state comptroller, a Democrat unhappy with the manipulations of his Republican colleagues.[19] Impatient with Gamble's foot-dragging, Gleason later induced a majority of the IIF trustees to transfer the power of approving payments to the treasurer of the IIF, John S. Adams, a faithful friend of the canal project.[20]

Governor Reed continued to cooperate closely with his recent enemies, Gleason and Senator Osborn. To help induce New York investors to put up money for the project, Reed, Gleason, Osborn, Adams, and Marcellus L. Stearns, the U.S. surveyor general for Florida, all signed a letter to Willis Gaylord, the contractor, stating that, from their knowledge of the lands granted to the Southern

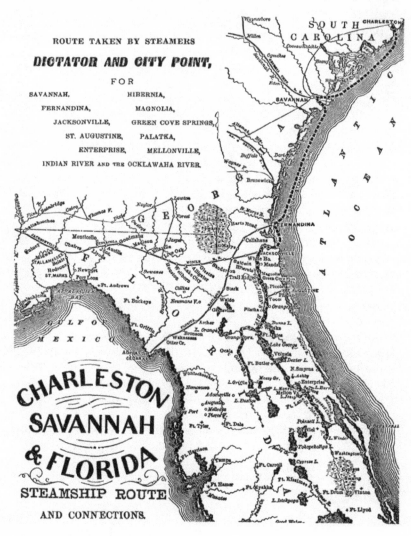

Steamship routes to Florida, 1875. Since railroad connections were still bad, northern tourists reached Florida most comfortably by embarking on steamships at Charleston and landing at Jacksonville or at some other port on the St. Johns River. Map Collection, Strozier Library.

Inland Navigation Company, they would "appraise their value at from Eight to Ten Dollars per acre upon the Completion of the Canal and Improvements contemplated by the Charter. . . ."[21]

But the Southern Inland Navigation Company was by no means the only enterprise to gain special favors from the Reed administration. In October 1869 the IIF trustees promised to sell 1.1 million acres of land to the New York and Florida Lumber, Land and Improvement Company for ten cents an acre on condition that the company settle at least one new inhabitant for each 320 acres it received from the state.[22] This deal offered huge profits to the speculators and politicians. Unlike the Gleason schemes, which involved mostly the southeastern swamplands, this one gave the promoters their pick of public lands in all parts of the state. Since timber was the real prize, the company could hardly lose. In October 1870 the IIF trustees conveyed the first 100,000 acres and accepted as payment $10,100, paid in coupons of the defaulted construction bonds of the Florida Railroad.[23]

Still a third land-grabbing scheme involved a new corporation bearing the exotic name "Aquatic and Tropical Plant Propagation Company," chartered by the legislature in February 1870. This organization proposed to encourage the growth of tropical fruits, drain the Everglades, and reclaim waste lands by cutting canals and drainage ditches from Lake Okeechobee west to the Gulf of Mexico and east to the Atlantic Ocean. To encourage these good deeds, the legislature promised huge grants covering all unsold land in South Florida that the state already held or might acquire from the federal government. The IIF trustees were directed to make the conveyance as soon as the company expended $100,000 on its improvements. The incorporators included New York financiers and such important Florida Republicans as former Lieutenant Governor Gleason, Speaker of the Assembly Marcellus L. Stearns, U.S. Congressman Charles M. Hamilton, Commissioner of Immigration John S. Adams, and State Senators William J. Purman and William M. Hunt.[24]

The great giveaway was brought to a halt, not by an outraged citizenry but by the maneuvers of a rival capitalist. After the Civil War the Democratic IIF trustees had attempted to get rid of the troublesome debt created by the state guarantee of the construction bonds by ordering seizure and sale of the bankrupt railroads. But the liquidation had had an unfortunate outcome. David Yulee and other investors in the Florida Railroad were able to buy back the now debt-free line from the state, while the IIF received much less money from the foreclosure than was necessary to pay what was due on the defaulted bonds. The IIF trustees offered 20 cents on the dollar to the bondholders, which many of them accepted, but a few held out for the full amount of the debt. Among these was Francis Vose, a New York iron manufacturer who had taken construction bonds in payment for rails sold to the Florida Railroad. Protesting that the IIF trustees were squandering assets pledged for the payment of these, Vose appealed to the courts for protection. In December 1870 a U.S. circuit court judge issued the first of several orders prohibiting the trustees from disposing of their land except at the official price, payable in cash. To protect the interests of Vose and other creditors, the court eventually appointed a receiver to handle the assets of the Internal Improvement Fund. The Vose litigation put a prompt halt to the schemes of the New York and Florida Lumber, Land and Improvement Company when the court ordered the company to reconvey to the state the 100,000 acres already deeded to it.[25]

But Gleason adroitly eluded the coils that Vose was winding around the Reed administration. In December 1870, when the federal court issued its first injunction, the IIF trustees had not formally conveyed any land to the Southern Inland Navigation Company, and thus it was not covered in the judge's order that recently deeded lands be reconveyed.[26] Over the next several months Gleason made a feverish effort to carry through his plans in spite of the Vose obstruction. What he needed was to get his inland waterway into actual construction, thus proving the good faith of his company and its right to buy the 3 million acres of land it had been promised. The only trouble was that the company had no money and could not sell its bonds unless it first received part of the land. With the cooperation of Harrison Reed and his fellow trustees, Gleason tried to lift the company by its own bootstraps.

Why did Reed continue to help Gleason, his recent enemy? One reason may have been Reed's sincere desire to promote railroads and canals for the benefit of the state; another was certainly his need to maintain détente with a rival political faction. But a third reason must have been the confused condition of Reed's personal finances. A careless man with money, he had occasionally dipped into his own funds to aid the depleted state treasury; on other occasions, he apparently accepted loans and gifts from promoters seeking benefits from the state. On 22 January 1871—only a month after the first Vose injunction—Charles L. Mather, the treasurer of the Southern Inland Navigation Company and a Jacksonville friend of the governor, wrote a letter to Gleason imploring him to deposit $9,000 for Reed's benefit in another man's name. Mather wrote: "I have pledged my word that the money should be paid in New York on Wednesday & I care not what it costs it must be done. The Governor here is involved in this matter to an extent that I can not *write to you*, but it is a matter of utmost importance to him & all of *us* that this matter is arranged and to you I look for its being done no matter what you have to promise or do. See that $9,000 is placed to the credit of F.E. Little with Jay Cooke & Co. on next Wednesday."[27]

Between April and September 1870 Gleason had paid into the IIF trustees about $56,000 in the past due coupons of four different Florida railroads.[28] On the basis of this he now asked the trustees to deed some 1.3 million acres of the 3.1 million total promised to the Southern Inland Navigation Company. This was desperately needed because the company was already building a dredge at Palatka and had to establish a market for its bonds. The Gleason group could count on Governor Reed, Immigration Commissioner Adams, and State Treasurer Simon B. Conover, but Comptroller Gamble continued to make trouble. In February 1871 Dr. Moragne, president of the company, wrote to Conover: "I hope you will persuade Col. Gamble to sign the Deeds as a refusal to do so now on the part of the Board will not only suspend our work but may abolish it altogether."[29] And to Gleason Moragne wrote that he had enlisted the help of Adams in trying to get the deeds. The dredge was nearly ready, and he was expecting the New York contractors, Gaylord and Flanagan, to come down soon, especially since he had sent them word of the discovery of phosphate beds near Lake Washington on the route of the proposed canal.[30] Late in March, Gaylord wrote to Gleason reminding him of steps that were needed before the construction bonds could finally be issued. Most important was an actual deed signed by the IIF trustees.[31]

On 10 February 1871 Reed and a majority of the board finally put their names on a deed conveying 1,360,600 acres of swampland to the company. After hurriedly getting the deed recorded in six county seats,[32] Gleason took his precious document to New York, where he was able to put through a deal with the Union Trust Company whereby the company issued $5 million worth of construction bonds secured by a mortgage on its land. This coup allowed Gleason's company to move the new dredge up the St. Johns River to Lake Harney and to begin digging out the river channel toward Lake Washington.[33] The Reed administration continued to help the scheme. Acting as secretary of the IIF board, Adams issued a certificate declaring that the land grant had been "perfected by absolute deed in fee simple, duly recorded," that nobody had any lien or legal claim upon the lands, and that the company's title was "clear and perfect." Governor Reed added an affidavit swearing that this certificate was "true and correct."[34]

This misleading document could not alter the actual situation. Neither Gleason's scheme nor that of other speculators could proceed unchallenged so long as Francis Vose persisted in his litigation. But Milton S. Littlefield, the most audacious promoter operating in Florida, now concocted a gigantic deal that proposed to take care of Vose and all the other hungry parties. On 31 May 1871 the IIF trustees promised to convey to Littlefield's Jacksonville, Pensacola and Mobile Railroad all of the lands held by them in trust except lands deeded or contracted to be conveyed to the Southern Inland Navigation Company, the Aquatic and Tropical Plant Propagation Company, and Hubbard L. Hart. For its part, the railroad agreed to do three things: complete a railroad between Quincy, Florida, and Mobile, Alabama; pay off Vose and other holders of the defaulted railroad construction bonds; and turn over $100,000 to the Internal Improvement Fund. Vose was willing to accept this settlement, and the federal circuit judge at Jacksonville approved it in December with a modification to enable the New York and Florida Lumber, Land and Improvement Company to have a share in the lands.[35]

If these plans had been carried out, the Internal Improvement Fund would have been stripped of all its vast acreage in return for a paltry $100,000 and the liquidation of the pre–Civil War railroad construction debts. But the scheme miscarried. News of what was happening reached the lower house of the legislature, which demanded the arrest of Littlefield for refusing to appear before an investigating committee. This anti-Littlefield move may have been motivated more by avarice than by zeal for reform; some of the legislators were alleged to be trying to extort money from the high-flying promoter.[36] In any event, the Littlefield scheme became lost in the general political confusion of the next few months. Still suspicious of Governor Reed, the Osborn ring made another attempt to remove him. The assembly passed a bill of impeachment, and from February to April, when the senate finally cleared him, Reed remained on his Jacksonville farm while Lt. Gov. Samuel T. Day served as acting governor. Although Day was supposed to be more compliant with the schemes of the ring than Reed, the IIF trustees bowed to public opinion and called a halt to the schemes of the promoters. On 6 March they repudiated the Littlefield deal by a

Embarking for a voyage up the Oklawaha River. Small specially built steamboats were required for the trip from Palatka to Silver Springs. SPA.

three-to-two vote, and on the next day they voted to support a legislature-directed policy of securing homesteads to actual settlers and ordered the lands claimed by the New York and Florida Lumber, Land and Improvement Company to be restored to the market.[37] Soon after Reed resumed the governorship, an attempt was made to revive the big deal, but by this time Littlefield was in such disgrace that his scheme never went through.

Also lost in the political turmoil of 1872 was a bill which Gleason had tried to push through the legislature. This would "authorize corporations to change their names, consolidate their capital stock and merge their corporate powers." A coalition of Democrats and dissident black Republicans successfully opposed the bill, and one of the latter bitterly denounced Gleason himself: "The gentleman who introduced this bill, it would seem, has a hobby for corporations. I am credibly informed that his signature is attached to no less than eight articles of association in this State. Doubtless the true intent of this bill is to consolidate these eight corporations, with their powers and capital stock, into one grand scheme for the controlling of future public works requiring State aid."[38]

The protracted Vose litigation became a more and more troublesome obstacle to Gleason. Suspicious investors refused to buy the Southern Inland Navigation Company bonds, and the contractors stopped their work. In January 1873 Harrison Reed's term in office ran out, and Ossian B. Hart, another Republican, became governor. Continuing to cooperate with Gleason, the new IIF trustees extended the time allowed for construction of the waterway. Gleason's company was given until 1 May 1875 to connect the St. Johns and Indian rivers and until 1 January 1877 to complete the entire project.[39] In an effort to meet the new deadlines the company ordered the contractors to put three more dredges on the job.[40]

But trouble for Gleason mounted. The Panic of 1873 and the subsequent depression dried up the bond market. Even more serious was the latest development in the Vose case. On 4 December 1873 the attorney general of the state gave his assent to a new federal order voiding the deed to Gleason's company.[41] Not a man to admit defeat, "Governor" Gleason simply added a still more grandiose project to his schemes. Taking advantage of a new general incorporation law for railroads and canals, Gleason and two other Republican politicians, Lt. Gov. Marcellus Stearns and Adj. Gen. John Varnum, organized "The Gulf and Atlantic Transit Canal Company" with the announced purpose of constructing 1,500 miles of waterway from the Rio Grande in Texas, across the Florida peninsula, and up the Georgia coast to Charleston, South Carolina.[42]

Gleason's new company was not the only one proposing to build a canal across Florida. This dream of pre–Civil War days had become vivid again during the early 1870s. Farmers in the Mississippi Valley had opened up thousands of acres of prairie soil and were producing bumper crops of wheat and corn. How was this produce to reach its most profitable markets on the East Coast and in Europe? Railroads were not enough, and existing waterways were inadequate. Ships from Texas ports and New Orleans still had to make the long voyage around the Florida peninsula with its treacherous reefs. In 1873 the Key West salvage court handled 700 shipwreck cases. So dangerous was the voyage that shippers were paying $3 million a year in extra insurance premiums, and the insurance companies paid out between $2 million and $2.5 million in wreckage claims.[43] In the early 1870s both the Texas and Alabama legislatures requested Congress to explore the possibilities of a ship canal across Florida.[44] And in 1873 the mayor of Savannah and the city's chamber of commerce asked for information on the subject from the Army Corps of Engineers.[45]

The Savannah inquiry probably reflected the ambitions of another group of capitalists, among whom Gen. Lawson McLaws of Savannah was a leader. In 1875 McLaws and other men, mostly from northern Florida, organized the Gulf Coast and Florida Peninsula Canal Company. The incorporators included George A. Drew of Ellaville, Florida, soon to be governor of the state, and Samuel A. Swann, a Fernandina merchant interested in land and railroads. The new company proposed to do just what Gleason's latest enterprise wanted to do—build a waterway from Pensacola along the Gulf coast and then across northern Florida to the east coast. And like Gleason's company, the McLaws company counted heavily on generous land grants from the state to induce capitalists to invest in its project.[46]

During the next few years Congress, no doubt responding to lobbying by various groups, authorized two surveys. The sums appropriated were too small to permit a thorough study of the canal project; the engineers were ordered to survey not all suggested routes but one particular one following the St. Marys River, through the Okefenokee Swamp, and down the Suwannee River to the most suitable point on the Gulf of Mexico. Concentration on this route to the exclusion of the often-discussed St. Johns–Oklawaha River route suggests the influence of the McLaws group, since the St. Marys route would benefit the ports of Fernandina and Savannah rather than Jacksonville. On 30 December 1876 Lt. Col. Q.A. Gillmore of the Army Corps of Engineers made the first of his reports. Two very different types of waterway had been proposed— one a barge canal that could be used only by vessels drawing no more than nine feet, the other a ship canal that could be used by oceangoing vessels. In this first report Colonel Gillmore said that a barge canal could probably be built along the proposed route, and he estimated the distance to be about 226 miles. The feasibility of a ship canal was, he said, "vastly more problematical." He pointed out the great economic benefits that a ship canal would bring, but he warned that much more extensive surveys would be required to evaluate the project.[47] A year later Congress responded by making a small appropriation for further surveys, and in 1880 Gillmore made a second report concentrating on the ship canal possibilities. Although the survey was far from thorough, Gillmore estimated that a ship canal could be built along the St. Marys route at an estimated cost of $50 million. The proposed route, 170 miles long, would save steamships running between New Orleans and New York twelve hours in time and $175 worth of coal on each voyage.[48]

But enthusiastic promoters like Gleason and McLaws did not wait for the final surveys before trying to enlist the backing of European

investors. Gleason chose as his salesman "Judge" John H. Fry of
New York, a glib operator in the realm of high finance. Fry was
commissioned to sell not only the construction bonds of the Southern Inland Navigation Company but land in the Panhandle as well.[49]
In 1874 Gleason had made a contract under which the IIF trustees
promised to sell him all IIF land west of the Apalachicola River—
some 1.1 million acres—at prices ranging from 25 cents an acre if he
took it all to 55 cents if he took 50,000 acres.[50] Gleason and Fry
ignored the Vose injunction, either because they hoped that European investors could be kept in ignorance of it or because they
believed that a really big deal would bring in enough money to pay

Dredging Santa Fe Lake. During the 1870s and 1880s local enterprisers opened up parts of
central Florida by digging short canals and dredging out lakes. The Santa Fe project,
northeast of Gainesville, helped to provide local orange growers with an outlet to the railroad at Waldo and to bring in tourists. SPA.

off the bondholders and remove the legal obstacles. Since Fry was a man prone to even bigger dreams than Gleason, he offered increasingly inflated projects to European investors. In a proposal put together in August 1874 the stock of the Southern Inland Navigation Company was to be enlarged to a face value of $26 million, of which $18 million was to be offered to foreign purchasers at the bargain price of $6 million. From this amount the company would pay Gleason $1 million for the Panhandle land. This 1.1 million acres of valuable timber land plus the 2 million acres which the company hoped to get in southeastern Florida would give it 3.1 million acres and provide security for its construction bonds. Five million dollars would be left for building the canal, retiring the construction bonds, and clearing the title to the land. Stockholders would be permitted to exchange their stock for land according to an agreed schedule.[51] Two years later the Gleason-Fry deal had become still more grandiose, involving not only the Atlantic waterway but the cross-Florida canal as well. The Atlantic and Gulf Ship Canal Company, with a potential capital of $40 million, would hold all the assets of the old Southern Inland Navigation Company, now its "Eastern Division," plus a franchise to build a waterway from Fernandina to the Gulf of Mexico.[52] In 1875 Gleason spent four months in London trying to nail down the elusive deal. It never quite came off, although Fry preserved his extraordinary confidence. "Be encouraged," he wrote to Gleason in November 1876, "I think the end of the long lane is near."[53]

Meanwhile Gleason had been thwarted in a much more modest effort. In May 1875 he reported to the IIF trustees that he had dug a canal from Lake Worth to the Atlantic Ocean, lowering the water in the lake and reclaiming all the adjoining land. Claiming that he had excavated some 300,000 cubic feet, he tendered $240 and requested a deed for 3,840 acres in accordance with the old drainage contract. Had he been able to complete this transaction, Gleason would have purchased at 6.25 cents an acre land near the soon-to-be-developed resort city of Palm Beach. Unhappily for the promoter, the IIF trustees decided that the Vose injunction forbade them to make the conveyance.[54] Gleason's ditch silted in but later was reopened; it became the well-known Lake Worth Inlet.

Once again Vose proved to hold all the aces in this game for high stakes. He offered to scale down his claim against the Internal Improvement Fund from $560,000 to $400,000, but the trustees were unable to sell enough land to pay him off.[55] Only a big deal would rescue the fund, and Marcellus Stearns, who became governor in 1874 after Hart's death, hoped to find saviors among English investors. In July 1875 the IIF trustees commissioned Reverdy Johnson, a well-known Maryland lawyer and former diplomat, to sell 3 million acres of state land at 30 cents an acre.[56] Johnson died in London the following February before he could make the hoped-for sale.

Neither Johnson's death nor the return of the Democrats to power at Tallahassee in January 1877 killed the dream of the big deal. Gov. George F. Drew and the new trustees first appointed George Norris, a Baltimore merchant, as their agent and later turned to Samuel A. Swann, the Fernandina specialist in lands.[57]

In June 1877 Swann wrote a long letter to a London investment house explaining the Florida situation. By selling 2 million or 3 million acres of land the IIF trustees hoped to raise enough money to pay off $850,000 owed to Vose and other holders of the guaranteed railroad construction bonds. Furthermore, they hoped that an infusion of foreign capital would bring about rapid development and a tide of immigration, thus compensating the state for selling off its lands. Without any further inducement the trustees expected a great program of internal improvements to result. Most important of the anticipated projects would be a ship canal to connect the Gulf of Mexico with the Atlantic Ocean. Others would be the east coast waterway from Fernandina to Key West and two railroads—one from Georgia down the east coast to Key Largo, the other across central Florida to Port Charlotte. The syndicate controlling the lands, Swann wrote, would be most likely to control these projected works. According to him, hard times made an investment in Florida land all the more inviting. Earlier depressions had spurred the frontier movement, and already people from the rural districts of the East and West were coming to Florida. Investors could make a short-run profit by cutting off the timber and a long-run profit by selling land to the new settlers. Swann offered tracts of 500,000 acres for 60 cents an acre and larger amounts for less. The price for 3 million acres would be 30 cents an acre. Swann emphasized that both political parties and the courts had endorsed the current plan to get the Internal Improvement Fund out of debt.[58]

More impatient than ever, Vose now proposed that the trustees turn over 4 million acres of land to him in satisfaction of all his claims, but they rejected this and waited for good news from Swann. The agent arrived in London on 29 July 1877 and sent back a shrewd analysis of the situation. He found English investors worried about the possibility of war in Turkey and suspicious of distant enterprises, but even so, he was encouraged to see that land investments and canal projects continued to be popular. He reported that Gleason's prospects appeared to be promising. "Judge" Fry was living in style at the Grand Midland Hotel and had been successful in selling his project to a syndicate of Amsterdam speculators. He had combined the trans-Florida ship canal with the Atlantic waterway in what he described as the "grandest and most acceptable investment now before the European public." The Amsterdam group had deposited a substantial sum of money, which would have been turned over to Fry already had the investors not "got an inkling that the title to the Canal Lands could not be perfected till the Vose decree was out of the way." Fry's problems had been complicated by the arrival in London of John T. Drew, an attorney representing Vose. Swann hoped to turn the situation to the IIF's advantage. In order to get out whole, he believed that Fry was going to have to raise the money to buy the 3 million acres being offered by the IIF trustees. If he could not, Swann believed that there were other parties in Europe ready to throw Fry and Gleason overboard "and go in with the Dutchmen" to buy the lands and build the canals themselves. "I have a good case, a good thing to sell," Swann wrote to the trustees, "and as land is in the ascendant, I look for success."[59]

As Swann had predicted, Fry put together another of his superschemes, one designed to take care of all the interested parties: European investors, Francis Vose, IIF trustees, Gleason, and, of course, Fry himself. Fry proposed to purchase the proffered 3 million acres for $900,000. More than two-thirds of this amount— $617,658—was to go to Vose to pay the interest on his railroad bonds. (Vose cannily reserved his rights to the principal that would not come due until 1891.) The IIF trustees would receive $282,342, out of which they would still have to pay off other bondholders. Fry, Gleason, and their backers would not only obtain 3 million acres of land at the bargain price of 30 cents an acre, but they would clear their title to 2.3 million more acres granted earlier, on the basis of which they had issued the bonds of the Southern Inland Navigation Company.[60]

The London negotiators—Fry, Swann, and Vose's attorney—all signed this agreement, but the IIF trustees refused to approve it.[61] Unwilling to go along with a scheme so favorable to Gleason and Vose and so unfavorable to the state, they looked to Swann to come up with something better. Swann stayed on in London until December 1877, when the IIF trustees ordered him to give up the effort unless he had a promising offer. They praised his activities, which would have been successful, they believed, "but for the interference of Vose and others."[62] Reporting on other developments, a member of the board wrote Swann that Vose was trying to get all the IIF land out of the control of the trustees and into his own hands.[63] The Drew administration continued to play a waiting game, stalling off Vose's lawyers in the courts while angling for the great land sale that would release the Internal Improvement Fund for other purposes. The governor pinned most of his hopes on the cross-Florida canal. In November 1879 the IIF trustees offered any company having the ability to carry out the project a free 200-foot right-of-way, and land lying within one-eighth mile of this, at five cents an acre. As soon as construction began, the trustees promised to sell the company 2 million acres more at 30 cents an acre; when construction was completed the company could purchase still another million acres at five cents an acre.[64] Two months later the trustees sweetened the offer, promising to sell any such company 3 million acres at 30 cents an acre as soon as construction was begun and carried on in good faith.[65]

Although Drew's canal policy was probably intended to attract foreign investors to the McLaws enterprise in which he and Swann had an interest, the indefatigable Gleason continued to boost his own rival project. Even before Fry's London deal fell through, Gleason had begun to lose faith in his agent. An inquiry about Fry had brought this disquieting reply: "My impression of him is extremely unfavorable. I would not trust him in any way whatever."[66] After the collapse of the latest deal, one of Gleason's associates described Fry as "the very worst and most difficult man I have ever known.... D——n the old fool. We would have had things very lovely if he had been half decent."[67] But Gleason was in no mood to give up his schemes. Firing Fry and hiring Frank Sherwin as his new agent, he continued to dangle bait in the financial waters of London.

In March 1878 Gleason achieved a major coup in getting the backing of Sir Edward Reed, one of England's boldest enterprisers, who had made a fortune in the construction of battleships for the Royal Navy. To resuscitate the Southern Inland Navigation Company, Reed loaned it £50,000 and took the old construction bonds as security. The Gleason-Reed strategy was first to raise enough money to build the Atlantic waterway from the St. Marys River to Key West, thus fortifying the company's claim to over 2 million acres of land at a bargain price. Gleason estimated that the project would require 20 dredges and cost $3,655,100.[68]

But this plan did not mean that Gleason had lost interest in the cross-Florida ship canal. On the contrary he had spent the spring of 1878 in Washington lobbying for the second Gillmore survey. Informing Sherwin of his success, he assured him that the survey would be made "in our interest." Gillmore was "fully committed to our route." Moreover, Gillmore's assistant, a Professor Mahan formerly of West Point, would probably make the actual survey. Gleason described Mahan as a "very able and efficient officer," who was "much impressed with our proposed route" and desired to "make it a success." "He is our friend," Gleason wrote, "and calls almost daily at our office." Gleason wrote Sherwin that it was very important for Reed to advance the promised money so that they could commence construction "and maintain the standing of the Atlantic & Gulf Transit Company."[69] Despite Gleason's confidence that the engineers making the survey would be friendly to his enterprise, the Corps of Engineers, perhaps under pressure from the McLaws group, replaced Mahan with S. L. Freemont, a Savannah engineer.[70] In any event, the second Gillmore report of 1880 followed the first one in concentrating on the northern St. Marys River and ignoring routes farther south that might have been Gleason's preference.

While Gleason pulled wires in Washington and Tallahassee, Sir Edward Reed tried to promote the canal project in London. But the Vose litigation still caused great difficulties. In August 1879 Reed complained to Gleason that the liens caused a "want of value" in the Southern Inland Navigation Company bonds, "and this difficulty you & the Co. have unfortunately not succeeded in any way in removing or diminishing." Reed had therefore been making efforts of his own to free the state lands from "the existing oppressive liens" and believed that he was making substantial progress.[71]

But Sir Edward did not find the magic key, and in January 1881, when William D. Bloxham succeeded Drew as governor, the impasse still continued. A score of eager speculators were offering to build a wide range of dazzling improvements—canals, drainage ditches, railroads—always contingent on generous land grants from the state. The politicians, often stockholders in the petitioning companies, were eager to cooperate, but Vose still barred the way, determined that no one else should make big money out of the growth of the state unless he was paid off first.

# 4 The Flow of Northern Dollars

I n the 1880s Florida began to climb out of its post–Civil War poverty. The state's recovery came as part of the national boom that increased railroad mileage by almost 68 percent in a single decade and created new fortunes in oil, steel, and electrical equipment. As northern capitalists grew richer and bolder, they looked to underdeveloped Florida as a field for their next exploits. The state also benefited by the emergence of a new leisure class. No longer content to enjoy pleasant summers at Newport and Saratoga, fashionable people now sought to escape the rigors of winter by patronizing the new Florida hotels.

Although southern planters had paid winter visits to Florida's lakes and springs before the Civil War, few northerners had made the long trip to these resorts. In 1870 the state still seemed a remote and mysterious region. In April of that year a northern physician described Florida in a magazine article: "It is a land of many wonders," Dr. J. P. Little reported; "No more singular country is to be found on the broad continent than this mixture of sand and mud, called the land of Florida." If one wanted to take a walk in East Florida, he said, he had first to wade through ankle-deep sand and then step into a mud puddle, "and some of these mud puddles cover a whole county."[1] Even Florida's famous springs aroused his professional suspicion. The surface water came from swamps that swarmed with "invisible animalcules," and the underground water was even worse because it passed through rotton shell-limestone. "The deeper the well, therefore," he warned, "the cooler and more dangerous the water."[2] In another article, he described Florida as "the tail-end of the country." Just as a horse's tail was useful only to brush off the flies, Florida was worthless except "to brush off the annoyance of ill-health."[3]

Yet even to the jaundiced eye of Dr. Little, Florida soon began to look better. While the St. Johns River had formerly seemed to him

62

"a great solitary highway leading to nothing," he saw it changing. In 1871 he wrote: "Since the war a large stream of emigration has poured in, the river banks are thickly strewn with settlements, and marks of cultivation are seen. An increasing crowd of Northern immigrants, energetic and restless, are planting fruit-farms and raising vegetables for the great cities of the seaboard."[4]

Among the new orange groves was one belonging to Harriet Beecher Stowe, then the most famous woman in the country. The author of *Uncle Tom's Cabin* made her first trip to Florida in the winter of 1866–67. She spent a few months at Laurel Grove, an old plantation on the west bank of the St. Johns, but she found a more promising site at Mandarin, a pretty little village on the east bank, about fourteen miles south of Jacksonville. Here she bought a thriving orange grove and had a house built. Arriving in January 1870 the Stowe household spent fourteen happy winters here before the failing health of Mrs. Stowe's husband made the long trip from Hartford, Connecticut, no longer possible.[5] A contemporary description conveys something of the charm of the place: "No one who has ever seen it can forget the peaceful beauty of this Florida home and its surroundings. The house, a story and a half cottage of many gables, stands on a bluff overlooking the broad St. John's, which is five miles wide at this point. It nestles in the shade of a grove of superb, moss-hung live oaks, around one of which the front piazza is built. Several fine old orange trees also stand near the cottage, scenting the air with the sweet perfume of their blossoms in the early spring, and offering their golden fruit to whomever may choose to pluck it during the winter months."[6]

Filled with missionary zeal, Mrs. Stowe endeavored to help the black people of the community. She was largely instrumental in building a pretty little Episcopal church, where the blacks worshipped at one service and the whites at another. She helped former slaves learn to read and write. But she combined these good works with money-making activities, shipping oranges from her grove and writing for the northern press. Yet with all this busyness Mrs. Stowe felt the languid enchantment of the region: "And when I get here," she wrote to her English friend, the novelist George Eliot, "I enter another life. The world recedes, I am out of it; it ceases to influence; its bustle and noise dies away in the far distance; and here is no winter, an open air life — a quaint, rude, wild wilderness sort of life, both rude and rich...."[7] In another letter she described the weather as "heavenly, neither hot nor cold; cool, calm, bright, serene, and so tranquilizing."[8]

Mrs. Stowe became one of the state's best boosters. She wrote little vignettes of Florida life for the religious press and published a book entitled *Palmetto Leaves* (1873). "No dreamland on earth," she wrote, "can be more unearthly in its beauty and glory than the St. John's in April."[9] Her enthusiasm made a strong impression on northern readers. If the author of *Uncle Tom's Cabin*, denounced as a disturber of the peace in the antebellum South, could find a happy second home in Florida, other Yankees could also expect to be well treated there. And more and more of them visited the state each winter.

A steamboat voyage up the St. Johns River became one of the feature events of such a Florida trip, and Mrs. Stowe's cottage was the point of greatest interest to most tourists. In brash disregard of the Stowes' privacy, the ship captains landed their passengers at Mandarin, and the sightseers trooped across the famous author's property, picking her flowers and breaking off branches from her trees. This rude behavior occasionally aroused the ire of Prof. Calvin Stowe, Harriet's husband, who liked to sit on the broad piazza reading weighty books in German and Latin. Outraged by some piece of insolence, Calvin would deliver a thundering rebuke. "I would have you understand, sir," he told one miscreant, "that I am the protector and proprietor of Mrs. Stowe and of this place, and if you commit any more such shameful depredations I will have you punished as you deserve."[10]

Mrs. Stowe was not the only writer to advertise the state. Sidney Lanier, whose health had been ruined by confinement in a Union prison camp during the Civil War, had been scratching out a precarious living in Baltimore when the Great Atlantic Coastline Railroad Company hired him to write a guidebook to Florida.[11] Lanier's *Florida: Its Scenery, Climate, and History* (1875) provided a vivid picture of the wild beauty of this unspoiled region. Published in the same year was a *Guide to Florida*, written under the pseudonym "Rambler." Subsidized by the advertising of transportation companies and hotels, Rambler's *Guide* specialized in practical information about steamship lines, railroads, and hotels. Still another addition to this growing literature was George M. Barbour's *Florida for Tourists, Invalids, and Settlers* (1882). Written in cooperation with a state agency for promoting immigration, Barbour's book contained a wide range of information useful not only to visitors but to farmers and businessmen who might want to move to the state.

This travel literature provided potential visitors with excellent advice on what to see and do. Directions on how to get to Florida varied according to who paid the author. Lanier, on the payroll of a railroad, carefully listed the various rail routes then in operation between New York and Jacksonville.[12] On the other hand, Rambler, responsive to steamship advertising, recommended the exhilarating voyage by sea. One could embark at New York and dock at Charleston or Savannah some 60 hours later. From either of these ports one could continue the voyage to Florida through sheltered waters. "By any other route," Rambler explained, "many changes of conveyance are made imperative, causing great inconvenience and suffering to the invalid traveller." By sailing on the *Dictator* or the *City Point* all this trouble was avoided, and the visitor was landed at the very door of the principal Florida hotels. The steamers proceeded directly to Fernandina, Jacksonville, Magnolia, Green Cove Springs, Picolata, Tocoi, and Palatka. Rambler assured his readers that the staterooms were clean and comfortable, "whilst the table is provided with every luxury that Charleston, Savannah, and Florida markets can produce."[13]

In the 1870s the visitor was likely to spend most of his time along the St. Johns River. Varying in width from one to six miles, the lower St. Johns seemed more like a string of lakes than a river. The same steamships that brought passengers from Charleston and Savannah could navigate as far up as Palatka, fifty-five miles south of Jacksonville, and other good-sized vessels sailed ninety miles further to Enterprise. "Here on the St. John's," wrote Mrs. Stowe, "a water-coach is more to the purpose, in the present state of our wood-roads, than any land carriage, and the delight of sailing is something infinitely above any other locomotion. On this great, beautiful river you go drifting like a feather or a cloud; while the green, fragrant shores form a constantly-varying picture as you pass."[14] Along the lower St. Johns attractive villages and well-kept premises impressed the travelers. Barbour described the scene: "Large estates, having commodious residences, with wide, roomy verandas, standing in the midst of neatly cleared house-grounds, and surrounded by broad fields and thrifty, green-leaved orange-groves, the home pier projecting into the river (for every one residing on the St. John's River *must* have a pier and a fleet of boats to complete his happiness), are everywhere in sight, lining the shores on either hand and charming the traveler with their manifest evidences of comfort and content."[15]

Several of the river towns became important resorts. In 1875 Jacksonville was the most important city in Florida. Every winter a

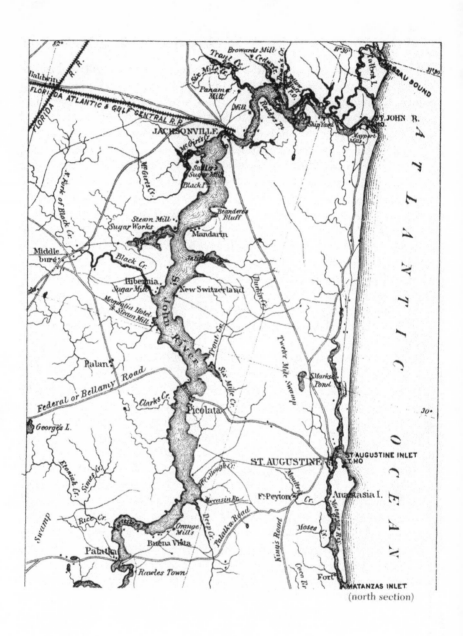

(north section)

The St. Johns River. During Florida's first tourist boom, a cruise up the St. Johns was a very popular attraction. From Daniel Brinton, *A Guide-Book of Florida and the South*, reproduced from the 1869 edition by University Presses of Florida, 1978.

(south section)

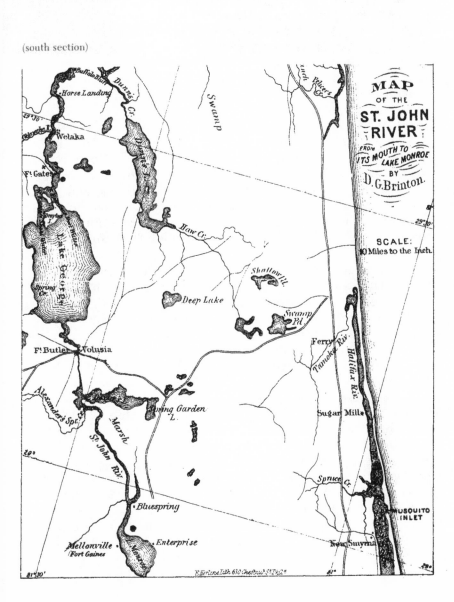

large influx of visitors was added to its year-round population of some
15,000. The new arrivals found imposing hotels, good banking facilities, and railroad and steamboat connections with the rest of the
state. Twenty-four miles to the south of Jacksonville was Green Cove
Springs, "the Saratoga of the St. Johns." Wealthy visitors strolled
through the grounds of two of Florida's best hotels, soaked in the
tubs, and drank the water, described as "slightly sulphurous and remarkably clear, sparkling and copious."[16] Thirty miles farther up the
river Palatka was a popular stopover place. Continuing their voyage
ninety miles farther, travelers reached Lake Monroe, the turn-
around point for most of them. The town of Enterprise boasted such
attractions as the De Barry estate with fine orange groves, a sulphur
spring, and a large hotel, which Barbour described as eclipsing any
other in the South at the time of its construction in the early 1880s.[17]

For the last eighty miles of the voyage, through the stretch that
Barbour called the Middle St. Johns, the river narrowed to a crooked
channel some 50 to 300 feet in width. A dense growth of oaks, cypress, sweetgum, and willow trees covered the shores, and great
clusters of Spanish moss hung from the branches. Along the river-
banks grew a jungle of tropical grasses, reeds, and brilliant-hued
flowers. Tourists crowded the decks to admire the snowy egrets,
white herons, and bright-colored birds of many species. Along this
stretch travelers might catch their first glimpse of alligators, but
these creatures had learned to be wary of the gun-happy visitors.
"The managers of the steamer-lines," Barbour reported, "have recently issued strict orders forbidding any shooting from their steamers, a wise and timely regulation, for, by their insane shooting at everything, the tourists were driving all birds, alligators, and animals
from this portion of the river."[18] Most males seem, indeed, to have
cherished shooting as their favorite pastime, and alligators appealed
to them as perfect targets. As a visitor to Florida in 1874 explained: "I
disapprove of killing animals for mere sport and destroy not deliberately, except when I wish to use them for food; but the alligator is the
enemy of all living creatures, the tyrant of the waters, and the death
of one saves the lives of hundreds of other animals. So blast away at
the 'gators, O ye Florida tourists!—you will not kill many of them,
anyway: their skulls are too thick—but spare the pelicans, who are a
harmless race of fisherfolk, like ourselves."[19]

Although most tourists did not go farther south than Enterprise,
the St. Johns wound on for 214 miles more to its headwaters in Lake
Washington. Adventurous sportsmen embarked on a small steamboat only about twenty feet wide. This tough craft pushed its way

through channels so narrow that it brushed the tall cane on either side and so crooked that it had to inch its way around the bends. "After hours of travel," Barbour wrote, "we could look back, and within one or two miles' distance see the outlines of the stream zigzagging across to the right and left, like a great letter S." Occasionally the river would broaden into shallow little lakes, "the paradise of alligators, fish, birds, and cattle." The entire region was alive with game—bears, deer, ducks, loons, coots, pelicans, storks, cranes, herons.[20] It was through this difficult country that William H. Gleason had tried to push his Southern Inland Navigation Company canal during the early 1870s.

Excursions on the upper St. Johns were not the only side trips that tourists could take from the river ports. No visit to Florida was complete without a few days in St. Augustine, and the most popular way to get there was by the St. Johns River. One took the steamboat to Tocoi, thirty-four miles from Jacksonville, and then transferred to a railroad for a fifteen-mile trip through the pine barrens to the picturesque old Spanish city. At first horses drew the coaches, but in the early 1870s a locomotive was substituted. From Palatka small steamboats took travelers to several nearby lakes and rivers, and from Enterprise there were other interesting points to visit, especially the new towns of Sanford and Mellonville.

The most delightful side trip was the voyage from Palatka to Silver Springs by way of the Oklawaha River. This was made possible by the entrepreneurship of Hubbard Hart, who had first contracted with the state to make the Oklawaha navigable and then had put into operation specially built little steamboats. "Our vessel," wrote Dr. Little in 1871, "was a mere canal boat, fitted up with a steam engine, ninety feet long by twenty feet wide and drawing only two feet of water. A wheel at the rear, with a rudder on each side of it, propelled us four miles an hour."[21] Sidney Lanier, who made the trip three or four years later, described the *Marion* as "a steamboat which is like nothing in the world so much as a Pensacola gopher with a preposterously exaggerated back."[22] Passengers embarking at Palatka went to bed in one of the little staterooms the night before. A few hours before dawn the ship began its voyage up the St. Johns, and about sunrise passengers could watch as the pilot made his way into the Oklawaha—an impressive feat because the entrance "resembled a little brook pouring out from a jungle of overhanging trees." The pilot continued to demonstrate extraordinary skill in finding the channel. "It would be difficult," Barbour said, "to imagine anything short of a bow-knot more crooked, and there were many places where half a dozen" streams, all looking exactly alike, would converge at one place. "The wonderful ability of that pilot, his foresight, or eyesight, inspired us all with profound admiration, not to say awe."[23]

All day long the little boat pushed its way up the narrow crooked channel, while the passengers lounged on deck. It was, Lanier said, "the sweetest water-lane in the world, a lane which runs for more than a hundred and fifty miles of pure delight betwixt hedgerows of oaks and cypresses and palms and bays and magnolias and mosses and manifold vine-growths, a lane clean to travel along for there is never a speck of dust in it save the blue dust and gold dust which the wind blows out of the flags and lillies, a lane which is as if a typical woods-stroll had taken shape and as if God had turned into water and trees the recollection of some meditative ramble through the lonely seclusion of His own soul."[24] The trip up the Oklawaha may have been for the poet an insight into the soul of God, but to the ordinary passenger it was a shooting gallery with something new to blaze

Shooting alligators. Although the Oklawaha voyage offered rich opportunities to enjoy the beauties of nature, male passengers preferred to blast away at the wildlife. *Scribner's Monthly*, November 1874, and SPA.

away at round every bend—white cranes, herons, curlews, snake-birds, buzzards, alligators, and more alligators.

When darkness finally dropped the curtain on this exciting show, the travelers experienced still further thrills. The crew lighted pitch-pine knots in an iron box above the pilot house, and under this flaring blaze the little steamboat puffed on through the blackness, disclosing an extraordinary scene. Barbour remembered the great trees arching over the channel: "These covered passages are solemn and impressive at any time; but in the night, when lighted up by the blaze of the brilliant bonfire burning on the roof of the wheel-house, then the scene is quite indescribable. The inky water, the lights and shadows of the foliage, the disturbed birds as they wheel gracefully out of sight, all leave an impression never to be forgotten."[25] Lanier had similar impressions: "Startled birds suddenly flutter into the light, and after an instant of illuminated flight melt into the darkness. From the perfect silence of these short flights one derives a certain sense of awe. Mystery appears to be about to utter herself in these suddenly-illuminated forms, and then to change her mind and die back into mystery."[26]

The Oklawaha voyage culminated the next morning when the boat left the river and steamed nine miles up Silver Springs Creek to the springs themselves. From its earliest discovery this place had delighted visitors. They still dropped pebbles and buttons into the basin and watched them sink sixty feet to the bottom where they were clearly visible. "I have seen many wonderful things, and many beautiful things in Florida," wrote Dr. Little, "but nowhere have I ever seen such a gem of perfect beauty as Silver Springs."[27] Silver Springs was the end of the journey for most tourists, but by 1875 the Hart Line steamers were venturing still farther up the Oklawaha River, to Lake Harris and Lake Eustis. This remote section of the state offered one delightful spot after another. Barbour recommended Lake Apopka as "a superb body of water" surrounded by unusually fertile land. He reported that T.G. Spear, a member of the Florida senate, was cutting a series of short canals that would give water communication from Lakes Apopka, Dora, Eustis, and Griffin into the Oklawaha River. Short railroad lines were also connecting some of this potential resort country with the river towns along the St. Johns.[28]

In 1880 Florida already had a flourishing tourist trade, yet where are the familiar names? The travel guides do not mention any of the Atlantic beach resorts soon to be famous—Daytona Beach, Palm Beach, or Miami Beach. And the Gulf coast receives only passing notice. Lanier speaks briefly of Pensacola as an isolated lumber port recently connected by rail with the nearby Alabama cities. Cedar Key had railroad connections with Jacksonville, but its hotel accommodations were primitive. Tampa was located on a magnificent bay, but it could be reached only by a weekly mail steamer from Cedar Key or by a stage coach arriving three times a week from Gainesville.[29] Charlotte Harbor was beautifully situated, but inaccessible to tourists. Pointing out the fact that existing tourist centers did not really have an ideal climate, Barbour wrote: "It is apparent that the time is near at hand when a vast winter 'Coney Island' with Newport and Long Branch combined, must be established at some point in the southern part of the peninsula, beyond any possible danger of cold, frosts, or extreme changes, where a sea-beach drive, islands for pleasure-yachts, a race-course, polo-ground, base-ball park, etc., etc., can be established, and where the health seeker, the hunter, and the fisher, as well as the lover of strange scenes and excitement, may find special attractions. Charlotte Harbor, with a railroad, would present just such a location; and railroads must go there. Each season the army of tourists to Florida is increasing, and the farther south they can get the better they like it. And this spot offers attractions not possessed by any other in the whole country for such a resort."[30]

Charlotte Harbor never became the fashionable resort that Barbour envisioned, but Palm Beach soon filled his prescription. In the 1860s the first settlers, people willing to forsake civilization for a remote Eden, had begun settling on the shores of Lake Worth. By 1880 there were still only a handful of these, dependent on salvaging lumber from shipwrecks to build and furnish their homes and on killing enough deer and fish to supply their tables. Only the hardiest of northern sportsmen ever ventured this far down the coast. Some of these hired boats at St. Augustine and made their way through sheltered waters along the Halifax River, Mosquito Inlet, and Mosquito Lagoon to the "Haulover," an 800-yard-long canal built during the Seminole Wars to connect the lagoon and the Indian River. Usually travelers ended their trip at Jupiter Inlet, the mouth of the Indian River. But, said Rambler, if anyone were disposed to go further through this swampy terrain, he would finally get to Lake Worth, "where perpetual summer crowns the ever-green foliage."[31]

Biscayne Bay was still more remote from the customary itinerary. The easiest way to get there was to take a steamship to Key West and then transfer to a small boat for the voyage to this beautiful stretch of water, near which a small number of settlers were living in happy isolation from the rest of the world. Lanier gave a bit of publicity to the schemes of William H. Gleason: "It is in contemplation to connect the lower end of Indian River with the waters of Biscayne Bay and Barnes' Sound by a canal from Indian River to Lake Worth, and from the latter to Biscayne Bay. The same company ('the Southern Inland Navigation and Improvement Company') propose to connect the St. Johns with Indian River by a canal across the narrow strip between Lake Washington and the latter stream, and thus to afford an inland water-route from Jacksonville entirely down the length of the Florida peninsula to Biscayne Bay, It is said that twenty-five miles of canal-cutting would suffice for the whole line."[32]

Although a few northerners were learning the delights of Lake Worth and Biscayne Bay during the 1870s, most people still considered South Florida to be a remote and forbidding region. Reporting on an expedition to Lake Okeechobee, a magazine writer in 1874 noted that the Seminoles were still living south of the lake. "Hitherto they have not been hostile to the whites," the author said "but as they increase in numbers faster than the white settlers, it is not impossible that they may reoccupy Southern Florida, sooner or later, it being, in fact, a region suited only to the roving hunter."[33]

Conditions changed dramatically during the 1880s. Earlier big dealers—Gleason, Fry, McLaws, Swann—had grandiose dreams but lacked the funds to carry them out. A new group of men—Hamilton Disston, Henry Sanford, Henry Flagler, and Henry Plant—had access to the millions of dollars needed to develop the state. The newcomers began their operations soon after William D. Bloxham became governor in January 1881. Bloxham was a Confederate war hero, a plantation owner, and a conservative Democrat, but despite these impeccable southern credentials he had no prejudice against northern money. A handsome man of great charm, the governor paid respectful attention to any rich man, southern, northern, or European, who indicated an inclination to invest in Florida. Fortunately for Bloxham, the state no longer had to go out in search of the investors. Wealthy individuals began to compete for the privilege of plowing their dollars into these promising fields. A surplus of capital in the North and a promising situation in the underdeveloped state brought striking consequences.

First to place a heavy bet on Florida's future was Hamilton Disston of Philadelphia. In 1878, when his father Henry Disston died, the thirty-four-year-old Hamilton came into control of the largest American company manufacturing saws and files. He now had the resources to pursue a project that had obsessed him since he began fishing trips to Florida in 1877. Disston's dream was the ancient one of draining the Everglades.[34] On 23 January 1881 John A. Henderson, a prominent lawyer and Democratic politician, presented Disston's proposal to the recently inaugurated Governor Bloxham and his fellow-trustees of the Internal Improvement Fund, and on 26

A view of the Oklawaha, about 1886. Extraordinary skill was required to navigate the narrow, winding channel. SPA.

February the board approved a contract. Disston and a group of associates promised to drain all the lands overflowed by Lake Okeechobee, the Kissimmee River and its branches, and contiguous lakes. In order to render these lands fit for cultivation, the associates pledged themselves to lower the level of Lake Okeechobee, to deepen and straighten the channel of the Kissimmee River, and to cut canals and ditches to connect Lake Okeechobee with the Caloosahatchee River on the west, the St. Lucie River on the east, and the Miami and other rivers on the southeast. For their part, IIF trustees promised to grant the associates one-half of all the reclaimed land already belonging to the state or later turned over by the federal government. Although the land grant was generous, it was less so than the legislature's proffered gift eleven years earlier to Gleason's Aquatic and Tropical Plant Propagation Company. If Gleason's company had been able to drain the Everglades, it would have received all the unsold state land in southern Florida; Disston and his associates were promised only half of it. Moreover, the contract stipulated that within six months Disston must put at least one hundred men to work and keep them on the job until the project was finished. He was to receive no land until he had drained 100,000 acres and made it suitable for cultivation.[35]

Even before the contract was finally signed, the *New York Times* praised Disston as "a young gentleman of great business energy and ample fortune." Describing the proposed works, the *Times* said: "These canals will entirely drain the swamp, and from ten to twelve million acres of the richest land in the world will be reclaimed," and it estimated this area to be approximately one-third of all the land in Florida. Because of its frost-free climate every tropical product— indigo, sugarcane, oranges, lemons, coffee, and jute—could be grown. The Disston group planned to form a company and sell one million shares of stock at $10 a share. Each share would entitle its owner to an acre of this remarkable soil.[36]

On 1 September 1881 the IIF trustees approved an assignment of Disston's drainage contract to the Atlantic and Gulf Coast Canal and Okeechobee Land Company, in which Disston was the largest stockholder.[37] On 22 November the company reported that it was employing the equivalent of one hundred men on its works, and on 3 January 1882 it asserted that it had spent $20,000 in building at Cedar Key a dredge to be sent to Fort Myers. A further $10,000 was earmarked for building a dredge and steamboat at Kissimmee City.[38] Barbour's guide book, published in 1882, was enthusiastic about the project: "A company of Philadelphia capitalists are proposing to drain a large portion of this Everglade region, by cutting a series of canals connecting it with both the Gulf and the Atlantic. The enterprise is one of considerable magnitude, and, if fully successful, will be of immense value to themselves, to the State, and indeed to the entire country, as it will open to profitable cultivation millions of acres of the richest soil in the world, especially and peculiarly adapted to the production of sugar."[39]

Although the IIF trustees hoped that these drainage operations would soon increase the value of the state's half of the reclaimed land, this did nothing to relieve them of their immediate need for money. Francis Vose was now dead, but his heirs and other litigants were pressing claims totaling some $900,000, and federal court injunctions blocked all state land grants for railroads and canals. Like his predecessors, Bloxham was desperately seeking to sell some 3 million or 4 million acres of swampland for enough cash to pay off this indebtedness. The situation had now become critical because the creditors were petitioning the federal court to turn over all the IIF's unsold land—some 14 million acres—to the receiver to be sold for whatever it would bring. The big deal could wait no longer. Fortunately for Bloxham, the sale that had been so difficult to make during the depression of the 1870s became relatively easy during the booming 1880s. The governor found himself in the happy situation of being able to choose between competing offers. Now convinced that thousands of newcomers from the North and from Europe would be moving into Florida, rival investors began to bid against each other. One group was based in New York but had the backing of a German banking house. A second was based in London but was headed by Gen. Henry Sanford, American minister to Belgium, a wealthy man already owning extensive lands along the middle St. Johns River. A third powerful competitor was Sir Edward Reed, the millionaire English shipbuilder who had backed Gleason's canal projects and was now heavily involved in the Atlantic and Gulf Coast and West India Transit Railroad, a successor to the old Florida Railroad, running between Fernandina and Cedar Key.[40] Still a fourth party with a major stake in any big land deal was Samuel A. Swann, the Fernandina merchant and investor, who held a power of attorney to sell the swamplands. Since he had been promised a commission of three cents an acre, he was eager to find customers.

In May 1881 Swann reported to the trustees that he had made the long-sought-for sales. To a certain James MacLaren he had sold 1 million acres at 40 cents an acre, receiving a payment of $110,000 to clinch the transaction. To James Hastings, Phillip Blythe and others of London, he had sold 3 million additional acres at 30 cents an acre, allowing them until 1 July to make a first installment of $200,000.[41]

But by this time still another would-be purchaser had emerged. In addition to the land involved in his drainage contract, Hamilton Disston had decided that he wanted to buy 4 million acres outright. Maneuvering at first in the background, he outgeneraled his rivals and negotiated the purchase with the governor himself. On 30 May 1881 Bloxham reported to his fellow IIF trustees that he had gone to Philadelphia and had signed articles of agreement with Disston for the purchase of 4 million acres at 25 cents an acre. The trustees unanimously approved and signed the formal contract on 1 June. Disston was to pay $200,000 immediately and the balance in three installments, the final one being due on 1 January 1882. He was to be allowed to select his own land in 10,000-acre tracts and acquire title as he made the stipulated payments.[42]

Samuel Swann was distressed at the news because he felt that he was being cheated out of $120,000 in commissions on the sales that he had arranged with other parties. "I claim," he wrote to the IIF trustees, "that in effecting these desirable sales, I have accomplished what I undertook and the duty that was assigned to me. I further claim that the other propositions made direct to your Board were occasioned by, and were the result of the competition brought about by me in popularizing the undertaking and bringing it (through my parties) to the notice of the present competitors." Still hoping that Disston would fail to make the specified payments, Swann offered to buy the whole 4 million acres and pay $40,000 more than anyone else was willing to offer.[43]

But Disston paid his first installment, and the trustees brushed off Swann's complaints. Why did Governor Bloxham choose to deal with Disston rather than with other parties who appeared to be offering more? One probable reason was the belief that Disston could produce cash faster than his rivals—and speed was imperative. Other reasons were undoubtedly personal: the southern governor and the northern businessman liked and trusted each other.

Disston's purchase created even more of a sensation than the drainage contract had. With probable exaggeration, the *New York Times* described it as "the largest purchase of land ever made by a single person in the world."[44] To market his latest acquisition Disston organized the Florida Land and Improvement Company. In a large map published in its advertising brochure, this company portrayed Disston's 4 million acres as a broad band of red covering most of central Florida. On the Gulf coast the purchase stretched from the

Withlacoochee River to Marco Island, a distance of over 200 miles; on the Atlantic coast it narrowed to a short stretch north of Titusville. Even more extensive were the lands colored green on this map to indicate that they were to be drained by Disston's Okeechobee Land Company. These potential holdings stretched along the east coast some 260 miles from Rockledge to Cape Sable and extended across all of southern Florida until they joined the 4-million-acre purchase lands. The map was misleading because Disston was entitled to only half the areas colored green even if he had been able to drain them all, and he had not purchased all the regions colored red but only selected tracts. Even so, however, the Disston lands constituted a huge empire sprawling over almost two-thirds of peninsular Florida.[45]

Disston's empire was, in fact, too large for him to retain intact. Even for a man of his large resources, it was not easy to raise $1 million in cash within a period of seven months. His agents were soon negotiating with other capitalists who had been competing for the big deal. In December 1881 Disston signed a contract with Sir Edward Reed, under which the latter was to assume half the agreed payments and acquire half the land. Associated with Reed were Dr. Jacobus Wertheim of Amsterdam and other Dutch investors in Florida railroads. Reed and his allies organized the Florida Land and Mortgage Company to sell land to English and Dutch immigrants.[46] Cramped by his financial commitments, Reed soon sold 500,000 acres to William B. Barnett, a Jacksonville banker, and in 1887 Reed retreated from the Florida real estate business completely by selling out his holdings to Gen. Philip Dale Roddy, formerly an officer in the Confederate army, now a promoter living in England.[47]

Disston and Reed had been able to purchase 4 million acres of land at the bargain price of 25 cents an acre, but Governor Bloxham was well satisfied with the deal. At long last the Internal Improvement Fund had enough cash to pay off not only the heirs of Francis Vose but other litigants under the old railroad construction bonds. The U.S. circuit court released the trustees from the troublesome injunctions on 8 July 1881.[48] This encouraged the legislature and the IIF trustees to accelerate the policy, already begun, of making lavish land grants to the railroads. The Pensacola and Atlantic Railroad was promised 20,000 acres per mile of railroad constructed across the Panhandle from Apalachicola to Pensacola. Completed in 1883, this 161-mile stretch formed the basis of the railroad's claim for 3,220,000 acres from the state. The Gainesville, Ocala, and Charlotte Railroad, incorporated in 1879, had been promised 10,000 acres a mile. Reorganized as the Florida Southern Railroad, it built 288 miles to Tampa and Fort Myers and established a claim for 2,882,200 acres. Smaller railroads, connecting other points in northern and central Florida, were promised grants ranging from 6,000 to 15,000 acres a mile. Eventually the wisdom of this policy was certain to be challenged because the state had promised the railroads not only more than it owned at the time, but more than it could ever expect to get from the federal government. For the time being, however, the miraculous progress of the state made everybody happy. Defending the Disston sale in August 1884, Governor Bloxham claimed that it had already

A town on the St. Johns River, 1915. Each little riverside settlement had its own busy dock. SPA.

opened the way for the construction of 700 miles of railroad and that 100 miles more would soon be completed. "When this great incubus of impediments upon our Internal Improvement Fund was lifted," the governor said, "Florida rose up and at once bounded forward more rapidly than any State in the Union. No State can show a development that about doubled her resources in the last four years. Few States can show as many miles of railroads built in the same period; and if you take our population and wealth and calculate the percentage, no State can equal us."[49]

Meanwhile, Disston's Okeechobee Land Company appeared to be making impressive progress in its reclamation efforts. Transforming the remote cow town of Kissimmee City, ninety miles north of Lake Okeechobee, into its forward base, the company pushed its

dredges through the Kissimmee Valley, deepening and straighten-
ing the river itself and cutting canals to connect the various lakes—
Tohopekaliga, East Tohopekaliga, and Cypress—at the river's
source. State engineers inspecting the project were impressed to
find cattle grazing on grasslands that had recently been several feet
under water. The company engineers planned to drain the whole region north of Lake Okeechobee by diverting the excess water into
the lake and then to lower the lake itself by digging canals and
deepening the natural streams to the Gulf of Mexico and the Atlantic
Ocean. As a first phase, one of the company dredges worked its way
up the Caloosahatchee River from Fort Myers, deepening the channel and blasting through the rock rim that held in the waters
of a series of small lakes lying between the river and Lake
Okeechobee.[50] By this dredging Disston's engineers opened a water
route from Fort Myers through Lake Okeechobee and on to Kissimmee City. In 1882 a company vessel made the first steamboat trip
over this entire distance.[51]

Already well publicized, Disston's great reclamation project enjoyed a publicity bonanza when President Chester A. Arthur visited
the region in April 1883. Arriving in Kissimmee City from Sanford
over the recently completed railroad, the president and his party
fished and cruised in the hastily painted company steamboat. Newspaper reporters sent back amusing accounts of this frontier outpost
with its cracker cowboys and absurdly costumed Seminole chiefs.
But they also wrote in all seriousness of the 12 million acres of land
which Disston was in the process of draining and the fabulous crops
of sugar and tropical fruit that would result.[52]

In this honeymoon period of the great Disston venture, the state
engineer readily supported the company claim that it had already
reclaimed over 2 million acres. By the end of 1884 the IIF trustees
had deeded about 1,175,000 acres to the company as its share under
the drainage contract.[53]

But not all Floridians shared Governor Bloxham's admiration for
the activities of Hamilton Disston. Farmers and ranchers already living on tracts deeded to Disston complained loudly. Some were mere
squatters, but others had valid claims under the Armed Settlement
Act of Seminole War days or other federal laws. Much of the Disston
land, they argued, was not swampland at all and never should have
passed to Florida under the Swamplands Act. The state quieted
some of this clamor by offering to sell disputed land to actual settlers
for one dollar an acre, crediting the sales to Disston's account. Other

critics asserted that it was absurd to believe that Disston had drained anything like 2 million acres. There had been several years of abnormally low rainfall during the early 1880s, and Disston was claiming credit for what nature had done in drying up this region. Responding to these complaints in 1885, the legislature ordered an investigation of the whole matter.[54] In 1887 a special committee reported that Disston's company had permanently drained only about 50,000 acres and that a much larger effort would be necessary to fulfill the terms of the agreement with the state.[55] Disston made an indignant reply, asserting that his company had dug 40 miles of canal at an expenditure of $250,000 and had actually reclaimed more than 2 million acres. In 1888 the state under Gov. Edward Perry compromised its differences with the promoter by a new agreement, under which the company agreed to spend an additional $125,000 to provide more adequate drainage for the land it had already received. Thereafter, the company was to have the right to purchase additional reclaimed land at 25 cents an acre. By 1894 when the Disston drainage efforts came to an end, the Okeechobee Land Company had acquired 1,652,000 acres. It claimed 347,000 acres more, but the state refused to recognize this.[56]

For over a decade Disston pushed ahead with his ambitious projects. The company dredges dug canals east of the Kissimmee Valley in the direction of the St. Johns River and south of Lake Okeechobee toward the Shark River in the heart of the Everglades. To demonstrate the fertility of his soil Disston invested in a wide range of experiments. He planted over a thousand acres of sugarcane, and at St. Cloud, about ten miles east of Kissimmee City, he built a sugar mill capable of processing 75,000 pounds a day. He prepared two thousand acres for rice culture and built a rice mill. He set out thousands of peach trees. He turned over land to the U.S. Department of Agriculture for crop experiments.[57]

In order to make a profit on these heavy investments Disston needed to build up a steady flow of cash from land sales. From the start he took energetic steps to do this. He established emigration offices, not only throughout the United States but in Europe as well. His advertising brochures provided a wide range of information about transportation, household expenses, soil conditions, and costs of clearing land and building houses. The pamphlets described opportunities for growing early vegetables for the northern market and had tempting sections on "How to Make an Orange Grove" and how to grow sugarcane, bananas, peanuts, and other exotic crops. The

Florida Land and Improvement Company offered to sell 40-acre tracts for $225, payable in ten quarterly installments of $22.50 without interest.[58]

Disston attempted to found several model communities. He laid out a city at Tarpon Springs and built a hotel there, hoping to accommodate its patrons by providing stagecoach transportation to Tampa, the terminus of Plant's railroad. He made even more ambitious plans for Disston City (now Gulfport) with 100-foot-wide

Silver Springs. The Oklawaha excursion culminated in a visit to one of Florida's most beautiful natural features. SPA.

streets and a business section large enough to serve the 50,000 expected inhabitants.[59] On Lake Constance near Orlando he settled some 250 carefully selected families, each with savings of at least $1,000. They had to purchase their own farms, ranging in size from 20 to 80 acres at prices from $1.25 to $5.00 an acre, but were assisted in selecting suitable crops and nursery stock.[60] As the years went on, the Disston companies made increasingly exaggerated advertising claims: twenty acres in this "favored spot" would produce as much as one hundred acres of ordinary farmland in the North; "You secure a home in the garden spot of the country, in an equable and lovely climate, where merely to live is a pleasure, a luxury heretofore accessible only to millionaires."[61]

Despite Disston's aggressive promotion, income from his land sales could not keep pace with his heavy expenditures. The Panic of 1893 buffeted his Florida empire, and one of his companies was compelled to mortgage its holdings for a loan of $2 million. As the depression deepened, Disston's situation became increasingly desperate. No longer able to pay his workmen, he had to suspend his dredging and steamship operations. The banks called his loans, and he was compelled to default on his bonds. After attending a Philadelphia theater on the evening of 30 April 1896 he filled his bathtub with water, climbed into it, and fired a bullet through his head. The Disston family, which had never approved his Florida ventures, allowed the state to recover some of the land for taxes and eventually sold the rest for a mere $70,000.[62]

In the early years of his Florida operations Disston had dreamed of building both of the great waterways that the state was believed to need. The map in his advertising brochures showed an east-west canal using the Caloosahatchee–Lake Okeechobee–St. Lucie River route and a north-south canal along the Atlantic coast from the mouth of the St. Johns River to Lake Worth. The brochure explained that, through its control of the Atlantic Coast Steamboat Canal Company, the Okeechobee Land Company was planning to build a 330-mile project connecting the inlets along the eastern coast.[63] Except for connecting the Caloosahatchee with Lake Okeechobee, Disston was unable to carry out either of these canal schemes.

Meanwhile, William H. Gleason was still trying to strike it rich, but he was rebuffed on both political and financial fronts. With the return of the Democrats to power in 1876 he lost the influence he had exercised in both Tallahassee and Washington during the years of Republican supremacy. On 25 February 1879 the IIF trustees voted to rescind the old drainage contracts under which Gleason and his partner, William H. Hunt, had retained a shadowy claim to much of South Florida.[64] And on 20 July 1882 the trustees voided the notorious deed of 1871 that had conveyed 1,360,600 acres of land to Gleason's Southern Inland Navigation Company.[65] In his relations with the big financiers Gleason was also a loser. He tried in vain to sell the old corporation charters acquired under the Reed and Stearns administrations. In June 1882 he offered his Aquatic and Tropical Plant Propagation Company to Sir Edward Reed for £25,000 and 100,000 acres of land. Gleason argued that by putting all his Florida lands and railroads into this holding company Reed would derive huge benefits—the right to construct canals, generous land grants, and liberal tax exemptions.[66] But Reed, perhaps because he had been burned in his previous dealings with Gleason, took no action. Similar frustrations attended Gleason's efforts to find English purchasers for his interests in the Atlantic and Gulf Transit Canal Company.[67]

In touting his cross-Florida scheme Gleason was struggling to hold his own in an increasingly crowded field. In March 1881 "Judge" John H. Fry reappeared on the Florida scene with a proposition whereby he and unnamed associates would receive 6 million acres of state land in exchange for assuming all the obligations of the Internal Improvement Fund and building a canal across the state.[68] In July 1881 Hubbard Hart, the steamboat operator and developer of the Oklawaha River route, urged a proposal in behalf of Gleason's Atlantic and Gulf Transit Canal Company, of which Hart was now president.[69] In 1883 the legislature chartered two new canal companies. The first of these, the Florida Ship Canal Company, included among its incorporators some of the most powerful figures on the national scene, men like Simon Cameron of Pennsylvania, Ben Butler of Massachusetts, and Gen. William Mahone of Virginia; the second, the Atlantic and Mexican Gulf Canal Company, included former Gov. George Drew, Gen. Lafayette McLaws, and Samual A. Swann—the group associated with the McLaws' Gulf Coast and Florida Peninsula Canal Company of 1875.[70] To confuse the situation still further, R.R. Peeler, a London promoter, was endeavoring in 1883 to merge the Gleason and McLaws interests in still another corporation, the Atlantic and Mississippi Canal and Transportation Company.[71] In the end, none of these projects for a cross-Florida canal went anywhere. The smart money was flowing into railroads, just as it had during the 1850s.

But another old idea, that of an intracoastal waterway along the Atlantic coast, finally led to action. The man who partially succeeded where Gleason and Disston had failed was another stubborn dreamer, Dr. John Westcott. Before he took up the idea of a coastal canal, he had been involved in other local schemes. During the 1870s he had been associated with the St. Johns Railroad, the short line connecting Tocoi and Jacksonville. In 1876 he had asked for state aid in building a "no gauge or single-track railroad" between Orange Lake and the Oklawaha River.[72] In 1881 Westcott organized the Florida Coast Line Canal and Transportation Company and filed surveys for an inland passage from the mouth of the St. Johns River to Biscayne Bay, about 340 miles away. Under the general incorpora-

tion law of 1879 for railroads and canals, the new company thereby
became eligible to receive alternate sections of state land for a distance of six miles on either side of its canal, or 3,840 acres for each
mile of construction. Utilizing the services of the well-known banker
Jay Cooke of Washington, the promoters mortgaged their franchise
and land rights to raise enough money to start construction on the
Matanzas River south of St. Augustine.[73]

Inspecting the project in 1883, a state engineer was amazed at its
amateurishness. The company had prepared no profile of its route or
detailed plans for excavation. Instead, Westcott and his associates
improvised as they went along. When they were not on the scene the

Hamilton Disston. Inheriting a fortune
from his father, who manufactured saws,
Disston plunged heavily into drainage
projects and purchases of Florida land.
SPA.

work either stopped or was carried on in a blundering fashion: "Thus
it happened that the great dredging giant sometimes forgot his bear-
ings, and with main strength and stupidity, gouged his way in circuitous routes and awkward elbows."[74] Despite this errant behavior
the company had managed to open up about six miles of waterway
about three feet deep and thirty feet wide, just deep enough for a
stern wheel steamboat to navigate but not wide enough for two such
boats to pass. To reward this somewhat dubious achievement, the IIF
trustees deeded a first installment of land, some 4,489 acres, to the
company in July 1883.[75]

To protect the interests of the company the IIF trustees had reserved from sale over a million acres of swampland lying along the
projected route of the waterway. Would-be settlers grumbled at this

restriction, and the trustees modified their policy to permit sales to actual settlers with the proceeds credited to the company's account. Both the IIF trustees and the legislature continued to defer to the wishes of the company. They continued the reservation of land all the way south to Key West and repeatedly extended the time limit for completion of the project. At the same time, however, the state authorities laid down somewhat more stringent terms: the company was to provide a waterway at least five feet deep and fifty feet wide, and it was to receive land grants only for the stretches of canal where excavation was necessary and not for naturally navigable streams along its route.[76]

At first the canal work went very slowly under Westcott's rough-and-ready management. But in the 1890s northern capitalists began pouring in the money and engineering skill needed to speed it up. The president of the reorganized company was George L. Bradley of Washington, who had made a fortune in the telephone and linotype businesses. Bradley formed a strange alliance with Henry L. Flagler, the Standard Oil millionaire, who was pushing his Florida East Coast Railroad down the peninsula through St. Augustine, West Palm Beach, and Miami. Although the canal promoter and the railroad magnate appeared to have competing interests, they supported each other's efforts. Flagler invested in the canal company, and the canal company turned over to the railroad 270,000 acres of the land granted by the state. Flagler's great hotels at St. Augustine, Ormond Beach, Palm Beach, and Miami were all built close to Bradley's canal. Through the efforts of Sen. Mathew Quay of Pennsylvania, Bradley also received some federal aid. In 1892 Congress appropriated funds for improving the Indian River from Titusville to Jupiter, a stretch for which the company agreed to collect no tolls.[77]

In 1896 the *New York Times* reported impressive progress on the Florida Coast Line Canal. The company had spent almost $1 million, mostly on two sections, one between St. Augustine and Lake Worth and the second between Lake Worth and Biscayne Bay. Company dredges had opened up forty miles of waterway, but there was still a fourteen-mile barrier to penetrate between the Matanzas and Halifax rivers and a few hundred feet between Jupiter Inlet and Lake Worth. The company was already beginning to work on a four-mile stretch needed to connect the mouth of the St. Johns River with Pablo Creek and the North River. With the completion of these projects "in a year or two" there would be a continuous intracoastal waterway from Jacksonville to Miami, some 340 miles down the coast.[78] The *Times* proved to be far too optimistic. Work on the canal again bogged down, and the last of the gaps was not closed until 1912.[79]

Probably the interlocking investment between the Florida Coastal Canal Company and the Florida East Coast Railroad had a good deal to do with the delay in completing the waterway. Only by withholding the coveted land grants did the IIF trustees finally get the canal company to finish the job. Even then, however, it provided no real competition for the railroad. Only five feet deep and fifty feet wide, the privately owned waterway was worthless for cargo ships and most other commercial vessels. On the other hand, its sheltered channel offered a lovely facility for the wealthy residents of Palm Beach and other coastal resorts who owned sailboats, yachts, motor boats, and fishing vessels.

# 5 The Progressive Challenge

Draining the Everglades was an idea whose hour finally arrived in the early years of the twentieth century. Why was the ancient dream so powerfully revived? The answer lies largely in the populist and progressive movements that swept across Florida in overlapping waves during the years between 1890 and 1920. The politicians who authorized the digging of an ambitious system of canals and ditches saw themselves as champions of the people redeeming millions of acres of soil from wealthy monopolists and transforming these swampy tracts into an agricultural paradise for small farmers.

Floridians regarded the railroads with a mingling of love and hate. In a generally favorable political climate the promoters had laid mile after mile of track between 1880 and 1890. The Florida legislature had encouraged this outburst of building by promising the railroads some 15 million acres of land. Since this was more than the state actually owned, the railroads had received deeds to only about three-fifths of this acreage but were still claiming the rest.

Like the railroads in other parts of the country, the Florida lines had gone through a ruthless Darwinian process in which scores of local companies had been born but relatively few had survived. During periods of depression many of the smaller lines were absorbed into a few great systems. By acquiring the Pensacola and Atlantic, the Louisville and Nashville Railroad became the most powerful force in the economic life of Panhandle Florida. It received deeds to 2.2 million acres of state land and claimed over 1 million more. One of its officers, William D. Chipley, exerted potent influence in Florida politics. A second masterful figure until his death in 1897 was Henry B. Plant, a Connecticut expressman, who had bought control of the South Florida Railroad, the Florida Southern, the Jacksonville, Tampa and Key West, and other lines to add to his holdings in Georgia and other southern states. The Plant System had acquired title to over 3 million acres of state land and claims to another million. Plant's great rival was the Standard Oil executive Henry M. Flagler, who had been investing in Florida hotels and railroads since 1883. Flagler first bought up existing lines between Jacksonville and Daytona Beach and then pushed his Florida East Coast Railroad farther south to Palm Beach, Miami, and Key West. Flagler became a great Florida landowner by acquiring the grants of the older lines. Besides these, he had been promised 8,000 acres a mile for new construction and had thus laid the basis for a future claim of over 2 million acres.[1]

The railroads exerted great power in state politics. The principal newspapers supported pro-railroad candidates and policies. The legislature passed the laws that the railroads wanted, and state officials carried out cooperative policies. Yet in politics as in physics action brings reaction, and a growing number of politicians began to court the voters by taking an anti-railroad line. In 1887 the legislature authorized a state railroad commission. Criticized as ineffective and expensive, the commission was abolished in 1891, but in 1897 the legislature established a new commission on a permanent basis.[2]

As populist sentiment intensified during the late 1880s and 1890s, the state's huge land grants to the railroads encountered increasing criticism. As early as 1885 U.S. Sen. Wilkinson Call, member of a famous Florida family, accused the state authorities of conniving with the Federal Land Office to get control of lands that were not truly swamplands.[3] Although such charges were repeated in later years, the governors hotly defended the conduct of the state. In 1890 Gov. Francis Fleming argued that everything had been done in accordance with the law: "No matter what proportion of the land heretofore patented to the state may be high and dry, it can in no manner affect the right of the state to the unpatented selections which come within the terms of the grant." Specifically Fleming called upon the federal authorities to complete a survey of the Everglades, preparatory to turning them over to the state. There were, he said, "over 4,000,000 acres of unpatented selections within the Everglades region, which to anyone familiar with the topography of Florida are as certainly known to be 'wet and unfit for cultivation' as that the east coast of the state is washed by the waves of the Atlantic."[4]

These 4 million acres, still held by the federal government but claimed by the state, were the last great prize to be competed for. In the ensuing contest the railroads held a strong position since their claims aggregated more than the amount of unpatented lands, but the rival systems weakened their position by struggling against each other. Moreover, other businessmen were eager to assert their rights. First, there was Disston's Okeechobee Land Company, and after his death the United Land Company, which claimed extensive acreage under the old drainage contract. Then there was the Florida Coast Line Canal Company, which kept digging away during the 1890s, thereby establishing claims to more and more land. And finally there were the politicians. Since so much power lay ultimately in the hands of the trustees of the Internal Improvement Fund and the legislature, it was inevitable that there would be a movement to

Henry M. Flagler and party on Stock Island, February 8, 1906. Left to right: J.E. Ingraham; unknown; Howard — —, dredgeman; J.C. Murdick, construction engineer; unknown; George W. Allen; Henry M. Flagler; W.D. Cast. SPA.

snatch what was left of the state lands out of the hands of the competing railroad and canal companies and to use it for the benefit of the farmers.

During the 1880s and 1890s the old dream of draining the Everglades had been revived, in part through the activities of Hamilton Disston but also because of a few well-publicized expeditions through the region. In 1882 and 1883 the *New Orleans Times-Democrat* sought to capitalize on interest in the Disston operations by sending two different exploring parties into the mysterious areas west and south of Lake Okeechobee. In March 1892 a third group headed by James Ingraham, president of the South Florida Railroad, an affiliate of the Plant System, made a hazardous twenty-three-day trip across the Everglades to see whether a railroad could be built across this wilderness to connect Tampa and Fort Myers with Miami, thereby strengthening Plant's domination of the Cuba trade.[5] To Ingraham's shrewd eyes this watery empire did not look suitable for a railroad, but it did appear to have exciting potential for agriculture. Convinced that nothing held back the water except a rock ledge along 160 miles of the eastern coastal belt, Ingraham argued that by digging vents through this ridge a vast region could be reclaimed for agriculture. In May 1892 Ingraham sought to make a contract for this purpose with the IIF trustees, but other railroad executives, jealous for their land claims, opposed the project.[6]

A year later Ingraham moved from the Plant entourage to that of Flagler, accepting a position as "land commissioner." According to a report in the *New York Times*, Ingraham sold the idea of draining the Everglades to his new boss. The land was described as worthless so that it might be obtained by the Flagler group at a nominal price or as a subsidy for extending the Florida East Coast Railroad to Key West. "In five feet of loam, and the richest soil never requiring such a thing as fertilizer, and with the climate tempered by favorable natural conditions," the *Times* reported, "it would be possible to cultivate almost any tropical fruits or vegetables."[7]

Ingraham's drainage schemes surfaced again in February 1898 when Capt. Rufus E. Rose appeared before the IIF trustees to ask for a contract. Rose had been an engineer for Disston's Okeechobee Land Company and was associated with Ingraham and other Flagler allies.[8] On 29 June 1898 the trustees signed a contract with Rose, Ingraham, and others, authorizing the associates to reclaim at their own expense 800,000 acres in the southeastern Everglades. In return for this work the associates were to have a right to buy the drained land for 25 cents an acre.[9] The contractors were to begin operations within one year and excavate at least 200,000 cubic yards each year. In October the associates organized the Florida East Coast Drainage and Sugar Company.[10] Despite its Flagler connections the company found it difficult to raise enough money to launch operations, and in December 1900 it had to ask for a two-year extension of the time limit for beginning the project.[11] A major obstacle to the scheme was probably the legal situation. The federal government had not yet patented the Everglades to the state. If and when it did, the Florida East Coast Drainage and Sugar Company would have to compete for the land with the other powerful claimants.

In 1901 there was a drastic change in the political climate. William Bloxham, friend of the railroads, who had been serving another term as governor, was succeeded by William S. Jennings, a man of very different temperament. The new governor was not only a cousin of

William Jennings Bryan but a politician who shared Bryan's hostility to corporate power. Jennings and Byran had had somewhat similar careers. Both were born in small Illinois towns, attended Illinois colleges, and studied law in the Union College of Law in Chicago. Both practiced their profession briefly in Illinois, then moved to frontier communities—Bryan to Lincoln, Nebraska, Jennings to Brooksville in west-central Florida. Jennings served as a county judge and as member and speaker of the Florida House of Representatives. He was a delegate to the Democratic National Convention in 1896 and presumably heard his cousin electrify the assemblage with his Cross of Gold speech. Only thirty-eight years old when he became governor, Jennings was not afraid to say no to the railroads' demands.[12]

In July 1901 a representative of the Louisville and Nashville Railroad appeared before Governor Jennings and the IIF trustees to complain that the state had deeded to other railroad and canal companies millions of acres which had been earned by its subsidiary the Pensacola and Atlantic. To enforce its rights, the Louisville and Nashville was bringing suit against one of the purchasers. If the railroad won the case, it would unsettle the titles of railroads and landowners in all parts of the state. To prevent this happening, the Louisville and Nashville offered to accept a compromise suggested by former Governor Bloxham. Under this plan the trustees would certify to the railroad 1.4 million acres of unsurveyed land in the Everglades. "While the lands thus proposed to be deeded to your petitioner are of much less value than the lands in Middle and East Florida, to which it is entitled, yet to cause a cessation of the present litigation and avoid the necessity of future litigations...the petitioner is willing to accept a settlement upon the basis proposed."[13]

In dealing with this and other claims, the Jennings administration was handicapped by the extreme confusion of the state records. A month before Jennings took office the Bloxham administration had ordered a printing of all the minutes of the trustees of the Internal Improvement Fund since 1855. Jennings repeated this directive and also instituted an intensive search for other relevant material in the archives.[14] This investigation revealed that the legislature had passed 115 land grant acts, under which approximately 9 million acres had been granted to the railroad companies and 6 million more were being claimed. In addition to this, canal companies had received deeds to 2,250,000 acres and were claiming 870,000 acres more.[15]

If all these deeds and claims were valid, the state had no more land to sell or grant, having already promised more land than it owned or could ever hope to get from the federal government. But Governor Jennings refused to recognize any such limitations. In June 1901 the IIF trustees sold Charles H. Scott and associates of Montgomery, Alabama, 202,240 acres in the southwestern Everglades for 30 cents an acre, or $60,672 in all. Scott's attorney explained that "a vast scheme of drainage" was in contemplation, which would "result in very great benefit to the State of Florida."[16] In July 1903 the trustees agreed to deed Scott 100,000 acres more of Everglades land for $30,000.[17]

Unsuccessful in getting the settlement that it had offered to accept, the Louisville and Nashville tried to get the U.S. District Court in Jacksonville to order the trustees to issue deeds for the full amount of its claims.[18] While this case was still pending, the Jennings administration affronted the railroad still further by selling 103,000 acres of land in northern Florida—land specifically certified to the railroad—to Neill G. Wade of Levy County for $233,000. The trustees defended their action: it provided needed cash for the Internal Improvement Fund and promoted "the drainage and cultivation" of the swamplands.[19] Denying the validity of the sale to Wade, the Louisville and Nashville asked the court to order that the proceeds be turned over to the railroad. While the case was being heard, the court enjoined the trustees from expending the funds.

The Louisville and Nashville was only one of the claimants trying to compel the IIF trustees to issue deeds. In 1903 and 1904 the Florida East Coast Railroad sued the state for 2,040,000 acres, the Florida Coast Line Canal Company for 523,000 acres, and Matilde Kittell, who had inherited a minor railroad claim, for 110,000 acres.[20] Holding out against all these claims, Governor Jennings argued that the legislative grants since 1879 had all been invalid because the federal act of 1850 had specified that the purpose of giving the swamplands to the state was to provide for their drainage and reclamation. Furthermore, the Florida Internal Improvement Act of 1855 had placed the lands in the hands of the trustees with a mandate to use them for this sole purpose. On 21 November 1904 Jennings and his associates unanimously resolved "That the Trustees adhere strictly to the provisions of the act of January 6, 1855, Chapter 610, Laws of Florida, as to their powers and duties and the purposes for which said trust was created, and that they will assert their rights and defend the title to the lands granted and irrevocably vested in them for the purposes therein set forth of reclaiming said lands by means of levees and drains."[21]

Stubbornly refusing to deed anything more to the railroads, the

Jennings administration tried to sell the land to parties like Scott and Wade, who would promise to reclaim it. The Ingraham-Rose group, doing business as the Florida East Coast Drainage and Sugar Company, asked for a further extension of its contract in October 1902, but the trustees refused.[22] The company then offered to buy 800,000 acres at 30 cents an acre, payable in installments over a period of fifteen months. But the Jennings administration rejected this offer also. "It is the policy of the Trustees," their resolution stated, "to secure the drainage and reclamation of the swamp and overflowed lands belonging to the Internal Improvement Fund by making sales of portions of such lands for cash to parties who will undertake to drain the purchased lands, the proceeds of such sales to be used for the purposes of the trust."[23]

In March 1903 floods in South Florida caused a half million dollars damage to farmers who had been attempting to grow vegetables on partially drained lands. This disaster prompted Governor Jennings to send a special message on drainage to the legislature. He said that the various expeditions through the Everglades had proved that it was entirely practicable to reclaim 3,760,000 acres of "The most valuable agricultural land in the Southern States." Acknowledging the great difficulty in financing reclamation by selling the swamplands in their unimproved condition, Jennings asked the legislature to ask the U.S. Congress for a $1 million appropriation.[24]

Federal money for the reclamation of the Everglades was not forthcoming, but on 29 April 1903 President Theodore Roosevelt did sign a patent transferring 2,862,080 acres of Everglades land to the state.[25] Having secured title for the Internal Improvement Fund, Governor Jennings fought doggedly to fend off the claims not only of the railroads, but of the Florida Coast Line Canal Company and the successor companies still claiming land under the old Disston drainage contract.

The future of the Everglades provided a key issue for the gubernatorial election of 1904. Ineligible for a second consecutive term under the Florida constitution, Jennings threw his support to Napoleon Bonaparte Broward of Jacksonville. As befitted a man bearing such a name, Broward had had a colorful career in which he had demonstrated shrewd intelligence, iron determination, and a flair for decisive action. He had sailed the St. Johns River as pilot and steamboat captain; he had been sheriff of Duval County until a governor removed him for excessive zeal in policing an election; he had defied federal neutrality laws by running guns into Cuba before the Spanish-American War.[26]

In the tradition of southern politics the contest for governor was fought out in two Democratic primaries held in May and June 1904. Although four candidates competed for the nomination, the strongest two were Broward and Robert W. Davis, prominent lawyer, state senator, and U.S. congressman. Denouncing Davis as a tool of the railroads, Broward promised strong support for the regulatory commission and continued resistance to railroad land grabs. In his campaign literature he denied that the Florida legislature had any power to grant land to the railroads except for the odd-numbered sections within six miles of their right-of-way. He claimed that the state owned over 8 million acres of land and had $400,000

Gov. Albert W. Gilchrist. During Gilchrist's administration (1909–13) the state compromised in its disputes with the large landowners and accelerated the drainage program. SPA.

cash in the Internal Improvement Fund, and he said, "I most emphatically will not grant these lands, or any part of them, nor turn over this money, or any portion of it, to the railroads of the State, but save both to the people of Florida."[27] Broward assured the voters that the state had enough money to begin draining the Everglades. Such a program would bring fabulous rewards. The reclaimed land would sell for $5 to $20 an acre, thereby bringing from $15 million to $60 million into the state treasury. This fund would earn more than $1 million in annual interest—twice the amount then being raised by state taxes. The profits from drainage would pay all the expenses of the state government and provide an additional $500,000 a year for education.[28]

Condemning these proposals as reckless, the conservative newspapers of the larger Florida cities strongly supported Davis. But
Broward, a popular figure in the rural counties, eked out a precarious victory, coming in first in the earlier primary, then beating Davis
by a very narrow margin in the runoff and swamping the Republican
and Socialist candidates in the November election.[29] As governor,
Broward acted with the same virile energy that he had demonstrated
in his earlier career. By no means a one-idea man, he pressed for a
broad progressive program of tax reform, state-supported education
at every level, stronger election laws, a state life insurance program,
and game conservation laws. But it was the drainage program that
dramatized Broward's iron determination to defy the railroads and
reclaim the Everglades, whatever the obstacles.

Although Jennings turned the executive office over to Broward on
3 January 1905, the former governor continued to exert strong influence. The new board of IIF trustees appointed him its general counsel to represent the board in the many lawsuits arising out of the new
land policy. Jennings urged his successor to build dredges and start
digging out either the Miami River or some other outlet from the
Everglades.[30]

Wasting no time, Broward made one steamboat trip to inspect
Lake Okeechobee shortly before the election and a second a month
after his inauguration. On the second excursion he took as his companions Jennings and Captain Rose, the state chemist who, as an associate of Ingraham's, had promoted drainage. They embarked at
Fort Myers and proceeded up the Caloosahatchee River and
through the old Disston canals into Lake Okeechobee. They made a
leisurely circuit of that great body of water, measuring its depths and
examining the surrounding terrain. Experienced through many
years of river life, Broward concluded that it would be possible to
lower the level of the lake as much as six feet without hampering
navigation. Doing this would drain both the region south of the lake
and the swampy terrain to the north as well, some 6 million acres in
all—more than six times as much as "the entire cultivated acreage of
Florida, including gardens as well as farms."[31]

On 3 May 1905 Broward sent the legislature a long special message, reviewing earlier drainage proposals, summarizing expert
opinion on the feasibility of reclamation, and praising the fertility of
the muck. "Ultimately," he said, "about 6,000,000 acres of the finest
land in the country would be rendered cultivable—an area capable
of producing the entire tonnage of cane sugar used in this country, a
crop which alone would be of untold value to the State."[32] In his

analysis of the problem, the governor pointed out that about half of the 6 million acres to be reclaimed belonged to the Internal Improvement Fund; the other half had been deeded to various railroad and canal companies. Since these owners would benefit greatly, Broward proposed the creation of a drainage commission with power to levy drainage taxes on landowners.[33]

The legislature promptly gave Broward what he wanted. It approved, subject to ratification by the voters, a constitutional amendment providing for a board of drainage commissioners to be composed of the same five state officials who were already trustees of the Internal Improvement Fund. The new board would have power to build canals, drains, levees, ditches, and reservoirs, to establish drainage districts, and to levy an annual tax not exceeding 10 cents an acre.[34] On the theory that a constitutional amendment might not be necessary, the legislature passed a bill embodying the same provisions.[35]

Broward hoped to use the drainage tax to finance a long-range state drainage program, but he was in no mood to wait until the new revenue started to come in. Thanks largely to the Jennings administration's policy of large land sales, the Internal Improvement Fund had a cash reserve of almost $400,000, which the governor intended to use without delay. Only two things were necessary to make the dirt fly: to build dredges and to decide where to put them to work. Broward spent little time on either problem. In August 1905 he and the attorney general negotiated contracts with a Chicago firm for the machinery needed for the dredges and within a month the IIF trustees gave their approval.[36] Meanwhile, he had arranged for three cursory surveys of possible canal routes—a northern line from Lake Okeechobee to the St. Lucie River, a central route to Lake Worth, and a southern one to the New River near Fort Lauderdale. Although Broward had at first inclined toward the St. Lucie project, the IIF trustees decided to begin their first canals on the New River. Political, rather than economic, reasons probably dictated their choice. The Stuart– Fort Pierce region that would benefit from a St. Lucie Canal was a stronghold of anti-Broward sentiment, but Fort Lauderdale and its environs had given the governor strong support. Moreover, canals through the southeastern Everglades would increase the value of state-owned lands that the trustees wanted to sell. To supervise the work, the trustees appointed John W. Newman, a civil engineer who had led Ingraham's expedition across the Everglades in 1892 and was now recommending the New River route to the state authorities.[37]

Taking keen interest in every aspect of the venture, Governor Broward made frequent trips to Fort Lauderdale to inspect the dredges being built there. On 2 April 1906 the Broward family participated in the christening of *The Everglades*, which the *St. Augustine Record* praised as "the largest and finest dredge boat south of Philadelphia." On 4 July *The Everglades* moved up the New River and began work on what became known as the North New River Canal. In his haste Governor Broward had not wanted to spend the time or money for a careful survey. With only the most general instructions, surveying parties worked just ahead of the dredge putting in stakes for the huge machine to follow. In the same awkward fashion the second dredge, *The Okeechobee*, began to dig the South New River Canal on 1 April 1907.[38]

Spending money freely, the Broward administration needed to start collecting the drainage tax as quickly as possible. Donning their new hats as drainage commissioners, the state officers designated a huge drainage district spreading over five counties both north and south of Lake Okeechobee and levied a tax of five cents an acre on all landowners. The amounts assessed for this tax throw a revealing light on the consequences of earlier Florida land policy. Nonresident owners of land within the drainage district (mostly railroads, canal companies, and land companies) held 4,044,500 acres; resident owners (farmers, ranchers, townspeople) had title to only 185,020 acres. Under Broward's plan, the nonresident owners would pay $211,476 a year for draining the Everglades, the resident owners only $9,250.[39]

The great corporations did their best to thwart the governor. They appealed to the courts; they stirred up the prorailroad newspapers; they scared the voters. First to take up the fight was the Southern States Land and Timber Company, organized in 1902 by New Orleans and New York investors, among them Herbert Lehman, later to be governor of New York. Having bought from the railroads some two million acres of land in the region around Lake Okeechobee, the Southern States Land Company obviously wanted it drained, but the promoters had no confidence in the Broward program. They were displeased because the Board of Drainage Commissioners was composed of five politicians without any representatives of the land companies or railroads. They were equally shocked by the headstrong way in which Broward was plunging ahead without any study of the problem, ignoring the contention that piecemeal drainage of small sections would make more sense than this grandiose attempt to drain the Everglades as a whole. Arguing that the Drainage

Act of 1905 was an unconstitutional delegation of the taxing power, lawyers for the Southern States Land Company applied to the federal district court at Pensacola for relief. The other great landowners soon followed this example, and by the end of March 1906 the state was handcuffed by injunctions prohibiting it from collecting the tax. Many of the small owners also clamored against the levy, and on 4 April the Board of Drainage Commissioners ordered a suspension of the tax until the courts had made their final decisions.[40] Despite this setback Broward pushed ahead with his drainage program, spending every dollar the IIF trustees could scrape together.

The prorailroad newspapers opened up a heavy barrage against the governor. Accusing him of using money from the good roads fund to buy dredges, the *Jasper News* said: "Of all the foolish ideas that ever entered the brain of man the draining of the Everglades is the most nonsensical."[41] The *Florida Times-Union* of Jacksonville, reputedly controlled by Flagler, published savage cartoons: one showed the IIF trustees robbing a schoolchild; another depicted the trustees dipping into a barrel labeled "School Fund" and using money belonging to "underpaid school teachers" for "drainage schemes." The *St. Augustine Evening Record*, the *Gainesville Sun*, the *Lake City Index*, the *Tampa Tribune*, and the *Tallahassee True Democrat* joined in lambasting the governor, despite his indignant denials that he was misusing any of the funds set aside for roads and schools.[42]

The drainage controversy continued throughout the summer and fall of 1906. Broward was trying to get the voters' approval for the drainage amendment. Lacking even the money for postage to send out his appeals, Broward had to ask his supporters for postage stamps and other small donations. He made speeches in every part of the state, welcoming debate with his opponents. He gained support from many independent newspapers, particularly in South Florida. The *St. Petersburg Independent* called the proposed amendment "the fairest, speediest and most practicable method yet proposed for reclaiming the Everglades, and it should be adopted by the largest vote ever given a measure in Florida."[43] But opponents were able to scare the voters by emphasizing the broad powers proposed for the Board of Drainage Commissioners. "This Constitutional Amendment," one pamphlet said, "is the most dangerous piece of legislation ever attempted to be incorporated in the Constitution of any State in the Union. It will place in the hands of the administration a weapon of tremendous power for unscrupulous use against their political enemies. Under it they can establish drainage districts of any size, anywhere in the State."[44] According to this pamphlet, only about one-third of the Everglades, the "Big Saw Grass" immediately south of Lake Okeechobee, was worth reclaiming. Broward's dream of draining the whole vast region was absurd.[45]

In the November election the voters decisively rejected Broward's drainage amendment.[46] Complaining that the opposition had misled the voters, the governor kept the dredges at work and sought new laws to make the landowners pay. He defined the issue in a special message to the legislature on 3 April 1907: "The contest is on between the people and the corporations, and especially between the Legislature and the corporations. The Legislature has passed a law—the corporations refuse to obey it. The Legislature has said that the corporations shall contribute a just proportion of the cost of such improvements—the corporations decline to do it, and say that the Legislature has no right or power to require them to do so."[47]

Once again—this time after bitter debate—the legislature bowed to Broward's wishes and passed a new drainage law. Drafted by ex-Governor Jennings to meet the constitutional objections to the Act of 1905, this measure established a single somewhat smaller district with definite boundaries and fixed the drainage tax at five cents an acre.[48] Broward signed the bill on 28 May 1907, but the corporations still refused to pay, contending that the canals under construction would benefit only a small part of the drainage district.[49]

At the suggestion of the governor, the legislature appointed a joint committee to inspect the drainage work. Reporting on 21 August 1907 the legislators painted a rosy picture of what they found at Fort Lauderdale. *The Everglades* and *The Okeechobee* were sturdy dredges that had dug over a mile of canals and drained some 750 acres of land, on which farmers were already growing tomatoes. The reclaimed land was estimated to be worth $30 an acre. According to Engineer Newman, drainage would result in an average of 906 acres per mile of canal; therefore, six miles would drain 5,440 acres, worth $163,200 when drained.[50]

Unable to collect the drainage tax and rapidly depleting the surplus in the Internal Improvement Fund, Governor Broward desperately needed to make new land sales. But these were almost impossible to arrange so long as the railroads, canal companies, and land companies continued to press their various suits against the trustees. Although ex-Governor Jennings, as special counsel, denied the validity of the legislative land grants, the Broward administration began to seek a way out of this spider's web of litigation. On 1 December 1906 the IIF trustees accepted a settlement with the Florida Coast Line Canal Company, under which the company agreed to pay the trustees $50,000 and to complete two unfinished sections of their waterway, one between St. Augustine and the St. Johns River, the second between the Matanzas and Halifax rivers. In return, the trustees would deed 200,000 acres to the company immediately and the balance of its claims—some 230,000 acres—on completion of the canal.[51]

During 1907 Jennings was able to win one important ruling for the IIF trustees, while losing others. Judge Charles Swayne in the Federal District Court in Pensacola recognized the right of the trustees to carry on their reclamation program. In granting an injunction requested by the Southern States Land Company, the judge gave the trustees the right to sell not more than 100,000 acres "for the purpose of using the proceeds for reclamation and drainage"; furthermore, after six months they might apply for permission to sell more.[52] On the other hand, Judge Swayne decided against the trustees on their sale of land claimed by the Louisville and Nashville Railroad. The hard-pressed Broward administration thus found itself confronted with a judgment of $250,000, the proceeds of the Neill Wade sale plus interest.[53] This decision demonstrated that the trustees were in a bad legal position concerning certain land that had been "certified" to various claimants. The right of the railroads and land companies to this unpatented land specifically reserved for them was much stronger than to the unspecified acreage covered in the general legislative grants.

In November 1907 Jennings reviewed the whole situation in a memorandum to the IIF trustees. He praised their courage in undertaking "what many have considered an impossible task, beginning as you have after legislative enactments have granted a greater area than the Trustees possess." The task, as he saw it, was twofold: "first, to defend and retain the lands vested in the Trustees for the uses and purposes for which they were granted; second, to reclaim those lands, thus carrying out the contract of the State and making fit for cultivation and habitation an area equal to and greater than some States of this Union." The trustees had done well, but now they faced a crisis: "Your available funds on hand are exhausted. The money on hand you are enjoined by the United States Court from using, therefore you are limited to the resources of sales of land to carry on this work, in the absence of which the work must cease." Unreclaimed land was bringing only 25 cents an acre; reclaimed land would be worth $10 to $20 an acre. Therefore, the trustees should settle pending law suits on the best terms possible in order to be able to sell land at a decent price and keep the dredges at work.[54]

Everglades, near Miami, 1912. Miami River at left, Miami Canal under construction at right. The sawgrass prairies and tree islands of the Everglades then covered the area where the International Airport and the cities of Hialeah and Miami Springs now stand. SPA.

Accepting Jennings's advice, the IIF trustees approved a sweeping compromise involving the Louisville and Nashville Railroad and the Southern States Land Company. With a payment of about $114,000 the trustees cleared the judgment against them in the Wade case. Since the judgment plus interest now amounted to $265,000, Jennings claimed a savings of $151,000 for the Internal Improvement Fund. The trustees also wiped out the claim of the L&N Railroad to 1,477,000 acres of land by giving a deed for 374,831 acres, the acreage covered by certificate. Since the L&N had sold this certified land to the Southern States Land Company, the settlement freed the trustees from another suit against them. The State Board of Education benefited from the settlement, because the IIF trustees decided that 1,072,199 acres of land saved from the L&N claim should go to the education fund to make up in part for the state's earlier failure to devote 25 percent of the proceeds of the Internal Improvement Fund to education as required by the constitutions of 1868 and 1885.[55]

A week later the trustees approved another compromise arranged by Jennings. The Wisner Land Company, which had purchased the rights granted or certified to various railroads to some 860,000 acres of land in seventeen counties in central and southern Florida, agreed to accept a deed for 60,000 acres of relatively good land and a cash payment of $17,456. Once again, the land saved to the Internal Improvement Fund was turned over to the State Board of Education.[56]

A third major land claim took much longer to settle. The United Land Company, which had purchased the assets of the Atlantic and Gulf Coast Canal and Okeechobee Land Company and another Disston company, had sued IIF trustees for 347,900 acres of land claimed under the old drainage contract. Jennings was opposed to making any concession to the company. He argued that the IIF trustees had never approved the assignment of the Disston rights and that Disston had never fulfilled the terms of his contract in any case. Only 80,000 acres of land to the north of Lake Okeechobee had been permanently drained, and the level of the lake had not been reduced. "I find... ," said Jennings, "that the drainage operations under these various contracts has failed to reclaim one single acre of land within fifty miles of Lake Okeechobee in any direction."[57] In deeding 1,652,000 acres to Disston's original company, the trustees had already granted 839,000 acres more than the company had earned under the terms of the contract. Despite Jennings's remonstrances, the trustees by a three-to-two vote approved a compromise whereby they deeded to the United Land Company 68,834 acres—less than one-fifth of its claim. Governor Broward voted with the majority.[58]

The settlement with the United Land Company took care of all the major railroad claims except those of Flagler's Florida East Coast Railroad. Since Flagler was still constructing the extraordinary series of island-linking bridges that finally carried the railroad to Key West, a final settlement could not be made until then. On 14 December 1912 Gov. Albert Gilchrist and his fellow trustees deeded 210,000 acres to the railroad in settlement of claims amounting to 2,674,692 acres.[59]

By alternately defying and dickering with the big corporations Broward had saved some 2 million acres of the Everglades for the Internal Improvement Fund. His original strategy had been to hold back this land and finance drainage by the drainage tax, thus making it possible for the trustees to sell the reclaimed land at $5 to $20 an acre. But continued resistance to the tax made it necessary to sell large tracts for whatever they would bring. This became all the more imperative as the trustees gained a clearer idea of the magnitude of the task. By the end of 1907 two dredges working out of Fort Lauderdale had dug little more than four and one-half miles of canal and only about 12,000 acres had been reclaimed—even by the most optimistic definition. At this rate, one of Broward's opponents charged, it would take a century to reclaim a million acres.[60]

The need to enlarge the effort was underlined on 6 January 1908, when the trustees considered a request from the Miami Board of Trade for a dredge on the Miami River "to be used for the purpose of digging a canal or canals into the Everglades west of this city, with the object of reclaiming all the land possible in this vicinity." The trustees promised to provide the dredge if they could sell enough land in the vicinity of Miami at a satisfactory price.[61] In response to this pledge, a group of Miami citizens agreed to buy 20,000 acres at $2 an acre. The trustees also promised to sell approximately 100,000 acres near Miami to various large private investors.[62] In July 1908, while this deal was still pending, R. P. Davie of Colorado Springs agreed to buy about 27,500 acres of these lands at $2 an acre. In addition, Davie and the trustees agreed to a contract under which Davie was to have a five-year lease on about 2,000 acres of land on which he would conduct an experimental vegetable farm and sugar plantation and dig at his own expense a drainage canal to connect with the South New River Canal.[63] Negotiations involving the other Dade County lands were finally concluded in October 1908. Walter Comfort of New York City bought 6,422 acres at $2 an acre, and the J. H.

Tatum Company of Miami took 80,000 acres of the more western and less desirable land for $1.25 an acre.[64] Even before these deals were completed the trustees had doubled their drainage program by contracting for two new dredges, one to work on the Miami River and the other on the Caloosahatchee running into the Gulf of Mexico.[65]

But projects much more grandiose than these were being aired during the fall of 1908. Charles A. Scott of Montgomery, Alabama, who had purchased extensive tracts in the Everglades during the Jennings administration, now proposed to take over the whole drainage project. He offered to build 150 miles of drainage canals within ten years; as recompense he asked for 75 percent of the reclaimed land. When the trustees rejected this proposal, he modified his offer to ask for 65 percent, and finally 60 percent. But Jennings advised against accepting the Scott proposal. He argued that 150 miles of canals would be inadequate to drain the Everglades and that the contract would be much more profitable to Scott than to the state.[66] The trustees followed Jennings's advice, but they expressed more interest in a later proposal from the Scott family. On 14 October 1908 Gaston Scott offered to purchase 1.9 million acres of land. He promised to pay $1 an acre and to build a comprehensive system of drainage canals. The trustees agreed to sign a contract on this basis if Scott made an initial installment by 20 December.[67]

The Scott purchase was never made final, but the Broward administration did make a huge land sale to Richard J. Bolles of Colorado Springs, who had run up a fortune in Colorado gold mines and Oregon farmland. He contracted to pay $1 million over the course of eight years for 500,000 acres of land in the Everglades. The trustees promised to put half of the Bolles money into a special drainage fund that would be used to dig without delay five major and two secondary drainage canals.[68]

The Bolles deal was Governor Broward's last blow for his drainage program. When he turned over the governorship to Albert W. Gilchrist on 5 January 1909, only 15 miles of canal had been dug, but an irreversible process had been set in motion. This was true despite the fact that Broward had suffered a severe political defeat during his last year in office. Unable to run for reelection under the Florida constitution, he had attempted to win a seat in the U.S. Senate. In a four-man Democratic primary contest in May 1908 he had come in first, but in the runoff he had lost to Duncan U. Fletcher, the candidate favored by the railroad interests. Although in their younger years Broward and Fletcher had been political allies, they attacked each other savagely during this fight. Fletcher condemned the gov-

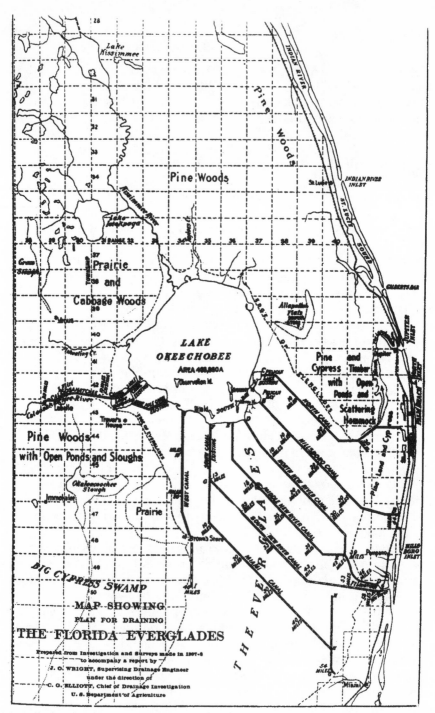

Wright's plan for draining the Everglades, 1909. The proposed canals encouraged belief that millions of acres could be reclaimed for farming. From U.S. Senate, *Everglades of Florida*, 62d Cong., 1st sess., 1911, Sen. Doc. 89.

ernor for persisting in his drainage program despite the voters' rejection of the constitutional amendment. According to Fletcher the program had cost between $300,000 and $500,000 and had reclaimed only 12,000 acres — dried up more by drought than drainage. Broward had promised never to give one foot of land or one dollar to the railroads, yet, Fletcher said, he had turned over to them 440,000 acres of land and nearly a quarter of a million dollars in cash.[69] Replying to these charges, Broward defended his settlements with the railroads and land companies: "By these compromises we saved the only land and the only money that have ever been saved in this fund." He had done his best to drain the Everglades. The project had already passed beyond the stage of experiment, as was evident from crops being grown on the reclaimed land "as well as by the interest which large and wealthy companies engaged in the beet sugar industry in the West have taken in the land."[70]

Not Broward's choice for governor, Gilchrist was a man of moderate views without a strong prior commitment to the drainage program. After the election Broward took him on an inspection trip through the Everglades and convinced him of the importance of the project.[71] Not so colorful and combative as Broward, Gilchrist followed a less exciting course but one that resulted in many more miles of canal than had been completed under Broward. The comparison is somewhat unfair, however, because Broward had to reverse the railroad-dominated policies of the state, whereas Gilchrist could take advantage of the momentum achieved through his predecessor's efforts.

During the Gilchrist administration the key figure in drainage matters was James O. Wright, an engineer from the U.S. Department of Agriculture, who had been studying the Everglades problem since November 1906. Sent at the request of Broward to advise the state, Wright had been given a broad assignment to determine the topography and make "plans and estimates of cost of a complete system of drainage." Under his direction, surveying parties carried out extensive work during the winters of 1907 and 1908. From the beginning, Wright acted not as a neutral expert but as a booster for the reclamation program. His Washington superiors soon had to reprimand him for making an imprudent speech to a Miami audience.[72]

In a message to the legislature dated 6 April 1909 Governor Gilchrist included an excerpt from the report that Wright was still preparing.[73] These preliminary findings were highly encouraging to the drainage backers. In Wright's oversimple analysis, excess water in the Everglades resulted solely from the overflow of Lake

Okeechobee. This might be remedied either by building a great
levee around the lower part of the lake or by opening up enough canals to reduce the water of the lake to a manageable level. The levee
would be too expensive and too uncertain, but the necessary canals
could certainly be built. Wright supplied a map showing eight canals. Four of these followed roughly the routes already chosen by
Governor Broward; four were new: a North Canal from Lake
Okeechobee to Lake Worth; a Hillsboro Canal from the great lake to
Hillsboro Inlet; a Middle New River Canal between the original two;
and a West Canal connecting with the remote Shark River and emptying into the Gulf. In estimating that these works could be built for
less than $2 million, Wright was far off the mark, as the later financial
history of the project proved. Wright also excited hopes that the
projected canals would provide the long-dreamed-for cross-Florida
waterway. By digging the Caloosahatchee and Hillsboro canals
deeper than the others, means would be provided for "transportation across the State."[74]

In May 1909 a joint legislative committee endorsed Wright's recommendations with enthusiasm. It pronounced the reclamation of
the Everglades to be "absolutely feasible and practical" and claimed
that "its success depends alone upon the number and size of the canals that are cut through them to Lake Okeechobee." The committee urged the trustees to "push with all possible dispatch the work on
the Glades, and if possible, let several of these canals on contract to
reliable, responsible bidders." The committee hoped that a resolute
policy would lead to federal aid to make part of the canals navigable,
"thus furnishing a public highway from ocean to gulf which will be
the pride of every Floridian and the wonder of the world."[75] The
legislators also stressed the importance of the Florida Coast Line
Canal: "The canals so far built have drained vast areas of swamp land,
which are now producing vegetables and fruits of various kinds in
large quantities...." When completed, the canal system would ensure reasonable freight and passenger rates all the way from Jacksonville to Key West. Once again the committee urged federal action,
hoping that a federal survey then in progress would result in "the
acquisition of the rights of the Canal Company by the government
(thus making it free to the public) and the enlargement of the canals
and natural inside channels along the whole coast."[76]

While legislators dreamed of federal sugarplums, Governor Gilchrist had to scratch for the dollars to keep four dredges in operation.
In June 1908 the U.S. District Court for Southern Florida had ruled
that the drainage tax was constitutional, and the following February
the U.S. Circuit Court at New Orleans had upheld this decision by a

two-to-one vote. But the big landowners still refused to pay and were preparing to take their case to the U.S. Supreme Court. In an attempt at compromise Governor Gilchrist proposed that the landowners give up their appeal and agree to pay arrearages on the tax, in return for which the legislature should reduce the tax from five cents to three cents an acres, retroactively to 1907.[77]

Although this suggestion was not acted upon, the two sides moved closer together during 1909. The big landowners were now ready to pay for drainage, provided they approved the plans and private contractors did the work. For their part, Governor Gilchrist and his fellow trustees were ready to turn the headaches of canal-digging over to engineers and businessmen. With all parties eager to work something out, a tentative agreement was signed on 3 January 1910. All the major parties—five great land companies, the Florida East Coast Railroad, and Richard Bolles—agreed to pay drainage taxes of five cents an acre for the period 1907–12. In addition to this, Bolles agreed to speed up the installments on his land so that he would pay them over the next two years instead of six. The state authorities in turn promised to appoint a competent chief engineer and arrange with private contractors for the digging of some 200 miles of canals in partial conformity with the routes recommended by Wright.[78] The two sides readily agreed that Wright himself should be offered the post of chief engineer of drainage. Rewarded by a salary twice as large as he was getting in the Department of Agriculture (but still only $5,000), Wright assumed his new duties in February 1910.[79] Some minor disagreements between the state and the great landowners remained, but these were ironed out in a final settlement of 7 April 1910.

On 1 July the trustees accepted the bid of the Furst-Clark Construction Company of Baltimore to excavate 184 miles of canals. The work was to be completed within three years, and the contractor agreed to purchase the state dredges and put others of its own on the job.[80] The company increased the tempo of the project over the slow pace of the state work. In addition to the four dredges purchased from the trustees, the contractor put five others into operation within the next eighteen months. Whereas the state had worked from the outside in—from the Atlantic Ocean and the Gulf of Mexico toward Lake Okeechobee—the construction company was able to dig canals in both directions. Bringing dredges up the old Disston canals now reopened from the Caloosahatchee River to Lake Okeechobee, the contractor started digging on the upper ends of the North New River and Miami canals. Since it was easier to excavate the terrain near the lake than it was to go through the rocky coastal

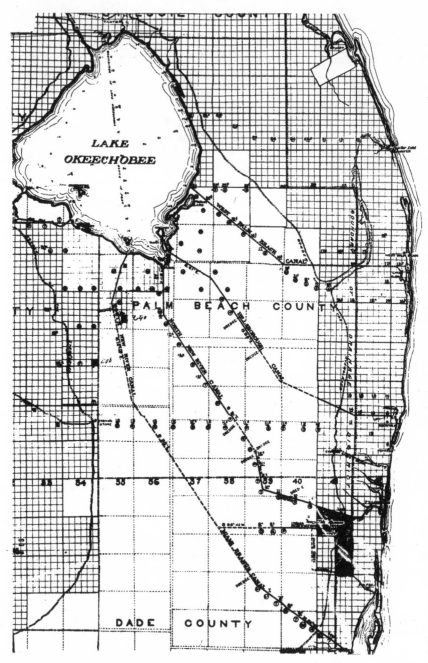

Canals built (heavy lines) and projected (broken lines), 1911. Detail of map of Everglades Drainage District. Map Collection, Strozier Library.

rim, the work went much faster. By the end of 1911 the North New River Canal was approaching completion: about 23 miles had been dug at each end, and only about 13 miles remained to be done. The other works were not so far along. Less than one-third of the 79-mile-long Miami Canal had been completed, and about three-fifths of the South New River Canal, now projected to extend 25 miles westward from Fort Lauderdale to connect with the Miami Canal. The 50-mile Hillsboro Canal, recommended by Wright, was begun in 1911 with 16.5 miles dug on its northern and 1.5 miles on its southern end by the end of the year.[81]

The state authorities were optimistic that all these canals would be completed by 1 July 1913, the time specified in the contract. But would this be enough to reclaim the Everglades? With every passing month it became clearer that the answer was no. To reduce Lake Okeechobee to the desired level, more outlets would be needed; to drain Everglades land already sold and still to be sold, additional canals must be dug; to make drainage effective, the main canals must be connected by lateral ditches; to facilitate navigation and provide water for irrigation, locks were needed; to prevent local flooding, levees must be built. The draining of the Everglades, which had seemed as easy to Broward as pulling the plug in the bathtub, loomed as an ever more complex problem. The prospect of having to spend more and more money on reclamation began to cause serious concern to the Gilchrist administration. At five cents an acre the drainage tax brought in only about $220,000 a year, but the trustees were now paying out about twice that amount on existing contracts. Only the great land sales had kept the project solvent, and these could not be expected to continue on the same scale. In March 1911 the state officials held a conference with representatives of the landowners who were parties to the agreement of 1910. Governor Gilchrist proposed doubling the drainage tax to ten cents an acre, but the big operators opposed this and promised instead to make additional payments to be used for new drainage works beneficial to their particular interests. In accordance with this agreement, Engineer Wright proposed building three auxiliary canals that would deepen small streams along the southeast Atlantic coast and extend these five or six miles into the Everglades. The additional drainage along this stretch of southeast Florida, the future Gold Coast, estimated to cost $70,000, was to be paid for by four great landowners who hoped to benefit—the Southern States Land Company, the Consolidated Land Company, the Florida East Coast Railroad, and R.J. Bolles.[82] In July 1912 the trustees contracted with the Miami Engineering and

Construction Company for the excavation of these short water-courses.[83]

The rising booster spirit in Palm Beach resulted in a more costly addition to the canal system. In March 1911 the Palm Beach Chamber of Commerce urged the IIF trustees to have a canal dug from Lake Okeechobee to Lake Worth. Explaining that all their resources were committed, the state officials invited the Palm Beach businessmen to raise money for the project.[84] In June 1911 two Palm Beach County officials appeared before the trustees to present the county's offer to contribute $75,000. The state, in turn, set aside 10,000 acres of land in the vicinity of the proposed canal. If the Palm Beach group could sell this land for $15 an acre, the trustees would earmark the proceeds of the sale for constructing the waterway.[85] It took many months, however, to carry this plan into operation. In December 1911 the trustees approved a route recommended by Engineer Wright and estimated the cost of construction at $328,000.[86] In March 1912 the Palm Beach representatives reported that they had a purchaser for the state land, and in December the trustees approved a contract with the National Construction Company of Birmingham, Alabama, to dig the canal for $594,000—some 80 percent above Wright's estimate.[87] But these arrangements fell through, and in November 1913 the state authorities had to contract all over again, this time with Johnson and Company of Miami. The West Palm Beach Canal was finally opened in 1917.[88]

On 1 July 1913, the date fixed for completion of the work that the Furst-Clark Construction Company had contracted to do, there were five main drainage canals open in South Florida, with a total length of 225 miles.[89] Since Furst-Clark had dug 181 miles of these since 1910, the work appeared to have made impressive progress. But the statistics were deceptive. None of the canals had been excavated to the specified width or depth, and an extension had to be given to the company to continue its work. By this time the state authorities were running into deep trouble in their drainage program. Most of the Everglades was still too wet for agriculture, and the trustees were finding it increasingly difficult to find the money to continue the effort. The progressives had been successful in saving millions of acres of Everglades land from the railroads, but not in transforming these acres into flourishing family farms.

# 6 Time of Troubles

For two years after the state officials made their peace treaty with the large landowners, the great reclamation project made good progress. The contractors kept a flotilla of dredges digging the drainage canals. The IIF trustees paid for the work with money collected from the speculators in the form of drainage taxes and installments on their purchases. The speculators in turn gathered in payments from more than 20,000 persons of small means who had signed up for farms in the Everglades. The whole operation depended on faith. As long as small purchasers remained convinced that they would soon be cultivating fertile, well-drained land, the flow of money continued, but by 1912 the required faith was beginning to collapse. Most of the land was still under water, and disillusioned buyers stopped paying their installments and clamored to have the speculators sent to prison. Salesmen could no longer find customers, and the large land companies fell into arrears in their payments to the state.

By 1913 the collapse of land sales was threatening to put an end to the whole project. But the state authorities could not back down. They had spent so much money that it seemed essential to keep going, and those who had invested in Everglades land insisted that the state make good on its promises. With great difficulty the authorities found ways in which to borrow the millions of dollars needed to build more canals, locks, and levees. Troubles continued to plague the effort. The great hurricanes of 1926 and 1928 took thousands of lives in the Lake Okeechobee region and destroyed houses and farms worth millions of dollars. Embittered farmers blamed the disasters on the bungling of the bureaucrats. Meanwhile, Florida real estate prices rose to dizzy heights, then plummeted downward, a portent of the great depression soon to engulf the country. By 1933 reclamation of the Everglades was one of the nation's bankrupt operations.

In 1909, when Richard Bolles began to map his sales campaign, these disasters lay far in the future. An old hand at real estate promotion, Bolles organized a series of companies to handle various tracts. His first such venture was the Florida Fruit Lands Company, to which he deeded 180,000 acres, or 641 square miles, in the eastern Everglades. The company offered land on an ingenious plan combining the convenience of installment buying with the gambling appeal of a raffle. For $240, to be paid in $10 monthly installments, a purchaser obtained a contract entitling him to a lot in "Progresso," a new town near Fort Lauderdale, and a farm in the Everglades, whose size and location would depend on the luck of the draw in a future lottery. Of the 12,000 farms to be allotted, two would be huge 640-acre ones, 8,000 would be small 10-acre ones, and the rest would be of intermediate size.[1] Glib salesmen distributed fancy brochures and added their own verbal embellishments. Thousands of customers signed contracts and began making their monthly payments.

So successful was this operation that several other outfits went into business. Most of them had their headquarters in distant cities like Colorado Springs, Kansas City, or Chicago, but others centered their operations in Miami and other Florida tourist centers. Some companies were handling Bolles land; others were selling that of other speculators. But they all copied Bolles's methods—exuberant advertising, insistent salesmen, installment plans, lottery drawings. Their brochures enticed customers with pictures of busy dredges, happy farmers, heavily laden orange trees, and flourishing sugarcane. The Everglades Land Sales Company of Chicago claimed that "the intrinsic value of the upper Everglades lands, based upon a minimum yield of $100 profit per acre in such commodities as sugar cane and figuring interest rates at 10 per cent is conservatively placed at $1,000 an acre." The same pamphlet boasted: "Added to the factor of climate, the soil, deep, uniform and black, is absolutely richer than the valley of the Nile. In all respects: in quantity, value and variety, these are the most productive lands in the world."[2]

In predicting the fecund future of the Everglades, salesmen loved to quote well-known personalities of the day. The Great Commoner, William Jennings Bryan, praised the reclamation project as "one of the greatest enterprises on record." Dr. Harvey W. Wiley, chief chemist of the Department of Agriculture, said that the mucklands south of Lake Okeechobee promised a development which "reached beyond the limits of prophecy." Secretary of Agriculture James Wilson said that doubting Thomases hesitant to buy Everglades land might regret it all the rest of their lives. The land promoters received their most useful boost in 1911 when the federal government issued a 208-page publication entitled *Everglades of Florida* (Senate Document No. 89). This included a treasury of material: Buckingham Smith's report of 1848, the texts of federal and state laws, an account of the Disston project, the messages of Jennings and Broward on drainage, the opinions of various experts, and Wright's report to the Department of Agriculture.[3] This congressional document seemed to give a stamp of federal approval to the enterprise. It was as though the U.S. government were somehow certifying that the Everglades would indeed be reclaimed and fabulous crops grown in their fertile soil. U.S. Sen. Duncan Fletcher of Florida had arranged for the publication, and Dr. Thomas Will, an employee of the Everglades Land Sales Company, had compiled the material.[4] The IIF trustees purchased 10,000 copies for distribution to the general public.[5]

One or two federal officials recognized the danger of establishing so cozy a relationship between the government and the land companies. Charles G. Elliott, chief drainage engineer in the Department of Agriculture, had inspected the eastern Everglades in 1904 and issued a brief, lukewarm report.[6] When Governor Broward had requested help, Elliott had sent his subordinate Wright to make a comprehensive survey. But Elliott strongly disapproved of Wright's rash endorsement of the reclamation scheme. Claiming the right to edit Wright's report, Elliott had toned down its optimistic findings. Wright had objected, and friction between the two engineers had hastened Wright's resignation and acceptance of the post of chief drainage engineer for the State of Florida.

While still postponing official publication of Wright's report, the Department of Agriculture had become entangled in another problem. Because it had received a number of inquiries from potential purchasers of Everglades land, a subordinate had prepared a circular letter to be sent out in reply. Reflecting Elliott's cautious point of view, the circular warned prospective purchasers that drainage was feasible, but the value of the land was "still largely problematical." Muckland might burn, and it might require large quantities of fertilizer.[7] Indignant that the department was supplying such timid advice, land company officials and state officeholders had protested to Secretary Wilson. In an effort to quiet the ruckus, Wilson had suppressed both the Wright report and the Elliott circular and ordered his subordinates to say nothing either for or against the Everglades project. But neutrality was not what the Florida boosters wanted, and Document No. 89 served the purpose of getting Wright's report—or at least one of its several drafts—into print.[8]

While the land companies and state officials, with occasional assists from the U.S. Department of Agriculture, were still extolling the fertility of reclaimed lands in the Everglades, thousands of small investors were getting their first glimpse of what they had purchased. Taking advantage of special railroad rates, they flocked to South Florida during the winter of 1910–11. They were drawn particularly by the news that the Florida Fruit Lands Company had sold all 180,000 acres of its land and would be holding its lottery in March. Thousands of contract holders arrived in Fort Lauderdale. Tom Watson, the Georgia populist politician who had a fishing camp nearby, wrote a sardonic account for his *Jeffersonian Magazine*: "Sale began March 15 and ran until about April 1. I was there when these bargain seekers (or I might say suckers) began coming to Fort Lauderdale. One day, about March 19, I saw three long, heavily-loaded trains come to the place; at one time they simply filled the woods, as there was not house room for one-fourth of the crowd in town. More than a thousand tents were put up through the piney woods between March 15 and 20. Fort Lauderdale two years ago had nearly 150 inhabitants, counting men, women, children, and dogs. The town had 5,000 inhabitants on March 20; I was there on the ground and counted. About 4,800 of these people came to this wonderful place to buy a small portion of the Everglades." Watson predicted that the Seminole Indians would continue to live unmolested in the Everglades, "as they are the only things that can possibly live there all year around except the alligators and rattlesnakes and mosquitoes."[9]

Most of the visitors were, in truth, cruelly disappointed. They accused the company of arbitrarily assigning land instead of holding the promised lottery and of failing to carry out its plans for the model town of Progresso. Their allotted farms were widely scattered and almost impossible to locate. The land was still unsurveyed, and the individual tracts existed only in the paper world of company maps. Most of the farms were, in fact, still under water. Only in the immediate vicinity of the half-finished canals was it possible to grow crops. The indignant contract holders sued Bolles for the return of their money. Those who had purchased from other land companies were no happier. The years 1911 and 1912 were a time of disappointment and anger.

Most of those who had fallen for the land promotion schemes went home in disgust, but a few stuck it out in South Florida. They found land to buy on the coastal ridge (often railroad or canal grant land), and in time many of them made good profits on their investments. Ironically the Everglades farms sold by Bolles and other promoters were usually worthless, but the town lots, thrown in merely as sweeteners, rose steadily in value as winter residents came in increasing numbers to Lake Worth, Fort Lauderdale, and Miami.[10]

Having been promised farmland richer than the Valley of the Nile and finding only sawgrass marsh, most of the contract holders complained bitterly that they had been cheated. Florida began to receive very damaging publicity. On 15 October 1911 the *Washington Times* published an article charging collusion among the land companies, the Florida East Coast Railroad, the state authorities, and the U.S. Department of Agriculture.[11] To demonstrate that he was not an ally of the land sharks, Florida Congressman Frank Clark called for a congressional investigation of the charges. Before the hearings could begin, Secretary Wilson poured gasoline on the fire by discharging Elliott and three associates on the ground that they had submitted false expense vouchers. Representative Clark charged that the firings had been made at the behest of the Florida land companies. "If the people want to be humbugged," Clark said, "I am perfectly willing to let them be humbugged; but not by a copartnership between a great government and the land speculators."[12]

Beginning in February 1912 and continuing at intervals until August, the House Committee on Expenditures in the Department of Agriculture conducted hearings on the Everglades business. Newspaper reports of the testimony were highly damaging to the drainage project. Wright was shown to have been responsible for the dismissal of Elliott, his old boss, by calling attention to some minor irregularities.[13] In this and in other matters, the testimony suggested that Wright was a tool of the land companies. When he had been sent to North Carolina on an earlier assignment, he had accepted favors from parties that would benefit from his recommendations.[14] No such allegations were made concerning his work in Florida, but the possibility of collusion had certainly been suggested. Other witnesses described the sales of methods of the land companies and the flooded condition of the Everglades land. In its report the congressional committee commented unfavorably on Wright's conduct and criticized Secretary Wilson for firing Elliott and his associates on a technicality.[15] The Department of Justice moved to quash indictments against the four men because further investigation had revealed no intention to defraud the government.[16]

Newspapers in forty-three states were reported to have published stories about the "Florida Scandal." Governor Gilchrist complained that northern and western railroads were conspiring to halt Florida's expansion.[17] On 10 April 1912 the IIF trustees passed resolutions deploring newspaper reports "derogatory to the practicality of the plans which are being followed for the drainage and reclamation of the Everglades and derogatory to the value and utility of the Everglades land for agricultural and horticultural purposes." In

Everglades survey party, 1913. In an effort to put reclamation on a sounder basis, Governor Trammell employed Isham Randolph, a New York engineer, to study the terrain and make recommendations. SPA.

order that the truth might be known, the trustees appropriated $1,000 to pay the expenses of "thirty or more influential representatives" of the leading newspapers of the country, who were to be invited to make a personal investigation of the scene.[18]

Eager for an expense-paid junket to distant parts, almost fifty reporters traveled from Chicago to Jacksonville aboard the "Hurry-Up Limited." There they were greeted by Governor Gilchrist, who accompanied them on the railroad trip to Fort Myers. At that city the party boarded a steamboat for a voyage up the Caloosahatchee River, through the connecting canals, and across Lake Okeechobee. After spending a night at the Bolles Hotel, they entered the newly completed North New River Canal. At this point the governor ceremoniously mixed the water from two coconuts, one containing water from the Gulf of Mexico, the other from the Atlantic Ocean. Having thus officially opened the "Gulf-to-Atlantic Canal," the party chugged down the narrow waterway to Fort Lauderdale for further festivities.[19] Impressed by what they had seen, the reporters sent enthusiastic stories to their papers. One wrote, "In the Everglades you simple tickle the soil and the bounteous crops respond to feed hungry humanity." Another said, "Florida must have been the first part of the world, made early Monday morning when everyone was feeling good without a care or a worry."[20]

But this favorable publicity did not last long. Soon the flow of damaging news arising out of the congressional investigation was resumed. In September 1912 Wright resigned, complaining that the "tirade of abuse and misrepresentation" had placed "the entire project and everyone connected with it in a false light." Perhaps relieved to get rid of a controversial official, the trustees ordered Fred C. Elliott, one of his subordinates, to take over as acting chief engineer. In March 1914 they appointed Elliott to the regular post, one which he was destined to occupy for many years. Wright had meanwhile taken a position with the Furst-Clark Construction Company, which was digging most of the canals.[21]

The anger of the small land purchasers resulted in a series of lawsuits. Contract holders sued Bolles and the Florida Fruit Lands Company for the return of their money. At the trial in Kansas City witnesses testified that the company had committed 12,000 contract holders to payments totaling $2,880,000—$2.5 million more than Bolles had paid for the land. The federal circuit court judge ruled that Bolles might keep $1.4 million already paid to him but that he should receive no more until the promised reclamation was completed.[22] In other cases the U.S. Department of Justice sought to have Bolles and his associates indicted on two criminal charges, one for conspiring to use the mails to defraud, the other for using the mails to conduct a lottery. In April 1914 a federal commissioner dismissed the first indictment on the ground that the evidence showed no criminal intent. The second indictment remained in force, but Bolles never came to trial.[23] Legal maneuvering delayed the case, and on 25 March 1917 the promoter suffered a fatal stroke aboard a Florida East Coast Railroad train traveling from Palm Beach to Jacksonville.[24]

In February 1914 a federal court in Kansas City tried Dr. E. C. Chambers and four associates for using the mails to defraud. The government claimed that Chambers had purchased 50,000 acres of undrained Florida land for $10 an acre and sold it for $50 to $65 an acre despite the fact that it was unfit for cultivation. Testifying for the defense, Governor Trammell and other state officials insisted that the land would eventually be drained. Nevertheless, the jury found the men guilty and the judge imposed prison sentences, but the sentences apparently were never served.[25]

The success of Bolles and Chambers in evading prison demonstrates not only the skill of their lawyers but the complexity of the issues. In making their large sales the IIF trustees were acting in good faith because they clearly intended to drain the Everglades, but they failed to realize that reclamation would be difficult and that some of the land would never be drained. In their advertising the speculators grossly exaggerated the fertility of the reclaimed muck and rashly assured their customers that frosts would never occur. They neglected to inform their prospects that most of the land was still under water. At what point did such misrepresentations become criminal? In April 1916 the U.S. Supreme Court pondered this question in a case involving swamplands in central Florida, where the promoters had used similar tactics in praising the land as high and well drained, capable of producing three crops a year, and accessible over good roads. A lower court had ruled that there was no fraud because the land was worth at least what the customers paid for it, but the Supreme Court reversed this decision. Justice Joseph McKenna said that "mere puffing" might not be within the statute's meaning, "but when the seller goes beyond that, assigns to the article qualities which it does not possess, does not simply magnify in opinion the advantages which it has, but invents advantages and falsely asserts their existence, he transcends the limits of 'puffing' and engages in false representations and pretenses."[26]

Attempts to punish the promoters usually failed, but the victims had at least one recourse. They could stop signing new sales contracts and making payments on their old ones. By the summer of 1912 this boycott was nearly complete, and the effect on reclamation was devastating. Up to the end of 1912 the trustees had spent about $2 million on drainage; of this amount about one-half had been derived from land sales and the rest from drainage taxes.[27] Once this flow of money stopped, the whole program was likely to collapse.

The Gilchrist administration was obviously worried about the situation. In May 1912 the trustees authorized Col. Cromwell Gibbons of Jacksonville to negotiate sales of Everglades land with any purchasers he could find in Europe[28]—a sure indication that things were bad, because state officials and promoters had always tried to hook foreign capitalists whenever domestic investors became wary. But this time no one took the bait. In December 1912 the trustees threatened to sue Bolles for the arrears on his payments and warned Chambers that they would cancel his contract if he did not pay up.[29] In 1912 the trustees took in only $231,000 while spending about $564,000. At the beginning of the year the Internal Improvement Fund had a reserve of almost $357,000; by the end of the year this had dwindled to $24,000.[30]

The managers of the great land companies were even more worried. If reclamation broke down, Everglades land would never sell. In July 1912, V.W. Helm, president of the Everglades Land Sales Company, employed three engineers to make an independent

Digging the St. Lucie Canal, 1921. Because of the inadequacy of the earlier canals the state authorities gave top priority to building a much larger one to serve as the principal outlet from Lake Okeechobee. SPA.

study. Their findings were disturbing. The current operations were hurting instead of helping because the water from Lake Okeechobee was overflowing the half-finished canals into the neighboring lands. The state's overall program was unwisely planned because it was too difficult and too expensive to drain the whole Everglades. It would be better to reclaim one area at a time, and to do this properly private owners would have to build their own levees and ditches to supplement the main canals of the state system. For this reason, the populist dream of ten-acre farms was unrealistic. Only large operators could invest the capital required to make Everglades agriculture profitable.[31]

In September officers of the Everglades Land Sales Company met with representatives of the other landowners in New York City. Governor Gilchrist was also present. Discussing the critical report, the owners made it clear that they were unwilling to make further payments to the trustees unless they received assurance that the state was going to carry through a soundly planned program. Gilchrist proposed a bond issue to raise the money needed to complete the drainage works. Six or seven million dollars, he said, would be enough to put the Everglades in splendid condition.[32]

Such was the condition of affairs in January 1913 when Park Trammell became governor. Having served as attorney general and therefore as IFF trustee, Trammell was well acquainted with the financial crisis in the reclamation program and the discontent of the land companies. Attacking these problems with energy, he and his fellow trustees arranged for a new survey. On 30 April 1913 they signed an agreement with Isham Randolph, member of a highly respected New York firm, providing for an Everglades Engineering Commission to determine the character and elevation of the terrain, recommend the location of needed canals, estimate their cost, and provide accurate maps.[33]

Without waiting for the recommendations of the commission, the Trammell administration asked for laws reorganizing the whole reclamation effort. To make it possible to speed up the program, the state officers recommended assessing drainage taxes on a sliding scale. "We believe that each acre of land in the territory should bear its part of the expense according to the benefit received." Higher drainage taxes would provide the security for drainage district bonds. This plan "would not create a State debt and would require a tax only in the drainage district upon lands benefitted." Emphasizing the urgency of the need, the Drainage Board said: "With the drainage tax entirely inadequate, and no demand for Everglades land at an adequate price, the situation is so critical that it is absolutely necessary for the Legislature to make provision other than that now proclaimed by law for the further financing of the drainage and reclamation project."[34]

On 6 June 1913 the governor signed into law a bill establishing an "Everglades Drainage District" to be administered by a board of commissioners composed of the same state officials who constituted the trustees of the Internal Improvement Fund. The new law levied drainage taxes in accordance with the anticipated benefits. The tracts nearest to Lake Okeechobee and the main canals would pay 15 cents an acre for three years, 18 cents an acre for the second three years, and 25 cents an acre thereafter. Tracts less directly benefited

St. Lucie Lock No. 1, 1921. The St. Lucie Canal was designed to link with the Caloosahatchee Canal and Lake Okeechobee to provide a navigable waterway across the peninsula. SPA.

would pay somewhat less, and those most remote from the drainage canals would pay five cents an acre for three years, eight cents for the second three years, and ten cents thereafter. On the basis of these revenues the Everglades Drainage Board was authorized to borrow money for periods not exceeding one year and also to issue "negotiable coupon bonds" at not more than 6 percent interest to a total amount of not more than $6 million.[35]

The legislature also provided for the establishment of special drainage districts. Landowners might either petition the county commissioners or apply to the circuit court of the county. Whichever procedure was followed, the petition had to bear the signatures of either a majority of the landowners of the proposed district or owners of more than half the land. If after public hearings the county commissioners or the circuit court believed the proposed reclamation would be of general benefit, they could order the project financed by assessing all landowners in the district. If the petition had been made to the county commissioners, this body would let the contracts and make the tax levy. If, on the other hand, the petitioners had chosen to apply to the circuit court, the judge would consolidate all the landowners into a public corporation to be managed by an elected board of three supervisors with one vote allocated to each acre of land.[36] This legislation favored the interests of the large landowners who could use the coercive powers of the government to obtain additional drainage, even though small owners might object to the taxes.

Plans for a bond issue made the work of the Randolph Commission all the more important because investors could not be expected to buy these securities unless reputable engineers recommended the expenditures. The commission report, issued 25 October 1913,

Sentinel cypress at Moore Haven, 1913. Located on Lake Okeechobee at the mouth of the Caloosahatchee Canal, Moore Haven was one of several settlements that grew up along the early canals. The "sentinel cypress" was a well-known landmark for boatmen on the lake. SPA.

was mildly critical of earlier drainage policy. "The existing system of canals, the commissioners said, "contemplates the reclamation of a greater portion of the Everglades in the immediate future than will probably be justified by the demand for new lands. It would have been much better to provide for an orderly progression of reclamation in accordance with the demand and with due regard to market conditions and transportation facilities." Nevertheless, a commitment had been made to the purchasers, and the commission therefore recommended "an earnest effort to reclaim in one continuous project and with the greatest possible expedition all the lands south and southeast of Lake Okeechobee, between the Miami Canal, the proposed West Palm Beach Canal, and the eastern boundary of the drainage district."[37]

The commission commended the policy of "progressive drainage," to which the state authorities were now supposedly committed. This would allow the work to proceed only as fast as there was need for those areas for farming. "We regard Lake Okeechobee as the key to the solution of the whole problem. When that great reservoir is brought under control and the territory to the south is freed from the overflow of the lake, then the emancipated region can be relieved by adequate main drainage outlets and subsidiary canals whose capacities may be adjusted to meet the needs of the territory which they serve."[38] To control Lake Okeechobee, a new canal was needed, wider, deeper, and shorter than those already built. "We propose to divert the entire flow of Lake Okeechobee into the St. Lucie River through a canal...."[39] Ironically this was the plan considered and rejected by Governor Broward eight years earlier.

The Randolph Commission argued that the St. Lucie Canal would serve several purposes. By a system of locks it would permit the authorities to control the level of Lake Okeechobee. It would also be useful for navigation: the existing canals were too narrow and shallow for boats of any substantial size, but the St. Lucie Canal would be 200 feet wide and 12 feet deep. If the state provided a navigable waterway of this character, the federal government might be expected to enlarge the Caloosahatchee waterway, thus providing the longsought cross-state canal. A final recommendation, which later proved to be impractical, called for building a hydroelectric plant at the eastern end of the St. Lucie Canal.[40]

The Randolph Commission estimated the cost of the St. Lucie Canal at $2,259,000. It recommended in addition the enlargement of the existing canals and the digging of three new ones between Miami and West Palm Beach at the cost of $4,281,000.[41] For the more distant future, the commissioners suggested a network of canals with outlets on the Gulf of Mexico, Florida Bay, and Biscayne Bay to drain the western and southern Everglades. Despite its sobering portrayal of what remained to be done, the report offered a rosy vision of the future. To be sure, the canals already dug had made the Everglades wetter than ever, but all would be well in the end. "They are there to serve a useful purpose in the great scheme of reclamation upon which the State has embarked: a scheme which has only to be carried to completion to make fertile fields of a watery waste and a populous land where now no man dwells."[42]

But the Randolph Commission's recommendation could not be carried out without money, and money was still very difficult to get. The Everglades Drainage District was unable at first to sell its bonds, and the drainage tax did not bring in enough revenue to permit work on a large scale. The state authorities loosened the deadlock in March 1915 by signing a new contract with the Furst-Clark Construction Company, under which the company would accept one-third payment in cash and the rest in two-year notes at 6 percent interest with the new Drainage District bonds serving as collateral. The new contract radically reordered the priorities. Work on the Miami and South New River canals was to be discontinued; the North New River and Hillsboro Canals were to be completed to modified specifications within twenty months. Preference was now given to the St. Lucie Canal, which was to be dug to half its designated size within two and a half years and completed in four years. Ever the optimist, Governor Trammell assured the legislature that "the work under this contract, with other work planned, no doubt means the ultimate success of the drainage and reclamation of the Everglades."[43]

But the program continued to drag, and the state officials found themselves the targets of bitter criticism. In 1915 a group of Fort Lauderdale citizens organized a "Back to Broward League," dedicated to insuring justice for "20,000 men and women in the United States who have bought Everglades land." Rebuffed in an effort to get the U.S. Attorney General to bring suit against the state, the league in 1917 instituted its own case in U.S. district court. Contending that the state had forfeited its claim to the swamplands because of failure to drain them and that the drainage taxes were illegal when used to secure bonds, the plaintiff asked to have the Internal Improvement Fund placed in receivership. The receiver should be directed to collect $1.5 million in unpaid drainage taxes on state-owned land, reclaim 2 million acres and large sums of money from the railroads, and use these assets to complete the drainage works.[44]

Nothing came of this suit, but early in 1917 the reclamation program fell into another of its recurrent crises. The Everglades Drainage District bonds were still unsold; drainage taxes were hard to collect; even the IFF trustees were delinquent in paying on state-owned swamplands. Disgusted with the situation, the new governor, Sidney J. Catts, recommended that the legislature pass a law putting all 1,250,000 acres still held by the Internal Improvement Board up for sale at from $5 to $8 an acre, and "that the same be sold at private or public sale and the amount of money gotten from these sales be, after the debts of the Board have been paid, turned over to the State School Fund, whereby each and every child of the State shall obtain its pro rata share, and allow the drainage of these lands to continue after they pass into private hands."[45]

Hillsboro Lock No. 1 at Belle Glade, early 1920s. The Lake Okeechobee towns grew substantially in the years before the floods and hurricanes of the 1920s. SPA.

Despite the governor's hostility to the reclamation program, the state finally came up with the money to continue it. Spitzer, Rorick and Company of Toledo, Ohio, bought the $3.5 million issue of Everglades Drainage District bonds, and the state and other land-holders resumed payment of their drainage taxes. Assured of pay-ment, the contractors started work again on the canals. The St. Lucie Canal, which the Randolph Commission had so strongly rec-ommended, was finally opened, although not to its specified size; other new canals proposed by the commission were undertaken; the original ones were improved.[46] All this cost more money than ex-pected. The Everglades Drainage District gained the consent of the legislature for new bond issues until the total amount outstanding reached $10,255,000 on 1 January 1927. The legislature kept changing the drainage tax; it was briefly reduced in 1915 but thereafter raised several times until 1925 when the tax on the lands most directly benefited reached $1.25 an acre.[47]

Supporters of the drainage program were able to point to some gains. State Chemist Rufus Rose, who had worked on drainage for Disston and Ingraham, wrote a highly optimistic pamphlet in 1916. The level of Lake Okeechobee, in earlier years about 21 feet above sea level, had been reduced to 16.5 feet. "Its shores, formerly impassable swamps, are now being cultivated, and are yielding phenomenal crops of all kinds, cane, corn, tropical fruits, and particularly native pasture grasses of the best quality on which are rapidly being established immense stock farms of pure bred cattle, with a rapidly increasing, energetic population of vigorous, industrious, sanguine, and contented people."[48]

But flourishing fields and bustling population were not what most visitors to the region reported. A travel book, published in 1918, described Moore Haven, located near the junction of the Caloosahatchee Canal and Lake Okeechobee, as a raw frontier village. In the surrounding countryside pioneer farmers were living in little temporary shacks while they tried to clear the land for crops.[49] Other small settlements maintained themselves with difficulty. In 1913 Dr. Thomas Will had founded the village of Okeelanta along the North New River Canal some four miles from the lake on a sawgrass tract purchased from the Florida Everglades Land Sales Company. In 1920 Okeelanta had about 200 inhabitants. Most of the new residents of the region settled along the drainage canals close to the lake. Thus the village of South Bay slowly grew near the mouth of the North New River Canal, Lake Harbor near the entrance of the Miami Canal, Belle Glade and Chosen near the Hillsboro Canal, and Pahokee and Canal Point near the West Palm Beach Canal. Farmers also settled on Ritta and other islands near the southern shore of the lake, where they enjoyed the benefits of particularly good soil and climate.[50] But the villages continued to be small, and the dramatic expansion of agriculture expected to result from reclamation had not yet materialized. In 1920 there were an estimated 34,000 acres under cultivation and 23,000 people living in the Everglades Drainage District.[51] Many of these were probably located along the canals on the outskirts of Fort Lauderdale, Miami, and West Palm Beach.

A combination of difficulties hampered the growth of the region. The first problem was isolation. The only way to get there was by boat, either up the Caloosahatchee from Fort Myers or up the North New River Canal from Fort Lauderdale. From 1912 to 1921 small steamboats carried passengers over these waterways, and frontier farmers sent their tomatoes, beans, and other produce down to Fort Myers and Fort Lauderdale for rail shipment to the North. But the drainage canals were always dangerous to navigate, and by 1921 the North New River Canal was so choked with silt that steamboats could no longer use it. Meanwhile, the opening of the West Palm Beach Canal in 1917 had provided another transportation route, but it had the same limitations as the earlier canals. The Miami Canal was too long and shallow to be useful for navigation.

Canal Point. Another Lake Okeechobee town located at the entrance to the West Palm Beach Canal. SPA.

Railroads began to reach the region in 1915 when the Florida East Coast built a branch line to Okeechobee City, a new town developed by the railroad's Model Land Company. In 1918 the Atlantic Coast Line, the old Plant System, opened a line connecting Fort Myers with Moore Haven. In subsequent years both railroads extended their tracks: the Florida East Coast reached Canal Point in 1925 and Belle Glade in 1928; the Atlantic Coast Line built down to Clewiston in 1921; and in 1929 the two railroads met at Lake Harbor at the southern end of the lake.[52]

Even more important was the opening of the region to automobiles and trucks. The prime mover in achieving this was William J. ("Fingy") Conners, an improbable character said to have been the inspiration for Jiggs in George McManus's comic strip "Bringing Up Father." After making a fortune on the Buffalo, New York, waterfront, Conners moved to Florida and invested heavily in land near Lake Okeechobee. Unable to attract customers because of the poor transportation, Conners obtained the permission of the legislature to build a private toll road from West Palm Beach to the lake. Completed in 1925, the 52-mile highway cost Conners $1.8 million but brought him rich returns both in tolls and land sales.[53]

Farmers expecting to find a new agricultural heaven in the reclaimed Everglades ran into unforeseen difficulties. Although the politicians and promoters had boasted that the muck was richer than the Valley of the Nile, the early settlers found that it had strange properties. The land was difficult to clear and break with the plow, and the first planting were likely to fail. Young plants either shriveled up or went all to leaves and stalk. The muck had to be purged of its toxic rawness by being broken up and exposed to the atmosphere; even then it seemed to lack certain minerals necessary for healthy growth. The U.S. Department of Agriculture had pointed out some of these problems in C. G. Elliott's report of 1904, and in 1915 the department issued another cautionary document emphasizing the difficulty of preparing the soil and warning that frost damage was not impossible: "It is such land as this, untried for agriculture and a large part of it still under water that... is being sold for $20 to $65 per acre." These gloomy tidings were so distasteful to the citizens of Fort Lauderdale, according to local tradition, that they consigned all available copies of the report to a public bonfire.[54]

But it made more sense to seek the scientists' advice than to burn up their findings. As early as 1913 Governor Trammell asked the legislature to establish an experimental station to study the peculiar qualities of Everglades soil, but the lawmakers took no action until 1921 when they ordered the IFF trustees to set aside not less than 160 acres and to appropriate $10,000 a year for two years and $5,000 a year thereafter for this purpose. The state treasury was ordered to match these contributions.[55] Located at Belle Glade, the Everglades Experiment Station was soon providing valuable advice on fertilizers and farm management. During the 1920s the farms around Lake Okeechobee began at last to bear the bumper crops that the promoters had promised.

To the astonishment of newcomers, the Everglades muck would burn. During dry seasons any mishap — a bolt of lightning, an abandoned camp fire, trash carelessly burned — might start a blaze that would consume not only the sawgrass but the soil underneath to a depth of one or two feet. So serious was the problem that in 1919 the legislature made it a misdemeanor punishable by a $500 fine or six months in the county jail to "carelessly, wilfully, maliciously, or otherwise" start a fire within the Everglades Drainage District.[56] In 1925 the law was stiffened: penalties were increased to a $5,000 fine or one year in state prison.[57]

As the growing menace of fire demonstrated, the Everglades were drying out. Indeed, it seemed that some sections were overdrained and in need of irrigation. Although canals and ditches had helped to

West Palm Beach Canal, Lock No. 1. SPA.

remove the surplus water, a shift in the weather had done even more. From 1912 through 1920 there was less than normal rainfall. Reduced flooding in the region around Lake Okeechobee attracted more settlers. Between 1920 and 1927 the acreage under cultivation and the population of the Everglades Drainage District both doubled, reaching as estimated 46,000 acres and 92,000 inhabitants.[58] Many factors contributed to this boom: more drainage, more railroads, new highways, improved agricultural methods.

Especially important to the region's growth was the expansion of the sugar industry, the realization of another ancient dream. The earliest proponents of draining the Everglades had argued that the soil and climate were ideal for sugar plantations. During the 1880s Hamilton Disston had grown cane and operated a sugar mill at St. Cloud near Kissimmee, and the U.S. Department of Agriculture

Dredging near Miami, 1926. The building boom encouraged extensive drainage to the west of the city. Fishbaugh and SPA.

had established a 40-acre experimental farm nearby. Results were excellent, but Disston plunged in too deeply and lost heavily on his sugar operations. In 1915 the Southern States Land and Timber Company began experimental plantings of sugar at Canal Point and in the region east of Lake Okeechobee. In 1920 the U.S. Department of Agriculture established a cane breeding station at Canal Point, where it developed three important new disease-resistant strains.[59]

Thereafter, sugar growing expanded rapidly. The Moore Haven Sugar Corporation, which opened a small mill in 1920, failed within a few years, but the Florida Sugar and Food Products Company, which built a plant near Canal Point in 1923, was a major promotion. Frank W. Bryant, an English engineer who had helped to develop the city of Lake Worth, provided the driving force. Running into financial trouble, Bryant reorganized his enterprise as the Southern Sugar Company. He bought out his principal competitor, the Pennsylvania Sugar Company with its extensive land holdings and its

$1,500,000 sugar mill built along the Miami Canal. In 1925 a still more masterful figure, Bror G. Dahlberg, Swedish-born president of the Celotex Company of Chicago, came onto the scene. Needing sugarcane residue for making wallboard, Dahlberg bought control of the Southern Sugar Company and took Bryant into the new management. Dahlberg moved the Pennsylvania Sugar Company mill to the new town of Clewiston on the southwest shore of Lake Okeechobee, and this became the center of a rapidly expanding agricultural empire. In 1929 the Southern Sugar Company was reputed to own 130,000 acres of land: 11,000 acres was devoted to sugarcane and other acres were used for vegetables and fruit.[60] By one of the ironies of Florida history the reclamation of the Everglades, which was supposed to invigorate family farming, was working out mostly for the benefit of agricultural big business. Instead of white yeomen, black laborers were tilling the fields.

But the Everglades boomlet was no more than a side show to the great Florida circus that was drawing visitors by the thousands and sending real estate prices soaring. Although this speculative fever invaded most of the state, it took a particularly virulent form along the southeast Atlantic coast. In their zeal for development, promoters turned water into land and land into water. In one such miracle Carl Fisher of Indianapolis, who had made a fortune manufacturing automobile batteries, transformed a swampy island into the glittering resort of Miami Beach. Armies of black laborers hacked away the mangroves with machetes, and great dredges pumped sand from the bottom of the ocean and spread it over the swamp to provide land for hotels, polo grounds, golf courses, tennis courts, yacht basins, and bathhouses.[61] George Merrick attempted a similar marvel at Coral Gables, south of Miami. Although most of his land was at some distance from the coast, he transformed an old drainage ditch into a 40-mile-long grand canal intended to wind through his model city and provide a romantic vista of yachts and gondolas.[62] But the dream of creating an American Venice was more nearly realized at Fort Lauderdale, where Charles Green Rodes discovered that he could create valuable building lots by a method known as "finger islanding." He dredged a series of canals at right angles to the New River and used the fill to make new land. Down each artificial peninsula he built a street, dead-ended at the river for privacy. Each building lot had its own waterfront with easy access to the New River and the whole East Coast canal system.[63] Rodes's success with this dredge-and-fill technique inspired other developers to turn mangrove swamps into high-priced waterfront property. Glad to have the mosquito population reduced, residents would not worry until many years later about the ecological consequences of destroying the mangroves.

The Florida real estate boom soared to its dizziest height in 1925. Developers opened one new subdivision after another, some of them on poorly drained land. A horde of speculators bought and sold options, often dealing with customers a thousand or more miles away and pushing prices higher and higher. Carpenters and masons threw up bungalows and apartment houses with careless haste, until the railroads could no longer handle the southward flow of materials, and freight embargoes delayed the work. The bubble broke in January 1926. Becoming wary, the banks began to refuse to make new loans or renew old ones. But the retreat came too late, and many of the banks failed. No longer able to get credit, speculators found themselves ruined. Many of the recent arrivals returned to the North. Land prices dropped sharply and construction stopped. After a depressing tourist season, hotelkeepers and merchants looked forward to recouping some of their losses during the winter of 1926–27.[64]

But the great hurricane of 18–19 September 1926 blasted these hopes. Winds, estimated at 130 to 150 miles an hour, lashed the southeast coast and roared across interior Florida, killing some 372 people, injuring 6,000 more, and destroying 5,000 homes. Ships and boats were smashed onto the beaches and into city streets; tent cities and tourist camps were leveled; flimsily built houses collapsed in ruins. The damage was estimated at $76 million, and 18,000 people were left without shelter.[65] Local boosters were appalled at the bad publicity. According to some northern moralists, Miami was a modern Sodom singled out by God for punishment. "And yonder is beautiful Florida," declared John Roach Straton, a fundamentalist preacher in New York City. "How beautiful. But how she did depart from God's way! She turned after the worship of Mammon. Racetrack gamblers were welcomed. The Sunday sermons were forgotten in the mad rush for gold. But God did not forget them. It is to be hoped that Florida will return to God, and it seems now that she will."[66]

The National Red Cross launched a drive to raise $5 million for Florida relief, but Florida Gov. John Martin and Miami Mayor Edward Rompfh gave out assurances that the hurricane stories had been exaggerated. Regarding these statements as sabotage of the relief effort, John Howard Payne, national chairman of the Red Cross, denounced the Florida officials for regarding "the poor people who suffered...as of less consequence than the hotel and tourist business of Florida." Hampered by this controversy, the reflief drive bogged down after raising $3.8 million.[67] It was years before the Gold Coast recovered from the twin blows of the real estate bust and the hurricane. Thousands of disillusioned retirees and workmen returned to the North, and the next great wave of sunseekers did not move in until after the Great Depression.

Injurious though the hurricane was to Miami, it took a still more tragic toll in the towns around Lake Okeechobee. The great storm of 1926 was not the first but the third serious blow that the region had suffered since 1922, when the cycle of dry seasons came to an end. After extensive rains in 1922 Lake Okeechobee overflowed its banks and ruined the farmers' crops. In 1924 there was still more serious flooding. Only one life was lost, but according to a Florida congressman, "the whole country was destroyed."[68] The trouble was caused not only by the protracted rains but by the subsidence of the lands bordering on the lake. Because of drainage, oxidation was consuming the dried-out muck. In some places the ground had settled by as much as four and a half feet.[69]

To prevent further trouble the Everglades Drainage District had

Dredging the Miami Canal, 1926. Even for these huge machines progress was slow because dynamite had to be used to blast through the rocky terrain. Fishbaugh and SPA.

built a dike of muck and sand around the southern end of the lake from Bascom Point to Moore Haven, about 47 miles. But the new barrier was only five to nine feet high and about 40 feet thick at the base. Beaten upon by the hurricane of 1926, it was worse than useless. The water of the lake piled up behind the frail structure and then broke through, bringing death or injury to more than 400 people. Some 1,200 survivors had to be evacuated from Moore Haven, where the main streets were still under water three weeks after the storm. The disaster resulted in bitter criticism of Governor Martin and State Engineer Elliott: the former was blamed for undercutting the Red Cross relief effort, the latter for contributing to the tragedy by mismanaging the drainage works. For weeks before the hurricane, lakeshore residents had been warning that the lake had reached a dangerously high level, but state officials failed to release more water down the canals. The officials had been caught between the conflicting demands of various factions. Farmers living close to Okeechobee wanted a low level to prevent flooding, but the federal government had insisted on a level high enough to meet the needs of boatmen and fishermen. Farmers living on the lower reaches of the canals had also objected to the release of too much water because they were afraid that it would overflow the banks and damage crops.[70]

Bitterly condemned for the Moore Haven disaster, the state officials held Lake Okeechobee to a low level during subsequent summers. In the early summer of 1928 the lake stood at only 13.3 feet above sea level, to the disgust of the boatmen. But this was not low enough to prevent the greatest disaster of all. During August and September rain fell almost continuously, backing up water in the lake faster than the drainage canals could carry it off. And then on the night of 16 September another hurricane blasted a path of destruction from West Palm Beach across the peninsula. The churning waters of Lake Okeechobee pounded through the fragile earth dike and inundated Belle Glade and the whole south shore. As houses and buildings tumbled through the deluge, so many people were swept to their deaths that an accurate count was impossible. Relief workers had to pile the bodies like cordwood and burn them in great bonfires. It was estimated that somewhere between 1,800 and 2,000 people—three-quarters of them black laborers—lost their lives.[71]

This disaster came as one more blow to the Martin administration. Ever since he took office in January 1925, the governor had been struggling with the tangled finances of the reclamation program. The Everglades Drainage District had already issued bonds amounting to $10,750,000 and was authorized to issue $3.5 million more. But the new issue could not be sold. Potential purchasers were scared off by the project's halting progress and the slow growth of the population. Property in the district was assessed at only $15 million. Not only the Drainage District bonds but all Florida securities were becoming suspect. When the legislature met in the spring of 1925, the governor presented a plan for refinancing that included an ad valorem property tax, but the lawmakers rejected it. In order to carry out the construction contracts signed by the preceding administration, Governor Martin had to scratch up money wherever he could. The Drainage District borrowed $400,000 from the Internal Improvement Fund and gave notes to the contractors for $380,000 to keep the work going through 1925 and 1926.[72]

Miami waterfront after the 1926 hurricane. Wrecked ships and houseboats are piled up against the Flagler Street bridge. SPA.

With its finances in this perilous condition, the Martin administration was battered by bitter criticism after the hurricane of 1926. On 28 October 1926 the governor confronted an angry group of Everglades landowners in West Palm Beach. Martin provided a plaintive description of his predicament: "Now we stand in this condition, with this great problem confronting us with no funds to carry it on, in debt to every source from which we would borrow money, without a market to sell bonds in, with our notes given to contractors to keep up the work, and the notes coming due, and with eternal and ceaseless criticism aimed at the Board charging them with neglect of duty, inability, incompetency, lack of foresight, and every other thing that can be thought of."[73] The governor warned the landowners that their fault-finding might ruin the whole program. Unless a "sane and sensible policy of co-operation" were adopted and "reckless and foolish statements and criticism" ceased, the state might have to halt the work altogether.[74]

The governor's critics were not silenced. Shortly after his speech, the president of the Pennsylvania Sugar Company wrote a bitter letter to Martin, blaming the state's mismanagement of the drainage program for ruining the interests of his corporation. "For twenty-four years we have been feasting on disaster. Millions have been spent, and with no result except an impotent indignation meeting. Really, isn't it time that some other ideas are considered that may at least result in betterment?" "Low-grade, sub-surface canals" would never reclaim the Glades, he insisted; dyking and pumping would be necessary.[75] Other landowners were demanding a reorganization of the Everglades Drainage District Board of Commissioners in order to reduce the influence of Tallahassee politicians and transfer power to representatives of the district.[76]

During the early months of 1927 the governor attempted to cut his way out of this financial jungle. Chief Engineer Fred C. Elliott published a report calculated to restore the faith of the bankers. Pointing out that the Drainage District had never failed to meet its obligations to bondholders, he set forth proposals for additional works that would reclaim 2.3 million acres of land. The cost would be $20.5 million, but this would not be excessive. For an expenditure of $15.48 per acre, agricultural land worth $50 to $500 per acre would be created.[77] With the help of S. Davis Warfield, president of the Seaboard Air Line Railroad, Governor Martin was able to negotiate a deal with two New York banking firms, Dillon, Read & Company and Eldridge & Company. If the Florida legislators would pass enabling laws, the bankers promised to purchase future issues of Everglades Drainage District bonds up to a total of $20 million.[78] In a special message to the legislature, Martin said that this arrangement would "settle forever the question of finance, not taxing the State of Florida a penny."[79] The lawmakers promptly authorized $20 million in bonds, revised the schedule of drainage taxes, and empowered the Board of Commissioners to levy an ad valorem tax on all real estate in the district.[80]

The Martin administration also obtained a favorable report from the Everglades Drainage Board of Review, a panel of three independent experts asked to examine the work already done and to make recommendations. The Board of Review emphasized the need for a plan of progressive drainage that would reclaim one section at a time. For the immediate future, it recommended completing the St. Lucie Canal, strengthening the Lake Okeechobee levee, and deepening the existing canals. After that, it called for new arterial canals "running east and west, and spaced at intervals of six to eight miles, as necessary for the most economical provision of proper outlets for the development of the Everglades lands."[81] These recommendations concentrated on the eastern Everglades and postponed indefinitely the reclamation of the southwestern part. The Board of Review findings differed in some details from Elliott's plans and estimated the costs at almost $26 million—$5.5 million more.[82]

On 11 May 1927 the governor announced that the New York bankers had purchased $10 million worth of the newly authorized bonds and agreed to take future issues until the work was completed. "The drainage of this great area means much to the State of Florida," he said, "and its success is now assured." But the purchase contract was

Lake Okeechobee areas damaged by 1926 and 1928 hurricanes. From A.J. Hanna and K.A. Hanna, *Lake Okeechobee: Well Spring of the Everglades.*

not to be binding unless the Florida Supreme Court decided that the recent laws passed by the legislature were "valid and constitutional."[83] Over the next year opponents of the new arrangements tied up the state in a straitjacket of litigation. The Florida Supreme Court upheld the validity of the bond issue, but the federal courts were not so accommodating in an action brought by Spitzer, Rorick & Company, which had been financing Everglades drainage since 1917. This Toledo firm contended that the new bond issue violated their rights under the earlier contracts. Without waiting for the outcome of this case, Governor Martin tried to force the issue by delivering the disputed bonds to the New York group, but he was thwarted by Nathan Mayo, the commissioner of agriculture, who refused to join other officials in signing the securities.[84] This blow was followed by the issuance of a federal court injunction forbidding the sale.[85]

Thus, by the time of the hurricane of 1928, the state's reclamation program had broken down completely. The Everglades Drainage District was heavily in debt and could borrow no more money. All reclamation work had come to a halt. More and more landowners, disgusted and broke, were refusing to pay drainage taxes. By the summer of 1929 these arrears had mounted to $3 million.[86] During the Great Depression the Drainage District sank still deeper into this financial quagmire. Unless new sources of money could be found, the dream of reclaiming the Everglades was shattered.

# 7 Tapping the Federal Treasury

The great hurricane of 1928 compelled Florida politicians to face a painful reality. Convinced that the state would transform swamplands into fertile fields, thousands of farmers had moved into the Lake Okeechobee region and capitalists had invested millions of dollars in sugar fields and cattle ranches. Yet the state's $18 million expenditure on canals and levees had been insufficient to save these people from disaster. To prevent future floods and complete the reclamation work, engineers now estimated that some $20 million more would have to be spent. But the Everglades Drainage District was paralyzed. It could not collect the drainage taxes; it could not borrow money; it could not meet the payments on its bonds.

Confronted by this situation, Florida authorities appealed to Congress for federal aid. In doing so, they were acting in keeping with a tradition as old as Florida politics. The territory's first representatives to Congress had sought federal dollars for harbors, lighthouses, highways, and canals. After statehood was achieved, Florida senators and representatives regularly filed bills seeking construction of federal buildings and military and naval bases, improvement of rivers and harbors, and surveys for projected canals. This was not, of course, a proclivity peculiar to Florida politicians. Legislators from all the states boasted about how much federal money they had been able to win for projects within their own districts. Since they all had similar needs, they gladly supported each other's pet proposals.

But the pork-barrel politics of the nineteenth century had operated within certain constraints imposed by the constitutional theories of the day. It ws indisputably within the power of Congress to build post offices, establish military and naval bases, and dredge rivers and harbors. But could Congress appropriate money for irrigation works, electric power plants, flood control projects, and aid for the unemployed? Before 1900 most legislators would have said no; during the days of Theodore Roosevelt and Woodrow Wilson they would have said maybe; during the days of Franklin Roosevelt they were ready to say yes. This withering away of the old constitutional scruples is not particularly shocking. As early as 1791 Alexander Hamilton had set the precedent by arguing that Congress must have the power to charter a bank because the new government needed one so badly. Thereafter, whenever the necessity became sufficiently urgent, legislators, presidents, and judges could usually be counted upon to find the necessary powers in the Constitution.

The new element in the situation was the interconnectedness of American life, both economic and emotional. Local crises sent shock waves thousands of miles away. Dust storms in Oklahoma, sharecropper poverty in Mississippi, and bank failures in Michigan brought injurious consequences to people in other states. The local crises of the twentieth century became too severe for local resources to handle. Local politicians appealed to Washington because that was where the money was. While the states clung stubbornly to antiquated tax systems, the federal government derived the greater part of its revenues from personal and corporate income taxes, the only sources destined to expand with the rapid industrialization of the country. And when legislators felt it necessary to spend more money than the U.S. Treasury took in, they did so, confident that the government could borrow enough money to cover the deficits.

These patterns of spending are commonly blamed on Franklin Roosevelt and the New Deal, but events were moving in this direction well before 1933. As early as December 1924 Florida Congressman Herbert Drane began to push for federal help in dealing with his state's flood problem. Shocked by an inspection tour of the flooded fields around Lake Okeechobee, he introduced a bill providing for a survey to see whether a deepening of the Caloosahatchee waterway might serve the needs not only of navigation but of flood control. At first Drane had a hard time. Congress appropriated $1,000 for such a study, but the Army Corps of Engineers said it was insufficient. Subsequently Congress authorized an expenditure of $40,000, but the corps allegedly mislaid the project. At all events, it still had not reported when the Moore Haven disaster of 1926 shocked the country. Even after that the corps's report of February 1927 recommended no federal action.[1] Congress was sufficiently impressed by Florida's troubles to pass a special bill authorizing a more comprehensive flood-control study of the region. This time the corps took its assignment more seriously. It conducted public hearings in the lake towns, and on 9 April 1928 Maj. Gen. Edgar Jadwin, chief of the Army Corps of Engineers, transmitted his recommendations to Congress. Jadwin was still highly conservative: "Until the resources of local interests and the State of Florida have been exhausted in providing flood control," he said, "it is believed that no action should be taken in this respect unless it is in direct connection with navigation."[2] Within this restraint he found it possible to recommend that the federal government spend $642,282 for improving the Caloosahatchee and St. Lucie waterways.[3]

After the great storm of September 1928 took 2,000 lives in the Belle Glade region, the clamor for federal help grew louder and prospects for success brighter. Congress had set a precedent by authorizing huge projects in the Mississippi and Sacramento valleys. In November 1928 Governor Martin and his cabinet passed a resolution asking the federal government to build a high levee around the southern shore of Lake Okeechobee and offering to have Florida pay half the costs.[4] But would the state legislature actually be willing to do this? For over twenty years Florida officials had carried on a drainage program in the Everglades without using any of the general revenues. Their first recourse had been to sell swamplands, their second to collect drainage taxes from landowners within the Everglades Drainage District, their third to sell the bonds of the Drainage District. Should taxpayers elsewhere in the state be compelled to contribute?

The House Committee on Flood Control probed this sensitive issue during hearings in January 1929. Committee members expressed their willingness to consider federal aid, but they reminded Florida spokesmen that the recently approved projects for the Mississippi and Sacramento valleys had provided for one-third of the costs to be borne by local interests and the state. Congress was not likely to pass any bill that did not require a substantial local effort. Representative Drane wobbled on the issue; at first he argued that the whole problem was a federal one since the federal government required Lake Okeechobee to be kept at a high level to facilitate navigation. He questioned whether the state "should be required to protect human life coming in there from every section of the Union when the danger is from waters owned and controlled by the United States." When pushed by the committee, however, Drane conceded that the state ought to make "a reasonable contribution."[5] Florida Attorney General Frederick Davis was pressed on the same point, and he first argued that the state had already made a large contribution by selling the swamplands to pay for canals. But a committee member objected that these lands had been given to the state by the federal government in the first place. Expressing strong doubt that the voters would approve the necessary bond issue, Davis explained that the people living near Lake Okeechobee were people coming from other states, "and it is mighty hard to get people in other parts of the State interested in whether they perish or not."[6]

On 31 January 1929 General Jadwin submitted a new plan combining improvement of navigation with flood control. Warned by the latest hurricane, the corps now recommended a 31-foot-high levee around the south shore of the lake and a barrier around the north shore as well. If this construction were combined with a deepening

Caloosahatchee Lock No. 3, near Fort Thompson on the Caloosahatchee Canal. SPA.

of the Caloosahatchee and St. Lucie waterways, the total cost would be about $10.7 million, of which General Jadwin recommended that the state and local interests contribute 62½ percent, not to exceed $6.7 million, leaving a federal share of only $4 million.[7]

To harassed Florida officials, a state contribution of over $6 million was out of the question. Hoping to get a much better deal, the new governor, Doyle E. Carlton, assiduously paid court to Herbert Hoover when the president-elect visited Florida a month before his inauguration. Hoover was taken on a tour of the devastated region and was guest of honor at a dinner in Clewiston. Keeping a tight mouth even to the extent of walking out on the speech-making, the distinguished visitor avoided making any commitment.[8] But the Florida leaders had good reason to believe that he would prove a friend to their project. Florida was one of four southern states that had given him its electoral votes, and the Republican leaders were eager to consolidate these gains. Equally important was Hoover's well-known interest in flood control. As secretary of commerce, he had pushed for the Mississippi and Sacramento projects despite the penny-pinching reluctance of President Coolidge.[9]

Attempting to pave the way for federal action, Governor Carlton proposed new state laws. "Reclamation of the Everglades," he said, "has developed into a national as well as a state problem with the Federal Government giving promise of co-operation that will insure the completion of this project in a proper way." He asked the legisla-

Caloosahatchee Lock No. 3 during flood of 1922. A series of floods during the 1920s revealed the inadequacy of the old canals to prevent flooding. SPA.

ture to authorize some agency "to accept such terms and conditions as Congress may establish and fully co-operate with the Federal Government in carrying out this program."[10] Since it was questionable whether the Everglades Drainage District was authorized to embark on a program of flood control, the legislature created a new "Okeechobee Flood Control District," beginning a little north of Lake Okeechobee and extending over all South Florida except the Keys. The new agency was to be administered by a board of ten commissioners composed of the usual five state officers plus five landowners of the district to be appointed by the governor—a partial recognition of local interest. This board was to have power to build flood control works and to enter into agreements with the U.S. government. It might issue bonds to an amount of $5 million, to be secured by revenue derived from a tax of one mill per dollar on all taxable property within the district, including that owned by the Internal Improvement Fund. The law also imposed acreage taxes on a sliding scale.[11] To harmonize with the new policy, the legislature reorganized the Everglades Drainage District to add five appointed commissioners to the board and to provide that acreage taxes paid to the Okeechobee Flood Control District might be deducted from those paid to the Everglades Drainage District.[12]

Establishing its headquarters at West Palm Beach, the Okeechobee Flood Control District employed George B. Hills, a Jacksonville engineer, to prepare a report on Florida's needs. On 8 February 1930 Hills transmitted to the Army Corps of Engineers a wide-ranging document dealing not only with the Lake Okeechobee levees and the Caloosahatchee—St. Lucie waterways but with flood protection for Miami and the enlargement of the old drainage canals—a $29 million program.[13]

On 15 March 1930 the corps submitted new recommendations on the Florida situation. Three factors may have combined to liberalize the corps's position. One was the Hills report; a second was a change in personnel, with Maj. Gen. Lytle Brown succeeding General Jadwin as chief; a third—probably the most important—was the inauguration of Hoover as president. The corps proposed building a 34-foot high levee around the south shore of Lake Okeechobee, another levee around the north end, and an improved waterway. They estimated the total cost at $9,692,000 and recommended that the state of Florida or other local interests contribute $3,812,000. But they could find no justification for building federal works to protect the Miami area.[14]

The corps had apportioned Florida's share of the costs at more than the state officials wanted to pay, but Congress was more generous. In December 1929 a bill to deal with the Okeechobee problem had been introduced in the house and referred to the Committee on Flood Control. Because continued constitutional scruples about assuming flood control as a federal responsibility clouded the bill's prospects, friends of the measure succeeded in having it transferred to the Committee on Rivers and Harbors for consideration as a bill to aid navigation. After an equally friendly reception in the Senate Committee on Commerce, the project slipped quietly through Congress as part of the general Rivers and Harbors Act, signed into law by the President on 3 July 1930. Florida's share had been reduced to a cash contribution of $2 million and the obligation to provide the necessary land and rights-of-way. The federal government was to construct and maintain the project.[15]

The Okeechobee Flood Control District Board accepted the conditions of the act, and President Hoover saw to it that work proceeded without delay. In November 1930 construction began, and in March 1938 the original project was completed. The Hoover Dike stretched for 85 miles around the north, northwest, south, and southwest shores of the lake. Rising from 34 to 38 feet above sea level, the new barrier was three times as high as the old state-built mud levee had been. It was also massive in width, extending from 125 to 150 feet at the bottom and 10 to 30 feet at the top. At the places where the main drainage canals left the lake, 34-foot-high locks and hurricane gates were installed. The lock gates were operated by electricity, but the hurricane gates were hand-operated for greater protection. The commissioners of the Okeechobee Flood Control District confidently reported, "The levee effectively prevents the overflow of water from the Lake along its location under any conceivable conditions including hurricane tides."[16] The dike was not fully tested until 26 April 1949, when a hurricane with winds of 75 to 122 miles per hour beat upon the barrier for seven hours, three times as long as any previous storm. Except for minor erosion the structure went through the ordeal without mishap.[17] Also important in controlling the lake was the greatly enlarged St. Lucie Canal.

Once begun, federal aid to the Lake Okeechobee flood control project became increasingly liberal. In 1935 Congress reduced the state contribution from $2 million to $500,000. Including the cost of acquiring rights-of-way and land, the state's outlay came to about $1.3 million. The federal government paid the rest of the bill. The total cost of the original project was $19,146,000—about twice the estimate. The Rivers and Harbors Act of 1937 provided for a new lock and spillway for the St. Lucie Canal. Not until the need for military preparedness dictated a new order of priorities did President Franklin Roosevelt bring about a temporary halt by vetoing an appropriation of almost $4 million for strengthening the Hoover Dike along the east shore of the lake. By 30 June 1942 the United States had spent $23,370,000 for construction and maintenance of the South Florida project.[18]

But if federal aid for flood control was new, federal appropriations to promote navigation were as old as the nation. During the first three decades of the twentieth century the amount of money allotted to Florida projects increased significantly. Up to 1929 the federal government had spent more than $8 million to improve the Jacksonville harbor and provide a safe channel to the ocean. Federal money had flowed into other Florida ports: almost $5.3 million to Tampa, $3.9 million to Fernandina, $3.8 million to Miami, $1.1 million to Key West, and $846,000 to Pensacola. In contrast to this, two Florida ports had been developed without federal aid. By 1929 the Port of Palm Beach had raised almost $4.3 million through the sale of

Hoover Dike and drainage canal, 1958. Part of the flood control works on the east side of Lake Okeechobee. SPA.

bonds, and the Broward County Port Authority had sold $6 million worth of bonds for the construction of Fort Lauderdale's Port Everglades.[19]

Early schemes for an inland waterway along the Panhandle coast were finally being realized. By 1931 federal projects had linked the various bays and lagoons to provide a Gulf Intracoastal Waterway extending some 200 miles from Pensacola to Carrabelle. Federal dredging of the Apalachicola River had given southwestern Georgia an outlet to this system.[20]

Along the Atlantic coast, the Florida Coast Line Canal had become an unloved orphan after the death of George L. Bradley in

1906. The waterway had served its purpose when the company received the last of its 1,030,128-acre land grant upon completing construction in 1912. Thereafter it was rarely maintained at its required size, a meagre 50 feet wide and 5 feet deep. Because the canal was useless for most commercial vessels, the company never collected enough tolls to show a profit. In 1923 it was forced into receivership, and the Rhode Island Hospital Trust, trustee for the Bradley estate, sold it to Harry S. Kelsey of West Palm Beach. The new owner probably hoped to rebuild the waterway and make it profitable, but all such dreams were shattered by the collapse of the Florida boom.[21]

Disgusted with this mismanagement, civic leaders hoped to get the federal government to take over the canal. Gov. Park Trammell had recommended this as early as 1913,[22] and a decade later Charles F. Burgman of Daytona Beach began to mobilize public opinion along the east coast. The Florida delegation succeeded in getting Congress to adopt the canal as a federal project in the Rivers and Harbors Act of 21 January 1927. This authorized the enlargement of the waterway to a width of 75 feet and a depth of 8 feet at a cost of $4.2 million, conditional upon local interests acquiring the existing canal and transferring it to the federal government.[23]

By a law approved 25 May 1927 the Florida legislature created the Florida Inland Navigation District as a special tax district to be administered by eleven commissioners, one from each county in the district. The governor would appoint the original board; the voters would elect subsequent commissioners. The board was authorized to purchase the existing waterway for a price not to exceed $800,000.[24] Thereafter matters moved along smoothly. In 1929 the commissioners purchased the canal and transferred it to the United States government. In the Rivers and Harbors Act of 3 July 1930, Congress provided for an enlargement to a width of 100 feet and a depth of 8 feet. Local interests were required to purchase the wider right-of-way and also land for the deposit of dredged material and other construction needs. To meet these obligations, the legislature increased the powers of the Inland Navigation District, authorizing it to spend $1,037,000.[25]

In October 1933 the *New York Times* reported that the Army Corps of Engineers had nine dredges at work on the "Florida Intracoastal Waterway." The work had been in progress for ten months and was expected to be completed the next fall. The news was reported in the paper's sports section, an appropriate place because the enlarged canal was still largely worthless as an artery of commerce but provided yachtsmen and fishermen with a splendid facility.[26] Up to

1935 the United States government and the Florida Inland Navigation District had spent a total of more than $9 million on the project.[27]

Meanwhile, boosters had never allowed the dream of a cross-peninsula canal to die. Duncan U. Fletcher, who represented Florida in the U.S. Senate from 1909 until his death in 1936, was a persistent advocate of the scheme. Running against Governor Broward for the senate seat in 1908, Fletcher had told the voters, "I favor the construction of a Ship Canal across the peninsula of Florida by the National Government."[28] In November 1908 the senator-elect was chosen president of the newly organized Mississippi to Atlantic Inland Waterway Association.[29] This group succeeded in getting an appropriation for a survey of possible routes for a barge canal into the Rivers and Harbors Act of 3 March 1909. In 1913 the Army Corps of Engineers made a preliminary report, but nothing further was done until after World War I.[30]

In 1921 Congressman Frank Clark of Florida revived the issue by introducing a bill calling for a survey exploring the possibilities for a ship canal. The legislature requested the state's congressional delegation to support the Clark bill and also created a Florida State Commission for Securing the Construction of the Atlantic, Gulf and Mississippi Canal.[31] The Floridians failed to get the requested ship canal study, but the corps did review its earlier findings on a barge canal. Reporting on 8 December 1924 the corps concluded that a lock canal would provide the only feasible plan and would require water sources at the summit adequate to work the locks. Four possible routes were suggested: through the Okefenokee Swamp as proposed by General Gilmore in 1880; by way of the Santa Fe and Suwannee rivers; using Orange Lake as a summit supply; using Lake Harris and other lakes at the head of the Oklawaha River.[32]

Like most corps reports, this one had avoided final recommendations and suggested further studies. To move matters along, Congressman Lex Green of Florida succeeded in getting into the River and Harbor Act of 1927 an authorization for a preliminary examination and survey of "a waterway from Cumberland Sound, Georgia, and Florida to the Mississippi River." In a progress report of 19 February 1929 the corps said that it had examined two possible routes, one using the St. Marys River and Okefenokee Swamp, the second the St. Johns and Oklawaha River, Lakes Griffin and Harris, and the Withlacoochee River. The engineers involved were unanimous in their preference for the second route.[33] In 1930 Congress authorized a much more extensive study of possible routes for either a barge

canal or a ship canal. Proceeding slowly, the corps studied twenty-
eight different routes but finally settled on "Route 13-B" as the most
feasible one. This would have its western terminus near Yankeetown, about seventy miles north of Tampa, and follow the Withlacoochee River to Dunnellon; then it would be dug in an easterly
and northeasterly direction south of Ocala and Silver Springs until it
joined the Oklawaha River, which it would follow to the St. Johns
River near Palatka; finally, it would use the St. Johns to the Atlantic
Ocean at Jacksonville. On 30 December 1933 a special board estimated that a lock canal 30 feet deep could be built from Yankeetown
to Palatka for $171,382.[34]

For over one hundred years the cross-peninsula canal had been a
hardy perennial of Florida politics. From time to time the state's
senators and representatives had introduced bills proposing surveys, and congressional log-rolling had resulted in small appropriations for this purpose in 1826, 1830, 1852, 1875, 1878, 1909, 1921,
1927, and 1930. But the corps's earlier reports, emphasizing the difficulties and dubious benefits of the project, had always chilled enthusiasm for the idea. Why did matters change dramatically after
1930? The most important new circumstance was the Great Depression and the need to provide jobs through public works. Seeing the
opportunity, champions of the cross-peninsula canal demonstrated
remarkable success in competing with rival claimants for federal
dollars.

Perhaps the most persistent advocate of the canal was Mayor A. F.
Knotts of Yankeetown, who had moved to Florida soon after World
War I. In the North he had been active in the waterways movement
and had learned how to wangle provisions for Army Corps of Engineers's surveys into federal river and harbor bills. He made his
Florida home near the mouth of the Withlacoochee River and began
a long agitation for a cross-peninsula canal that would follow the
Withlacoochee-Oklawaha route. He wrote thousands of letters, attended meetings of waterway associations in other states, and made
over thirty trips to Washington. In 1927 Knotts organized the Florida
Inland Coastal Waterways Association, of which he became president. This organization claimed credit for directing the attention of
the reluctant Army Corps of Engineers to the advantages of the
Withlacoochee-Oklawaha route.[35] Civic leaders in Jacksonville also
took up the cause with enthusiasm. The city commission engaged
Gilbert A. Youngberg, a retired colonel in the corps, to make an economic study. In a report transmitted to the corps in October 1931
Youngberg estimated that, if a ship canal had been in use in 1929, the

savings to commerce would have been $15.5 million; in 1945 the savings would be $47.4 million.[36]

The cross-Florida project gained increased muscle when boosters from other states joined the movement. On 31 March 1932 representatives from five states—Texas, Louisiana, Mississippi, Alabama, and Florida—met at New Orleans and organized the "National Gulf-Atlantic Ship Canal Association." In choosing Gen. Charles P. Summerall to be president of the new organization, the members achieved a public relations coup. The recently retired general was a well-known, if somewhat controversial, public figure. Born in Florida, Summerall had been decorated for bravery during World War I, had risen to the rank of four-star general (the first southerner to do so since the Civil War), and had been chief of staff from 1926 to 1930. In accepting his new post, the general said: "It is estimated that more tonnage will pass through the canal than through any ship canal in the world. It will handle each year one and a third times the tonnage which passes through the Panama Canal."[37] Henry H. Buckman, a Jacksonville engineer, was the new association's hard-working secretary.

Prompted by the growing movement, politicians and editorial writers began to issue statements supporting the project. Huey Long, Louisiana's flamboyant senator, gave it his backing in April 1932. Arthur Brisbane, influential editorial writer for the Hearst chain, endorsed the idea the same month. Regional mercantile and shipping groups announced their support: the Mississippi Valley Association, the Intracoastal Canal Association of Louisiana and Texas, the Atlantic Deeper Waterways Association, and the Alabama State Docks Convention.[38]

Backers of the cross-Florida canal recognized a golden opportunity in the summer of 1932 when Congress granted Hoover's Reconstruction Finance Corporation (RFC) enlarged powers to lend money for "self-liquidating" projects. On 31 August 1932 the National Gulf-Atlantic Ship Canal Association applied to the RFC for a loan of $160 million—later reduced to $118 million—to dig a ship canal across Florida. A nonprofit corporation would build and operate the canal, collecting sufficient tolls to repay the construction costs.[39]

While the association's loan application was still pending, Roosevelt became president and the canal backers promptly went to work on him. As early as 22 March 1933 Congressman Lex Green wrote that he had been conferring with the president and was "well pleased with the interest which he is manifesting in the project."[40] Eager to get federal dollars, the Florida legislature created the Ship

Canal Authority of the State of Florida, a public corporation empowered to acquire, operate, and maintain a ship canal across the state.[41] Gov. Dave Sholtz appointed General Summerall chairman of the board of directors, and the new authority took over the loan application to the RFC.[42] On 27 May the legislature passed a memorial urging President Roosevelt "to approve of said construction project as an effective measure in relieving unemployment and stimulating industry."[43]

Ex-President Herbert Hoover at dike dedication. Clewiston, 1961. Left to right: Gov. Farris Bryant; Herbert Hoover; ex-Gov. Doyle Carleton. From *Clewiston News*/Beryl Bowden.

The National Industrial Recovery Act of 13 June 1933 gave the President authority to spend an unprecedented $3.3 billion on useful construction projects. Florida's application to the RFC was transferred to the new agency, and the first Public Works Administration (PWA) reports were encouraging. But the final say would have to come from Harold Ickes, Roosevelt's secretary of the interior and PWA administrator, a notoriously tight man with federal dollars. For well over a year the PWA kept the Florida project on a slow burner.[44] Meanwhile, the corps was continuing its methodical investigations.

Boosters for the project had no patience with these bureaucratic delays. On 2 March 1934 senators from all the Gulf states joined in a letter to President Roosevelt, pointing out the wide discrepancy in the preliminary estimates of the PWA engineers and the corps. The senators asked the president to appoint a special board of review.[45] In May, Roosevelt appointed such a panel, and Senator Fletcher transmitted the thanks of the group. "We all believe that the canal is one of the most appropriate and useful public works which the government can undertake," wrote Fletcher. "Its immediate widespread benefits both to labor and industry and to commerce in the long run are not questioned."[46]

On 28 June 1934 the special board of review sent Roosevelt a report highly favorable to the project. Noting that the previous findings by the Army Engineers and the PWA engineers had dealt almost exclusively with a lock canal, the new board stated its preference for a sea-level canal since it would be not only cheaper to build but more economical to maintain and would have a greater ship capacity. The board favored the Withlacoochee-Oklawaha route and recommended a 30-foot-deep canal, to be increased to 35 feet as soon as there was enough traffic. The initial cost was estimated at $142.7 million.[47]

Elated by this report, Senator Fletcher and his allies urged the president to undertake the project "which has been so amply justified, measured by every yardstick of experience and every rule of prudent valuation."[48] But nothing happened. Roosevelt seemed disposed to leave the matter in Ickes's hands, and Ickes gave a very strict interpretation to the words "self-liquidating." Despite its approval of the canal, the special board had cautioned that the anticipated tolls at eight cents a ton would not provide enough revenue to pay back construction costs. On 29 January 1935 Ickes handed down his long-delayed decision, disapproving a loan to the Ship Canal Authority.[49]

The Florida delegation now launched a campaign to get the canal built as a toll-free federal waterway. Representative Green argued for the project in a nationwide radio broadcast on 9 February 1935. But it seemed more promising to center the campaign on the president rather than on Congress. On 8 April 1935 Roosevelt signed into law the Emergency Relief Appropriation Act, giving him extraordinary powers to combat unemployment.[50] The canal boosters immediately concentrated their energies on winning the support of the new Works Progress Administration (WPA), headed by the free-spending Harry Hopkins. As early as 1 June 1935 the *New York Times* reported that the WPA had given tentative approval to spending $25 million for the first year's construction costs of the canal.[51]

On 1 June the Florida legislature did its part by creating the

Florida Ship Canal Navigation District, composed of six counties along the route of the proposed waterway. This special tax district was authorized to sell bonds to a limit of $1.5 million, to purchase the necessary rights-of-way, and to convey them to the federal government free of charge.[52] Notifying Roosevelt of this, Senator Fletcher wrote, "I very earnestly hope that you will be able to approve this splendid undertaking, which is so well fitted to the needs of your work-relief program from every point of view, and which will yield increasing benefits to the whole country as time goes on."[53]

News of FDR's lively interest in the cross-peninsula canal startled the people of Florida. For over a hundred years successive generations of boosters had tried to drum up support for the idea without much success. Suddenly the situation was completely different, and it seemed probable that the great ditch would actually be dug. Chambers of commerce in Jacksonville, Palatka, Ocala, and other communities along the route were ecstatic, but other residents of the state felt strong misgivings. The earliest to sound the alarm were the railroad executives, traditionally jealous of competition from tax-free waterways. As early as 10 February 1933 a spokesman for four great systems doing business in Florida—the Atlantic Coast Line, Florida East Coast, Seaboard Air Line, and Southern—stated the railroad position in a hearing before a board of the Army Corps of Engineers. J. E. Willoughby, chief engineer of the Atlantic Coast Line, predicted that the canal would cost $300 million and require $19.5 million in annual interest and maintenance charges. With its long, narrow, and tortuous channel, the canal would be dangerous to navigate, particularly during Florida's frequent periods of storm and fog.[54] The state's highway and railroad development would be hampered by the need for bridges. Finally—and most ominously—the deep cut would threaten the water resources. In the words of the railroad engineer: "The excavation of the canal through the Ocala limestone may have a very decided effect on the underground flow in the Ocala limestone, and on the wells and water supply remote from the canal, and on Silver Springs Run, as well as on many of the streams that come to the surface in this part of Florida."[55]

Opposition to the cross-peninsula canal also developed in Tampa. Fearing the growth of a rival Gulf port, the Tampa Chamber of Commerce sent a telegram to the chief of the Army Corps of Engineers in July 1933, criticizing the proposed route and urging new surveys along lines that would terminate at Tampa Bay. Two years later, when Roosevelt seemed to be on the point of approving the

Palatka-Yankeetown route, the Hillsborough County Commissioners adopted resolutions condemning the scheme as exorbitantly expensive and threatening "possible disastrous results."[56] On the east coast there were similar fears that the projected canal might injure the ports of West Palm Beach, Fort Lauderdale, and Miami.

Marvin H. Walker of Tampa, editor of *The Florida Grower*, made a series of attacks upon the project. In a speech before the Winter Haven Chamber of Commerce, Walker said that, if a Mephistopheles wanted to ruin the people of Florida, he could "cunningly achieve his diabolical purpose" by poisoning the water they drank and used to raise crops. The devil would only need to cut a big ditch to drain off the fresh water and allow salt water to rise into the wells. "In the big ditch separating the world from this infernal region of Florida's wasted splendors and hopes he would have a River Styx. An appropriate name for it would be the Stygian Canal."[57] Fear that the big ditch might cut off the underground flow of water vital to the citrus and vegetable growers was particularly strong in Seminole County, with Sanford its largest city.

Disturbed by this adverse publicity, Senator Fletcher and General Summerall sought reassurance from Maj. Gen. Edward Markham. The chief of the Army Corps replied that the special board of review had found that "with a sea-level canal any possible damage to agriculture beyond the right-of-way to be secured for the canal would be negligible, and that any damage to water supply would be small and would consist only in lowering the levels of nearby wells."[58]

By July 1935 the battlelines were becoming clear. Newspapers in the northern cities—Jacksonville, Palatka, Ocala, Gainesville— supported the proposal; newspapers in the central and southern part of the state—Tampa, St. Petersburg, Sarasota, West Palm Beach, Miami, Sanford—opposed it.[59] For the Florida politicians, the issue was a troublesome one. Eager to increase federal spending within the state most of the congressional delegation supported the canal, but Rep. J. Hardin Peterson of Lakeland was a bitter opponent.[60] He scored an important point when Secretary Ickes released a statement from the U.S. Geological Survey: "To summarize, there appears to be no reasonable doubt that serious adverse effects will be produced upon the important underground water supplies of the Ocala limestone in a wide zone extending from the canal line by the construction of a sea-level canal along route 13-B. The particular dangers herein discussed apply to a sea-level canal only and not to a lock canal so constructed as to avoid deep cuts into the Ocala limestone and thus to leave undisturbed the present water level in this important water-bearing formation."[61]

But President Roosevelt had already decided to act. On 14 August Senator Fletcher and George Hills, a prominent Jacksonville engineer, called at the White House to urge the president to allocate $26 million for the project. The next day Roosevelt sent back word that money would be forthcoming, although it might be less than requested.[62] On 30 August 1935 he ordered the Treasury Department to transfer $5 million from WPA funds to the Army Engineers to begin construction of the canal. On 3 September General Markham established a new district at Ocala and designated Lt. Col. Brehon B. Somervell as district engineer.[63] This news was greeted with jubilation all along the projected route. "Great President to Build Great Canal" read the caption under Roosevelt's picture in the *Ocala Evening Star*. In Jacksonville, Mayor John T. Alsop called for a full week of celebration.[64]

Colonel Somervell appeared to be the very incarnation of New Deal energy. Arriving in Ocala on 6 September, he announced that he would employ four shifts to work day and night. "We are going to push the canal right along as long as the money holds out," he said. "It's up to the other fellows to provide us with additional funds."[65] First on the construction schedule was "Camp Roosevelt" to house workers and equipment on a site a mile and a half south of Ocala. But almost simultaneously workmen began to hack away the underbrush along the canal right-of-way seven miles south of the city.

On 19 September President Roosevelt pressed a telegraph button at his Hyde Park estate, thereby setting off the dynamite charge that began the actual evacuation. Hundreds of Ocala citizens had thronged to the construction site to witness the great event. Senator Fletcher, the orator for the day, praised the project as the greatest waterway to be built anywhere in the world since the completion of the Panama Canal. Only one miscalculation marred the celebration. Through some error FDR pressed the telegraph button while Fletcher was still in the middle of his speech. The explosion shook up the onlookers so much that most of them failed to doff their hats for the National Anthem.[66] A superstitious observer might have regarded this turn of events as a kind of "thunder-on-the-left"—an unpropitious omen for the cross-peninsula canal.

Near the end of November the *New York Times* reported that the corps was creating in Florida "what is perhaps the most opulent single symbol of the New Deal." It had erected 97 buildings on a 215-acre site and was constructing five other camps along the right-of-way. Employment had reached 4,600 and was expected to climb to 6,500 as soon as the project moved from camp preparation to full-scale excavation.[67] But a $5 million allocation could be only a token commitment on a project estimated to cost $146 million. Senator Fletcher continued to pay court to FDR in search of $21 million to continue construction through its first year. Acting on behalf of thirty-six governors and sixty-one senators, Fletcher gave the president a silver tray to commemorate the commencement of the canal.[68]

Public opinion in Florida continued to be sharply divided. Along the route of the canal the project had overwhelming support. By a vote of 15,394 to 571 (a ratio of 27 to 1) citizens in the six counties approved a bond issue of $1.5 million to acquire the right of way.[69]

Cross-Florida ship canal project, 1936. President Franklin D. Roosevelt allocated Works Progress Administration funds to begin construction. National Archives.

The first $300,000 worth of these bonds was purchased by the Florida National Bank of Jacksonville and by DuPont, Ball, Inc.[70] The head of the latter firm was Edward Ball, brother-in-law of the deceased Alfred I. DuPont. As trustee of the DuPont estate, with vast holdings in Florida industries, banks, and land, Ball was becoming one of the most powerful men in the state. He described the canal as "a splendid public improvement" that would "probably advance the commercial development of Florida by 100 years."[71]

But opposition was still bitter. The Central and South Florida Water Conservation Committee, organized at Sanford, ran large advertisements asking the question "What Will We Do Without Water?" Supporters of the canal charged that the railroads were financing the Sanford campaign, but this was hotly denied. In December 1936 the Sanford organization merged with a similar one at Bradenton to form the Florida Water Conservation League, which claimed support in nineteen counties.[72]

To quiet these opponents Colonel Somervell appointed a special board of five civilian engineers and geologists to study the impact of the project on water resources. In a report made public on 26 December the board concluded that there would be no damage to municipal water supplies or to agriculture. The only effect would be to reduce the ground water level for a distance of not more than ten or fifteen miles from the cut. In this belt shallow farm wells would have to be deepened, but even here crops would not be injured. There was no danger of saltwater intrusion, either from the ocean or from upward movement out of the rock formation deep below the canal.[73] But the anticanal faction pounced upon the experts' admission that the water level would be lowered in the vicinity of the canal and charged that the damage would extend much further.[74]

Doubly warned by hostility in Florida and misgivings in Congress, President Roosevelt announced a change in tactics on 17 December. In the future, he said, he planned to ask Congress to pass on such large requests for funds.[75] In conformity with this policy, the administration included an item for $12 million for the Florida canal in the army appropriation bill introduced into Congress in January 1936.

Sen. Arthur Vandenberg of Michigan immediately launched a strong attack upon the administration. The canal issue provided this leading Republican with an opportunity to denounce the president for starting a dubious and expensive project and then leaving it to Congress to vote the necessary funds. On 4 January the senator introduced a resolution asking for an investigation of the whole matter. In subcommittee hearings Vandenberg struck a damaging blow by introducing letters from leading steamship operators saying that they would not use the waterway if it were built. Such shippers as Standard Oil of New Jersey, the Texas Company, Gulf, and Cities Service contended that the canal would be too crooked and dangerous to navigate.[76] Since the business community was now becoming bitterly anti–New Deal, Vandenberg probably found it easy to recruit allies for his campaign against the project.

The subcommittee hearings were inconclusive, but Congress could not evade the issue raised by the canal item in the army appropriation bill. The project suffered a defeat when the House Committee on Appropriations cut $29 million from funds requested for unauthorized projects started by the president under his emergency powers. These included not only the ship canal but the Passamaquoddy, Maine, tidal power scheme and projected dams and reservoirs in Mississippi, New Mexico, and West Virginia. Despite protests from Florida congressmen the house upheld the committee decision.[77] President Roosevelt countered this setback by allocating $400,000 more in emergency funds to the project, but this only stiffened the opposition in Congress.[78]

In the Senate, Fletcher moved to add $20 million to the House bill, $12 million for the Florida canal and $8 million for three other rejected projects.[79] Bringing all his guns to bear on the Fletcher amendment, Vandenberg reminded the Senate that the canal had never been approved by either the Army Corps of Engineers or Congress. "This is the Senate's last chance," he said, "to decide whether it wants to build the Florida canal, because if Congress upon its responsibility once makes one appropriation in this direction I will freely agree hereafter with the able Senator from Florida that Congress is under moral obligation to continue and conclude the undertaking."[80] Vandenberg argued that Fletcher's proposal was "just the admission fee." The canal would cost much more than estimated, and there was not "one scintilla of economic justification for this burden of from $150,000,000 to $200,000,000, which is proposed to be placed on the Treasury of the United States."[81]

Senator Fletcher responded with a fine display of southern oratory. Referring to a large map that had been hung in the Senate chamber, he called attention to some 900 red marks indicating ships coming from England, Holland, France, Germany, and the United States en route to the Gulf of Mexico. Those ships, Fletcher claimed, would all use the canal. "This is the greatest stream of ocean-borne traffic in the world, and is equivalent to one ship every 47 minutes, day and night, throughout the year.... This is nearly double the traffic on the Suez Canal and almost one-half again as great as that on the Panama Canal.... Mr. President, is it possible that the Senators will oppose a mighty stride of progress, the greatest undertaking in this generation on the part of this government? Is it possible that Senators will block the way of the greatest accomplishment achieved by the government in this century?"[82]

The Senate replied by turning down Fletcher's amendment 39 to 34. All the Republicans except the progressives George Norris and Hiram Johnson voted no, as did such anti–New Deal Democrats as Bennett Clark of Missouri, Royal Copeland of New York, and David Walsh of Massachusetts.[83] They rejected the treaty not because it might jeopardize the state's water supply and natural beauty but be-cause it stood for so much that congressional conservatives hated—big spending, headstrong action by the president, and disregard for conventional legislative procedures.

The supporters of the canal were by no means ready to surrender. WPA workers continued to clear the right-of-way, and Jacksonville and Ocala boosters redoubled their efforts to line up support. With a reelection campaign requiring his attention, Roosevelt was cautious in dealing with the issue. Testifying before a congressional commit-tee on 10 April 1937 Harry Hopkins promised that none of a re-quested $1.5 million in relief funds would be used for the Florida canal or the Quoddy project, as the tidal power scheme was popu-larly called. The president made a similar pledge a few days later.[84]

Prospects for the canal became still bleaker when the Senate Ap-propriations Committee amended a deficiency bill to provide that no work-relief money could be allocated for any project that could not be completed with the funds on hand. But Sen. Joseph Robinson of Arkansas, the majority leader, tried to soften this stand by proposing an amendment that would authorize the president to appoint two boards of impartial experts, one to study the Florida canal, the other Quoddy. If the board reports were favorable, the president might allocate relief funds up to $10 million for the canal and $9 million for Quoddy.[85] There was another sharp Senate debate with Vandenberg repeating his denunciations, while Robinson stressed the need to provide employment. If the two great projects were closed down, some 11,000 relief workers would lose their jobs.[86] Not wishing to link Quoddy's fate with that of the canal, the Maine Republican senators asked to have separate votes taken on the two projects. The strategy misfired because the Senate approved the waterway study by a vote of 35 to 30 and rejected that for the tidal power study 39 to 28.[87] But the House of Representatives refused to accept the Senate action, the conference committee upheld the House version of the deficiency bill, and the Senate, rushing toward adjournment, went along with this. To culminate this chapter of disasters, Duncan U. Fletcher, who had championed the idea of a cross-Florida canal for three decades, died suddenly on the morning of the House vote.[88]

Having exhausted the $5.4 million allocated by the president, the Army Corps of Engineers had to suspend work on the canal. The project had provided work for crews numbering at times 6,000 men. Left as melancholy souvenirs of the venture were the buildings erected to house the workers, some 4,000 acres of land cleared along the right-of-way, almost 13 million cubic yards of excavation, and a half-finished cross-over bridge.[89] The empty buildings were turned over for temporary use to a WPA school.[90]

Although construction was never started again during the Roosevelt years, canal boosters continued their agitation. Indeed they won several tactical victories in their long campaign. In the first place, they gained support from the Army Corps of Engineers. One of Vandenberg's most persuasive arguments had been that Roosevelt had started the project before the corps had made its final recommendations. All this was changed during the next year when the slow machinery of the military bureaucracy ground out three reports. Two of these favored the canal; one did not. In November 1936 the Revisory Board recommended continuance of the project with a deeper and wider channel—33 feet deep, 250 feet wide—to make it safer for navigation. Because of these changes, it estimated the cost at $163 million ($17 million more than the President's Board of Review had calculated).[91] But the Board of Engineers for Rivers and Harbors under the chairmanship of Brig. Gen. George Pillsbury reported that a much bigger canal would be necessary—35 to 37 feet deep and 400 feet wide—and that therefore the cost would be much greater, nearly $264 million. Because of the "undeterminable possibility" that a sea-level canal might cause "extensive damage to ground-water supplies," the Pillsbury report recommended giving the secretary of war authority to substitute a lock canal if this seemed advisable during the progress of the work.[92] And finally it made a still more damaging finding: "The Board of Engineers for Rivers and Harbors reports that the reasonably assured present and prospective benefits from a canal across Florida do not establish the economic justification for the large expenditures necessary for its construction."[93]

But the negative conclusions of the Pillsbury report were largely overruled in the most important report of all, that of the Chief of Engineers on 1 April 1937. Dismissing worries about the water supply problem, General Markham asserted that "a sea-level canal will not to any consequential, or vitiative, degree influence the ground water levels of the State, or result in serious intrusion of salt water." He agreed with the Pillsbury board in recommending a width of 400 feet, but thought that a 33-foot depth would be adequate. He estimated the cost to the federal government at $197,921,000. Fixed charges plus maintenance would cost the United States about $8,641,000 a year and local interests about $264,000. Annual benefits to shipping would be $8,741,000. "These figures indicate definitely," the general said, "that the canal would not be, in any sense, a bad investment at the present time." Most important of all, from the New Deal point of view, was the chief's assertion that "for a period of years it may be advisable to finance public works with the dual purpose of constructing useful facilities and of employing those who would otherwise require relief."[94]

Encouraged by Roosevelt's landslide reelection and Markham's recommendations, canal backers tried to get funds to resume construction. By gaining the approval of the Rivers and Harbors Committee of the House, they cleared a major hurdle in 1937, but the bill died without further action.[95] On 16 January 1939 President Roosevelt tried to revive the proposal with a letter to the chairman of the Senate Commerce Committee asking approval for both the

Building a bridge across the projected canal, 1936. Despite early progress on construction Congress refused to appropriate funds for continuing the project. National Archives.

Florida canal and the Quoddy power projects. FDR suggested spreading out construction of the canal over ten or fifteen years and collecting tolls to repay the government. He emphasized the military and naval advantages of a shortcut through the Florida peninsula.[96] The Senate debated the issue in May with Sen. Claude Pepper of Florida making a strong appeal for the canal and Senator Vandenberg leading the opposition. This time the canal lost more decisively than in 1936; only 36 New Deal loyalists supported it and 45 conservatives (23 Democrats, 21 Republicans and 1 Progressive) opposed it.[97]

As the United States came closer to full involvement in World War

II, arguments for a shipping shortcut across Florida became more plausible. The Florida lobbyists saw a great opportunity in Roosevelt's deep desire for the St. Lawrence Seaway. They pressured the two Florida senators, Claude Pepper and Charles Andrews, to withhold their support for the St. Lawrence project unless the administration would link it with the cross-Florida canal. In March 1941 Henry Buchman explained this strategy to editor Bert Dosh: "The only weapon with which we now enforce our rights is a pistol pointed at the heart of the northern project, and there must be no doubt as to its being loaded. There is manifest no effective desire to help us, but fate has given us the millionth chance of being able to use coercion to secure the performance of the promises made to us by higher authority. We shall receive only the cooperation we can enforce."[98] Apparently responding to this pressure, the House Rivers and Harbors Committee voted in August 1941 to include both the ship canal and the St. Lawrence Seaway in an omnibus bill.[99]

Continued opposition to a deep canal stalled this omnibus bill, but Pearl Harbor and subsequent naval disasters created a new situation. On 20 January 1942 the president met with congressional leaders to plan a strategy that would win both the St. Lawrence and Florida projects. Roosevelt wanted authority to start digging a ten-foot barge canal, postponing for future decision the question of the ship canal.[100] Walter Coachman, Jr., one of the canal's Jacksonville promoters, wrote to his allies in other cities to mobilize support for the president's initiative. The recent sinking of four tankers off the Atlantic coast, he said, increased the chances of action.[101] On 2 February Coachman wrote, "The submarines and Adolph are helping us, but the opposition is also intensely active."[102] But he was reluctant to have a barge canal permanently substituted for the ship canal. The better strategy, he said, was to request Congress to authorize the ship canal and then to have it dug to barge depth as a first stage.[103]

During the spring Hitler and the submarines continued to aid the canal faction. Despite wartime censorship, reports circulated that the enemy had sunk fifty tankers. Even more important were the fuel needs of a global conflict. Suddenly thrust into war with Japan, Germany, and Italy, American ships, troops, and supplies had to be deployed across two oceans. The ocean tankers that had been carrying oil from the Gulf ports to the Atlantic ports were now required for more important missions. To relieve the growing oil shortage, Harold Ickes, acting as petroleum coordinator, was urging rapid construction of pipelines from Texas to the east coast. Arguing that barges would also help, the House leadership pushed through a bill on 17 June authorizing the president to build a barge canal and two pipelines across Florida.[104] The chief of the Army Corps of Engineers cooperated in a report asserting that a barge canal would not alter existing groundwater conditions. He estimated that a barge canal would take three years to build and cost about $44 million.[105]

In the Senate the measure ran into strong opposition, not only from Vandenberg but from the conservative Democrat Josiah Bailey, chairman of the Commerce Committee. Since the barge canal could not be completed in less than three years, Bailey argued that its construction would hamper rather than help the war effort. The Florida senators, Pepper and Andrews, responded that provisions had to be made for a long conflict and that, in any case, the canal would not be dug unless the president deemed it to be in the interest of national defense. The Florida faction gained the support of a group of midwestern senators eager to line up support for a synthetic rubber program that would benefit grain growers.[106]

When the showdown came on 17 July 1942 the Senate approved the Florida barge canal by a single vote, and that vote was cast by Vice-President Henry Wallace. When the senators divided 30 to 30 on a crucial amendment proposed by Bailey, Wallace with a broad grin broke the tie.[107] The authorization became law with President Roosevelt's signature on 23 July. But the measure carried no appropriation, and the defense planners preferred to deal with the oil problem through other means. Fuel shortages the next winter stirred the canal faction to a new effort. On 16 January 1943 General Summerall, chairman of the Florida Ship Canal Authority, wrote to the governors of the eastern states, promising to get the barge canal dug in ten months if Congress and the president would act promptly.[108] But this rash proposal found no support, and the canal project went on the back burner, not only for the duration of the war, but for fifteen years thereafter. After the death of Franklin Roosevelt, the canal did not win effective support in the White House until John F. Kennedy took up residence there in 1961.

Yet even without the cross-state canal, Hoover's support of the flood-control works around Lake Okeechobee had established an important precedent. When torrential rains again inundated city streets, suburban tracts, farms, and ranches in South Florida, Congress would be ready to appropriate large sums for the levees and canals needed to manage the unruly waters.

# 8 Struggle for Conservation

No progressive cause of the early twentieth century was more sa-
cred than the conservation of natural resources. But conservation was a loosely defined goal, and conservationists could advocate
significantly different courses of action. Some were preservationists,
lovers of unspoiled nature, eager to halt the encroachment of
technology and safeguard large tracts of wilderness. Others were
managers, people who admired efficiency and hated waste. The
managers wanted to use timber, minerals, oil, and water but to handle these resources prudently, replacing, replanting, recycling
whenever possible in order to prevent wasteful depletion.

Both schools of conservationists deplored the abuses that had
flourished in nineteenth-century Florida. Lumbermen had grabbed
millions of acres of public land through bargain purchases and construction grants for railroads and canals. They had chopped down the
timber but had made no attempt to replant. In similar fashion commercial hunters had ruthlessly destroyed the wildlife, slaughtering
alligators, deer, bears, herons, and egrets. Canneries and pack-
inghouses had depleted the supplies of clams, shrimp, and fish.
When the state embarked on its drainage program in 1905, most
progressives applauded this effort to reclaim the swamps and foster
agriculture. At first only a few farsighted naturalists like John K.
Small warned that reckless drainage might disrupt South Florida's
unique plant and animal life and destroy the soil itself through muck
fires, erosion, and subsidence. As these dire predictions began to
come true, a wider public came to realize that water was not a nuisance to be gotten rid of but a resource to be husbanded. The organization of water conservation leagues to combat the ship-canal
scheme during the 1930s gave evidence of this new awareness.

The preservationists achieved their most significant Florida victory on 9 December 1947, when President Harry Truman formally

opened Everglades National Park. This event climaxed almost half a century of effort by nature lovers. Even before 1900 naturalists had begun making excursions into the Everglades to observe the rare and beautiful birds. But other visitors had preceded them. Commercial hunters were killing egrets and other birds to sell their feathers to the millinery trade. To stop this slaughter, the National Association of Audubon Societies induced the Florida legislature to pass a protective law in 1901. Because there were not enough regular game wardens, the Audubon Societies employed four of their own to watch over the rookeries. In 1905 plume hunters murdered Guy Bradley, one of the Audubon wardens, near Florida Bay; in 1908 they killed a second, C.C. McLeod, near Charlotte Harbor. The blood of these martyrs nourished the conservationist cause. In New York State, center of the millinery trade, the legislature prohibited the commercial use of wild bird feathers. When the plume hunters sought to circumvent this prohibition by selling to foreign middlemen, the U.S. Congress banned the importation of feathers. Meanwhile, rising sympathy for the birds was making the wearing of hat feathers unfashionable.[1]

Admirers of exotic trees and plants had also learned to cherish the Everglades. Visiting naturalists particularly admired Paradise Key, a hammock located some 15 miles southwest of Homestead. This beautiful island had a fine growth of royal palm trees and other tropical vegetation. In the bordering mangrove swamps alligators and wading birds flourished. At first reached only by boat or rough footpath, Paradise Key attracted more visitors after a road was built by the Model Land Company, a subsidiary of Flagler's Florida East Coast Railroad. But the new road threatened to bring in citrus growers, farmers, and developers, who would destroy the natural beauty of the spot. James Ingraham, head of the Model Land Company, discussed the problem with Mrs. Kirk Munroe of Miami, chairman of the Florida Federation of Women's Clubs. In 1910 Mrs. Munroe suggested that the Model Land Company give Paradise Key to the federation to be maintained as a public park. Ingraham, a nature lover himself, was willing, but since half the hammock still belonged to the Internal Improvement Fund the politicians had to be won over. In this effort the preservationists received strong support from former Governor Jennings and his wife. The IIF trustees agreed to donate 960 acres to the project, and the Model Land Company matched this gift. On 22 November 1916 Royal Palm State Park was dedicated. To the original 1,920 acres the state added a further grant of 2,080 acres in 1921.[2]

The federation women hoped to make the park self-supporting by renting rooms in their lodge, collecting donations from visitors, and leasing tomato plots in outlying fields, but they suffered a series of disappointments. Park income was less than expected, and hurricanes and fires caused serious damage. In 1929 the federation, acting on the recommendation of Mrs. Jennings's park committee, offered to donate its faltering project to a national park if one could be established.

Hattie Bower Hammock, Dade County. Looking into lime sink, 1916. Ferns and shrubs. A John Small photograph. SPA.

The idea of such an addition to the national park system was not new. As early as 1905 naturalists had begun to suggest it, but there was no concerted effort until the 1920s. In 1922 a Miami group organized the Florida Society of Natural History, which set as one of its objectives the establishment of a national park in the Everglades. Ernest R. Coe, a landscape architect who came to Miami in 1925, became a zealous convert to the idea. In 1928 he organized the Tropical Everglades National Park Association with Dr. David M. Fairchild, an expert on tropical plants, as president. In 1929 the Florida legislature gave nominal support by authorizing a Tropical National Park Commission. Appointed executive secretary, Coe redoubled his efforts to get action. Congress cooperated by ordering a study of the proposal, and Hoover's secretary of the interior, Ray Lyman Wilbur, gave the idea his support in 1931. Three times the U. S. Senate passed bills approving the park, but the house killed the "Alligator and Snake Swamp Bill," as some Republicans called it.

When conservation-minded Franklin D. Roosevelt moved into the White House, prospects for the measure improved. The Civilian Conservation Corps worked on restoring Royal Palm State Park, and on 30 May 1934 Roosevelt signed a bill authorizing Everglades National Park, whose borders would encompass more than 2 million acres. Not until thirteen years later, however, did this projected park actually materialize. Because Congress provided no federal funds, it was up to the State of Florida to acquire the designated lands, some of which belonged to the state and some to private parties. Coe tried to prod the legislature, but by this time a formidable alliance of game hunters, orchid merchants, real estate developers, and oil prospectors were lobbying against the plan. The Great Depression prolonged the delay. A new state administration failed to reappoint the gadfly Coe to his official position, and the park project went into eclipse during most of World War II.

In 1944 the plan was revived through the joint efforts of the outgoing governor, Spessard Holland, and the governor-elect, Millard Caldwell. With the consent of the National Park Service, they reduced the size of the park to about two-thirds of the area authorized in 1934. The exclusion of privately owned lands north of the Tamiami Trail and on the Keys was a bitter disappointment to Coe and other conservationists, but it reduced the opposition of private interests and made the cost more manageable. Even so, a hard selling job had to be done to get the necessary appropriations. August Burghard of Fort Lauderdale became an effective chairman of the reactivated state commission, and John Pennekamp, editor of the *Miami*

*Herald,* carried on a spirited publicity campaign. Reports that oil had been discovered within the proposed boundaries threatened to wreck the proposal, but in 1947 the battle was finally won. The legislature appropriated $2 million for acquisition of privately owned property; the Internal Improvement Fund turned over the state lands; and a few large landowners like the Collier family donated tracts. On 9 December 1947 President Truman formally opened Everglades National Park in a ceremony at Everglades City.[3]

It was a great victory for the conservationists, but they still had stiff battles ahead of them. An adequate flow of water was vital to the plant and animal life of the park. Because of the peculiar cycle of the Florida seasons—copious rain during the summer and fall and very little during the winter and spring—it was imperative that the southward flow of the Everglades water should continue. Whether the park would receive enough of this water depended on how it was handled in the region to the north of the park. Here the other conservationist ideal prevailed—not preservation of ever wild nature but management of water and soil for the use of man. Would the managers regard the park only as a dumping ground for unwanted surplus water, or would they see to it that enough water continued to flow down into the park in dry years as well as wet?

Throughout southern and central Florida the ideal of prudent water management was on the march. The state had run out of money for building big drainage canals, and privately managed sub-drainage districts had to provide for the reclamation of additional acreage, thus insuring a more orderly expansion of crop production. This did not mean, however, that government was not playing an essential role. The Everglades Experiment Station, established by the state at Belle Glade in 1921, continued to study the peculiarities of muckland soil and other regional problems. Federal agencies were active: the Department of Agriculture gathered information about rainfall, soil subsidence, and water use; the Geological Survey investigated surface and groundwater resources; the Biological Survey explored the impact of new conditions on the fish, animals, and birds of the area. In the late 1930s an attempt was made to bring all this federal and state data into some kind of master document. Conservative suspicion of government planning and the reordered priorities of World War II combined to abort this enterprise, but the preliminary studies that had been completed were important to the evolution of water policy.[4]

Also important was the work of the Soil Science Society of Florida, established in 1939 with R. V. Allison of the Everglades Experiment

Station as its secretary-treasurer. Experts with long experience in drainage and soil conservation problems became members, and the society published a series of valuable studies of the situation. By 1940 these studies had produced a substantial consensus about what needed to be done for the prudent management of South Florida's natural resources. The experts agreed that the existing canal system worked badly, underdraining some areas and overdraining others, thereby destroying soil, vegetation, and wildlife. To prevent this overdrainage and to provide the reserves of water necessary for irrigation, industry, and urban needs, certain parts of the Everglades

Hattie Bower Hammock, Dade County, 1916. Ferns shown are Maidenhair, Wood, Boston, Triangular. A John Small photograph. SPA.

should be allowed to revert to wetlands. The proper management of
the region's water resources was so important that there was great
need for some central agency to be established to collect data, make
plans, and administer policy.[5]

The Everglades Drainage District was in no condition to undertake such a program of reform. In 1931 the legislature had bowed to
the demand for home rule by dropping the state officers from the
board of commissioners and giving sole authority to five residents of
the district appointed by the governor. The new board inherited an
enterprise that had been in serious trouble in 1928 and had sunk still
deeper during the depression. The commissioners found themselves defendants in a million-dollar suit brought by the bondholders to collect defaulted interest. The federal court prohibited
the district from spending its tax revenues for any purpose other
than paying off its indebtedness. So tight was the noose that the district had to release all its employees and operate with volunteer
help. New construction was out of the question, and the old canals
silted in. But the creditors' intransigence was self-defeating. The
more the drainage system deteriorated, the less able and the less

Dr. Charles Torrey Simpson, naturalist, John Soar, nurseryman-naturalist, and Paul
Matthaus, an aide, carrying plants of saw cabbage palm. A John Small photograph. SPA.

willing were the landowners to pay their acreage taxes. Almost all of them, including the trustees of the Internal Improvement Fund, fell into arrears. The legislature tried to remedy the situation by reducing rates and forgiving past taxes, but the courts invalidated these laws as impairing the obligation of the contract with the bondholders. In 1937 the Reconstruction Finance Corporation promised to help with a refunding loan, but the bondholders were unwilling to accept a 30-cents-on-the-dollar settlement of their claims. In 1939 the offer was raised to 38 cents, but the creditors still held out.[6]

Meanwhile the debt continued to mount. At the end of 1940 the district owed about $16 million—$13 million to the bondholders, the rest to the contractors for unpaid bills. By this time the discouraged creditors were ready to settle for the best terms they could get. Unwilling to come within the jurisdiction of Florida courts, the bondholder representatives met with Gov. Spessard Holland in Georgia, where they agreed to a plan of action that was carried into effect the next year.

On 3 June 1941, Governor Holland signed a bill by which the legislature reorganized the finances of the Everglades Drainage District. The new law defined seven zones according to the amount of drainage provided: landowners in the most benefited zone were to pay $1.50 an acre; those in the least benefited only three cents an acre. Those who owed taxes for 1940 could pay them at the new lower rates; those who owed for earlier years could clear their debt by paying for two years at the new rate. The defaulters were given two years to pay up; at the end of this period the Everglades Drainage District would acquire title to all land on which taxes for two years were owed. The district was authorized to refund its debt by a new issue of bonds.[7] On 10 June the Reconstruction Finance Corporation agreed to purchase $5,660,000 of these new bonds, and the creditors accepted a division of the proceeds. Most of these went to the old bondholders, who received about 57 percent of the face value of their securities.[8]

Having scaled down its debt to a manageable size, the Everglades Drainage District began to lay plans for the future. Meeting with the trustees of the Internal Improvement Fund on 3 August 1943, the district commissioners pointed out that recent studies by the U.S. Soil Conservation Service had identified certain regions in the Everglades as having soil too shallow for cultivation. The commissioners suggested that publicly owned lands in Palm Beach and Broward counties unsuitable for agriculture should be withheld from

Royal Palm State Park Board, 1918. In 1916 the Model Land Company and the State of Florida donated Paradise Key to the Florida Federation of Women's Clubs for preservation as a public park. Mrs. Kirk Munroe (6) and Mrs. William Jennings (10) led the movement to establish the park. Board members are: Mrs. Evans (1), T.U. Moore (2), Mrs. Edwards (3), Mrs. Moffat (4), Mrs. Stranahan (5), Mrs. Kirk Munroe (6), Mrs. Taylor (7), Mrs. Jennison (8), Mrs. Lewis, president (9), Mrs. Jennings (10), kitchen maid (11), Mrs. Waite (12), Miss Kate V. Johnson (13), Mrs. Loveland (14), Dr. Safford (15), Mrs. Byrd (16), Miss Meggs (17), Mrs. Goodrich (18), Mrs. Jarrott (19), Mrs. Judge Young (20). Man at far left is Charles A. Mosier, first warden of the park. Hetty Mosier, his wife, is at the center of the door in the back row. Charles I. Mosier, their child, is in front of Dr. Safford.

sale and designated "a water holding and soil conservation area." Giving the idea tentative approval, the IIF trustees placed a temporary ban on sales and requested the district to prepare more specific plans.[9] For ten years the district had been too poor to employ an engineer; on 13 August it hired Turner Wallis of West Palm Beach, who brought with him his assistant, Lamar Johnson. Both men had worked on the drainage projects of the 1920s. Wallis's first assignment was to cooperate with an advisory committee from the Soil Science Society of Florida in developing a plan for land use and conservation.[10]

With Johnson doing much of the work, the advisory committee submitted a report in May 1944. It recommended that the old canals be dug out again to improve drainage for existing agricultural land but that drainage of wild lands should stop. By retaining the rainfall on tracts unsuitable for farming, these could be conserved for wildlife and recreation and for retarding soil subsidence. The advisory committee estimated that a relatively modest $3 million would put this program into operation, but the Everglades Drainage District needed all its tax revenue for debt services and administration.[11]

Too poor to do much, the district placed its greatest emphasis on conservation. To the extent that the land already belonged to public agencies, it would cost nothing to reserve it for storing water. Succeeding Wallis as chief engineer in April 1946, Johnson prepared an elaborate map designating three water conservation areas—one in Palm Beach County, a second mostly in Broward County, and a third mostly in Dade County. In October 1946 Johnson explained his varicolored map and accompanying plan to the trustees of the Internal Improvement Fund. Happy to save $14,000 a year in acreage taxes paid by the IIF itself, the trustees approved the designation of the Palm Beach and Broward conservation areas, reserving for the state any oil or minerals that might be discovered and making the transfer contingent on action by the legislature.[12] In February 1947 the trustees took similar action in regard to the Dade County conservation area.[13]

Everything now hinged on favorable action by the state legislature. The Everglades Drainage District requested a number of laws—for authority to donate land to the conservation areas, to lease part of these areas to the U.S. Fish and Wildlife Service, to donate certain lands to the proposed Everglades National Park, and to construct pumping stations and other works to make the old drainage canals more effective. But the district ran into formidable opposition from a combination of landowners, cattle raisers, and dairy operators who wanted to force the state to sell its land and apply the proceeds to the debt, thereby relieving them of the burden of paying drainage taxes. Leaders of this faction were Sam Collier, son of the famous Baron Collier, who had acquired vast holdings in the western Everglades, Joseph Lykes, a great rancher, and Ernest R. Graham, a former state senator who operated a large Miami dairy. The Collier-Lykes-Graham faction called upon the legislature to abolish the Everglades Drainage District.[14]

Forced into a free-for-all with its enemies, the Everglades Drainage District emerged from the legislative session bloodied but still alive. The bill to abolish the district failed, but so did the bill to authorize new works. Bills permitting donation of land to the three conservation areas were passed, but in each of the three counties — Palm Beach, Broward, and Dade—the action was made contingent upon approval by the voters.[15] Since Floridians usually voted against such referenda, prospects for the new conservation policy did not seem very promising. Without waiting for the results of these votes, the Collier-Lykes-Graham faction began litigation to try to get the courts to invalidate the new legislation.[16]

But in the fall of 1947 two rampages of Florida weather changed the whole situation. All spring and summer more than the usual amount of rain had fallen so the Everglades were unusually wet when a hurricane struck on 17 September. The winds did relatively little damage, but the heavy rains flooded the farms of the upper Everglades. While the region was still repairing the havoc caused by this storm, a second hurricane hit on 11 October. Once again farmers, ranchers, and dairy operators suffered heavy losses, but this time residents of the Gold Coast cities and their suburbs were also mauled. In two hours six inches of rain fell in Hialeah; overnight from 13 to 15 inches poured down on Fort Lauderdale. High tides retarded the runoff and two feet of water stood in the streets of the business sections. Septic tanks overflowed, polluting household wells. Towns on the outskirts of Miami were particularly hard hit. Between 10,000 and 12,000 people had to be evacuated from their homes in Miami Springs and Opa-Locka. The Army Corps of Engineers estimated that the 1947 floods caused $59 million worth of damage.[17]

The hurricanes produced an outburst of wrath against the Everglades Drainage District and its chief engineer, Lamar Johnson. The drainage canals had carried excess water from the Everglades down into the coastal regions, and Johnson was accused of protecting upstream farming interests at the expense of downstream homeowners. Defending himself vigorously, Johnson argued that he had tried to serve all sections but that the two storms and the earlier rains had dumped more water on the region than the existing works could handle. As tempers cooled, public leaders began to rally around proposals for preventing similar disasters. The most promising way to do this would be to build a great levee a few miles west of the Gold Coast. Such a huge barricade, longer than the Hoover Dike, was far beyond the feeble resources of the Everglades

Royal Palm State Park, 1916. Temporary quarters of Warden C.A. Mosier. Everglades National Park later evolved from this modest beginning. A John Small photograph. SPA.

Drainage District or any other state agency. Once again South Florida appealed to Washington for help. Despite the unpopularity of the drainage district the voters decided that approval of the three conservation areas was essential to gaining federal aid. Some 97 percent of the Palm Beach County voters approved the plan, as did 86 percent in Broward County and 96 percent in Dade County.[18]

Prospects for federal action were good. Even before the hurricane the Army Corps of Engineers had been working on flood control for Florida, and they now speeded up these efforts. Spessard Holland, who became U.S. Senator in 1946, was a stubborn conservative on social issues but a master operator in getting federal money spent in his home state. The convenient death of the veteran Mississippi senator Theodore Bilbo opened the way for Holland to get himself appointed to the Public Works Committee in November 1947. "I shall do everything in my power," Holland wrote to a constituent, "to bring about early Congressional consideration of a permanent flood control project that would be designed to protect the Everglades and other sections which suffered because of recent water damage in Florida."[19]

Returning home for the Christmas recess, Holland discussed the flood control problem with influential leaders at a ranch house near Kissimmee. Irlo Brownson, chairman of a group seeking protection for the Kissimmee Valley, arranged the meeting, attended by both Florida senators, Holland and Pepper, and five wealthy landowners, some from the Kissimmee area, others from places as far away as Fort Pierce and Clewiston.[20]

Holland kept in close touch with the Army engineers as they prepared their flood control recommendations. He passed on suggestions from his landowner friends and saw to it that Governor Caldwell had a chance to review the report before it was released.[21] The Florida leaders had every reason to be pleased with the corps's findings, made public in February 1948. As expected, the report recommended the building of a levee roughly paralleling the coastal ridge to protect both the Gold Coast cities and an intervening belt of land suitable for farming and suburban development. This so-called perimeter levee would be combined with other levees radiating from Lake Okeechobee to retain water in the three new conservation areas. Other levees and pumping stations would provide protection for a 700,000-acre Everglades Agricultural Area to the south of Lake Okeechobee. In all, the plans called for 780 miles of new or improved levees and 492 miles of canals, as well as pumping stations, spillways, and culverts. The Army Corps would build these primary structures with funds supplied both by the U.S. government and by state and local agencies in Florida. Construction would be in two phases: the first, costing an estimated $70 million, would take care of the region south and east of Lake Okeechobee; the second would provide benefits for the vast region lying north and west of the lake, including the Upper St. Johns River and Kissimmee River valleys, the area south of Orlando, and the Caloosahatchee Waterway. In all, the works would cost $208 million and would take at least ten years to build. In addition to this network of primary structures, the corps recommended that subdistricts, using both public and private funds, build secondary levees and canals to serve the needs of their particular localities. Because of earlier state expenditures on drainage and flood control, the corps proposed that the federal government pay 85 percent of the construction costs on the primary structures, leaving only 15 percent to be contributed by state and local districts.[22]

The Florida delegation to Congress had two major goals. To provide speedy help, they prevailed upon the Army Corps to request an appropriation of $1.6 million to deepen the St. Lucie Waterway. For the longer run, Senators Holland and Pepper introduced a bill to authorize the flood control plan recommended in the engineers' report. Not all Floridians liked these proposals. Sam Collier opposed the flood control scheme as impractical.[23] And leaders in Stuart were unhappy with plans to enlarge the St. Lucie Waterway. The Stuart City Commission opposed them, and Edwin Menninger, publisher of the *Stuart News*, wrote Senator Holland a bitter letter complaining that the community had recently lost $500,000 worth of business because of mud brought down from Lake Okeechobee. "Our St. Lucie River, around which the entire tourist and commercial picture revolves, has been turned into mud soup."[24]

Senator Holland tried to appease his Stuart critics by explaining that the enlargement of the St. Lucie was being pushed only because it was the most feasible way to get quick help on the flood problem. For a long-range solution he was counting on congressional approval of his bill, "under which flood waters will be stored and ultimately discharged through the Park rather than lost to the Atlantic."[25] But Menninger was still highly critical of the project. In another letter to Holland he said: "Some hard-shelled conservationist needs to arise in Congress and awaken his associates to the fact that we are not interested in getting rid of the water. The engineers think only in terms of ditches. The greatest service you could render Florida would be to organize a comprehensive program to preserve, impound, and treasure that water, as it is our life blood. The longer I live here, the more I am impressed with the necessity of stopping this infernal ditch-digging." As a specific alternative, Menninger suggested planting 100,000 water-resistant, swamp-type trees in the Kissimmee watershed.[26]

But if people in Stuart did not want the new projects, those in West Palm Beach, Fort Lauderdale, and Miami definitely did want them. To enlist congressional sympathy the supporters put together a book of photographs recording the havoc caused by the 1947 floods. Because the cover bore a picture of a bawling cow shoulder deep in water, the publication became known as the "Weeping Cow" book. Among those receiving copies was President Truman himself.[27]

Senator Holland welcomed the support of Florida Republicans. C.C. Spades of West Palm Beach, chairman of the Republican State Executive Committee, and other state leaders lobbied for the flood control program among key Republican congressmen and senators.[28] Holland also received a timely boost from R.Y. Patterson, president of the United States Sugar Corporation, who sent supporting telegrams to congressional leaders.[29]

Ernest Coe (fourth figure from left, with bowtie), 1929. A landscape architect who moved to Miami in 1925, Coe energized the movement to establish Everglades National Park. Historical Association of Southern Florida and SPA.

The measure easily passed through Congress and was signed into law by President Truman on 30 June 1948. It approved the entire first phase of the Army Corps's flood control plan, estimated to cost $70 million. It authorized $16.3 million to start work, contingent upon contributions from state and local sources of $3.7 million in land and money. Careful to share the glory with others, Senator Holland wrote: "The whole Florida delegation has stuck together in this matter and will, I am sure, continue to do so, and each member of the delegation is entitled to his full share of the credit. The Florida citizens, industries, and public units have also cooperated to the fullest degree as has the Republican delegation. I want you to remember that this is not a partisan project and that it should continue to merit the united efforts of all our people."[30]

Construction of the authorized flood control works did not begin for almost two years. Because the Army Corps could not spend any federal money on the project until the state had contributed its share, the governing bodies of the Internal Improvement Fund, the Everglades Drainage District, and Palm Beach, Broward, and Dade counties advanced $150,000 to enable the corps to start designing the necessary structures.[31] Cooperation was a two-way street. When South Florida again suffered flooding in September 1948, the corps dipped into its emergency funds to build protective barriers.[32]

Meanwhile the state authorities were putting together a legislative package for the session that began in April 1949. After some maneuvering the lawmakers passed a general law authorizing the establishment of flood control districts anywhere in the state with power to cooperate with federal agencies in the interest of protecting inhabitants and property "from the effects of water, either from its surplus or deficiency, or both."[33] The legislature also created the Central and Southern Florida Flood Control District, a new agency to replace the Everglades Drainage District and the Okeechobee Flood Control District.[34] Its authority extended over about 15,500 square miles, including all or parts of seventeen counties. The governing body was to be composed of five resident landowners, not more than one from the same county, to be appointed by the governor for staggered three-year terms. For the first time in the reclamation history of Florida, the legislature authorized the use of general revenues for both the state's share of construction costs and the cost of purchasing private lands for the conservation areas. The new flood control district was to pay for rights-of-way and maintenance. The sharpest legislative battle was over district taxes: should landowners be assessed on the basis of the benefits they would derive, or should there be an ad valorem tax on all assessed property? The first method would lay substantial burdens on the great agricultural corporations; the second would shift most of this to the taxpayers of the Gold Coast cities. Legislators from the small rural counties insisted on the ad valorem tax, and the representatives from the cities, now desperately afraid of floods, gave in to them. As a result, three counties—Palm Beach, Broward, and Dade—were obligated for 95 percent of the total bill. Dade's share, in fact, was about two-thirds.[35]

In January 1950 the corps began constructing the 100-mile-long perimeter levee. At first the work did not proceed as rapidly as its sponsors had hoped. One problem was the plodding pace of the engineers themselves. Their master plan had been hastily drawn, and they needed many months to work out the details. A second problem was financial. Despite its approval of the program Congress was niggardly in its annual appropriations. The engineers used these small allocations as an excuse for delay, and Congress used the failure of the corps to spend current appropriations as a justification for not increasing them. This dilemma played into the hands of the Eisenhower administration, eager to apply the brakes on federal spending. In 1954 Congress made no new appropriation at all. Actually this was a dubious economy. If the projected works were going to be built, they needed to be built quickly because Florida was enjoying a new boom. Real estate prices were going up rapidly, which meant that the state had to pay much more for the required land with each year's delay.[36]

Despite these difficulties the flood control program kept moving along. The state legislature continued to appropriate funds for the project, and the Central and Southern Florida Flood Control District (FCD) collected a substantial revenue from the ad valorem tax. Indeed, the rapid growth of the Gold Coast increased FCD income from $390,000 in 1950 to over $2 million in 1956, permitting the governing board to reduce the tax rate by one-quarter. Enjoying a dependable income, the FCD rapidly expanded its staff of engineers, lawyers, and clerks. In 1950 it was employing only 34 persons; by 1954 it had a staff of 100, crowded together in two West Palm Beach office buildings.[37]

In 1949 Lamar Johnson and Turner Wallis, both of whom had served as chief engineers for the old Everglades Drainage District, were under consideration for a similar post in the new FCD. Because Johnson had made enemies as a consequence of the 1947 floods, the position went to Wallis, who was appointed not only chief engineer but secretary-treasurer. For the next seven years Wallis was the most powerful individual in the flood control program. The first governing board, composed of political friends of Gov. Fuller Warren with little experience in drainage and flood control matters, gave Wallis a free hand. And Wallis was a born empire builder. Although somewhat brusque and combative in temperament, he commanded respect both as engineer and businessman.

Realizing that earlier efforts had been poorly supported because they benefited only one part of the drainage district, Wallis sought to spread the benefits of the new program as widely as possible. Traveling and speaking throughout the Flood Control District, he encouraged the organization of county water conservation and flood control committees. In eleven of the seventeen counties such local groups took shape, combining the energies of a wide range of people—county agricultural agents, cattlemen, farmers, citrus growers, real estate developers, and newspaper publishers and editors. But Wallis knew that this mobilization of local support would soon evaporate unless the levees and canals close to home were promptly built. For this reason he was unwilling to be bound by the Army Corps's timetable. He developed an emergency works program estimated to cost $3,350,000, about two-thirds of which he hoped would eventually be reimbursed to the FCD with federal and state money.[38]

Resentful of the legislation under which Dade County taxpayers provided two-thirds of the FCD revenues, the *Miami Herald* looked with suspicion on Wallis's emergency program. "Are pressure groups—some of them politically favored—menacing the great $208,000,000 federal-state water control plan so vital to the future of South and Central Florida?" asked Steven Trumbull in a special article. He listed several projects which seemed to benefit a few big landowners in Central Florida. The most suspect was an 18-mile-long canal under construction along the St. Lucie—Martin county line. "This canal," said the *Stuart News*, "is a political pork barrel for the sole benefit of a small group of wealthy landowners who are well able to pay for their own water control projects." Turner Wallis indignantly replied: "We make no apologies for the fact that some 15 landowners own most of the property along this canal. This is an area that lends itself only to a large-scale development. We look forward to the fact that this will open up thousands of new acres to agriculture, and we see full justification for this project."[39]

Wallis survived these newspaper attacks, but his position became less secure in January 1953 when Dan McCarty succeeded Fuller Warren as governor. Although the law had provided that the terms of FCD board members would run out at different times, circumstances allowed McCarty to replace four of the members. The new board kept Wallis on a much shorter leash, particularly in promoting his emergency program. Moreover, he soon had to deal with other governors. Governor McCarty died in September 1953 and was succeeded by Charley Johns, president of the state senate. In January 1955 LeRoy Collins, winner of a special election, became governor. Thus within a three-year period Wallis had to deal with four different governors and four different boards. He also had to contend with dissension within his own staff. Lamar Johnson had accepted a subordinate post in the agency but was soon at odds with Wallis. Late in 1954 Johnson resigned and sharply criticized FCD policies in an interview published in the *Miami Herald*. The Collins-appointed board took away Wallis's administrative powers and shifted him to a newly created post of director of planning and research.[40] Unhappy with these new arrangements, Wallis resigned in January 1957, and the guidance of the FCD passed to the hands of less controversial men. [41]

Through all the shifting winds of FCD politics, the great project kept moving along. The Army Corps made its requests, and Congress, sometimes willingly, sometimes grudgingly, passed authorizations and appropriations. The Flood Control Act of 1954 authorized Phase 2 of the comprehensive plan; the Flood Control Acts of 1958, 1960, and 1965 provided for still additional work. Dissatisfied with the formula that had the federal government paying 85 percent of the construction costs, Congress reduced the federal share to about 61 percent in later appropriations. In the late 1950s and early 1960s Congress and the state legislature both became more generous. By 1964 the federal appropriation had increased to $16.3 million for the year and the state's to $10 million. [42]

Summarizing its achievements at the end of fifteen years, the Flood Control District reported that it had completed the East Coast Levee and built lesser canals and levees in two regions—just south of Lake Okeechobee to protect the Everglades Agricultural Area and east of the East Coast Levee to improve drainage on the coastal belt. It had established three conservation areas, covering 1,300 square miles, enclosed these with levees, and installed giant pumps to pull in excess water to be released during periods of drought. The FCD was raising the level of the Hoover Dike and continuing it around Lake Okeechobee. It had started to build works in the Kissimmee Valley to improve drainage for a vast region in Central Florida. It was deepening and widening the Caloosahatchee River. In 1965 the FCD was operating 11 pumping stations, more than 1,300 miles of canals and levees, over 60 major spillways and dams, and several hundred secondary control structures. It had installed barriers in all canals leading to the ocean to prevent saltwater intrusion. [43]

Up to 1965 the FCD project had cost $174 million. In return for this investment, FCD officials claimed that the district had received $200 million in benefits through flood prevention, expanded acreage for agriculture, and improved water supply for the cities. But inadequate funding had delayed construction, and the project was only 40 percent completed. The FCD and the corps stressed the need for works in the upper St. Johns Basin, important for protecting the state's "fastest growing area"—the region around the Cape Kennedy space center. They also called for protective works in southern Dade County and in central Florida to provide growing room for Miami and Orlando. [44]

The FCD was proud of its success in protecting the area where al-

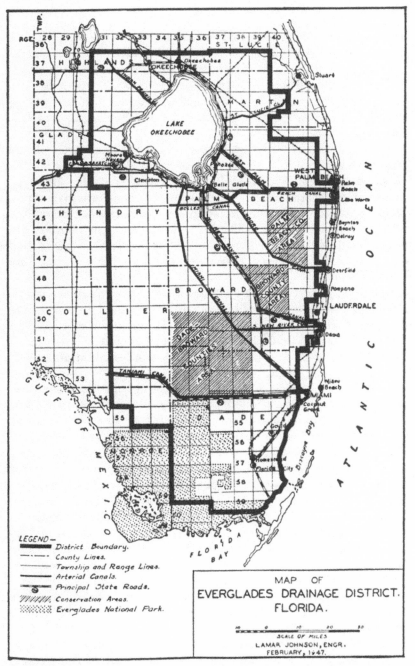

Proposed conservation areas, 1947. Lamar Johnson, engineer for the Everglades Drainage
District, urged a halt to drainage of areas unsuitable for agriculture and the establishment of
water storage areas. From A.J. Hanna and K.A. Hanna, *Lake Okeechobee: Well Spring of
the Everglades.*

most 40 percent of the state's population lived. Yet from the beginning the agency was a storm center of controversy. It was accused of favoring special agricultural interests, of giving priority to the needs of farmers and cattlemen at the expense of other water users, of designating too much land for agriculture and not enough for wildlife and recreation, of overtaxing city dwellers for the benefit of the rural counties.[45]

The FCD turned over supervision of Conservation Area 1 to the U.S. Fish and Wildlife Service and of Areas 2 and 3 to the Florida Game and Fresh Water Fish Commission.[46] Under these arrangements the area offered recreational sites conveniently near the Gold Coast cities. There were launching ramps and docks for those who wanted to go fishing or boating. Visitors could buy, rent, or hire almost anything they needed—motorboats, airboats, swamp buggies, tackle, bait, guides. There were camp sites with electrical and sanitary hookups.

Cherishing these recreational opportunities, sportsmen—among the state's most powerful lobbies—could be counted upon to oppose any changes that would encroach upon the conservation areas. This was an obvious political advantage to the FCD, yet there were serious problems involved in the situation. The conservation areas were created to retain water, not just to provide recreational opportunities. And sometimes one purpose conflicted with the other. Consider, for example, the plight of the deer. Before man interfered with natural conditions, the deer avoided the so-called sawgrass Everglades with its deep water, grazing instead on the drier lands on the edge of the Everglades. When the state drainage program dried up much of the former sawgrass region, the deer moved into this new habitat. In dry years they flourished, but in years of heavy rainfall when their grazing places were flooded they suffered from stress and starvation. And they were still more vulnerable in the conservation areas. In the summer of 1966 there were heavy rains, and the FCD pumped excess water from the farmlands into the conservation areas. Hundreds of deer were drowned, and smaller animals like wild hogs and raccoons died because the high water covered their natural food supplies. Deploring this "man-made flood," the *New York Times* said: "In the Everglades, mindless technology is triumphing over life."[47]

In 1968 and 1969 the deer again suffered when the FCD pumped large quantities of water into the conservation areas. Even rescue efforts of conservationists and sportsmen miscarried. Hoping to move the deer to higher ground, the animal lovers pursued them in airboats, but the frightened animals exhausted themselves running away. Contending that kindness was killing more deer than was high water, one naturalist advised the conservationists to leave the animals alone.[48] But the deer who found shelter on the hammocks were not any safer, for they were easy targets for hunters. The state cut short the hunting season, but illegal killings continued. In the five years between 1966 and 1970 Florida's deer population was estimated to have been reduced from 7,000 to less than 1,000.[49] A member of the state game commission admitted his agency's helplessness. Speaking of the FCD, he said: "They're more interested in draining farm lands than protecting deer. But then flood control is their function."[50] Acknowledging that recreation and wildlife preservation were only secondary objectives of the FCD, Lamar Johnson recommended that the state establish a real sanctuary in the Big Cypress Swamp so that the deer would move west again.[51]

Even more bitter were the clashes over the water needs of Everglades National Park. Ample water for the park had been one of the good deeds promised by the FCD. By reducing runoff through the old drainage canals and storing surplus water, the new works were supposed to take care of all needs. But construction of two cross-state highways—the Tamiami Trail and Alligator Alley—had already substantially interrupted the southern flow of water. Now with the Army Corps of Engineers building a new network of levees and canals, the lower Everglades became ever more dependent on the FCD managers. So long as there was adequate rainfall the park was reasonably safe, but in years of scarcity, who would get the water?

The threat to the park became serious during the early 1960s. In 1961 southern Florida received only 30 inches of rain—about one-half the annual average. During the first four months of 1962 there was practically no rain at all. As the water holes in the park dried up, a struggle for survival developed. The rain finally came in time to prevent further disaster, but for several years the flow of water through the park was dangerously slight.[52] Fires and drought damaged plant life, thus threatening the food supply on which the wildlife depended. Responding to the protests of the U.S. Department of the Interior, Congress authorized a $400,000 study of the water needs of all of South Florida.[53] The Army Corps took several years to carry out this assignment, and in the meantime park officials continued to complain of niggardly FCD releases.

In its pleas for more water the Park Service had the fervent support of Audubon Societies and other preservationist groups. Television news reports depicting the plight of the wildlife provoked nationwide protests. But the values in jeopardy were economic as well as sentimental. At the most obvious level, a flourishing national park drew tourists to Florida for the benefit of motel owners, service stations, and airlines. Less understood, except by marine biologists, was the relationship of the park's estuaries, tidal flats, and bays to the state's valuable shrimping and fishing industry. The coastal waters were the nursery grounds for shrimp and minute marine life on which the larger fish fed, and an adequate freshwater flow through the estuaries was necessary to maintain the proper salinity of this habitat. As the environmentalists saw the situation, the Army Corps of Engineers and the FCD were ignoring these ecological facts of life in building and operating their canals and levees.

A number of efforts were made to relieve the park. The park administration drilled wells but was unable to tap a dependable supply. The FCD tried to pump Lake Okeechobee water down through the canals, but they were too shallow. The conservation areas were not yet providing the water storage that had been planned. One problem was the succession of abnormally dry years; another was the failure of Congress to appropriate enough money to complete the project.

Accepting the fact that completion of the FCD project would take many years, the Army Corps in 1965 proposed an "interim" project for getting more water into the park. Since the 100-mile intervening territory between Lake Okeechobee and the park was too flat for an adequate natural flow, the Engineers wanted to enlarge the canals through the conservation areas and install pumping stations to move the water southward. The Park Service liked the idea, but Gov. Haydon Burns attempted to add another feature. He asked to have a low earthen levee built across the southern part of the park to prevent excess runoff into the ocean. Claiming that this would disrupt the ecology of the region, park officials refused to approve it.[54] Despite this skirmish, the three parties—corps, Park Service, and FCD—did agree to back the interim project, estimated to cost $3 million. In the spring of 1966 Congressman Dante Fascell of Miami steered the first $1.5 million appropriation through Congress.[55]

To give the park some security while these new works were being built, the FCD promised to release a "minimal" supply of 90 million gallons a day, provided that the surface of Lake Okeechobee did not sink below the safety level fixed by the Army Corps at 12.5 feet above sea level.[56] But this pledge, given in March 1966, was severely tested the next year when South Florida experienced its worst drought in twenty-five years. Crops were parched; cattle were dying; urban water supplies were running short; brushfires were burning out of control. The level of Lake Okeechobee sank to one-tenth of an inch above the critical 12.5 foot level. On 7 May Gov. Claude Kirk announced that if the drought continued the release of water to the park would have to be halted. "Those who are solely concerned about the national park," he said, "have got to remember that there

Flood in Palm Beach County, 1947. Extensive damage to farms, cattle ranches, and homes created a demand for federal aid in flood protection. From *Tentative Report of Flood Damage*, Florida Everglades Drainage District, 1947 (the "weeping cow" book).

are more than one million people involved in this drought also." The wrath of nature lovers across the nation promptly descended upon the governor's head. The *New York Times* asserted that there was as yet no threat to the Miami water supply: "The choice is not between alligators and people. Rather it is between farmers who will suffer a diminished crop and a park of national importance and unique quality. Crop insurance and government indemnities can make up the financial loss to farmers but there is no way to compensate the nation for the untold harm done to its only subtropical park."[57]

As it turned out, Governor Kirk scarcely deserved this scolding. Florida's first Republican governor since Reconstruction days was a flamboyant politician who shocked liberals by his high-handed actions, but he was less beholden than most of his predecessors to the agricultural and ranching interests. Cast in the role of villain in the fight to save the park, Kirk chose to play a hero's role instead. He interceded with the Army Corps and the FCD to continue the minimal flow of water into the park until the crisis eased in June. Another unexpected hero was Robert Padrick, a Republican whom Kirk had appointed to the FCD governing board. Although this Fort Pierce auto dealer came from the same small town political background as had earlier FCD officials, he proved to have a much broader concept of water management. The preservationists learned to their surprise that at heart Padrick was one of them. For his leadership in safeguarding wilderness areas, Padrick was designated "Florida's outstanding conservationist" for the year 1969. To emphasize the FCD's new direction, the agency in 1967 adopted "Freddy the Friendly Alligator" as its symbol.[58]

By this time protection of Everglades National Park had become a rallying cause for nature lovers in every corner of the country, and even the Army Corps seemed to be influenced by the new mood. On 19 July 1967 it unveiled its tentative findings on South Florida water needs at a meeting attended by Park Service representatives, FCD board members, Florida Board of Conservation officials, and other interested parties. Pleased with what he heard, Harthon L. Bill, acting park director, wrote that this suggested "very promising indications that the water needs of Everglades National Park are not only being recognized, but there is also a resolve to skillfully and equitably end these long standing problems."[59]

The corps proposed major new works that would permit an increased release of water to the park of up to 315,000 acre-feet every year, the minimum quantity the Park Service considered necessary. Randolph Hodges, director of the Florida Board of Conservation, regarded this recommendation with considerable suspicion.

Characterizing the park as just one of several "customers," he said that it "should share the shortages and the surpluses along with all other customers." Since floods and droughts were characteristics of the natural environment, it would be unwise to protect the park completely against these conditions. It was all right to establish "an irreducible minimum needed for survival," but it would "not be realistic to guarantee the Park an assured annual flow contrary to that previously provided by Nature." Hodges argued that the park ought to protect itself by building water storage and conveyance structures within its own boundaries. As for new works outside these boundaries, the park should share in construction costs. Hodges insisted that such construction for the benefit of the park should not be allowed to delay construction of the original FCD project, still only 52 percent completed.[60]

During the next few months the preservationists and the state officials continued to struggle over the corps's study. The preservationists wanted stronger guarantees that the park would receive enough water in dry years as well as wet, whatever the future growth of South Florida population and industry might be. The state officials had no objection to meeting the demands of the park in normal years but insisted on the principle of "shared adversity" in years of drought.

In the final draft of its report dated 7 May 1968, the Corps of Engineers accepted the Park Service's definition of its basic needs. In the words of the report: "The Service has asked that water be delivered to the park on an annual schedule of 315,000 acre-feet, with varying monthly schedules patterned closely after the historic distribution of flow throughout the year. The Service also desires the water greatly in excess of 315,000 acre-feet whenever excess to the needs of other users."[61] But the park was not the only party needing assurance of an adequate supply. Taking note of South Florida's rapid growth of population, the Army Corps warned that the region might suffer water shortages after 1976 even if all authorized FCD works were completed. To meet these new needs, the corps proposed additional facilities to collect and backpump excess water from the East Coast canals into Lake Okeechobee and the conservation areas, additional canals, levees, and pumping stations to convey water to areas of need, and higher levees around Lake Okeechobee so that the maximum level of water could be four feet higher. Other parts of the new plan were designed to provide better protection for farmlands, a deeper channel across Lake Okeechobee, and more recreational facilities. The corps estimated that the new construction would cost about $70 million, the federal share to be $55 million.[62]

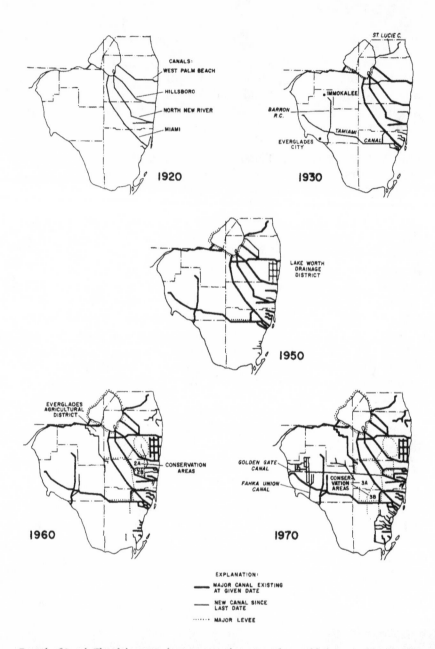

Growth of South Florida's regional water control system. The establishment of the Central and Southern Florida Flood Control District in 1949 resulted in a steadily more complex network of canals and levees, especially along the southeast coast. From Florida Division of State Planning, *Final Report on the Special Project to Prevent Eutrophication of Lake Okeechobee.*

Despite earlier misgivings the Florida Board of Conservation formally endorsed the corps plan on 7 May 1968, and Governor Kirk wrote a strong supporting letter. He recognized Everglades National Park as "a legitimate water user" and as a unique place that could exist only in South Florida. The state, Kirk said, "accepts the responsibility of guarding this treasure for generations unborn. Authorization of the Corps of Engineers study is vital to the Park, and to our citizens, whose lives and livelihood depend on the Central and Southern Florida Flood Control District."[63]

But even this strong statement was not enough to calm the fears of the Park Service. Stanley A. Cain, assistant secretary of the interior, complained that the corps report failed to establish unequivocably that the basic water supply to the park would be unaffected by future demands of urban and agricultural growth. "We, therefore, cannot recommend the plan," Cain wrote "without written assurance by the Secretary of the Army that he will provide the water supplies as set forth in the report, undiminished by new incursions." On 14 June Maj. Gen. F.C. Clarke, acting chief of engineers, responded in a letter to Secretary of the Interior Stewart Udall: "Under authority of the Secretary of the Army, the Chief of Engineers will insure the project is regulated to deliver the water requirements of the Everglades National Park as set forth in the report."[64]

With all parties promising to cooperate, Congress authorized the new $70 million project in 1968, but the preservationists still felt uneasy. For one thing, until the new works were actually built, the water supply of the park was highly vulnerable. Moreover, the lines of authority were far from clear. The army had promised that the water needs of the park would be met, but most of the corps's responsibilities ended with construction. Except in certain contingencies, the actual management of the complex works lay in the hands of the FCD. For the moment, the board seemed to be sympathetic to the preservationist cause, but what would happen if South Florida's phenomenal growth continued? As the demand for water grew, how would the FCD of the future respond to the pressures of real estate developers, corporate farmers, and cattle raisers?

Friends of the park received another promise in March 1969 when Walter Hickel, Nixon's secretary of the interior, visited Florida. Just emerging as a champion of the environmentalist cause, the secretary made a two-day tour of the Everglades to publicize his intention of cracking down on alligator poachers. In what the *New York Times* described as a "summit meeting" held in a trailer at a ranger station on the Gulf of Mexico, Hickel and Governor Kirk discussed the park's water requirements. Once again Kirk recognized the legitimacy of these and promised that they would be met.[65]

Actually there was no shortage at the time of the Hickel-Kirk meeting. The cycle of dry years had been followed by several wet years. In 1969 the park received 1.7 million acre-feet of water, more than ever before and more than five times the 315,000 acre-feet specified in the annual schedule.[66] But all concerned knew that these years of abundance would be followed by years of drought, and the preservationists still feared for the park's future. In 1970 two congressional friends of the movement, Senators Gaylord Nelson of Wisconsin and Edmund Muskie of Maine, pushed through Congress, over Senator Holland's opposition, a stipulation that as soon as new conveyances were adequate the park was to receive 315,000 acre-feet annually, or 16.5 percent of the total deliveries from the flood-control project, whichever was less.[67]

To the managers in Florida, this water guarantee was dangerously rigid. Lamar Johnson complained: "In times of plenty 16.5 percent is negligible; in times of scarcity, it's murder. When such a time of scarcity comes, the onus will fall upon the park, not the Congress." He complained that the park officials wasted the water they already had. They failed to build the engineering works within the park that would store water, convey it to where it was needed, and keep out the salt water. "It is inexcusable to allow fresh water to flow into the sea with no attempt to retard the runoff," Johnson wrote. "Florida saw too much of that practice in the all-out drainage period of its history. The park people know this, yet the park sits there like a fledgling egret on its nest, mouth open and squawking, waiting to be fed."[68]

The Everglades issue symbolized the whole clash between managers and preservationists in Florida. The older managers loved to plan and build the engineering works that would use water efficiently; the older preservationists hated this tampering with nature and sought to allow the water to flow freely through the unspoiled wilderness. Each group tended to become intolerant of the other. What was needed was a bridge between the two. The water managers needed to become less engineer-oriented and more sensitive to ecological values; the preservationists needed to undergird their love of nature's beauty with more scientific understanding of nature's mechanisms. The new environmentalist movement of the late 1960s and 1970s helped to build the required bridge.

# 9 Environmentalists to the Rescue

I n 1974 Patrick Caddell, a political pollster soon to be employed by Jimmy Carter, reported that attitudes in Florida had "dramatically changed." A "new issue structure" appeared to be emerging with "'Quality of Life' replacing 'Quantity of Life,' with environmental concerns clashing with economic concerns." People interviewed in other states gave priority to pocketbook issues like inflation, food prices, and unemployment. "Yet in Florida these issues have been overwhelmed by the issues of growth, overpopulation, pollution, water shortages, etc. This is not to say economic and other concerns are not important issues, but the surprising point is the overwhelming *saliency* of the environmental issue."[1]

If Caddell was right, if environmentalism had become not a mere piety but smart politics, why had this occurred? The shift in Florida was, of course, part of a national trend. Particularly among the young, the 1960s had been a period of rising concern over technology's threat to nature. Pesticides were killing the birds; detergents were fouling the rivers; automobile exhaust was contaminating the air. The new-style environmentalists were the heirs of the earlier preservationists. Like them, they longed to halt the rape of nature and preserve the unspoiled wilderness. But they were more sophisticated in assessing the threats. If people were to have safe food to eat, pure water to drink, and clean air to breathe, the environmentalists had to stand guard against a variety of enemies— manufacturers who adulterated food, factories that dumped industrial wastes into rivers and lakes, power plants that allowed noxious fumes to pour out of their smokestacks; campers and boaters who dumped sewage into the streams; motorists and hikers who cluttered the roadside with empty cans. Concern over these issues was everywhere on the rise, and Congress and the state legislatures were passing protective legislation.

The new environmentalism was rooted less in a love for the unspoiled beauty of nature than in a scientific understanding of ecology, that is, the relationship of living organisms with their environment. Concerned botanists and biologists emphasized the adaptive mechanisms of nature, the ways in which plant and animal life adjusted to cycles of wet months and dry months, floods and droughts, overpopulation and killings by predators. In the natural habitat, marshes and wetlands had their vital functions no less than arable uplands. Because man himself was involved in these ecological chains, he ought, before interfering with nature, to make a much more thoughtful analysis of environmental costs and benefits than the older engineers had provided.

The environmental movement hit Florida with particular force because it challenged the state's traditional boosterism. For 150 years progress had been measured in the number of new residents, tourists, railroads, highways, houses, condominiums, shopping centers, orange groves, sugar fields, cattle ranches, and phosphate mines. Whatever "developed" the state was good; whatever hindered development was bad. Then development became suspect. Builders who hacked down the mangroves to create waterfront lots were ruining the nursery grounds for shrimp and other marine life. Suburban expansion overdrew municipal wells and caused saltwater intrusion. Inadequate and overloaded sewage systems threatened to pollute underground water sources. Many Floridians began to believe the state had been growing too rapidly. Should there not be limits imposed on building permits, water hookups, and sewage system extensions? Should there not be serious planning for the state's future?

Leadership in the organized environmentalist movement was assumed by the old preservationist groups—the Audubon Societies, the Izaak Walton League, and the Wildlife Society—and by new groups like the Nature Conservancy. Long sneered at as mere "bird watchers," nature lovers gained new members and a new militancy during the 1960s. Highly influential civic groups like the Federation of Women's Clubs and the League of Women Voters began to emphasize environmental issues.

Crusading individuals preached the new gospel. Particularly zealous was Arthur Marshall, a marine biologist, who in 1960 became head of the Vero Beach office of the U.S. Bureau of Sport Fisheries and Wildlife. Convinced that the Corps of Engineers was paying scant attention to environmental impact in planning its projects, Marshall accepted every invitation he could get to speak before local groups. At first his audiences were small, but he gradually built up a substantial following. Eventually he left government service to head an applied ecology program at the University of Miami.[2] Universities were natural rallying grounds for the new movement, and important work was done by David Anthony, Archie and Marjorie Carr, Ariel Lugo, John Kaufmann, Martin Mifflin, and George Cornwell at the University of Florida, and John DeGrove at Florida Atlantic University. But nonacademics were also dedicated—people like Nathaniel Reed, a wealthy Hobe Sound investor, Lyman Rogers of Ocala, sporting goods salesman and influential Republican, and William Partington and Hal Scott, officials of the Florida Audubon Society.

The environmentalists gained a sympathetic hearing with Governors Claude Kirk and Reubin Askew. Although the first was a Republican and the second a Democrat, both represented a striking change from the unrestrained boosterism of their predecessors. In 1966 Kirk enlisted the support of Nat Reed and Lyman Rogers in writing a strong conservationist platform for his campaign. Kirk appointed Rogers chairman of the Governor's Natural Resources Committee and Reed environmental adviser to the governor. Supported by environmental groups and newspapers, Kirk obtained from the legislature two pieces of significant environmentalist legislation. The first created a Pollution Control Board with power to issue waste discharge permits and enforce compliance with air and water quality standards. The second, the so-called Randell Act, required a biological survey prior to the issuance of state or local permits for any alteration of tidal lands or the bottoms of state-owned lakes.[3] Reed, appointed chairman of the new Pollution Control Board, used his post to reduce drastically the state's sale of submerged lands to private developers. The ultimate decision in such cases lay with the governor and cabinet, the Republican Kirk's one vote against the Democratic officeholders's six. But Reed provided the pugnacious governor with sufficient ammunition to win cabinet support on many dredge-and-fill cases. Prior to 1967 the state had been routinely approving an average of over 2,000 such applications each year; during the last three years of the Kirk administration these approvals averaged only about 200 a year.[4] In 1970 Kirk was defeated in his reelection campaign, but Reed continued the battle for environmentalism as assistant secretary of the interior for fish, wildlife, and parks in the Nixon administration.

Kirk's defeat was not a defeat for environmentalism. Although Reubin Askew had not hitherto been a conspicuous champion of the cause, he soon became firmly committed. In a generous tribute to the Democratic governor in 1978, Republican Nat Reed said, "In my opinion, Florida desperately needed the quiet, sane Askew years to pull together, codify, and institutionalize the frenetic years of Kirk's assault on the outdated and corrupt."[5] Among Askew's influential advisers was Jay Landers, a young lawyer whose first assignment was to brief the governor on issues involving natural resources. After serving in other posts in the administration, Landers became in 1975 secretary of the new Department of Environmental Regulation. A second key figure was Joel Kuperberg, a land management expert who was appointed executive director of the Internal Improvement Fund. Kuperberg carried the protection of submerged lands still farther than had Reed. Even though he had to fight some of the most powerful developers in the state, he was able to bring a halt to the dredge-and-fill operations that had sacrificed the mangrove swamps to create expensive waterfront lots. Scores of other environmental scientists found posts in the Division of State Planning, the Department of Environmental Regulation, and other new branches of government. Askew also sought the advice of various university people, men like Arthur Marshall, John DeGrove, and Howard Odum.

At the same time that the environmentalists were gaining such strong influence in the governor's office, they were exerting pressure on the Florida legislature. In July 1969 Lyman Rogers took the lead in organizing a group called "Conservation 70s." All the older conservation groups joined in the effort, along with friendly politicians like Rogers and Reed and influential legislators like Representative John Robert Middlemus, a Democrat from Panama City, and Senator Warren Henderson, a Republican from Sarasota. After a successful appeal for donations the coalition employed Loring Lovell as its executive director, and his energetic lobbying gave it a remarkable win-loss record in the 1970 session of the legislature. Out of fifty-five bills proposed, forty-one were passed. They penalized oil spillage, protected state-owned submerged lands, restricted drainage, dredging, and filling, increased penalties for pollution, facilitated the financing of sewage disposal works, curbed the use of pesticides, created a state wilderness system, and banned the sale of alligator products. Although many of these measures were underfunded and otherwise emasculated, it was an impressive demonstration that the environmentalists were gaining political clout.[6] In the 1971 legislature Conservation 70s was able to pass still more laws. After 1972 the group became less active, but only because the major legislative battles had been won and protection of the environment had now become the responsibility of new state agencies.

Reaching its peak during the early 1970s, the environmentalist movement pitted its strength against powerful enemies. Especially formidable were the Jacksonville faction, determined to build a barge canal across the peninsula, and Miami's boosters, who wanted to build a giant jetport close to Everglades National Park.

At the beginning of 1951 the canal project had appeared to be moribund, but its Jacksonville backers had refused to allow it to die.[7] John H. Perry, owner of newspapers in Jacksonville, Ocala, and other Florida cities, induced an influential Democrat, Congressman Emanuel Cellar of Brooklyn, to take up the idea with President Truman.[8] After doing so, Cellar gave his Florida friends an encouraging report: "The President was even more favorably disposed than I had hoped. He confirmed the fact that he had been for it from the beginning, and was still for it, and thought it ought to be built."[9] Excited by this news, Congressman Charles Bennett of Jacksonville tried to get Sen. Spessard Holland and other Florida representatives to seek a joint meeting with the president, but Holland knew that the canal scheme was unpopular in southern Florida and wanted to let the administration take the initiative.[10] The results were disappointing. Truman did ask the Defense Department for a review of the project, but the report was lukewarm: "The Joint Chiefs of Staff consider that the military aspects of the proposed project are so limited that they should not be used as the primary basis for decision on this matter."[11]

Yet if the Defense Department did not need the barge canal, who did? In their summary estimates of 1942 and their more detailed plans of 1943 the Army Corps of Engineers had calculated the benefit-to-cost ratio at only 0.19 to 1. Since Congress expected such public works to have at least a 1-to-1 ratio, the outlook was bleak. Nevertheless, in 1954 the corps placed it in a "deferred for restudy" category, and Congress subsequently appropriated enough money for the corps to issue an economic restudy in 1958. The new figures were strikingly different from the earlier ones. Construction costs, estimated at only $44 million in 1942, were now projected at $164.5 million, but estimated benefits had risen from $482,000 a year in 1942 to $7,758,000 a year in 1958. The benefit-to-cost ratio was now 1.05 to 1.[12]

The corps's new figures revived the hopes of the canal backers. Gov. LeRoy Collins gave the project his blessing, and Senator Holland sought to get construction money into the corps's budget requests for fiscal 1960.[13] A presidential "no new starts" order blocked this, but Holland appealed to his friend, Sen. Allen Ellender of Louisiana, chairman of the Subcommittee on Public Works, to support an appropriation of $160,000 for planning. Ellender wrote back that he could not do so because 1.05 to 1 was still "a very slim margin."[14]

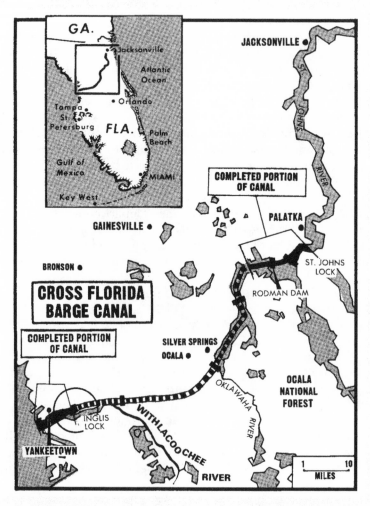

Cross-Florida Barge Canal. When construction was halted in January 1971, the parts of the canal indicated by a heavy black line were completed. The broken line shows the projected route of the uncompleted portion. SPA.

Canal prospects suddenly brightened during the campaign of 1960. Needing electoral votes in the South, John F. Kennedy named Lyndon Johnson as his vice-presidential choice and made a number of other carefully calculated moves. To Congressman Bennett he wrote: "I know of your persistent work for the early construction of a cross-Florida barge canal. If I am elected President I will be glad to cooperate with you in making this project a reality. I regard it not only as important to Florida but to the economy of our entire country, which must fully utilize all natural resources if we are to achieve necessary economic expansion."[15]

Although Kennedy did not carry Florida, he honored his campaign commitment by obtaining a new study of the project. Meanwhile, nature, which had so often provided plausible grounds for federal action, cooperated again. In 1959 and 1960 there was severe flooding along the proposed canal route, prompting John E. Wakefield, director of the Florida Department of Water Resources, to advise Senator Holland that "an incidental flood control benefit in excess of $7,000,000 for the Oklawaha River Basin and $1,000,000 for the Withlacoochee River Basin could have resulted had the canal been in construction prior to March 1960, and similar benefits can result from the construction of the canal in the future."[16]

In a new report issued in 1962 the corps calculated flood control benefits at $257,000 a year. Another new item was "land enhancement," estimated at $650,000. By these additions the corps came up with the more impressive benefit-to-cost ratio of 1.17 to 1. The cost of the canal was now estimated at $157 million, of which the federal government was to contribute $145.5 million and the state of Florida $12.4 million.[17]

During 1962 the canal backers waged an energetic campaign. "As you know," Gov. Farris Bryant, an Ocala man, wrote to Bert Dosh, editor of the *Ocala Star-Banner*, "I am most anxious to proceed with the Cross-Florida Barge Canal during my administration."[18] Giles Evans, manager of the Cross-Florida Canal Navigational District, consulted the governor on a promotional campaign that would include speeches, movies, and television programs but "no debates." All state agencies were to be asked for their support, and prominent industrialists were to be lined up. A special effort was to be made to interest leaders in other states.[19] Responding to the bugle call, the Florida Game and Fresh Water Fish Commission endorsed the barge canal in July 1962 and the Florida Board of Conservation fell in line in August.[20]

President Kennedy gave the project another boost by asking for an appropriation of $200,000 for final design and planning. This ran into stiff opposition from crusty Clarence Cannon of Missouri, chairman of the House Appropriations Committee, but Congressman Robert Sikes of Panhandle Florida adroitly tied the Florida project to others in Texas, Oregon, Washington, and Illinois. This logrolling, combined with White House pressure exerted through House Speaker John McCormick and Majority Leader Carl Albert, put the appropriation across. Chairman Cannon was reported to have said: "No bigger bunch of pirates ever sailed the Spanish Main. All the money that Captain Kidd and Long John Silver stole is infinitesimal compared to this raid on the federal treasury."[21]

But would Kennedy continue to muscle the scheme along? On 1 March 1963 Henry Buchman, a veteran of earlier canal battles, confided his misgivings in a letter to Bert Dosh. The president, Buchman said, was only interested in the canal as a possible "pawn" in his 1964 election campaign, and he was reputed to be turning to other "bait." It was absolutely essential, he wrote, to get word to Kennedy, either directly or through party channels, "that his chances of winning Florida will in all probability vanish if he fails to provide for the canal at this time."[22]

The Florida leaders went promptly into action. Editor Dosh wrote to John Bailey, chairman of the Democratic National Committee, warning him of growing Republican strength and urging him to use his influences to get action from the president.[23] Governor Bryant and other Florida officials went to Washington to confer with Bailey in person.[24] The message obviously got through because on 21 June 1963, Kennedy sent a message to Congress requesting $1 million for initial construction costs. "The project," he wrote, "will provide an impetus to the economy of the Southeastern United States and augment strategic materials transport capabilities in the event of a national emergency."[25] The House of Representatives voted the requested funds on 19 November, less than a week before the president made his fateful trip to Dallas.[26]

After Kennedy's death the Florida leaders went to work on his successor. On 28 December Dosh wrote to Chairman Bailey to applaud the report that President Johnson would ask for a $4 million appropriation to continue construction. "Such a recommendation I can assure you," wrote Dosh, "would be most appealing to Florida voters, including some Republicans."[27] On 27 February 1964 Johnson took the occasion of a swing through Florida to participate in a groundbreaking ceremony at Palatka. A crowd of 10,000 people waited in a driving rain for his arrival and were a little disappointed

when he made only a ten-minute speech. But the symbolic dynamite blast was entirely satisfactory. Thanks to the forethought of
those who had loaded the site with peat moss, a great mass of debris
went mushrooming skyward.[28]

The political auspices for the canal were now highly favorable.
Two presidents had bestowed their personal blessings. Florida's
governor-elect, Haydon Burns, a former mayor of Jacksonville, was
a fervent canal booster. Most other Florida politicians were supporting the project, and other powerful influences were at work. Although most railroads were as hostile to this as they were to other
proposals for toll-free waterways, the Florida East Coast Railroad
strongly supported it. This railroad was controlled by the Alfred I.
Du Pont estate and was part of an economic empire that included
pulpwood forests and paper mills in the Panhandle, banks and industries in Jacksonville, sugar plantations in Belle Glade, and real estate
holdings in downtown Miami. The cross-Florida barge canal would
benefit the Du Pont interest by linking the Panhandle and north-
central Florida with the port of Jacksonville. Edward Ball, Du Pont's
brother-in-law and trustee of his estate, was reputed to be one of the
most influential men in Florida politics. Other investors had also
gained a strong stake in the canal by buying up tracts of land along
the proposed route, particularly along its western stretches and in
the vicinity of Ocala. Some of these speculators were rumored to be
close associates of important Florida politicians. Still another
behind-the-scenes influence was the phosphate industry of north-
central Florida, eager for cheap transportation.

In this favorable political climate all went well for the canal at first.
Without protest the Florida legislature voted the appropriations
needed for the state's share of the costs. The corps refigured the
benefit-to-cost ratio from time to time, finally achieving a figure
of 1.5 to 1 in 1969. President Johnson continued to provide for the
canal in his budgets, and Congress voted a steady stream of appropriations.[29]

Florida environmentalists sought to play the role of David against
this Goliath. At first the odds seemed overwhelmingly against them:
they were weak and divided, and local societies concentrated their
attention on local issues. But Marjorie Carr of Gainesville proved to
be a woman of broader vision. Listening to a description of the
proposed canal at a meeting of the Alachua Audubon Society in
November 1962, she realized that the project would destroy the
lower stretches of the Oklawaha River, a region that had been
delighting nature lovers for over a hundred years. Under the leader-

ship of Mrs. Carr and David Anthony, the Alachua Audubon Society began a serious study of the ecological consequences likely to follow construction of the canal.[30]

In March 1965 the Gainesville group sent out a mimeographed letter to conservationists throughout the state, warning them that the canal as planned would obliterate forty-five miles of the Oklawaha River and submerge the riverine forest. Enclosed were several brochures, including one entitled "A Brief Outline of the Inadequate Economic Justification of the Cross-Florida Barge Canal." Col. F. W. Hodge, the author, argued that the Army Corps of Engineers had overestimated the anticipated benefits and underestimated annual costs, especially by asssuming a 2.625 percent interest rate at a time when the federal government was paying 4.1 percent on its long-term obligations.[31]

Early in 1965 the House Subcommittee on Public Works received letters opposing the project from local Audubon societies, the Florida Nature Conservancy, the Pinellas County Board of Commissioners, and other groups from various parts of the state.[32] A spokesman for the state cabinet condemned the troublemakers who had "violated every rule of fairness and objectivity" in their literature. He hinted that the railroads were behind this mischief: "We can only conclude that this letter-writing compaign has been inspired and masterminded by traditional opponents of waterway improvements as a last-ditch effort to inject confusion and misdirection into the path of progress which has been laid out by official acts of local, State and Federal government."[33]

Not yet sure that they wanted to kill the whole project, the "Save the Oklawaha" movement concentrated its early efforts on trying to get the route changed. At a public hearing at Tallahassee in January 1966 the conservationists crowded the chamber of the House of Representatives, but Secretary of State Tom Adams, the only cabinet member who took the trouble to attend, badgered the petitioners with hostile questions. Nor were the environmentalists any more successful in Washington, where Congress continued to vote appropriations for the canal.[34]

By now, however, the canal controversy was beginning to attract national attention. In 1963 an article in *Life Magazine* entitled "Pork Barrel Outrage: Too Much Money Spent Foolishly" identified the cross-Florida barge canal as one of twelve "glaring examples." In 1965 a *New York Times* editorial noted that a Wild Rivers Study Team had selected the Oklawaha as one of seventy-three streams worthy of inclusion in a national wild rivers system. "It is time to stop the work," said the *Times*, "and weigh the total public interest in the Oklawaha before irreparable, tragic damage is done to this stream for benefit of a project which is at best of dubious merit."[35] The *Times* also published a letter from William Partington of the Florida Federated Conservation Council, who warned that "massive interference in the natural water conditions of Florida" was "like playing 'Russian roulette.' "[36]

The canal's threat to the environment became highly visible as contractors began tearing up the landscape on both sides of the state. On the western end they knocked down palm and cypress trees and began digging a straight 12-foot-deep waterway bypassing the crooked Withlacoochee River. They rebuilt a dam and locks across the river near Inglis. Even more disruptive were the works pushed through on the eastern end. Again there was a straight cut bypassing the lower reaches of the Oklawaha River. But much more damaging were two dams built across the river at Rodman and Eureka. As the water in the Rodman Reservoir began to rise the consequences of man's interference became more and more disturbing. A cypress forest had been sacrificed. Less than 15 percent of the trees had been salvaged for lumber; the rest had been knocked down by a huge machine called a "crusher-crawler" by the engineers and a "tree-killer" by the environmentalists. The powdery debris rose from the bottom and began to float on the surface.[37]

Was this progress? In October 1966 Secretary of State Tom Adams was exuberant about the project. It would "put Florida at the apex of the greatest trade potential in the nation—a crossroads between the Atlantic Seaboard and the Gulf of Mexico and the Midwest." The final phase of the program would be to supply a "missing link," the 144-mile-stretch between the present terminus of the Gulf Intracoastal at Carabelle and the Anclote River at Tarpon Springs. A continuous route extending all the way from Texas up the Atlantic Coast would then serve shippers of lumber, ore, coal, petroleum products, fertilizer, industrial chemicals, paper products, and animal feed. It would facilitate the transportation of missiles and rocket engines to Cape Kennedy.[38] But the environmentalists were not impressed by this argument. Did it cost less to move goods by barge than by pipelines and railroads? Probably not, if the expense to the taxpayers of building and maintaining free waterways was included. Moreover, there was a danger that the barge canal would be out-of-date even before it was completed. Barge transportation of all types seemed to face an uncertain future as shippers depended more and more on large tankers and cargo ships.

Uneasy that their case for economic benefits was not more convincing, the boosters began to emphasize the canal's advantages for recreation. Not only would it provide good boating, but there would be excellent fishing in the newly created lakes with nearly 300 miles of shoreline. The public would have easy access at thirty-two projected recreational sites.[39] Once again, the environmentalists refused to concede any ground. They argued that the disruption of the wilderness was destroying more recreational opportunities than it was creating. Both sides quoted a 1963 report of the United States Fish and Wildlife Service, which had projected gains and losses over a fifty-year period. Hunting would be reduced, but fishing would increase.[40] Congressman Bennett argued that there would be "a net gain of 78,200 man-days of sports fishing."[41] But how long would the good fishing continue? Judging from their experience with shallow Florida lakes, the environmentalists predicted a growth of weeds that would spoil the sport within a few years. Even the Florida Game and Fresh Water Fish Commission, which had previously supported the canal, reversed its position. In a report of November 1969, the commission concluded that "the previously assumed benefits from fishing and hunting will not be realized throughout the project life of the Florida Barge Canal."[42]

Now convinced that the whole scheme ought to be scrapped, a group of scientists and other conservationists organized the Florida Defenders of the Environment in July 1969. Asserting that the Corps of Engineers had never made an adequate study of the project's ecological impact, the defenders began their own intensive investigation. Before this was completed, the group enlisted the help of the Environmental Defense Fund, a national group of lawyers and scientists. In September 1969 the Defense Fund applied to the federal district court in Washington for an injunction requiring the corps to halt construction of the canal until the project's social costs and benefits could be determined.[43] In January 1970 the *Reader's Digest* gave the cause a boost with an article entitled "Rape on the Oklawaha."[44]

The Florida Defenders of the Environment published their findings in March 1970. Their scientists warned that even a shallow canal might pollute the aquifer because of the porosity of the underlying rock structure. Both the surface water and the aquifer would be threatened by oil spills and other leakage from the barges and from the washoff of herbicides, pesticides, fertilizers, and the wastes that would accompany industrial and residential development along the canal route. The Oklawaha region, the only large wild area that still supported "the full spectrum" of plant and animal life native to north-central Florida, would be ruined. The artificial lakes backed up by the dams would quickly suffer overenrichment and invasion by weeds, ruining them for fishing and boating. Quite apart from these environmental factors, the report contended that an impartial study would condemn the project on economic grounds. On the basis of these findings, the Defenders of the Environment recommended an immediate halt to federal and state expenditures for the barge canal, a rescinding of the congressional authorization of 1942, reservation of lands acquired for the right-of-way for recreational

Crusher-crawler at work. In constructing Rodman Reservoir the Army Corps of Engineers leveled a forest area with this tanklike machine, denounced as a "tree killer" by the environmentalists. Environmental Information Center.

use, dedication of at least part of the Oklawaha River to the federal "wild and scenic rivers" system, draining of the Rodman Reservoir, and restoration of the Oklawaha to its free-flowing condition.[45]

Despite the fervor of their campaign, the environmentalists probably could not have succeeded if the corps had been able to push the canal project through as rapidly as planned. But a succession of events slowed the pace of construction. The first blows resulted from the Vietnam War. Hard-pressed to find needed dollars, President Johnson began to shave dispensable items in his budgets. For fiscal 1968 Florida officials asked $20 million for the canal and were allocated only $11.4 million. For 1969 the state asked $11 million, but this was cut to $4.6 million. Protesting to the House Committee on Public Works, Congressman Sikes said, "I find no other project of major significance before you which has been so drastically cut back in its construction as the Cross-Florida Barge Canal."[46] L.C. Ringhaver, chairman of the Canal Authority, accused the president of "wanton disregard" of the canal's importance to national defense.[47]

But at least Lyndon Johnson was a Democrat. The canal boosters had to deal with a much stickier situation when Claude Kirk became governor in 1967 and Richard Nixon president in 1969. Both were ambitious Republican politicians, aware of the strength of the environmental movement. Why should either of them feel committed to an expensive and controversial project associated with the names of Franklin Roosevelt, John Kennedy, and Lyndon Johnson? For some months Kirk and Nixon bided their time. Kirk went along with the Democrats of the Florida cabinet in asking the federal government for construction money, and Nixon included $6 million for the canal in his first budget, more than Johnson's 1969 request but much less than the $17.5 million program proposed by the Corps of Engineers.[48]

In January 1970, 162 environmental scientists from across the nation appealed to the president to suspend the project until an environmental study could be made. Nixon referred the request to his Council on Environmental Quality, recently appointed and eager for business. Could this agency review projects already approved by Congress? Russell Train, its chairman, said yes.[49]

Kirk was also tilting away from the canal. In May 1970 he sent word to the House Public Works Appropriations Subcommittee that he was withholding endorsement pending completion of the announced environmental studies. But other Florida officials argued that construction should continue. Congressman Bennett ridiculed the nature lovers. "I am a Florida man," he told the committee, "and I must say a lot of the Cross-Florida Barge Canal goes through what we call scrub oak and pine flats. This is not exactly even a deer's idea of the first Eden and so it is not all quite as glorious as some people would have us think."[50] Snubbing the environmentalists, the House Appropriations Committee approved $6 million for the barge canal and stipulated that construction should continue without waiting for the results of further study.[51]

In June, Secretary of the Interior Hickel asked the secretary of the army to halt construction for fifteen months to permit a detailed study of the canal's effects on the regional ecology.[52] The army secretary promised to study the suggestion, but the corps continued to dig. Hickel did not carry much weight because he had recently antagonized the president by defending student protests against the Vietnam War; in November he was fired.

During the fall of 1970 both Governor Kirk and President Nixon handled the hot issue with long tongs. Running for reelection against Reubin Askew, an opponent of the canal, Kirk avoided taking a strong stand either for or against it. Nixon also played a cautious game. Visiting Florida during the campaign, Nixon is reported to have pointed out signs reading "Stop the Barge Canal." "Governor," said the president, "there is opposition to your canal." To which Kirk replied: "No, Mr. President, not my canal, *your* canal."[53]

Despite Askew's victory, the procanal forces were still formidable. Randolph Hodges, head of the Florida Department of Natural Resources, cooperated with Congressman Bennett in countering the environmentalist arguments, and Dr. Robert Vernon, the state geologist, was quoted as saying that the canal could not hurt the state's water supply and would improve, rather than injure, the environment. The Canal Authority was reputed to be spending $1,500 a month on publicizing the canal project.[54]

Early in 1971 the environmentalists scored two spectacular victories. The first came on 15 January when U.S. District Court Judge Barrington Parker issued a preliminary injunction ordering the Corps of Engineers to suspend construction of the canal. The judge was acting, he said, because irreparable injury might occur to Florida's swamps and to the Oklawaha River while the court was holding hearings on a permanent injuction.[55] On 19 January President Nixon ordered a halt to the project "to prevent potentially serious environmental damage." He was doing this, not because of the court order, but because his own Council on Environmental Quality had found that the project "could endanger the unique wildlife of the

Construction of the Cross-Florida Barge Canal, 1964–71. Environmentalists deplored
the destruction of the lower Oklawaha River Valley and the construction of the shallow
Rodman Reservoir, likely to be choked with weeds. SPA.

area and destroy this region of unusual and unique natural beauty." Nixon declared that his action would "prevent a past mistake from causing permanent damage."[56]

The *New York Times* applauded Nixon's action as the "death of a boondoggle": "The President is apparently beginning to realize— and it is high time that Congress recognized—that the American people are becoming increasingly fed up with the expensive, boon-doggling, make-work, environmentally destructive projects that to a large degree characterize the civilian activities of the Army Corps of Engineers."[57] Two leading Florida newspapers, the *Miami Herald* and the *St. Petersburg Times*, also praised the president's decision, but other papers, especially those in northern Florida, condemned it. Congressman Bennett and other procanal politicians were pre-dictably indignant. More surprising was the reaction of Reubin Askew, the recently inaugurated governor. Although he had been arguing that work on the canal should be suspended, he was critical of the high-handed way in which Nixon had acted.[58]

Was the canal project really dead? Judge Parker had issued a temporary injunction, but the case still had to be tried on its merits. Nixon had issued an executive order, but was it valid? On 13 Febru-ary the Florida Canal Authority filed suit in the Jacksonville Federal District Court, challenging the constitutionality of the president's action. According to the agency's brief, neither the president nor anyone acting under his direction had any authority to override the will of Congress expressed in the project authorization and sub-sequent appropriation bills. The Canal Authority asked the court to order the corps to resume work immediately.[59] Suits brought by other parties complicated the legal situation still further. Eventually five cases were consolidated in a long trial that began in Jacksonville in July 1973.[60]

While this litigation was plodding through the courts, pro- and anticanal forces clashed over the Rodman Reservoir. The canal backers wanted to keep this intact so that construction of the canal could be speedily resumed, but the environmentalists were deter-mined to open the dam and allow the Oklawaha River to return to its natural channel. As a first step, they urged lowering the water level to save thousands of hardwood trees still standing in the upper end of the lake. To prevent this drawdown, the canal supporters rallied the boaters and fishermen who had been using what was now named "Lake Oklawaha." Both factions appealed to the federal judge, who ruled first for one side and then for the other. The corps obediently reduced the level of the reservoir for a time and then raised it again but all to no avail in preventing the steady deterioration of the lake.[61]

On 31 January 1974 Judge Harvey Johnsen made his decision. On the major point at issue, the procanal forces won a clearcut victory. The judge ruled that President Nixon's order of 19 January 1971 was invalid. Congress had authorized the barge canal and appropriated money for its construction, and only Congress could order it halted. However, the judge ruled that the Corps of Engineers could not resume the project without making the environmental impact study required by recent laws. He ordered the Office of Management and Budget to release immediately the $150,000 that Congress had appropriated for this purpose in 1972 and directed the corps to carry through this study within the next six months. He issued a permanent injunction against further work on the canal until Congress had received this and decided whether to resume funding the canal.[62]

Judge Johnsen's decision thus left it up to the Corps of Engineers and Congress to decide the future of the canal project. The environmentalists were unhappy because the corps could be expected to minimize the ecological damage and Congress to continue a project, one-third completed, for which some $74 million had already been spent. In reality, however, prospects for the environmentalists were not all that bad. Despite his suspicion of Nixon's motives, Governor Askew was clearly opposed to the canal. This did not mean that all Florida officials followed his lead. Under the Florida constitution, the principal state officers were separately elected, and some of them continued to support the project. But in August 1972 the cabinet voted to withdraw official support until an environmental impact study, new benefit-to-cost estimates, and a new evaluation of recreation factors had been made.[63]

In August 1976 the Corps of Engineers released a draft environmental impact statement and an economic restudy of the project. The corps now estimated that it would cost $370 million to complete the canal. Calculating the rate of interest at 2⅞ percent, the rate specified by law in 1964 when the project was authorized, the corps estimated the benefit-to-cost ratio at 1.28 to 1. The draft report did not attempt to place a dollar value on the environmental costs of the canal, but did include a $15 million item for applying a seal of grout on one section to prevent contamination of the Floridan Aquifer. The report minimized the danger of spillage from noxious substances. It admitted that construction of the reservoirs would be harmful to "dry habitat species," but claimed that it would be beneficial to "freshwater associated species."[64]

State officials subjected the Army Corps's reports to rigorous scrutiny. Jay Landers, secretary of the Department of Environmental Regulation, disputed the corps's findings in a letter to the State Clearing House,[65] and the Division of State Planning issued a scathing report in which it criticized not only the unrealistic 2⅞ percent interest rate but the corps's alleged overestimate of benefits and underestimate of costs. The division found that the canal would very seriously damage the environment. In the parts already built the canal water did not meet state quality standards. If completed, the canal would cut through a portion of the Floridan Aquifer, and approximately 40 million gallons of water a day would enter and leave the aquifer. The corps's plan to line a critical portion of the canal would be very expensive and might not work. Canal water polluted from oil or chemical spills might enter the aquifer. Through evaporation the canal and its reservoirs would consume some 50 to 75 million gallons of fresh water a day, thus diverting it from other uses. "It is the conclusion of the Division of State Planning," the report said, "that the Canal should not be completed, and that the project be deauthorized."[66]

A decisive showdown came on 17 December 1976 when the Florida cabinet wound up a two-day meeting on the subject. Governor Askew presided over raucous public sessions for over nineteen hours. Many businessmen and labor leaders wearing "I Support the Canal" buttons were there, and two former governors, Bryant and Burns, and Congressman William Chappell argued that the canal would bring great economic benefits to the state. But Marjorie Carr, president of the Florida Defenders of the Environment, and Hal Scott, president of the Florida Audubon Society, led a determined company of people wearing "Stop the Canal" buttons. The Army Corps had tried to make the project more acceptable by reducing the depth of the canal and rerouting it away from the Oklawaha River, but the environmentalists were in no mood to compromise. When it was over, the cabinet voted six to one to withdraw state support from the project. The only dissenter was Commissioner of Agriculture Doyle Conner. The cabinet gave further joy to the environmentalists by authorizing the Department of Natural Resources to make plans for restoring the Oklawaha River to its natural channel, designating it a "wild and scenic river," transferring a portion of it to Ocala National Forest, and reimbursing the counties for money spent to acquire land for the canal.[67]

Despite this seemingly lethal blow, the project was not completely dead so long as the congressional authorization remained on the books. Nor could any step be taken to restore the Oklawaha

River unless state and federal agencies could agree on a plan of action. President Jimmy Carter, both a conservationist and a foe of pork-barrel public works, advocated termination of the project in a 1977 environmental message to Congress, and a planning study ordered by the Department of the Army recommended draining the Rodman Reservoir, tearing down existing dams, and filling in three locks, thus effecting a partial restoration of the river. During 1978 Congress considered a bill cosponsored by the two Florida senators, Lawton Chiles and Richard Stone, that would deauthorize the canal project and authorize expansion of the boundaries of the Ocala National Forest to include about 60 percent of the canal route. The Oklawaha would be designated a "wild and scenic river." Strongly approved by the Carter administration and by Governor Askew, the Chiles-Stone bill passed the Senate but was ambushed in the House by three veteran canal boosters—Charles Bennett of Jacksonville, Bill Chappell of Ocala, and Robert Sikes of Crestview, in the Panhandle.[68] Thus the 150-year old canal scheme clung to life by a narrow thread.

During the years in which Gainesville environmentalists had been battling the canal, Miami-based groups had mobilized to meet a series of local threats. Between 1950 and 1960 Dade County's population had almost doubled, and speculators were eager to develop the region south of the city, particularly the Biscayne Bay waterfront and the offshore islands. In the absence of effective public planning there was danger of major ecological damage: the water of the bay, already tainted, might be further polluted; the mangrove swamps might be cut down; the marine life might be destroyed. Particularly threatening was the Seadade plan of 1962, under which investors proposed to develop a deep-water port and oil refinery. First gaining the attention of the local newspapers and politicians, the environmentalists then won over Governor Kirk, Congressman Dante Fascell, and Secretary of the Interior Stewart Udall. A survey ordered by the Interior Department supported the contentions of the environmentalists. In 1968 Congress responded by passing the Biscayne National Monument Act, which established a preserve of 96,000 acres where offshore development was prohibited.[69]

Although the new law did not cover the mainland, rising concern for the environment compelled the Florida Power and Light Company to make major modifications to reduce the danger of thermal pollution from a nuclear power plant at Turkey Point. In another significant victory the environmentalists forced drastic modification of a development that would have crowded apartment houses and commercial buildings onto two miles of bayfront in a new town called Saga Bay.[70]

Nature lovers were especially vigilant against threats to Everglades National Park. Throughout the 1960s they had kept the pressure on state and federal governments to guarantee an adequate southward flow of water. Looking with suspicion on new drainage canals close to the park borders, they particularly condemned C–111, built from a point below Homestead to Barnes Sound. Although only seven miles long, C–111 threatened the ecology of the eastern part of the park by diverting the natural flow of water and risking a saltwater backflow during dry seasons. Environmentalists charged that in overriding the objections of the Park Service, the Corps of Engineers had dug the canal not just to prevent floods but to serve the transportation needs of the Aerojet-General Company, a defense contractor with political influence.[71] The National Audubon Society and other groups applied for a federal court injunction to prevent removal of the earthen plug that would open the canal to the sea, and the Flood Control District agreed to leave the plug in place until the issue was resolved.[72] Although the plug was never removed, environmentalists complained that it leaked water in both directions. They argued that the ditch should be filled and that construction should be stopped on other South Dade canals as well.[73]

A more serious threat to the park was now taking shape. On 2 November 1967 the commissions of Dade and Collier counties agreed to a plan under which 12 square miles in Dade and 26 square miles in Collier would be designated as the site for a new airport to be built by the Dade County Port Authority. This would be 45 miles from Miami, but a search committee claimed that no nearer site was feasible because so much land was under the control of the Everglades National Park and the state water conservation areas.[74] The Dade County Port Authority boasted that this would be the world's biggest airport. The planes of the future—jets, jumbo jets, and supersonic transports—would arrive and depart every thirty seconds. The wide expanses of the Everglades would shield the Gold Coast cities from the sonic booms. The authority claimed that the existing airport was already too small: it had a rated capacity of only 437,000 takeoffs and landings a year, but in 1968 there were 445,000 flights, about one-quarter of them for the training of pilots. By 1975 about 750,000 flights could be expected. The first benefit from the new jetport would be to relieve the old airport of training flights.[75]

At first there was little fear that the planned jetport might harm the environment. When the Port Authority revealed its preliminary plans, officials of the Flood Control District, the state Game and Fresh Water Fish Commission, and Everglades National Park raised no serious objections.[76] Yet, from the conservationist point of view, a worse site could scarcely have been chosen. The new facility would be located in the Big Cypress Swamp, scarcely six miles from Everglades National Park. Noise from the jets would shatter the stillness, frightening the wildlife. Exhaust fumes from the great machines would pollute the air. Still more injurious would be the industrial and commercial complexes that could be expected to spring up in the vicinity. Any extensive development of the Big Cypress region threatened to mutilate one of the park's primary water sources. Not

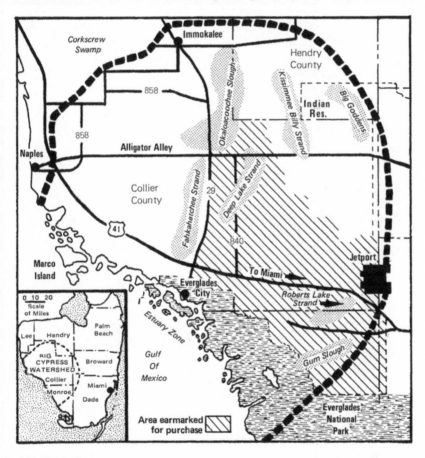

Big Cypress Swamp and proposed jetport. Environmentalists' concern over the proposed jetport helped persuade Congress to establish the Big Cypress National Preserve in 1974. Map by Michael Upham.

only would it reduce the vital southward flow, but it would pollute the water with sewage, pesticides, and industrial wastes.

Moving swiftly to acquire the needed land by sale and condemnation, the Port Authority started construction of the first runway before the environmentalists could organize an effective opposition. On 18 September 1968 various dignitaries, including a colorfully garbed Miccosukee Indian chief, gathered for a ceremonial groundbreaking "at an Everglades site hard by the end of the world," as a *Miami Herald* reporter described it.[77]

One of the first protests came from Robert Padrick, chairman of the Flood Control District's governing board. Attending a state road department meeting on 31 October 1968, Padrick learned that a planned extension of Interstate 75 from Tampa to Miami would be routed through the middle of the new jetport and then directly east through Conservation Area 3. In a letter sent out to more than a hundred "conservation-minded citizens," Padrick warned that in order to save six minutes time on the trip from the airport to Miami, the state was proposing to build "a sort of Chinese Wall, which will destroy the many values for which the area has been preserved."[78] In response to Padrick's warning a group of conservationist leaders including Nat Reed from the governor's office met with the FCD governing board in December. The Port Authority tried to quiet the growing protest by a public hearing in February 1969, but the environmentalists went away even more alarmed.[79]

Meanwhile, friends of Everglades National Park in other parts of the country had been alerted by a strong article written by Anthony Wayne Smith, president of the National Parks and Conservation Association (NPCA) and published in the January 1969 issue of the association's magazine. Two months later representatives of twenty-one national conservation groups, the United Automobile Workers, and the United Steel Workers met in the NPCA board room to organize a common front called the Everglades Coalition. The coalition promptly appealed to U.S. Secretary of Transportation John Volpe to withdraw federal support from the jetport.[80]

The Nixon administration was involved in the controversy because the Department of Transportation had granted the Port Authority $500,000 to build a runway for training flights and $200,000 to plan an access road to Miami. Briefed on the issue during a trip to South Florida in March 1969, Secretary of the Interior Walter Hickel wrote to Secretary Volpe expressing concern for the safety of the national park and asking what environmental studies had been made.[81]

In June opponents and supporters of the project testified at a

hearing of the Senate Interior Committee. Russell Train, undersec-
retary of the interior, promised to oppose the jetport if an environmental study then under way concluded that it would damage the
park. Nat Reed accused the Dade authorities of not keeping the state
government informed: "Before we knew it, that field was there."
Spokesmen for the National Audubon Society and the Sierra Club
warned that the park was in danger of "utter destruction." This was
denied by Nat Ratner of the West Dade Improvement Association
and Riley Miles of the Water Users Association of Florida, who testified that the site had been carefully chosen to minimize ecological
damage.[82]

During subsequent months backers of the jetport injured their
cause by brash statements. Alan C. Stewart, director of the Port Authority, dismissed the environmentalists as "butterfly chasers" and
sneered at the endangered birds as "yellow-bellied sapsuckers." He
boasted that "a new city is going to rise up in the middle of Florida.
You are going to have one whether you like it or not." Richard H.
Judy, Stewart's deputy, argued that the jetport would serve as a buffer between the park and developments that must be expected in
any case. "Big Cypress Swamp," he said, "is just typical south
Florida real estate. It's private property; eventually it's going to be
put to human use." Irritated by such talk, Sen. Gaylord Nelson of
Wisconsin came down strongly on the other side. "Either we stop
the jetport at the present site," Nelson said, "or we publicly admit
that we are going to destroy the Park." To stop it "would cause a hell
of an uproar, but it can be done." In an attempt to damp down the
controversy, the Dade County Commission announced that it was
employing a consulting firm headed by former Secretary of the
Interior Udall to study ways of minimizing airport damage to
Everglades National Park and to consider the possibility of other
sites.[83]

Before the Udall study was ready the jetport scheme had suffered
a succession of body blows. At the end of August the newspapers reported that an environmental study made by Dr. Luna Leopold of
the U.S. Geological Survey would be severely critical of the project.
This news jolted Governor Kirk out of his neutral posture. On 4 September he announced that he would try to have the jetport moved to
another site. Praising Kirk in an editorial entitled "A Jetless
Everglades," the *New York Times* pointed out that one long runway
had already been built and a second was under construction. "It is
the eleventh hour but not yet a lost cause." On 10 September Kirk
met in Washington with Hickel and Volpe. The three Republicans
tried to find safe middle ground by approving the new airstrip for

training flights but at the same time promising to protect Everglades National Park from harm.[84]

The Leopold report, made public 17 September, provided the environmentalists with all the ammunition they could have hoped for. "Development of the proposed jetport and its attendant facilities," the report concluded, "will lead to land drainage and development for agriculture, industry, housing, transportation, and services in the Big Cypress Swamp which will inexorably destroy the South Florida ecosystem and thus Everglades National Park." Even the training strip was "intolerable," not so much because of the training flights themselves as because of the pressure they would create for industrial development. Secretary of the Interior Hickel immediately announced that he fully expected the jetport to be relocated.[85]

Two other environmental reports followed the Leopold study. The first, made public 18 September, was the work of sixty scientists working under a grant from the National Academy of Science. It emphasized the need for regional planning and for reserving the whole Big Cypress Swamp as a water conservation area. Unless rigorous measures were taken to prevent development of the surrounding region, the scientists did not favor even a training field on the proposed site.[86] The Udall report outlined means by which the jetport might be built without environmental injury, but, released in December, it was too late to have much influence.[87]

The jetport issue had involved a power struggle between Volpe, who originally favored the project, and Hickel, who opposed it. In this situation everything depended on the White House, where a crucial role was apparently played by John Ehrlichmann, President Nixon's number 2 aide, who had been involved in land use cases as a Seattle lawyer.[88] On 25 November Volpe announced that he would approve of the runway for a one-year trial period but only with stringent safeguards for the park.[89] On 15 January 1970 representatives of the Interior Department, the Transportation Department, the state of Florida, the Dade County Port Authority, and Dade County signed a formal agreement permitting the completed runway to be used for training flights, but under strict environmental safeguards to be monitored by the federal agencies. If the flights were injuring the park or neighboring communities, the federal government might terminate them on ninety days' notice. The agreement recognized the need for a regional airport to be completed within ten years. The Port Authority was to begin an immediate search for an alternate site, and the federal government promised to provide funds for the new facility. When the new site was acquired, priority was to be given to building training facilities so that use of the Big Cypress field could be halted. Safeguards on the interim use of Big Cypress included a prohibition on flights at less than 5,000 feet above the park, culverts of sufficient size to maintain the historic water flow, and prohibition on fueling planes and on use of detergents and pesticides without the federal government's written consent. The agreement was to run for three years but might be renewed by mutual consent.[90]

Attorney Daniel Paul, who had been advising the National Audubon Society, called the agreement "a complete victory" for the conservationists. Philip Wylie, popular novelist and critic, exulted that "against all odds, the birds have won." He credited the victory to the new national mood. "It has been said that every Congressman has become an ecologist overnight, though few could have defined the word a year ago."[91]

But where in South Florida could such a huge airport be built without danger to the environment? In July 1972 a site selection committee recommended a 50-square-mile tract in northwestern Dade County near the Broward County line. But opposition soon developed. Residents in nearby communities objected to the anticipated noise. After some delay the Dade County authorities approved the recommendation and applied to the Federal Aviation Authority for a $115 million grant to buy the land and build a training runway. When the federal authorities balked, arguing that this was too much to pay to replace facilities that had cost the local authorities only $15 million, Dade County reduced the size of the proposed site to 23 square miles and cut its request to $69.26 million.[92]

The plan continued to encounter delays. Householders kept up their protests, and the FCD raised serious questions about the impact of the project on the adjoining conservation areas. Nature lovers protested that planes landing and taking off from this site would fly close to the nesting places of forty Florida Everglades kites—about 25 percent of the world population of this rare bird. The Federal Aviation Authority promised to restudy the location. In their campaign the environmentalists were aided by changing trends during the 1970s. Not only was the country becoming less tolerant of noise and air pollution, but plane travel was not expanding as rapidly as had been predicted. The changed situation was reflected at the Big Cypress training site. During 1972 there were 100,000 training flights; by 1975 they had fallen to 8,100 flights. Not only were fewer pilots being trained, but soaring fuel costs had forced the airlines to make increasing use of flight simulators. So lightly used was the Big Cypress field that some environmentalists were now suggesting that it might be less harmful to allow the training flights to continue there than to start bulldozing a new site.[93]

But the jetport idea was far from dead. In the late 1970s a new wave of tourism and a booming real estate market again crowded the older airports. In July 1977 strong pressure from businessmen induced the South Florida Regional Planning Council to drop its opposition to the northwestern Dade site. A prominent banker warned that South Florida might never be able to acquire enough land for a regional airport unless it acted promptly. Even if the jetport were not immediately built, it would be better to buy the land and "bank" it for future needs.[94] But opinion continued to be strongly divided. For the present the expansion of existing facilities at Miami International and Fort Lauderdale – Hollywood received priority, while for the more distant future some planners were arguing for a site farther north, perhaps in southwestern Palm Beach County, where it could serve all of South Florida.

The Florida environmentalist movement came of age in 1970 and 1971 with the successful campaigns to halt construction of the cross-Florida barge canal and the Big Cypress jetport. In both fights the state groups had the great advantage of alliance with leaders in the national conservation movement and with prominent Washington politicians. Because of the danger to the Oklawaha River and Everglades National Park, regions highly cherished by nature lovers, this outside support was readily mobilized. The emotional appeals of the preservationists were bolstered, moreover, by the scientific data supplied by ecologists and economists. The rigorous findings of the state Game and Fresh Water Fish Commission, the Department of Environmental Regulation, and the Division of State Planning weighed heavily in the Florida cabinet's turnabout on the barge canal, and the Leopold report was probably decisive in the Nixon administration's rejection of the Big Cypress airport.

It remained to be seen, however, how well the Florida environmentalists would do when they took up less glamorous questions of land use, water management, and water quality. For these emerging issues were no less important to the future of the state.

# 10 Florida Takes the Lead

I f governments were to be "judged solely on their response to the
environmental crisis," said Governor Askew in April 1973, "I'm
confident Florida would walk away with the honors. We passed last
year a program of environmental land and water use planning that
has rightly been called the best in the country, and rightly selected
as a model for the nation."[1]

The environmental movement that had been gathering force in
the late 1960s and early 1970s reached its high point in the legislative
session of 1972, when four key bills, strongly backed by the governor, were passed. The new laws not only laid down important
principles for regulating land development and protecting water resources but also created new agencies. In subsequent legislative sessions, the environmentalists had to fight to defend their gains and to
pass additional legislation.

Most of the new laws dealt with the protection of the state's water
resources. Why was there such a sudden sense of urgency about this
issue? For most of Florida's history the principal water problem had
been how to get rid of it. Hurricanes and tropical storms brought severe flooding, and even in normal years the land was so flat that vast
areas were too swampy to be used without drainage. The state had an
average annual rainfall of 53 inches. In the hot sun most of this water
evaporated or was utilized by trees and plants, but enough seeped
through the sandy soil into the limestone below to maintain a large
underground flow. Whatever the need might be—household use,
sprinkling lawns and golf courses, irrigating crops, watering cattle,
processing minerals—it could be met by drilling another well. For
decades these holes in the earth had yielded a copious supply, but
during the 1960s and 1970s there were warning signs that the underground reservoirs were being overdrawn.

Consider, for example, the frightening experience of two motorists whose cars dropped out of sight into a great hole near Lakeland that opened so suddenly that the drivers could not avoid it. Sinkholes were nothing new in this part of the state, but this was one of fifteen new ones that appeared between December 1966 and April 1967, indicating a serious drop in the water table.[2] Robert Vernon, the state geologist, reported that the underground level in this region of citrus groves, orange juice processing plants, and phosphate mines had dropped about 55 feet since 1920. Asked what the situation would be in the year 2000, Vernon replied, "It frankly scares the hell out of me."[3]

The Gulf cities experienced serious water shortages. In July 1972 after several months of dry weather the Pinellas County commission declared a moratorium on new building permits in St. Petersburg. Salt water was intruding into the municipal wells, and the city was searching for new well sites farther from the sea.[4] Tampa was unusual among Florida cities in that it did not depend on wells but on water pumped from the Hillsborough River, yet it too was suffering from severe shortages in 1972. The river level was low, and the facilities for pumping and treating the water were inadequate. Anticipating a 50 percent increase in water needs over the next twenty years, the Tampa authorities were looking for new sources.[5]

But if Central Florida's water shortages were serious, those of the southeast coast were even more so. In 1970–71 the region suffered its worst drought in forty years. From July 1970 through June 1971 it received only 34.6 inches of rain—the smallest amount ever recorded for any twelve-month period. The level of Lake Okeechobee dropped to an unprecedented 10.3 feet.[6] In May 1971 the municipal authorities in Palm Beach and West Palm Beach threatened to fine or jail those who ignored new water conservation ordinances. Miami and Fort Lauderdale reduced the quantity of water pumped from the municipal wells by 25 percent and appealed to the citizens to avoid waste. To relieve the situation the Flood Control District released Lake Okeechobee water down the canals but warned that this would have to stop if the lake level continued to drop.[7] Meanwhile fires in the Everglades raged through 750,000 acres of dry sawgrass and cypress, destroying the muckland and harming the wildlife.[8]

News of the water shortages was all the more alarming because of Florida's runaway growth. Since 1920 the state had been doubling in population every twenty-two years, almost three times as fast as the nation as a whole. And the seven counties of southern Florida were growing fastest of all, doubling in population every fourteen years during the 1950s and 1960s. In December 1971 a Federal Commission on Population Growth and the American Future predicted that for the rest of the century southeastern Florida would grow faster than any other area in the United States, jumping from 2.2 million in 1970 to 5.6 million in 2000. Other rapidly growing areas would be Orlando and Tampa– St. Petersburg.[9]

Governor Askew was keenly aware of the perils of the situation. Arthur Marshall, who preached the need of environmental repentance with the fervor of an Old Testament prophet, appeared before the governor and cabinet in April 1971 to warn that South Florida's water supply was deteriorating in quality. He urged such measures as reflooding the Kissimmee Valley, protecting the Big Cypress, and filling in unnecessary canals.[10] Robert Padrick, chairman of the South Florida Flood Control governing board, Jay Landers, a young lawyer who briefed the governor on natural resource problems, and Joel Kuperberg, newly appointed executive director of the Internal Improvement Fund, exchanged ideas on the situation and suggested that the governor sponsor a conference of experts to consider South Florida's water problems. Their plan called for a program of workshops on the model of the American Assembly. To serve as chairman, they recruited John DeGrove of Florida Atlantic University, who had been active in the American Assembly movement.[11]

In September 1971 this carefully prepared Governor's Conference on Water Management in South Florida convened at Bal Harbor. The 150 participants constituted a *Who's Who* among Florida environmentalists and water managers. Among them were people from the Audubon Society, Conservation 70s, the Flood Control District, the Army Corps of Engineers, Everglades National Park, state regulatory agencies, the legislature, county commissions, and business groups. In his opening address Governor Askew pointed out that cities, farms, and the Everglades National Park were engaged in fierce competition for Lake Okeechobee's dwindling supply of water. Florida's current population was expected to double before the year 2000. Should a limit be placed on population growth in South Florida? Who should manage the natural resources of the region, and what powers should be granted to them?

Taking an even more serious view of the situation, the conferees declared: "There is a water crisis in South Florida today. This crisis has long-range aspects. Every major water area in the South Florida basin, Everglades National Park, the conservation areas, Lake Okeechobee and the Kissimmee Valley is steadily deteriorating in quality from a variety of polluting sources.... The quantity of water, though potentially adequate for today's demand, cannot now be

Fire raging in the Big Cypress Swamp, May 1967. Environmental Information Center.

managed effectively over wet/dry cycles to assure a minimum adequate supply in extended drought periods."[12]

The conference agreed on a long list of recommendations, many of them involving a change in historic Florida practices: "no further draining of wetlands for any purpose"; reflooding the Kissimmee Valley and unused agricultural land; allowing a maximum high-level mark of 17.5 feet in Lake Okeechobee; purchase or zoning of lands to protect water recharge areas; filling in certain South Dade canals; and a state drilling code to regulate wells. But the most significant resolutions were those on planning. "For an adequate long range water supply, the State must have an enforceable comprehensive land and water use plan," a plan designed "to limit increases in population and machines" to a level that would insure "a quality environment."[13]

Acting in the spirit of these recommendations, Governor Askew appointed a fifteen-member task force to draft an environmental program for the next session of the legislature. John DeGrove was chairman of this group and Arthur Marshall and State Senator Robert Graham of Miami Lakes were influential members.[14] Transmitting their proposals to the legislature, Governor Askew said: "The *economy* of government planning is obvious when you consider that it might have kept us from spending $50 million ruining the Kissimmee River in the name of flood control...or $13 million endangering the Everglades in the name of jet travel...or $75 million on a barge canal which is in considerable doubt."[15]

Graham led the environmentalist fight in the senate while Speaker Richard Pettigrew of Miami and Jack Shreve of Merritt Island guided the bills through the house. Conservation groups lobbied vigorously for the governor's program, while some, but not all, of the large developers opposed it. Still suspicious of granting too much power to state agencies, the legislature did not go as far as the task force recommended.[16] Nevertheless, four bills passed, and Speaker Pettigrew called it "the best session for the environment in the history of the legislature."[17]

The Florida Water Resources Act of 1972 affirmed a policy of conserving and controlling the waters of the state "to realize their full beneficial use." General responsibility was vested in the Department of Natural Resources (DNR). Among other duties the DNR was directed to formulate a state water use plan that would inventory water resources and formulate measures for maintaining an adequate supply, preventing waste, preserving and improving water quality, and controlling the water for environmental protection, drainage, flood control, and water storage. The water use plan was to be developed in coordination with a water quality standards system that the Department of Pollution Control would establish. The water use plan and the water quality standard system would together constitute "the Florida water plan." The DNR was given extensive regulatory powers, but it was authorized to delegate many of these to regional agencies. The law provided for the establishment of five water management districts but left the determination of their boundaries to future legislatures. Among the most important powers to be exercised by the DNR and the districts was that of issuing permits for all water users except individual householders. Permits were to be issued for specific quantities, which had to be periodically renewed and might be reduced in times of scarcity.[18]

Equally important was the Florida Environmental Land and Water Management Act of 1972, the so-called ELMS Act. "To insure a water management system that will reverse the deterioration of water quality and provide optimum utilization of our limited water resources, and to facilitate orderly and well planned development," the legislature declared it necessary for the state to establish policies to guide and coordinate local decisions relating to growth and development. The act provided two major tools for this purpose. One provided that the governor and cabinet might designate "areas of critical state concern," where special regulations concerning land development must be formulated by collaborative action between local and state agencies. The other granted local and state agencies power to prohibit or regulate "developments of regional impact" that might have "a substantial impact upon the health, safety or welfare of citizens of more than one county." As a concession to get the bill passed, its backers accepted an amendment requiring final approval of the cabinet's regulations on development by the 1973 legislature. Despite this postponement Governor Askew praised the law as moving Florida "further along the road to land control" than any other large state.[19]

The 1972 legislature passed two other significant measures recommended by the task force. The State Comprehensive Planning Act undertook to "provide long-range guidance of the orderly social, economic, and physical growth of the state." The governor was designated as chief planning officer for the state, and a Division of State Planning within the Department of Administration was created to carry out these responsibilities. The Land Conservation Act authorized, subject to a referendum, a $240 million bond issue to finance state purchase of environmentally endangered lands.[20] In

November 1972 the voters approved the bond issue by more than a two-to-one-margin.[21]

In the 1973 session the governor encountered more resistance. He called for "protection by law of our wetland areas, both coastal and inland," but a bill for this purpose was killed in the senate Natural Resources and Conservation Committee after thirty-nine spokesmen for developers and farmers appeared to oppose it.[22] But the legislature did pass bills for the protection of the Big Cypress Swamp and clarifying certain parts of the 1972 environmental laws.

In 1975 the governor wrestled with the legislature over control of environmental policy. Responding to the complaints of developers who had to seek permits from a variety of local and state authorities, Senate President Dempsey Barron and House Speaker Don Tucker attempted to consolidate all the environmental agencies into a greatly enlarged Department of Natural Resources under cabinet control. Conservation groups opposed this "superagency" plan as an attempt to suppress certain independent bureaus like the Pollution Control Board, and the governor condemned it as an attempt to dilute his authority. The deadlock was broken by a compromise under which the disputed powers were divided between two agencies, a reorganized Department of Natural Resources (DNR), under cabinet control, and a new Department of Environmental Regulation (DER), directly controlled by the governor.[23]

The Environmental Reorganization Act of 1975 abolished the Trustees of the Internal Improvement Fund and transferred their functions to the Department of Natural Resources with final authority retained by the governor and cabinet. The DNR was to manage state-owned lands and parks and to carry on such other functions as boat registration, aquatic plant research, and beach restoration. The new Department of Environmental Regulation took over responsibilities previously exercised by the Pollution Control Board and a number of other agencies. It was authorized to establish environmental standards, apply these through the issuance of permits, and take enforcement action against violators. To speed up the permitting process, five environmental districts, paralleling the water management districts, were established with power to make most decisions. The 1975 law corrected one serious flaw in earlier water policy. Problems of water quantity had been the responsibility of the old Department of Natural Resources; the prevention of pollution had been the duty of the Board of Pollution Control; the establishment of drinking water standards had been the business of the Department of Health and Rehabilitative Services. Now these functions all passed to the new Department of Environmental Regulation, as did the supervision of the five water management districts and the preparation of the state water plan.[24]

For four years after the passage of the Water Resources Act of 1972 not much was done toward organizing the new water management districts. Two problems caused difficulty—the drawing of district boundary lines and the granting of taxing powers. Cutting loose from the hoary tradition that such boundary lines should follow county lines, the 1972 law had specified that they should "follow as nearly as practicable the natural river basin boundaries of the state." But local jealousies delayed the final implementation of the law for several years. Collier County's suspicion of the Gold Coast led the legislature to give tentative approval to a sixth district, the Gulf and Ridge, but this idea was abandoned in 1976 when the district boundaries were finally defined. To reassure the west coast, the legislature divided the South Florida Water Management District into two subdistricts, the Big Cypress Basin and the Okeechobee Basin, and specified that taxes levied in each should be used largely for the benefit of that area. On the other hand, the large eastern counties, which had complained of underrepresentation in the Flood Control District, were assured of at least four seats on the ten-man board of the new Water Management District. The governor was to appoint at least two persons from Dade County and one each from Broward and Palm Beach counties.[25]

The tax problem was also settled in 1976 when the voters ratified a constitutional amendment giving each water management district the power to impose an ad valorem tax, not to exceed one mill per thousand dollars, on all real property.[26] This power, already exercised by the old Central and Southern Florida Flood Control District and the Southwest Florida Water Management District, was extended to the new districts despite recurrent complaints that agricultural interests were favored and city dwellers penalized.

The new districts came into official existence 1 January 1977. The South Florida WMD was the old Flood Control District shorn of the upper St. Johns River basin in north-central Florida. It still covered the vast Kissimmee River—Lake Okeechobee—Everglades region extending from the Gulf coast to the Atlantic and northward through the southern part of Orlando. It included the Gulf coast cities of Fort Myers and Naples and the Atlantic coast cities of the Palm Beaches, Fort Lauderdale, Hollywood, and Miami. The Southwest Florida WMD covered the four river basins of west-central Florida, the Withlacoochee, Hillsborough, Peace, and upper Oklawaha. It included such major cities as Tampa, St. Petersburg, Clearwater, Sarasota, and Lakeland. The St. Johns River Basin WMD covered all of northeastern and east-central Florida, including such cities as Jacksonville, St. Augustine, Daytona Beach, and northern Orlando. The Suwannee River Basin WMD covered the Gulf coast region watered by the famous Suwannee, the Fenholloway, and other minor streams. Gainesville was its only substantial city. The Northwest Florida WMD covered the Panhandle with its important rivers—the Choctawhatchee, Apalachicola, and Ochlocknee. Pensacola, Tallahassee, and Panama City lay within its boundaries.

The Water Resources Act of 1972 had authorized the governor and cabinet to designate "areas of critical state concern," areas containing such important natural resources or historical remains that they required special protection from the developers' bulldozers and dredges. Disturbed by the cozy relationship that often existed between local governments and real estate interests, the law empowered state agencies to establish the principles that should guide the development of these critical areas and to insist on the establishment of suitable regulations.

The first "area of critical state concern" to be designated by the state cabinet was the Big Cypress Swamp. The jetport controversy had focused attention on this variegated terrain of swamps, lakes, sloughs, and hammocks lying west of the sawgrass Everglades. The Big Cypress watershed extended over 1.5 million acres, from the middle of South Florida west to the Gulf, north to Immokalee, and south to Everglades National Park. During the rainy season the region soaked up water like a giant sponge. Some of this water flowed into the northwest part of the park; some of it seeped into the shallow aquifer on which Collier County depended for its needs.

Even before the jetport scare, conservationists had begun to worry about the future of the Big Cypress. During the 1940s and 1950s lumbering operations had removed most of the timber, and after that developers had begun a high-pressure campaign to sell lots. The projected network of roads and drainage canals threatened total disruption of the natural flow of the water. Other speculators were seeking sites for oil-drilling. Existing state highways had already affected the environment. The Tamiami Trail, built during the 1920s to link Tampa and Miami, had altered watercourses in a vital area just north of Everglades National Park; still greater change had resulted from the construction of Alligator Alley, the toll road linking Naples and Fort Lauderdale. Now a superhighway was being planned, an extension of Interstate 75 from Tampa to Miami. What-

Dredging the "Tamiami Canal, 1921. In building an automobile road from Tampa to Miami it was necessary to use this 20-ton "walking dredge" to dig a drainage canal through the Big Cypress Swamp and the Everglades. It straddled the canal on its own mechanical legs and dug a cubic yard of sand with each scoop. Fishbaugh and SPA.

purchased or was already state-owned, or any balance from the $40 million fund, to the proposed federal reserve.[30]

What the *New York Times* characterized as Florida's "grand gesture" helped to get the administration bill through the national House of Representatives in October 1973, but the Senate took no action until after Nixon resigned. Then the bill rolled through with little opposition. On 23 August Senator Jackson, chairman of the Committee on Interior and Insular Affairs, presented a favorable report. Among the minor changes was one designating the region as a "national preserve," a new category intended to cover "nationally significant areas which differ from the qualities attributed to national parks and national recreation areas."[31]

Finally signed into law by President Gerald Ford on 11 October 1974, the bill authorized a federal expenditure of $116 million, contingent upon the state's contribution of $40 million. The secretary of the interior was authorized to make necessary rules regarding grazing rights, explorations for oil and minerals, and new construction within the preserve. Hunting, fishing, and trapping were to be permitted at suitable times and places, and present owners of one-family houses were allowed a right of residency and use of land up to three acres for twenty-five years after selling their land to the government. The Indians of the region were granted the right to continue their customary hunting and fishing and were granted preference in contracting for visitors' services.[32]

Although Congress had authorized a larger expenditure for the Big Cypress National Preserve than for any previous addition to the national park system, much remained to be done to safeguard the water resources. In the first place, the State of Florida and the federal government had to buy the land from its private owners. No one knew just how many there were. The initial estimate was about 35,000; later guesses were 50,000 or 60,000. A few were large-scale operators; many were petty speculators scattered across the United States and in foreign countries; others were sportsmen who had built fishing camps and hunting lodges. The Park Service would find it difficult to complete its purchase program within the six years stipulated by Congress and to keep within its $116 million authorization.[33]

But even after the Big Cypress National Preserve became a reality, it would contain only 570,000 acres out of a watershed of 1.5 million acres. As finally designated by the Florida cabinet, the area of critical state concern was 50 percent larger. Its 858,000 acres included all of the national preserve and 289,000 acres of buffer land to the west and north of it. Three regions of great ecological value—the

Okaloacoochee Slough, the Fahkahatchee Strand, and the northern part of the Ten Thousand Islands—were included. In the portions that lay outside the national preserve, the private ownership of land was permitted, but strict regulations were issued to prevent the overcrowding of sites, require restoration of vegetation, limit the size of parking lots, require methods of road construction that would not interfere with the natural flow of the water, prohibit the digging of finger canals, and prevent water discharge into the Gulf.[34] Developers denounced the restrictions as confiscatory of their property, but only the farmers had enough political clout to be exempted by the legislature.

Unfortunately state and federal efforts to protect the Big Cypress had come too late to save 121,000 acres of land in western Collier County. In the most scandalous promotion of the 1960s the Gulf American Corporation had induced an estimated 30,000 or 40,000 people to buy lots in a project called Golden Gate Estates. Since few families actually ventured to take up residence in these wide open spaces, the principal inducement to buy was the hope of making a profit on resales. When this artificial market collapsed and angry purchasers began to charge fraud, Gulf American sold out to the GAC Corporation, a conglomerate that tried to operate in a somewhat more responsible fashion. To restore credibility to the promotion, the new owners speeded up the building of about 800 miles of roads and 171 miles of canals. The environmental consequences extended over about 390 square miles of land. Regions on which water used to stand for half the year were now so thoroughly drained that trees and underbrush wilted and burned away in forest fires while white sand blew through the doors and windows of houses. In some places the groundwater level sank as much as three feet, a warning to the city of Naples because saltwater was already invading its wells near the Gulf coast.[35]

Paying a heavy price for its delay in developing land use plans, the Collier County Commission was beset with conflicting advice on what to do about the Golden Gate problem. Environmentalists urged plugging the canals to stop the runoff into the Gulf; developers called for public works to provide better water management and flood control. Among the proposed requests for federal works in 1978 was one calling for an Army Corps of Engineers study to develop a water management system to rescue the Golden Gate Estates area from the effects of overdrainage. One of the serious problems was the rapid encroachment of worthless Melaleuca trees at the expense of cypress and other valuable plant life.[36]

Environmentalists were also alarmed by schemes for development along the southwestern Gulf coast and on the neighboring islands, a region of great ecological value. In the shallow bays, tidal creeks, and mangrove swamps, minute marine life flourished, serving in turn as food for fish and water birds. Controversy centered on Marco Island with its beautiful natural beaches, good fishing, and exotic wildlife. In 1964 the Deltona Corporation announced plans for developing Marco and the surrounding region by dredging and filling the wetlands and cutting canals to provide several thousand waterfront lots. At first, all went smoothly. Deltona enjoyed an excellent reputation for respecting natural values, and state and federal agencies commended the company for planning a model community. Confident of governmental approval, Deltona resorted to the traditional method of selling its lots in advance of improvement and using the installments as a cash flow to finance its ambitious program.[37]

But the surge of environmentalism during the late 1960s and early 1970s brought condemnation for the Marco Island project. The first phase of construction had chopped up large stretches of shoreline, and the Florida Audubon Society led a campaign to save what was left. Deltona had applied for dredge-and-fill permits to develop three new sections containing 5,700 waterfront lots. According to conservationists, the proposed work would destroy mangroves along 50 miles of shoreline and would eliminate about 735 acres of shallow bay bottom. Although generally sensitive to such warnings, Governor Askew and the cabinet accepted a tempting trade-off with the company under which the state would receive 4,000 acres of Deltona-owned wilderness south of Marco Island. Final approval of the permits lay with the Army Corps of Engineers. In public hearings environmentalists urged the corps to deny them while purchasers of lots, contractors, construction workers, and Collier County boosters urged that they be granted. Governor Askew asked that the state's agreement with Deltona be respected, but such Nixon officials as Russell Train of the Environmental Protection Agency and Nathaniel Reed of the Interior Department opposed the application. In a final attempt to exert political leverage, Deltona employed Dean Burch, former chairman of the Republican National Committee, as its counsel.[38]

The engineers' decision, announced 16 April 1976, angered the company. The corps approved only one of the three requested permits, denying those for tracts in which Deltona had sold an estimated 3,700 lots and collected some $40 million in installments.

Unless the courts overruled the corps's decision, the company faced the unhappy prospect of either returning this money to the purchasers or getting their consent to an exchange of lots. Although some observers thought that Deltona had been penalized by a change of the rules in the middle of the game, environmentalists had little sympathy either for the company that had offered lots for sale before receiving the necessary permits or for the customers who had contracted to buy land that was under water.[39]

Dry cypress "swamp." This area burned a few days after this photo was taken in May 1967. Environmental Information Center.

Since curbing developments once begun involved bitter fights, environmentalists favored buying up ecologically sensitive regions before this happened. During the 1950s and 1960s officers of the National Audubon Society assumed leadership in a campaign to save the Corkscrew Swamp, a western Collier County region, where towering cypresses and other trees had escaped the lumberman's ax and where rare birds and animals lived in the marshy undergrowth. The Collier family and other large holders either sold or gave lands to the enterprise, and eventually the National Audubon Society was entrusted with the administration of a sanctuary of some 11,000 acres. Later the National Audubon Society cooperated with the Nature Conservancy and the Collier Conservancy, supported by wealthy nature lovers, in acquiring 3,608 acres of wilderness at Rookery Bay on the Gulf coast south of Naples. In 1977 the state accepted a 99-year lease of this tract to be used as an estuarine sanctuary and research center.[40]

In 1974 Joel Kuperberg resigned from his post with the Internal Improvement Fund to become director of southeastern operations for the Trust for Public Land, a California-based nonprofit corporation established to acquire ecologically valuable land and transfer it to public ownership. Three years later he became president of the trust. Under his leadership the trust acquired 1,168 acres of scenic wetlands in Volusia County, a gift from Robert and Radford Crane, two wealthy brothers. The Cranes also donated 1,459 acres of endangered lands in the Florida Keys. In another negotiation the trust was able to arrange a bargain price for the state's purchase of Cape Romano, the southernmost point on the Florida west coast.[41] Kuperberg's most remarkable coup was perhaps the deal arranged between the trust and the General Development Corporation, Florida's largest builder of new communities. Instead of fighting the state's new prohibition on dredge-and-fill operations, General Development agreed to sell 7,800 acres of mangroves and wetland, some located at Port Charlotte on the Gulf coast and some near the Atlantic coast in Central Florida. The trust bought the sensitive land at $50 an acre, far below its potential value if developed, with the intention of turning it over to the state.[42] In appealing for donations in cash and land, the trust did not rely entirely on love for the environment. It pointed out tax advantages as well as opportunities to dispose of land that it would be difficult or impossible to develop under the new environmental laws.

Florida's water problems were not confined to the south. In July 1974 the governor and cabinet designated the Green Swamp in Central Florida as a second area of critical state concern.[43] Located midway between Orlando and Tampa, the Green Swamp was a 500-square-mile region of soggy soil interspersed with flat hills, sandy ridges, and sinkhole lakes. This was a vital recharge source for the Floridan Aquifer on which 2.4 million people in northern and central Florida—city dwellers, farmers, ranchers, miners, manufacturers—depended for 90 percent of their water supply.

During the dry years of the 1960s and 1970s there had been mounting evidence that parts of the Floridan Aquifer were being overdrawn. In a U.S. Geological Survey map of 1969 an area in southwest Polk County had been colored red to denote "caution area." In this so-called Great Red Hole, the water table had dropped 5 to 20 feet in the preceding five years as a result of heavy consumption by phosphate mines, citrus groves, and citrus-processing plants. At first this was dismissed as a local phenomenon, but during the next five years the drop in the water table spread west and south into five other counties.[44]

Flood near Tampa, 1959. Severe floods in 1959 and 1960 led Congress to authorize the Four River Basins flood control project in 1962. SPA.

The environmental legislation of 1972 and 1973 had assigned responsibility for dealing with the water problems of this region to the Southwest Florida Water Management District (SWFWMD). This was not a new agency but one created a decade earlier to cope with a quite different situation. Between 1945 and 1960 seven major floods had swept through the region around Tampa Bay. Three particularly severe ones in 1959 and 1960 had inundated much of Tampa and nearly a million acres of farm lands and cattle ranches to the east of the city, causing an estimated $29 million worth of damages. In June 1961 the state legislature had created the SWFWMD with authority to cooperate with the federal government in building flood control works in a fourteen-county district. Obviously modeled on the Central and Southern Florida Flood Control District, the new agency was provided with a nine-member governing body and taxing powers.[45] In cooperation with the SWFWMD the Army Corps of Engineers prepared the so-called Four River Basins project to control the Hillsborough, Oklawaha, Withlacoochee, and Peace rivers and some smaller streams. Floodwaters would be diverted from populated areas by a system of channeled rivers, canals, reservoirs, and control structures, estimated to cost $100 million. The corps recommended that the federal government pay $59.5 million of this, the state and district to contribute the rest.[46]

Congress authorized the Four River Basins project in October 1962, but construction did not begin until April 1966. In 1970 the Army Corps reported that the project was 16 percent completed. But by this time the problem had changed. The threat was not floods but shortages. Environmentalists began to attack the Four River Basins project because no environmental impact study had been made. By draining swampland, the engineers were interfering with the recharge of the aquifer. By channelizing the rivers they were increasing the wasteful runoff into the Gulf and disturbing the habitat of wildlife. The *Tampa Tribune* warned that the SWFWMD might be doing the same kind of harm to the southern stretches of the Oklawaha River that the barge canal project was doing in the north.[47]

Uncomfortable at being cast in the villain's role, "Swiftmud," as the SWFWMD was popularly called, became much more conservation-minded. In 1970 it requested the Corps of Engineers to restudy the Four River Basins project for the purposes of increasing the water supply for urban, industrial, and agricultural needs, developing recreational facilities, and preserving environmental quality. Congress authorized this restudy in 1970, but did not provide the needed funds until 1975.[48] Meanwhile "Swiftmud" took steps to husband the area's resources. It refused to permit the drilling of wells to irrigate a 42-square-mile orange grove east of Sarasota; the wells would have had the capacity to pump 71 billion gallons a year—three times the amount used by residents of the Tampa Bay area.[49]

In June 1974 the Bureau of Land and Water Management of the Division of State Planning recommended that almost 323,000 acres in Lake and Polk counties be designated as the Green Swamp area of critical state concern. "If the central Florida region continues to grow and consume ground water at the current rates," the report said, "then by about 1985 water withdrawn and used from the Floridan Aquifer will equal that amount naturally recharged to the aquifer." Although the critical area was as yet sparsely settled, this condition would not continue much longer. The building of Disney World, whose western boundary was less than five miles from the Green Swamp, had set off a land boom. Between 1967 and 1974 more than 75,000 acres of land between Orlando and the Green Swamp had been purchased for development. Three major developments within the Green Swamp area had already been announced.[50]

When the recommendation came before the Florida cabinet in July 1974 the issue was sharply disputed by the conservationists and

Mangrove trees, 1916. Growing profusely in the wetlands near the ocean, the mangroves with their sprawling roots provided an ideal nursery for shrimp and small marine life, but thousands were destroyed to provide waterfront property. A John Small photograph. SPA.

the landowners. After five hours of clashing testimony Governor Askew and three state officers voted in favor of the proposal while three others opposed it.[51]

Hoping to start development of the region before new rules could be formulated, three land companies announced plans for draining a 16.5-square-mile area. Atty. Gen. Robert Shevin sued to stop them, and the contending parties turned to the U.S. Geological Survey for advice on how far the critical area extended. The government experts supplied ultramodern data in photographs taken from an orbiting satellite and U-2 plane. In a compromise settlement the state consented to a smaller development with reduced population densities and a prohibition on emptying drainage canals into the Withlacoochee River.[52]

Corkscrew Swamp Sanctuary. Through the initiative of the National Audubon Society, the Corkscrew Swamp was set aside as a wilderness preserve. National Audubon Society photograph. SPA. Photo by George Porter.

In July 1975 the governor and cabinet laid down detailed regulations for all developments within the Green Swamp area. To get a development permit the developer had to submit a plan showing the topography of the tract and the type of soil. This would determine the amount of site alteration permitted: relatively high (60 percent) for uplands, moderate (25 percent) for pine flatwoods, very little (10 percent) for wetlands. In any case, site alteration was permitted only when it would not reduce the natural retention and filtering capabilities of the wetlands. A dozen other regulations obligated the developer to maintain the natural surface flow, protect the Floridan Aquifer, and revegetate all altered sites.[53]

In April 1975 the governor and cabinet designated the Florida Keys as a third area of critical state concern. Except for Key West, a busy port and naval base, these islands, stretching southwest of the mainland for more than a hundred miles, had been sparsely settled during most of the nineteenth century. In 1912 Henry Flagler had completed an extension of the Florida East Coast Railroad across the Keys, but his hope of developing Key West as a shipping center and tourist resort did not pay off. The railroad lost money until it suffered its final disaster in the great 1935 hurricane. Three years later, however, the Overseas Highway, built as a New Deal project using the old bridges and right-of-way, opened up the Keys to tourists and campers.

Because of its important naval installations, Key West grew significantly during and after World War II, doubling in population between 1940 and 1950. But so few people lived on the other islands that the total population of Monroe County was only 30,000 in 1950. Things changed rapidly during the 1950s as fishing and boating enthusiasts began to buy homes in Key Largo, Islamorada, Marathon, and other communities. In 1960 the population of the Keys reached 48,000; in 1970, 52,500; in 1973, 56,000. There were at least fifty mobile home parks in the region, and high-rise apartment houses and condominiums were beginning to block off the ocean vistas. Developers were dredging the shallow bays, sometimes damaging the live coral and cutting up the mangrove swamps to generate canals and waterfront lots.[54]

Since many Keys residents loved the quiet isolation of the region, they allied themselves with the environmentalists in trying to put the brakes on growth. They pointed out that the region was highly vulnerable. One obvious problem was transportation. Except for what little could be brought in by plane or boat, all goods had to be trucked down a two-lane highway over dangerously deteriorating bridges. Even with the present population the old road was jammed with traffic, especially during the tourist season. What would happen if another hurricane swept across the islands? Even with the earliest of warnings, it would be impossible for all the residents to flee to the mainland over the antiquated highway.

But the 18-inch water pipe that ran beside the Overseas Highway was an even more fragile life support system. Water had always been scarce on the Keys. Early in the nineteenth century the Navy had dug a few wells at Key West, but these were soon fouled by sewage and saltwater. For many decades the island residents had depended on rainwater, collected in private and municipal cisterns. Early in the twentieth century an additional supply was brought in by barges and railroad tank cars. Needing a more dependable source, the Navy bored wells at Florida City on the mainland and laid a 130-mile-long pipeline down the island chain. This system, completed in 1939, had a capacity of 6.2 million gallons a day, far more than the Navy needed. The Florida Keys Aqueduct Authority bought the surplus to provide a water supply to residents living all the way from Key Largo to Key West.

Because the population jump of the 1950s created new needs, the Aqueduct Authority invested $3.3 million in a Stock Island plant to convert seawater into fresh water. The new installation was designed to produce 2.6 million gallons a day, enough to supply Key West and neighboring communities. On 20 July 1967, Vice-President Hubert Humphrey spoke at the opening ceremonies, praising the installation as the largest one-unit desalting works in the world. Hailing a revolution in the use of resources, he predicted that by 1980 nuclear-powered plants would be transforming billions of gallons of seawater into fresh water every day.[55]

Despite this jubilation, the Stock Island plant provided no permanent answer to the water problem. Storage tanks on the islands had a capacity of only 18 million gallons, so any mishap caused almost immediate hardship. In 1969 a broken main cut off the water along a 75-mile stretch, forcing some of the 7,000 affected residents to siphon out their swimming pools to meet household needs. Still more people lost their water in 1972 when an errant dump truck cut the pipeline.[56] The desalting plant suffered frequent breakdowns. In 1975 it had to shut down for a week for repairs. The next year the plant broke down 41 times in a single month.[57]

Even when all the facilities were working properly they did not supply enough water during the tourist season. In February 1975 the daily drawoff reached 9 million gallons, 500,000 gallons more than the supply. With the storage tanks depleted, residents of the Lower Keys were reported to be getting up at 4:30 A.M. to wash their hair, waiting an hour for the washing machine to fill, and postponing household chores until after midnight. "If someone down the line flushes the john," complained one woman, "we have nothing for five minutes."[58]

Since the Keys did not have enough water for their present population, how could they supply newcomers? The Key West experience did not encourage the building of more desalting plants. Not only were they subject to breakdown, but they gorged on fuel in a period of soaring fuel prices. Some engineers believed that the answer might be deep wells, drilled through intervening seams of seawater to tap the Floridan Aquifer. But an experimental boring at Marathon had to be abandoned when the water 2,115 feet below the surface was still too salty to use.[59] The only practical water source for the Keys lay in southern Dade County, a region with its own urgent water needs.

In 1974 the Florida Keys Aqueduct Authority sought approval for a plan to drill more wells at Florida City and to lay down a second pipeline to increase its potential supply to 20 million gallons a day. The Central and Southern Florida Flood Control District approved an increase to 13.5 million gallons a day by 1984. John DeGrove, an Askew appointee to the governing board, dissented on the ground that the Keys officials should have been required to formulate a plan for controlling growth. Commending this stand, the *Miami Herald* said that Dade County's limited water supply ought to be conserved for the Miami metropolitan area, "which is on the mainland and is better able to accommodate more people in already developed areas" rather than being diverted to "newcomers to the remote island chain where there is no plan for orderly development and where all the amenities which make the area so uniquely beautiful are fast disappearing because of overdevelopment."[60]

In May 1975 the Florida cabinet took up the Keys water request. By this time all parties conceded that the region needed at least 10 million gallons a day for its present population, but environmentalists argued against any additional allocation that would encourage growth. Brushing aside these objections, the cabinet granted permission for the Aqueduct Authority to increase its supply to 13.5 million gallons a day by 1980. A month later the authority lifted a 10-month ban on new water hook-ups for single-family residences.[61]

Meanwhile, environmentalists had been trying to stop the dredge-and-fill operations that were destroying the mangrove

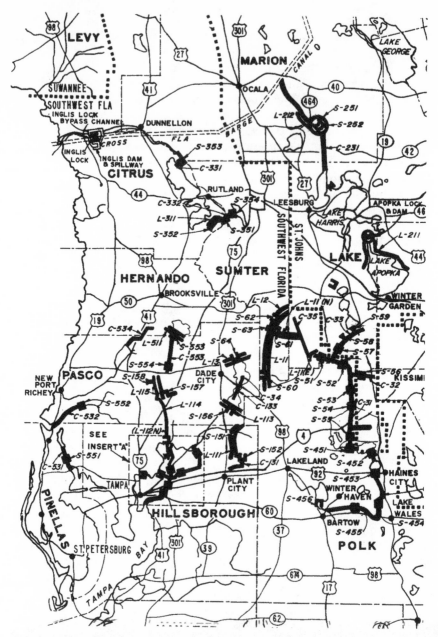

The Four River Basins project. To prevent floods in west central Florida the Army Corps of Engineers planned a complex network of channelized rivers, canals, reservoirs, and control structures. Map by Army Corps of Engineers.

swamps. Now charged by Congress with the duty of protecting the environment, the Army Corps of Engineers brought suit against several developers who had been dredging on Key Largo without the corps's permission. In December 1974 U.S. District Court Judge William Mehrtens ordered Joseph Moretti, owner of a 50-acre mobile home park, to refill certain unauthorized canals and restore all unsold lots to mangrove wilderness. Protesting that compliance would bankrupt him, Moretti appealed the decision. While this case was pending, Judge Mehrtens handed down tough rulings in three other cases, thus becoming a hero to the environmentalists. In an out-of-court settlement approved by Judge Mehrtens, the Ocean Reef Club, an exclusive resort on Key Largo, promised to restore seven acres of mangrove along a 500-foot stretch of oceanfront.[62]

In February 1976 the U.S. Circuit Court of Appeals in New Orleans drastically reduced the scope of Judge Mehrtens's decisions. Ruling that the Corps of Engineers had no authority over dredging unless the canals were linked to navigable waters, the court relieved the developers of much of the ordered restoration and directed Judge Mehrtens to apply reasonable standards in considering the developers' proposals for repairing the rest.[63]

Those who wanted to preserve the isolation and beauty of the Keys believed that the best safeguard would be to have it declared an area of critical state concern. In 1974 the president of the Upper Keys Association presented a petition with 2,170 signatures asking that this be done.[64] The Division of State Planning recommended it. But a powerful coalition of forces—developers, real estate agents, bankers, merchants, trade unionists—opposed any "Tallahassee takeover." Already plagued by the economic recession, they preferred to leave regulation in the hands of friendly Monroe County officials. They argued that the Keys were not wilderness like the Big Cypress Swamp and the Green Swamp but an area of flourishing towns and substantial population.

On 15 April 1975, the two sides argued their cases at a nine-hour public cabinet meeting. Charles Lee of the Florida Audubon Society, Monroe County Commissioner Jerome Shipley, and others argued that state action was necessary to prevent destruction of the natural beauty of the Keys, but Dr. Philip Dolbert, representing the Chamber of Commerce, compared state controls to Hitler's invasion of Poland and France. Governor Askew and four officers voted to have the Keys designated as an area of critical state concern, overriding the opposition of State Treasurer Tom O'Malley and Agriculture Commissioner Doyle Conner.[65]

Carrying out the procedures specified in the ELMS Act, state and local authorities enacted strict regulations on land use and development. Strong emphasis was placed on protecting the shoreline and the mangrove swamps, minimizing adverse effects on water quality, preserving scenic beauty and open space, requiring water-saving plumbing devices, and maintaining the unique character of historic Key West.[66] Bitterly resenting outside interference, the Key West city government joined with landowners and developers in contesting the new regulations in the courts. In August 1977 a Florida District Court held the ELMS act "unconstitutionally vague" because it did not set up specific standards for designating areas of critical state concern. In November 1978 the state supreme court unanimously upheld this decision. The ruling did not apply to the Big Cypress Swamp, which the legislature itself had specified as an area of critical state concern, but it did threaten the protection of the Keys, where local regulations went only part way, and the Green Swamp, where local laws were completely inadequate. Responding to this challenge to his environmental program, Governor Askew called the legislature into special session during his final month in office. Although there was still considerable local opposition, the lawmakers speedily passed a bill continuing the land-use restrictions while a joint committee studied the issue.[67]

The ELMS Act had provided state and local agencies with another potent weapon in restricting projects that threatened the environment. A "Development of Regional Impact" (DRI) was defined as "any development which, because of its character, magnitude or location, would have a substantial effect upon the health, safety or welfare of citizens of more than one county." Guidelines for determining whether any particular development fell into this category were to be recommended by the Division of State Planning and adopted by the governor and cabinet. As factors to be considered, the law specified pollution of air and water, noise problems, traffic congestion, number of residents and employees, size of site, likelihood of subsidiary development, and unique qualities of the region. The 1976 legislature added another timely consideration: amount of energy required. Actual designation of DRIs, issuance of permits, and imposition of conditions were functions left largely to local governments and regional planning agencies, with provisions for appeal to the governor and cabinet.[68]

As things worked out, major public and private projects, such as airports and power plants, clearly fell into the DRI category, as did new planned communities. In the Gold Coast counties, real estate

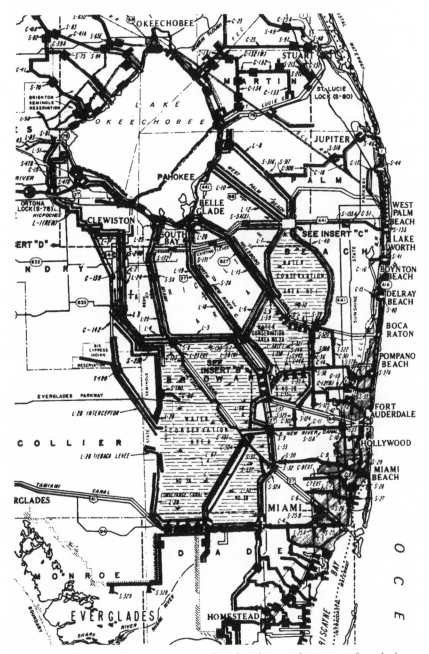

Central and Southern Florida flood control works. This complex system of canals, levees, and control structures illustrates the strong tendency of the Flood Control District and the Army Corps of Engineers to seek technological remedies for South Florida's water problems. Map by Army Corps of Engineers.

developments were not defined as DRIs unless they had at least 3,000 units. Environmentalists complained that enforcement of the law was not strict enough to apply the brakes to population growth, even in areas important for the recharge of the Biscayne Aquifer and other water-sensitive regions. Nevertheless, governmental bodies were now equipped to require builders to modify their plans to protect natural features and to reject outright developments to which there were serious objections.

Hurricane damage on the Keys, 1960. Workmen are repairing a break in the vital pipeline at Conch Key. Reprinted with permission of the *Miami Herald.*

Environmentalists gained another victory in 1975 when the legislature passed the Local Government Planning Act. Each county and municipality was required to prepare and adopt a comprehensive plan to guide and control future development. If a municipality failed to act before 1 July 1979, the county plan would govern. If both the municipality and county failed to act, the state land planning agency was to prepare plans for both county and municipality, and the governor and cabinet had authority to impose them. All decisions regarding development were to be consistent with the local comprehensive plans once adopted.[69]

But helter-skelter private development was not the only threat to the environment. For decades the Army Corps of Engineers had been dredging harbors, restoring beaches, digging waterways and ditches, and building dams and levees. Invariably local politicians and businessmen had lobbied for these projects, and congressmen and senators had happily appropriated the money. The purpose was always commendable—to improve navigation, protect beaches, prevent floods, store water, provide employment. Yet these public works had often brought deplorable consequences—scenic rivers mutilated, mangrove swamps destroyed, wetlands drained, waters polluted. Nor was the Army Corps of Engineers the only culprit. Other federal agencies, such as the Aviation Administration, the Highway Administration, the Atomic Energy Commission, and the Soil Conservation Service, had carried on activities that threatened to upset the ecological balance.

In an effort to remedy this situation, Congress passed in 1969 the National Environmental Policy Act, establishing a Council on Environmental Quality and requiring federal agencies to prepare environmental impact statements before embarking on new projects. Under procedures prescribed by the federal Office of Management and Budget (OMB), the draft environmental impact statements had to be submitted to other federal, state, and regional agencies. Feedback from this review process was used in preparing the final environmental statements for the information of Congress and the executive. The OMB recommended that state and regional clearinghouses be established to coordinate review not only of the environmental impact statements but of other material relating to proposed federal grants.

To cooperate with the new policy the Kirk administration set up a state clearing house in 1969. When the Division of State Planning was established during the Askew administration, the Bureau of Comprehensive Planning took over this function. Headed by Eustus Whitfield, the Environmental Clearing House sent out copies of the draft environmental impact statements to all state agencies affected and then held weekly discussion meetings. For the first time, experts from different fields had an opportunity to subject public works proposals to searching scrutiny. The clearinghouse then prepared a proposed state position for submission to the governor or some other authority for final approval before being forwarded to the federal agency involved.

The Environmental Clearing House provided environmental scientists working for the state a unique opportunity to influence scores of important decisions—location of airports, building of new flood-control works, granting of dredge-and-fill applications, building of interstate highways, and digging of waterways. Sometimes, as in the case of the cross-Florida barge canal, the Environmental Clearing House played a decisive role in killing the project. More often it achieved modifications in design.[70]

Completing his eight years in office on 1 January 1979, Governor Askew took his greatest satisfaction in the victories achieved for environmentalist causes. Continuing the course initiated during the Kirk years, the legislature had cooperated with Askew in passing important environmental laws; the cabinet supported him in imposing curbs on dredge-and-fill operations and in protecting "areas of critical state concern" against unwise development; new state agencies and invigorated old agencies calculated the ecological costs and benefits of proposed public works; municipalities, counties, regional authorities, and state bureaus all became involved in planning activities. Yet these victories gave no reason for complacency. In American history periods of reform are cyclical; interests subject to regulation have traditionally laid low until the progressive winds have blown themselves out, then reasserted themselves, often co-opting the very agencies created to control them. During the coming decade public opinion was likely to shift and blow from some other direction. Already a new real estate boom was generating projects for new condominiums, new suburban tracts, and new planned communities. And in the state elections of 1978 politicians vied with each other in schemes for attracting new industries to the state. As faith in the hypnotic cause of "growth" revived, knowledgeable environmentalists braced themselves to hold onto the ground already won and to win further protection for the state's vital water resources.

# 11 Rival Prescriptions for South Florida

There is "a water crisis in South Florida today": this finding, adopted by the Governor's Conference on Water Management in South Florida in 1971, referred to both the immediate situation and the unrolling future. The concern of the moment was the severe drought that had required emergency measures in the Gold Coast cities; the problems of the future related to the region's rapidly growing population. Would there be water enough for the newcomers? Would the water be pure enough to drink? The Biscayne Aquifer still provided a copious supply during normal years but afforded only a narrow margin during dry years. Lake Okeechobee and three conservation areas contained backup supplies that could be released down the old canals, but were these reserves adequate, particularly in view of the heavy demands of sugar growers and vegetable farmers? And would they continue to be safe, or were they becoming contaminated? Throughout the 1970s federal and state agencies, regional authorities, farmers, developers, and environmentalists struggled to influence water policy.

The two most firmly entrenched agencies in the region were the Army Corps of Engineers and the Central and Southern Florida Flood Control District. In close alliance they had built a vast network of levees, pumping stations, and drainage canals. These FCD works protected 1,200 square miles of farmland from floods and provided water for irrigation; they protected the Gold Coast against both inundation and drought. Proud of these accomplishments, the corps and the FCD made plans for new engineering works that would meet South Florida's future needs. But the environmentalists regarded this technological approach with increasing suspicion. Nature lovers deplored the massive structures that disrupted plant life and destroyed the habitats of birds, animals, and fish. And the preservationists were not the only people who challenged the engineers;

253

a new generation of hardheaded environmental scientists were now calculating the costs of soil depletion, ecological damage, water pollution, and reliance on fossil fuels to move water through artificial systems. The environmentalists recommended new techniques by which men would cooperate with nature to allow water to seek its historic levels, moving through swamplands and marshes, seeping into the aquifers, and purifying itself through natural processes. No longer confined to the role of outsiders, the environmental scientists were moving into increasingly powerful positions in such federal agencies as the Environmental Protection Agency and in Florida's Division of State Planning and Department of Environmental Regulation.

Even the Corps of Engineers and the Flood Control District were feeling the impact of change. Required by Congress to prepare environmental impact statements for its projects, the corps now added specialists in ecology to its staff, while the Flood Control District was also employing new personnel to meet the requirements of the Water Resources Act of 1972 and other environmental legislation. Agricultural interests were still heavily represented on the FCD governing board, but Governors Kirk and Askew infused new blood with the appointment of such conservationists as Robert Padrick, John DeGrove, and Nat Reed. When the Flood Control District undertook the task of preparing a water use plan for South Florida, it could build upon twenty years of collaboration with the Army Corps. This was an advantage in that a vast amount of data was available; it was a disadvantage in that the earlier planning had been heavily weighted toward technological measures.

In 1968 the corps had issued an important report on *Water Resources for Central and Southern Florida*. Three circumstances had strongly influenced their findings: the extraordinary growth of the population, the disturbing cycle of dry years during the early 1960s, and the nationwide protest over the water problems of Everglades National Park. Warning that the project's already authorized work would not meet the region's requirements beyond 1976, the corps suggested the need to store more water either in the conservation areas or in state-owned regions within the Everglades Agricultural Area to the south of Lake Okeechobee. But hunters opposed high water levels that might force the deer to move to other places, and the farm corporations hoped to lease additional acreage within the area. Avoiding controversy, the corps limited its actual recommendation to the type of public works that always appealed to politicans. To provide for the needs of a projected South Florida population of

4.7 million in 1985, 5.9 million in 1995, and almost 10 million in 2020, the corps recommended a $70 million program that included additional canals, levees, control structures, and pumping stations to move the water to places where it was needed and also added two major innovations to the system. To increase the storage capacity of Lake Okeechobee and reduce the runoff through the St. Lucie Canal, the corps proposed to raise the barriers around the lake so that a water level of 21.5 feet above sea level could be permitted — four feet higher than already authorized. To prevent the runoff through the southeast canals into the ocean, they recommended building the works necessary to save the water and pump it back into the conservation areas and the lake.[1] Congress authorized this program in 1968, but a decade later the key structures were still unbuilt.

The 1968 plan did not answer all the questions that would be asked during the 1970s. Environmentalists insisted that water quality was even more important than water quantity. Therefore it might not be a good idea to store more and more water in Lake Okeechobee, which was already showing ecological stress. Also doubtful was the wisdom of backpumping runoff from city streets and parking lots into the lake or the conservation areas. In an age of rising fuel prices, moreover, it was becoming more and more expensive to pump water from place to place. Might not better advantage be taken of the natural flow of water and its retention in marshes and swamps? Environmentalists became more interested in the Army Corps's unchosen alternative, that of storing more water in the conservation areas or in state-owned land within the Everglades Agricultural Area.

Even before the old Flood Control District was reorganized as the new Water Management District, its staff had taken up the task of preparing the water use plan. In 1973 William Storch, chief engineer for the district, presented what he called a "rough cut model" for the water use plan. Earlier plans had accepted the inevitability of growth and assumed that water consumption would increase proportionately. This left to the engineers only the task of recommending the means by which these needs could be met. But Storch pointed out that these trends could be influenced by public policy. He suggested that it might be desirable to modify both population growth and consumption habits. Planners ought to suggest a range of alternatives and then calculate not only the economic cost but the environmental impact of the suggested courses of action. "Each water supply option," he said, "would be associated with a certain population level, agricultural development level, and population distribution.... *An approach such as this, if soundly developed, would give the decision-makers a reasonable basis for matching people and activities with a water supply base and an environment of acceptable quality.*"[2]

Storch's "rough cut model" indicated the principal ingredients that he thought would have to go into the South Florida plan. It would be necessary to make "maximum effective, safe use" of the shallow water aquifers and to protect their recharge; to provide "carry-over" storage capability at various points within the region; and to provide storage "as close to the areas of demand as possible." Storch died in 1976, but the South Florida Water Management District continued to develop its plans in accordance with his ideas.

In evaluating alternatives the WMD planners concentrated first on the eastern counties, Dade, Broward, and Palm Beach, and two central counties, Glades and Hendry. In a draft report issued in 1977, the staff compared various predictions of future population and assumed that the three Gold Coast counties would reach their saturation points sometime after the year 2000. At that time Dade would have about 2.6 million inhabitants, twice its 1970 population; Broward would have 1.8 million, almost three times its 1970 population; and Palm Beach would have 2.9 million, eight times its 1970 population. To provide for these residents and to meet the irrigation needs of the farmers, a water supply of 1.5 to 1.8 billion gallons a day would be needed—twice the amount used in 1970.[3]

The most obvious way to meet these needs was to develop additional wellfields at a cost somewhere between $40 million and $150 million. By careful management of the old wells and the drilling of new ones already planned, urban water needs could be met until about 1985; after that, supplementary supplies from other sources would be required. But the full utilization of the eastern aquifers would require careful management. To prevent saltwater intrusion it was imperative to avoid overpumping in periods of drought and to keep the water in the coastal canals at a safe height above sea level. As new wellfields were opened farther west, the risk of environmental damage would increase. If the groundwater level were drastically lowered, the organic soil would oxidize and burn during the dry season and Melaleuca trees and other undesirable plant life would spread.[4]

A second alternative was to carry out the Army Corps plan for building the public works needed to backpump storm water from the West Palm Beach, Hillsboro, and Tamiami canals into the conservation areas, which would cost about $53 million. By combining this option with that of developing new wellfields, the projected water needs of the three Gold Coast counties could be met for an indefinite future, even in times of drought. But there would be grave environmental risks in pumping possibly polluted waters back into the Everglades, and it might be necessary to devise means of first purifying the drainage water.[5]

A better way might be to inject excess rainwater into deep wells. The theory was simple. Far below the shallow aquifers used for the coastal water supply lay the Floridan Aquifer, too salty in this part of the state to be used. If surface water were injected into this deep aquifer, it would not mix with the heavier salt water but would collect in an underground bubble of fresh water which might be retrieved for later use. After testing this theory in experimental borings, it was estimated that 20 wells could store some 7.2 billion gallons of water during the wet season. About half of the stored water, or 3.6 billion gallons, could be recovered during dry periods. A 50 percent recovery rate would compare very favorably with backpumping into the conservation areas, where a large proportion of the stored water was continually lost through evaporation. An additional advantage would be that the water would be stored close to where it was needed. Costs would be relatively high, $34 per million gallons recovered, but this would be cheaper than providing water by desalination.[6]

The actual costs of desalination were hard to estimate, particularly in an age of soaring fuel prices. Much would depend on the process and the type of water. To desalinate seawater was expensive, over $300 per million gallons. To treat brackish water, such as that in the Floridan Aquifer, would be much cheaper, under $100 per million gallons. Another variable would be the use to be made of the reclaimed water. Drinking water would be expensive; water freshened just enough for irrigating crops, watering lawns, and air conditioning would be cheaper. But the effluent would present serious environmental problems. It might be discharged into the ocean or into the sewer systems; it might be allowed to dry out in evaporation ponds; or it might be injected into deep wells. Each of these methods of disposal posed serious disadvantages.[7]

The draft plan also discussed the advantages of increasing the storage capacity of Lake Okeechobee. Raising the permitted level to only 19.5 feet above sea level (the engineers' plan called for 21.5 feet) would provide enough water to meet regional needs up to the year 2020 at a cost of $103.7 million ($71.7 million federal money, $32 million state). But the environmental risks would be substantial. More of the shoreline would be submerged, thus destroying vegetation and disrupting fish and wildlife. Pollution from Taylor Creek, Nubbin Slough, the lower Kissimmee, and the Everglades Agricultural Area would become a more serious problem.[8]

The WMD planners never advocated using Lake Okeechobee as a major water source for the east coast cities. In his "rough cut model," Storch had said: "Ideally, Lake Okeechobee should be counted on only to supply irrigation water to the agricultural lands adjacent to the lake and supplemental municipal water to northern Palm Beach County. The Park's minimum requirements should be supplied from the conservation areas. Finally, the lower east coast area should get its supplemental water from local storage (interim shallow ground water reserve and deep underground storage), in combination, perhaps, with the Everglades conservation area."[9] In times of drought, Lake Okeechobee water was used to help the cities not by the direct supply of water but by releasing water down the canals to replenish the aquifers.

The WMD staff conducted a series of public workshops where its alternatives were discussed. Neither taxpayers nor environmentalists displayed much enthusiasm for new public works to increase the storage capacity of Lake Okeechobee or to backpump the canals. Much more popular was the idea of developing a conservation program to cut down on water use. Proponents argued that conservation would be less expensive and more effective than new engineering works. Other well-received suggestions were to hold the brakes on overdevelopment by tighter regulation of water permits and to reuse sewer water for irrigation.[10]

The *Miami Herald* found the WMD draft report disappointing: "As we see it, the report leans too heavily on increased management of water resources and not enough on techniques which exploit or imitate natural systems to the fullest extent possible. Nor does it dwell sufficiently on priorities, failing to question certain questionable uses."[11]

During the same years that WMD planners with headquarters at West Palm Beach were proposing new engineering works to assure South Florida's future water supply, another group of planners operating out of Tallahassee was developing recommendations that placed primary emphasis on restoring historic water levels and conserving water in the natural reservoirs provided by lakes, streams, marshes, and aquifers. The new planners, many of them young men employed in the new Bureau of Comprehensive Planning, received their first great opportunity when they were assigned to study the Lake Okeechobee problem. Long famous for its good fishing, the lake was still full of sport fish, but the number of gizzard shad and other worthless species was increasing. Another danger signal was the spread of algae blooms and other weeds over wide expanses of the lake. To environmental scientists, these changes were evidence of "eutrophication," overenrichment of the surface water by nutrients such as nitrogen, phosphorus, potassium, and carbon. The U.S. Geological Survey reported that Lake Okeechobee was in an early state of eutrophication, and the Governor's Conference on Water

Kissimmee River during 1947 flood. In making its circuitous way to Lake Okeechobee, the old Kissimmee River often overflowed into the bordering marshlands and opened up new channels. From *Tentative Report of Flood Damage*, Florida Everglades Drainage District, 1947. SPA.

Management repeated the warning. Why was this taking place? Could the process be halted or reversed before Lake Okeechobee went the way of Lake Apopka near Orlando, once a fishermen's paradise and now ruined for sport and recreation?

But sportsmen were not the only group with a stake in the water quality of Lake Okeechobee. The lake provided public drinking water for the bordering towns and indirectly supplied the whole Gold Coast during times of drought, when water was released down the canals to restore the Biscayne Aquifer. The lake was also vital to the irrigation needs of the great Everglades Agricultural Area because of its situation in the center of a vast watershed extending from

Central Florida to the tip of the peninsula. In earlier times rainwater falling on the flat and marshy terrain south of Orlando gradually made its way southward through a string of pretty lakes to the Kissimmee River. This lovely stream meandered lazily through 90 miles of marshland to Lake Okeechobee. Serving as a natural reservoir, the lake periodically overflowed its banks to feed the slow moving sheet of water that flowed through the Everglades to Florida Bay. Because of its importance in receiving and discharging the life-sustaining fluid, Lake Okeechobee was described as the "liquid heart" of South Florida.

But by 1970 the engineers had largely replaced this natural arterial system with an artificial one composed of hundreds of miles of canals and channelized rivers as well as a wide assortment of levees, dams, control structures, and pumping stations. By an irony of history this manipulation of nature had begun and ended in the same vicinity. The Kissimmee chain of lakes and the Kissimmee River had been the scene of Disston's first dredging operations during the 1880s; the same bodies of water underwent "improvement" by the Army Corps during the 1960s.

The Central and Southern Florida Flood Control project had always included plans to tame the Kissimmee River. In 1947 a flood had inundated 600,000 acres in this basin, causing $4 million worth of damage. To protect themselves against future losses, cattle ranchers and landowners had sought the aid of Sen. Spessard Holland in getting the Army Corps of Engineers to include Kissimmee flood control works in its overall plan of 1948. Congress approved this phase in 1954, but nothing was done until a new series of floods led to calls for action. The Army Corps then proposed a $31 million program that included structures on the lakes to retain or release water, better connections between the lakes, and channelization of the Kissimmee River with five control structures to regulate its flow.[12]

The U.S. Fish and Wildlife Service and the Florida Game and Fresh Water Fish Commission opposed channelization, warning that it would seriously disturb the ecology of the region, but the Florida cabinet brushed aside these protests and Congress appropriated money for the project. The Army Corps began construction in the early 1960s. In 1965 a *Miami Herald* reporter contrasted the old Kissimmee River with Canal 38 that was replacing it. The old stream had "wound for nearly 100 miles down to Lake Okeechobee. It twisted from a couple of lakes near Kissimmee, across great marshbanks, past cypress head and live oaks and cabbage palm hammocks. Now under the assault of great, floating suction dredges and draglines—seemingly enough of them to build another Panama Canal—a straight-gut is being chopped through it, cutting its length in little more than half."[13]

When the project was completed in 1971, the whole Kissimmee-Okeechobee watershed became a plumber's masterpiece. By opening and closing gates and by pumping water, the managers could control the flow through 1,400 miles of canals. During the rainy seasons they could store water in the Kissimmee chain of lakes, Lake Okeechobee, and three conservation areas; during dry spells they could direct the water to the area of need. The FCD works protected 1,200 square miles of farmland from floods and provided water for irrigation; they protected the Gold Coast against both inundation and drought.

But, despite these benefits, environmentalists deplored the channelization of the Kissimmee. The old river, twisting in oxbows through the marshlands, had been a natural filtering system, delivering pure water to Lake Okeechobee. Now all was changed. Some 40,000 acres of marshes had been reduced to only 9,000 acres. Thousands of cattle grazed on neighboring ranchlands, and the runoff, heavily burdened with animal wastes, drained into a great ditch, 200 feet wide and 30 feet deep, that ran a straight course to the lake. All this was bad enough, but more trouble was in prospect. Central Florida was booming, partly because of Disney World, and the Orlando suburbs were growing rapidly. Much of this area drained into the upper lakes of the Kissimmee Valley. John V. Betz, a University of Florida microbiologist, described the consequences: "What was intended to help answer the coming water needs in South Florida has instead brought them to a crisis by forging a short circuit from the bathrooms and streets of central Florida to the major drinking-water reservoir of south Florida."[14]

Disturbed by the Lake Okeechobee situation, the Central and Southern Florida FCD began an experiment in reflooding some of the marshes by building a temporary structure across the Kissimmee about 25 miles north of Lake Okeechobee.[15] In 1972 the FCD governing board held public hearings on the problem and made a series of recommendations that included efforts to stop the discharge of wastes into the system, a program to plan and control all land and water activities in the river basin, and a study to determine whether there should be additional reflooding of the marshes. To carry out such a study, the FCD recommended establishment of an interdisciplinary team.[16]

In December 1972, when Governor Askew and the Florida

cabinet took up the FCD recommendation, they also had before them more drastic demands of a team of scientists headed by Arthur Marshall. Not trusting the FCD to correct its own mistakes, this group called upon the governor to appoint a "water quality master" for the Kissimmee-Okeechobee Basin. They wanted the legislature to mandate a restoration of the Kissimmee River based upon independent engineering studies. The entire program, Marshall said,

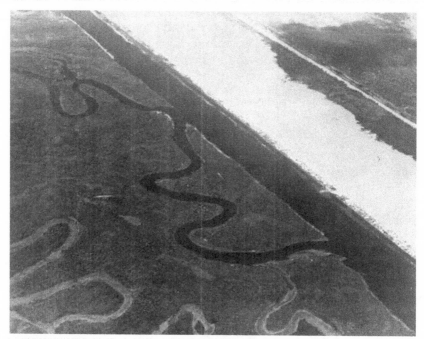

Canal 38. Diverting the Kissimmee River into this deep waterway reduced the flooding problem but carried the runoff from neighboring pastures into Lake Okeechobee. Environmental Information Center.

should be directed toward "reversing the process which has reduced the quality of water in Lake Okeechobee to its present condition" and should be centered "on action rather than study and monitoring."[17]

In his annual message on 3 April 1973, Governor Askew urged the legislature to address itself to "the correction of environmental problems within the Kissimmee River Basin...problems that are endangering Lake Okeechobee, the major water reservoir for the populous Gold Coast."[18] The lawmakers responded with a $1 million appropriation to set up a "Special Project to Prevent the Eutrophication of Lake Okeechobee." By agreement among the state agencies the primary responsibility for making the necessary studies and recommendations was given to the Division of State Planning, the Department of Environmental Regulation, and the Central and Southern Florida Flood Control District. The project leader was Dale Walker, now employed by the Bureau of Comprehensive Planning but earlier an official in the Game and Fresh Water Fish Commission, where he had been severely critical both of the cross-Florida barge canal project and the channelization of the Kissimmee. Walker appointed as his chief associate Curry Hutchinson, also employed by the Bureau of Comprehensive Planning and an earnest environmental scientist trained at the University of Florida. Walker and Hutchinson used the million-dollar appropriation to recruit a large team of experts and to commission a wide variety of special studies of the Lake Okeechobee problem in all its ramifications. Federal, state, and local agencies were all drawn in, as were university groups and private consulting firms.

Even before the special project was completed, its activities led to sharp controversy. In December 1975 Florida newspapers published portions of a draft report on the costs and benefits of South Florida flood control policies. Written by Paul Roberts, a former member of the University of Florida Department of Economics, Donald Patton of the Florida State University Department of Geography, and Curry Hutchinson, the report concluded that the FCD had been operating largely for the benefit of the great farming corporations. Agriculture consumed 58 percent of all water used in Palm Beach, Broward, and Dade counties, but the farmers paid only about 12 percent of the ad valorem taxes levied in these counties for FCD operating expenses. Real estate owners in the cities paid most of the balance. The report questioned the value of the flood control provided for the cities; indeed, it said, FCD policies encouraged unwise development of low-lying tracts that might be inundated in future floods. Even for agriculture the benefits of flood control and drainage needed to be weighed against heavy costs in ecological damage, soil depletion, and injury to Lake Okeechobee. To curb these abuses, Roberts recommended a user's tax, whereby large farmers would pay in proportion to the water they were drawing. He also suggested that farmers divert their acreage from sugar to rice and other wetland crops that would not require drainage. Summarizing its findings, Roberts's report advocated new management policies that would more nearly approximate the operation of the natural water system.[19]

Unhappy with these criticisms, Jack Maloy, chief executive of the FCD, released the draft to the newspapers where it provoked a hullabaloo. The sugar growers hotly disputed Roberts's findings, and Maloy pointed out that in the cities all the rainwater drained into the ocean but in the Agricultural Area the runoff was pumped back into the lake so that there was no net loss of water through irrigation.[20] The Askew administration wanted to damp down the controversy for fear that it would prevent the voters from approving a referendum extending the power of levying ad valorem taxes to the new water management districts. Therefore the Roberts report was never officially published.[21]

But even without the Roberts component, the final report of the Special Project was loaded with dynamite. It found that Lake Okeechobee's eutrophication problem was indeed serious, so serious that the discharge of nutrients into the lake would have to be substantially reduced. As suspected, the channelized Kissimmee River was found to be discharging substantial amounts of nitrogen and phosphorus into the lake. But the special project placed more blame on two other sources of overenrichment. One of these was the Taylor Creek—Nubbin Slough region, a 116,000-acre area to the north and northeast of the lake. Here a variety of drainage projects, financed by private parties, the U.S. Soil Conservation Service, the Army Corps of Engineers, the Flood Control District, and local governments had transformed the marshlands into an area of thriving dairies and cattle ranches. The wastes from thousands of animals washed off into the streams leading into Lake Okeechobee. The other culprit was the Everglades Agricultural Area, where an extensive system of levees enclosed about 700,000 acres of rich muckland to the south of the lake. Sugar growers used about 300,000 acres, vegetable farmers and cattle ranchers about 200,000 acres. The rest, most of it still state-owned, was drained but still uncultivated, an excellent place for deer hunting. Farmers in the area used large quantities of Lake Okeechobee water for irrigation but returned large quantities of runoff (about 480,000 acre-feet a year) to the lake through backpumping. This discharge was heavily loaded with nitrogen and phosphorus, mostly residues from the oxidized soil. To a lesser extent the backpumped water was polluted with fertilizers and pesticides.[22]

The special project made numerous recommendations for reducing the overenrichment of the lake. Rejecting the nature lovers' demand for a complete restoration of the old Kissimmee River as too expensive and too uncertain in its ecological consequences, the special project advised restoration of some of the marshes along the lower Kissimmee, upland retention structures to slow the runoff of rainwater, and improved pasture management to reduce the washoff of animal wastes. Although the upper reaches of the river chain were not yet contributing seriously to Lake Okeechobee's problems, the upper lakes had their own incipient eutrophication problems, and the special project recommended better sewage treatment, improved pasture management, and higher levels in the lakes.[23] For the Taylor Creek–Nubbin Slough Basin, the special project recommended an extensive system of structures to retain rainwater, the routing of runoff through natural and man-made marshes, and rigorous regulation to reduce the washoff of cattle wastes.[24]

The most explosive special project recommendations dealt with the Everglades Agricultural Area. Backpumping into the lake should be "eliminated or reduced to the maximum degree feasible." To dispose of surplus water during the rainy season, the Miami, North New River, and Hillsboro canals should be enlarged and used to convey the water to storage areas for recycling and irrigation needs. The recommended storage area was the Holey Land, a 30,000-acre state-owned tract in the southern part of the agricultural area. The special project also urged further interdisciplinary study to develop means of conserving the mucklands by the substitution of aquatic crops and other alternatives. By such recommendations as these the special project challenged the interests of two of the most politically powerful groups in the state. The sugar growers, long the beneficiaries of drainage projects and federal subsidies, were threatened not only with a ban on backpumping but with exclusion from the Holey Land into which they had hoped to expand. Even more alarming was a possible change of state policy to discourage sugar culture and substitute the growing of rice and similar wetland crops. And the deer hunters were irate at proposals that would flood some of their favorite hunting grounds—the Holey Land and parts of the conservation areas.[25]

Although the cooperating agencies had been able to agree on publication of the Final Report on the Special Project, growing hostility to the enterprise blocked the release of other key findings. The most important document to be aborted was a "Final Report on the Management Plans of the Special Project," written by Curry Hutchinson and three other experts from the Bureau of Comprehensive Planning. Intended as a companion volume to the consensus report, this long and detailed paper was still more rigorous in its criticism of current practices and its recommendations for change. Not limiting themselves to the narrow issues involved in the Lake Okeechobee problem, the Hutchinson group presented a broad indictment of the drainage policies of many years, policies that had lowered groundwater levels throughout much of South Florida. This diversion of water was changing the ecosystem of the region. Melaleuca trees and other exotic species were taking over, and the native vegetation was dying off. "If this continues to occur as it is certain to in the absence of management to elevate groundwater levels throughout the region," the report said, "South Florida will experience even more severe summer floods than occur historically, followed by longer and more pronounced dry seasons with acute water

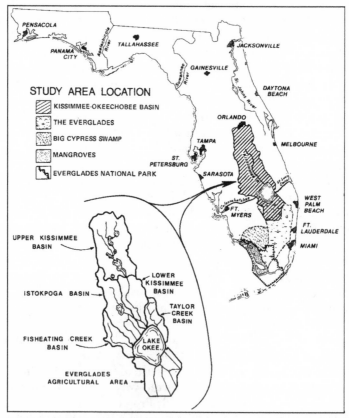

Kissimmee-Okeechobee Basin. Alarm over the deterioration of Lake Okeechobee persuaded the legislature to appropriate funds for study of regional water quality problems. From Florida Division of State Planning, *Final Report on the Special Project to Prevent Eutrophication of Lake Okeechobee.*

shortages and uncontrollable and disastrous fires." Despite the seriousness of this ecological threat the Hutchinson group was confident that environmental scientists now had the knowledge to restore the natural balance. Their prescription was to minimize reliance upon technology and to substitute measures that would retard runoff and retain rainwater in marshes and wetlands. "For South Florida," they said, "wise management of the unique subtropical region is the challenge of the present and the promise of the future."[26]

So outspoken was this "Final Report on the Management Plans" that the Department of Environmental Regulation and the Central and Southern Florida Flood Control District, two of the three agencies specially involved in the special project, opposed its release. Compelled to decide the matter, Governor Askew's office ruled against publication. Instead a much shorter *Summary Report on the Special Project to Prevent Eutrophication of Lake Okeechobee* was issued. Committee written, this document summarized the findings in a way that, in the view of the Hutchinson group, understated the problem and the steps needed to solve it.[27]

Bitterly opposed by a wide spectrum of interests—sugar growers, deer hunters, and nature lovers disappointed because full restoration of the Kissimmee had not been recommended—the special project had a rocky time during the 1976 session of the legislature. Ignoring its findings, the lawmakers gave most of their attention to a bill for full restoration of the Kissimmee, pushed by Johnny Jones of the Florida Wildlife Federation, one of the state's most effective lobbyists. In the end, however, Jones was frustrated when opponents cut out of his bill a key provision levying a special tax to finance restoration. Instead the law set up a new study group, the "Coordinating Council on the Restoration of the Kissimmee River Valley and the Taylor Creek–Nubbin Slough Basin." The legislature designated officials from five state agencies to compose the Coordinating Council but did not include anyone from the Department of State Planning, which had managed to antagonize so many powerful groups.[28]

The act called for "restoration" of the Kissimmee, but just what did restoration mean? In its report of April 1977, the Coordinating Council recommended measures for reducing pollution in the Taylor Creek area and controlling development in the Kissimmee Valley. But it threw the red-hot coal of "restoration" back to the legislature. The council proposed two alternatives. If the legislature really wanted to "restore" the river and "negate" the canal, the council advised against completely refilling the canal; instead it favored "partial backfilling," that is, filling in successive stages of Canal 38 and gradually forcing the water back into most of the old riverbed. This would cost at least $30 million and might run to two or three times this amount since it would probably involve compensating land-owners whose land would be transformed from pasture back to marshland. If the legislature decided it did not really want to under-take such an expensive restoration, the council recommended "im-pounded wetlands" as an alternative. This would abandon the old riverbed but re-create some 14,000 acres of marshland by raising a series of barriers across the canal and reflooding some of the valley. This program, which would cost some $14 million, mostly for land acquisition, was an extension of the experimental program that the FCD had initiated in 1970 and the special project had recommended in 1976.[29]

The 1977 legislature was unable to resolve the issue. Although many nature lovers still argued for filling in the whole canal and turning the river back to its old channel, there were powerful argu-ments against this: for one thing, it would be very expensive, costing perhaps $90 million; for another, it might add to Lake Okeechobee's problems by bringing down large amounts of sediment. So most en-vironmentalists accepted partial backfilling as less expensive and less likely to entail negative side effects. This plan called for filling in about 60 percent of the canal and restoring two-thirds of the marshes. Bills committing the state to this strategy passed their first hurdles in the house and senate but then ran into serious opposition both from landowners and from legislators belatedly impressed by the findings of the special project, which supported the less drastic impounded wetlands solution. In the end, the legislature sent the problem back to the Coordinating Council for further study.[30] Since federal consent would be necessary for alterations in the flood con-trol works, particularly if federal dollars were to be sought, the state agencies appealed to Congress to fund an Army Corps restudy to de-termine whether modifications were necessary to safeguard water quality, fish and wildlife resources, and other environmental values.[31]

While the Kissimmee controversy was monopolizing the attention of the politicians, the environmental scientists in the state agencies continued to press for measures they considered more important. The case for restoring water levels received important scientific support in the so-called *South Florida Report*, prepared by the Cen-ter for Wetlands headed by Howard Odum of the University of Florida and by the Bureau of Comprehensive Planning. Published in 1976, this document reported the findings of a study commissioned after the jetport controversy by the U.S. Department of the Interior and the Florida Division of State Planning to develop guidelines for land and water management in the region. The Odum group argued that because of rising energy costs South Florida's period of rapid growth was coming to an end. The region might soon enter a no-growth or "steady state" condition—a good thing because it would improve the quality of life, increase economic stability, and promote cultural health.[32]

The *South Florida Report* pointed out that it required a great deal of energy to move water from one place to another. It was much more efficient to let nature distribute the water and adapt land use to natural conditions. This meant protecting local aquifers and their recharge areas so as to minimize the need for more distant sources; it meant preserving wetlands and using them for water retention and waste recycling; it meant leaving the mangrove swamps intact and building homes along natural streams instead of canals. Odum recommended building suburban homes on pilings rather than draining tracts, building dikes around farms and pumping surplus water into local basins instead of digging large canals, and using cypress swamps to recycle partially treated sewage.[33]

The specialists who had been urging restoration of natural water levels had a unique opportunity to exert their influence in the drafting of the Florida State Comprehensive Plan. Mandated by the legislature in 1972, the comprehensive plan was intended to "provide long-range guidance of the orderly social, economic, and physical growth of the state...." In all important areas of policy—agriculture, economic development, education, and the like—task forces went through a long process of drafting reports and subjecting them to expert criticism and public hearings. Curry Hutchinson prepared a key draft for the water section of the comprehensive plan. It called for managing resources "to maintain ground and surface water levels which approximate the hydroperiod which existed prior to modification to the maximum extent practical within the constraints of existing development and planned land use."[34] Johnny Jones of the Wildlife Federation praised the Hutchinson draft as the best document he had seen during many years of lobbying. "When you look at the South Florida Water Management District report, it makes you sick. When you look at this one it makes you proud." But the Department of Environmental Regulation and the WMD protested that the restoration of historic water levels was unrealistic. "Our basic philosophy," said Peter Rhoads, WMD district planning director, "is that water resources need to be managed in view of what we have today, not attempting to simulate what you had 75 or 100 years ago."[35] Developers and homeowners warned against any restoration of ancient water levels that might threaten to flood their suburban tracts.

This struggle over the water section of the comprehensive plan involved the rival prescriptions that had emerged over the past decade. The older agencies (the South Florida WMD and the Army Corps of Engineers) still placed their principal faith in new public works—deep aquifer storage, desalination, higher dams, and more pumping stations. The newer agencies, especially the Bureau of Comprehensive Planning, distrusted technology and placed their principal reliance on scientific management to restore water levels to a more natural level. The Hutchinson draft successfully ran a gamut of committees and was approved by most of the specialists, once it was explained that existing developments would be safeguarded. But the Department of Environmental Regulation and the South Florida WMD asked for modifications.

Compelled to act as a referee among contending factions, the Department of Administration finally approved compromise wording suggested in meetings involving the DER, the South Florida WMD, and representatives of the Audubon Society and Sierra Club. Still further editing was done in the governor's office. But although the final phrasing differed from that of the Hutchinson draft, the essential principle of that document remained intact.[36] The disputed policy statement finally read: "Encourage restoration of more natural hydrologic relationships in areas where development activities have significantly and detrimentally altered the natural hydrology beyond the extent necessary to support existing development and planned land use. Where practical, ecologically desirable, and where adequate documentation exists, the hydrologic conditions which existed prior to modification should be utilized as a guide for restoration efforts."[37]

This statement was only one of forty-nine policies covering every aspect of water management: the protection of watersheds, the preservation of groundwater, the regulation of surface water and floodplains, the recycling and conservation of wastewater, the safeguarding of water supply, the coordination of legislative and administrative policy, and scientific planning at every level of government. Throughout the document the environmentalists' preference for reliance on natural systems rather than engineering works was evident. Thus the phrasing of such principles as these: "maintain runoff/infiltration and other hydrologic relationships... to achieve as

nearly as practical the natural hydrologic conditions...";  "ensure
that development does not diminish the functional values of wetlands...";  "encourage the use of non-structural means to prevent
flood damage...";  "utilize local water resources to the greatest degree...feasible before considering interdistrict, interbasin, and
other large scale transfer of water."[38]

In submitting the comprehensive plan to the legislature, Governor Askew asked that it be approved as "state policy." Instead of
this the legislature recognized the plan as "advisory only, except as
specifically authorized by law." But even in this form the com-

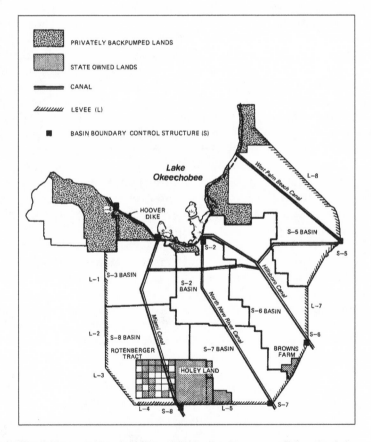

Everglades agricultural area drainage basins. Experts studying the Lake
Okeechobee problem advised a prohibition on backpumping from the great
sugar farms into the lake. From Florida Division of State Planning, *Final
Report on the Special Project to Prevent Eutropication of Lake Okeechobee.*

prehensive plan placed very important obligations on the executive branch of the state government. Acting as "chief planning officer of the State," Governor Askew issued an executive order directing that the comprehensive plan be used as guidance in the planning activities of all executive agencies. All budget requests were to be analyzed for compatibility with the plan.[39] In reviewing these budget requests the Bureau of Comprehensive Planning moved into a position of real power.

The State Comprehensive Plan gave the Environmental Clearing House leverage with which to modify the direction of South Florida WMD policy. The WMD board of governors had already responded to public criticism of its draft water use plan by recommending two more alternatives for meeting future needs: additional water conservation areas and reclamation and evaluation of new and existing structures "to optimize ground and surface water levels." But this shift away from the district's engineering bias did not go far enough to satisfy its Tallahassee critics. Curry Hutchinson recommended that the district's request for an Army Corps study of "technologically advanced methods to augment water supply in South Florida" should be "intensely" evaluated "to insure that all due emphasis and urgency is placed upon a highly coordinated effort to increase the water storage capacity of South Florida as a necessary adjunct to water supply and water conservation policies as contained in the Water Section of the State Comprehensive Plan."[40]

Because there had been no provision for storing more water, the Bureau of Comprehensive Planning opposed public works that would make additional demands upon Lake Okeechobee. One such project was the South Dade Conveyance System, first suggested by the 1968 Army Corps program but not actually begun until 1975. About 60 percent completed in 1977, the new works were designed to route 55,000 acre-feet of water a year into the eastern part of Everglades National Park and 350,000 acre-feet into the southern part of Dade County, a region of rapidly expanding suburban tracts and vegetable farms. In a review of the project, Curry Hutchinson emphasized the huge amount of water involved, more than that used for irrigation in the Everglades Agricultural Area. He warned that much of this might be wasted because of the porous nature of the Biscayne Aquifer, the overdrained condition of the soil, and leaky control structures, which would divert most of the additional water out to sea. He recommended that the works needed by the park be completed immediately, but that the rest of the project be halted until the overall water storage problem could be solved and other steps taken to prevent water loss and unwise use of the land.[41]

Meanwhile, state agencies were slowly taking steps to deal with the problem of Lake Okeechobee. Determined to force action, Barry Lessinger, a Broward County attorney acting for certain environmental groups, petitioned for a court order requiring the Department of Environmental Regulation to enforce water quality standards in the lake through the permit system. By this means the environmentalists hoped to compel the WMD to halt backpumping from the Everglades Agricultural Area. At first, the district denied that a permit was required, but in March 1977 Jay Landers, secretary of the DER, ordered measures to be taken either to stop the back-pumping or to clean up the water. No deadline was fixed, but the reform was to be carried out as expeditiously as possible and was to provide "ultimate compliance with water-quality standards in the water of the state."[42]

Required by Landers's order to apply for a temporary permit to continue backpumping, WMD staff members began to gather the necessary supporting data. In September 1978 WMD experts confirmed earlier findings concerning the seriousness of the eutrophication problem. They estimated that by rerouting runoff water within the Everglades Agricultural Area into the conservation areas, it might be possible to reduce backpumping by as much as 50 percent. But Jack Maloy and other key officials in the WMD were reluctant to order this to be done without further study and comparison with other alternatives. In November 1978 the DER and WMD worked out an agreement calling for a temporary permit to continue back-pumping for 30 months under carefully stipulated conditions. Water quality was to be carefully monitored, not only at the discharge points from the Agricultural Area but at all other critical points. Within 30 days the WMD must present a plan for immediate action to reduce undesirable loadings; within 120 days it must present written plans for analyzing each reasonable alternative for reducing the total nitrogen and phosphorous loadings to acceptable levels; within 24 months it must submit the finished analysis. In effect, the WMD, the sugar growers, and other interested parties had been given 30 months either to stop the backpumping or to devise techniques for purifying the water.[43]

But how was this to be done? The simplest solution would be to enlarge the old canals and allow the excess water to flow out to the ocean, but this would be a shocking waste. A second alternative would be to divert the water into the conservation areas and ultimately into Everglades National Park. WMD biologists argued that vegetation in the conservation areas could absorb the excess nitrogen and phosphorus without danger to the fish and wildlife, but nature lovers doubted this and were particularly opposed to allowing the suspect water to run down into the park. Too much water could be as disruptive to the ecology of the park as too little. The park needed more water in the dry season, not in the rainy season when water from the Agricultural Area would come pouring down. The most acceptable solution was probably that recommended by the special project in 1976, to store the runoff in the state-owned Holey Land in the southern part of the Agricultural Area. Here natural processes could safely operate, absorbing the nutrients and filtering out the pollutants. Thus restored, the water could be safely used for other purposes—release to the conservation areas and Everglades National Park, irrigation in the Agricultural Area, or return to Lake Okeechobee. But the deer hunters' lobby bitterly opposed any program that would submerge the Holey Land under four feet of water.

Another strategy recommended by the special project had been to convert sugar fields to rice culture. Since rice required flooded fields during 60 days of the growing season, it would be well adapted to the Florida cycle of seasons. Equally important, its cultivation would slow down the subsidence of the muckland soil which was depleting at the alarming rate of an inch per year. In the 1950s there had been experiments with rice in the Agricultural Area, but these were soon halted when disease attacked the plants. In the late 1970s a cautious new experiment began. Rice plantings on about 100 acres in Hendry County yielded an excellent crop in 1978, and plantings on 3,000 acres were planned for 1979. Also projected was the construction of a rice mill south of Clewiston. But no revolutionary transition from sugar to rice was to be expected. On the contrary, it was the sugar growers themselves who hoped to grow rice as a rotation crop on land that had periodically to lie idle and be flooded to kill worms and other pests before being replanted with sugar. Yet even as an auxiliary crop, rice held some promise for reducing the need for backpumping, maintaining more natural water levels, and conserving the soil. [44]

Although planners at Tallahassee and at West Palm Beach had written somewhat different prescriptions for South Florida's water ailments, there was hope that some kind of consensus would evolve. Compelled by the DER temporary permit to study once more the problems of Lake Okeechobee, the staff members of the Water

Management District would have to answer many of the same questions as those pondered in the special project. And, handling much the same data, there was a strong probability that the two studies would reach similar conclusions. The problems of Lake Okeechobee, however, were inextricably bound up with the problems of all other parts of South Florida—the problems of the Kissimmee and the Taylor Creek–Nubbin Slough Basin, the Everglades Agricultural Area, the conservation area, Everglades National Park, the Big Cypress Swamp, water supply for the Gold Coast and the Keys, and water supply for the southwest and Gulf coast. Piecemeal solutions would no longer do. What was needed was a master strategy for dealing not only with South Florida water problems but with those of the whole state.

# 12 Water for the Future

I n 1963 the Florida Geological Survey issued a pamphlet in which it confidently concluded that the state's water resources were sufficient to meet all expected growth. Annual average rainfall was 53 inches, or 148 billion gallons a day. Under the hot Florida sun some 108 billion gallons a day evaporated or were utilized by vegetation, but this left 40 billion gallons a day to replenish rivers, lakes, and aquifers and this was eight times the amount currently being used. The pamphlet boasted of Florida's many lakes, both natural and artificial. Four major dams on the Apalachicola, Ochlocknee, Withlacoochee, and Oklawaha rivers backed up a total of 187 billion gallons of water. There were 182 large springs, more than in any other state. Silver Springs alone discharged 500 million gallons a day, "enough to satisfy Florida's municipal and rural and domestic needs, if it could be distributed to the place of need." Underlying most of the state was the remarkable Floridan Aquifer, estimated to contain between 800 and 1,000 cubic miles of water—one hundred times the amount impounded in Lake Mead behind Hoover Dam.[1]

In other words, why worry? Yet nine years later the legislature was enacting a series of laws providing for conservation and management of the state's water resources to ensure an adequate supply for the future. Why this striking change of mood? The 1963 document was a typical example of Florida boosterism, extolling the state's resources and inviting more industry, more farming, more tourists, and more residents. The 1972 legislation reflected the rise of environmentalism with its insistence that not all growth was good. Growth was bad when it resulted in polluted lakes, rivers, and bayfronts; growth was bad when it led to breakdowns in the water supply and salt intrusion into the wellfields; growth was bad when it destroyed the mangrove swamps and drained vital marshlands. By 1972 it had become obvious that the state had water problems. For one thing, the most

276

abundant supply was not always close to where water was most needed. Many of the biggest rivers, lakes, and springs were located in the Panhandle and northern Florida, several hundred miles from central and southern Florida where the larger cities were located and where farming and mining made heavy water demands. Moreover, average rainfall was a somewhat misleading concept in a state where 70 percent of the rain usually fell between May and October and only 30 percent the other six months of the year. There were wet years when hurricanes, tropical storms, and heavy rains flooded farms and homes and dry years when municipal supplies ran dry, irrigation water had to be rationed, and uncontrolled fires raged through the Everglades. Public concern about water rose and fell in a counter movement to the water level. During six of the seven years preceding the complacent 1963 pamphlet, Florida had received more than average rainfall; during five of the seven years preceding the 1972 legislation it had received less than the average.

The Water Resources Act of 1972 required the Department of Natural Resources, in cooperation with the Department of Administration, Bureau of Planning, to formulate "an integrated, coordinated plan for the use and development of the waters of the state."[2] This water use plan, together with the water quality standards and classifications of the Department of Pollution Control, was to constitute the Florida water plan. The governing boards of the new water management districts were directed to gather data and advise in drafting those portions of the state plan that would apply to their region. The law obviously intended a vast coordinated planning effort to measure the water resources of the state, to estimate future water needs, and to determine how these needs might be met. At first the planning process proceeded rather slowly. Not until 1976 did the legislature finally draw the boundaries and the voters approve the taxing powers so that the water management districts could go into operation on 1 January 1977. At the state level responsibility was still divided until the Environmental Reorganization Act of 1975 charged the new Department of Environmental Regulation with responsibility for safeguarding both quantity and quality of water. The DER was to assume the duty of formulating both the water use plan and the quality standards for the final water plan.

Even before the formal planning process began, a number of agencies had been gathering important information about the Florida water situation. In 1975 a U.S. Geological Survey estimated that about 18.420 billion gallons a day were being withdrawn for all purposes. About 11.502 billion gallons of this was saltwater withdrawn from bays or estuaries, mostly for electric power plants. About 6.918 billion gallons of fresh water were withdrawn in nearly equal quantities from surface water sources and from wells. Popular assumptions to the contrary, the heaviest water users were not the city dwellers. Only 1.146 billion gallons a day were withdrawn for public supplies. The heaviest water users were farmers and ranchers, who withdrew 2.868 billion gallons a day to irrigate their fields and pastures. Second to them were industrialists, who withdrew 2.638 billion gallons a day for various purposes.[3]

In the politics of water, farmers, ranchers, manufacturers, miners, real estate developers, homeowners, sportsmen, and nature lovers all had vital interests at stake. Historically, the strongest of these groups had always been the farmers. Although less than 1.5 million acres, or about 4.3 percent of Florida land, were under cultivation in 1976,[4] three crops were highly important to the economy. Florida grew more citrus than any other state; in 1976 the orange crop was

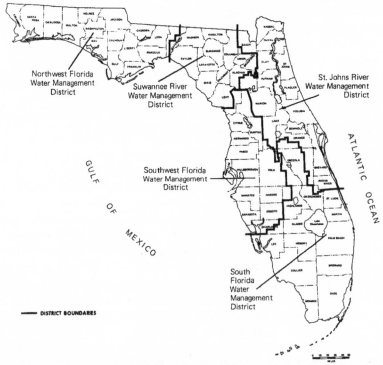

Water management districts. On 1 January 1977, five districts charged with developing and administering water policy for the entire state went into operation. State of Florida, Bureau of Natural Resources. Map Collection, Strozier Library.

valued at $538 million. Vegetables brought in another $409 million, with Florida producing more tomatoes than any other state except California. The third major crop was sugar, worth $192 million in 1976. Florida was now growing more sugarcane than either Hawaii or Louisiana. Also important to the state were the cattle ranches, dairies, and poultry farms, with an aggregate income of $693 million in 1976. With 1.4 million head of beef cattle Florida ranked ninth among the states.[5] The typical Florida farmer or rancher was not the sturdy individualist of American tradition. In 1971 the Florida Chamber of Commerce reported that one-third of the agricultural land was owned by corporations, a larger proportion than in any other state in the continental United States.[6]

Because of Florida's dry winters and springs, all of the major crops required extensive irrigation. In 1975 the state had 564,829 acres of irrigated citrus groves. Almost half of this acreage was in four counties of central and eastern Florida: Polk, 91,650 acres; St. Lucie, 73,000; Lake, 52,000; and Indian River, 50,000.[7] Although the groves required large quantities of water, their demands were mitigated by several factors. During the summer and fall this region had abundant rainfall. Many of the groves were in the central highlands where the rolling country constituted a splendid recharge area for the Floridan Aquifer. Even when the growers had to irrigate with water drawn from nearby streams, canals, lakes, and rivers, the demands were moderate, and much of the water seeped back into the aquifer. Indeed an Orange County farm agent traveled through the region displaying an empty rain barrel to dramatize the warning that urban development in the region north of Disney World was reducing the acreage in orange groves, thereby endangering the aquifer.[8]

The state had 317,716 acres of irrigated vegetable farms. Palm Beach County had 119,000 of these acres, more than 37 percent of the total, and other counties south of Lake Okeechobee—Dade, Collier, Hendry, Lee, and Broward—accounted for almost 80,000 acres more. In all, this usually frost-free region of South Florida, ideal for growing winter vegetables, had more than 62 percent of the total irrigated truck farming acreage of the state. The other 38 percent was widely scattered, with 19,910 acres in St. Johns County on the northeast coast and 12,500 acres in Jackson County in the northern Panhandle.[9] Although the vegetable growers of South Florida were heavy water users, they agitated for extensive drainage and a low water table. Only in this way could they farm low-lying acreage, especially that located near the coast in southern Dade County. The low water table was a threat, particularly in drought years, to the urban wellfields on which the Gold Coast cities depended. In other ways, too, the location of the southern vegetable farms created problems. As the metropolitan areas expanded, developers bought up more and more of the agricultural land. The farmers, therefore, had to open up new acreage to the west and south. But whenever they did so, they alarmed the environmentalists, fearful that wetlands important to the flow of water into Everglades National Park would be invaded. In 1976 two large companies announced plans to grow vegetables on tracts close to the eastern entrance to the park. Nature lovers protested that this would diminish the flow and pollute the water of Taylor Slough, which was vital to the Anhinga Trail, the most popular nature walk in the park. They pressed the Dade County planning agencies to save the wetlands from further encroachment. At stake were not only the beauties of nature but the recharge of the Biscayne Aquifer and the preservation of marine life in the southern estuaries.[10]

Sugar growers were very heavy irrigators. In 1975 Florida had 289,000 acres of irrigated sugar fields. Of this, 245,000 acres, or 85 percent, were located in Palm Beach County, and the rest was in three other counties bordering Lake Okeechobee—Hendry, Glades, and Martin.[11] Sugar growers argued that their heavy use of irrigation water was offset by the runoff that was pumped back into Lake Okeechobee. But the water thus returned was so loaded with oxidized muck, fertilizers, and pesticides that it contributed seriously to the eutrophication problem.

Environmentalists criticized the sugar growers on other grounds as well. To protect the Everglades Agricultural Area from flooding, the Army Corps of Engineers had built levees, canals, and pumping stations, mostly at federal taxpayers' expense. Thousands of acres of land had been drained before it was needed, interrupting the flow of water into the conservation areas and the aquifers as well as into Everglades National Park. All the drained lands, whether cultivated or uncultivated, were being rapidly depleted because this type of soil, unless it remained moist, oxidized and disappeared. Soil subsidence had, in fact, been a problem ever since drainage began in the region. Experts calculated the average rate of subsidence at one inch of muck soil per year. Unless the process could be halted or retarded, the famous muck soil—once advertised as richer than the soil of the Nile Valley—would become too shallow for cultivation before the year 2000. This was the reason why environmental scientists urged the state to sell no more Everglades land to the farmers and instead to allow as much as possible to revert to wetlands. They also urged experiments with rice and other wetland crops that would be less destructive of the soil.[12]

Sugar growers had always been heavily involved in national politics. Domestic producers, both of cane and beet sugar, had been adept in obtaining tariff protection and subsidies. At the beginning of 1979 warehouses in Belle Glade and other parts of South Florida were bulging with U.S.–owned sugar acquired during the Carter administration in the latest of these federal aid programs, a system of price supports based on government loans to sugar planters. At every level of government—federal, state, and regional—there were important decisions to be made for the future. Should tariffs, quotas, drainage policies, irrigation policies, and labor policies continue to foster the domestic cultivation of sugar? Environmentalists opposed these special privileges to an enterprise that was polluting the water and consuming the soil. Nutritionists joined in attacking a product whose overuse was injuring the health of millions of American children and adults. But the great sugar corporations continued to exert strong political power in defending their interests. They argued that domestic sugar production provided employment and retarded the outward flow of American dollars.

But sugar was not the only crop that created problems. In 1975 Florida had 537,600 acres of irrigated pasture land, more irrigated acres than for vegetables or sugar and second only to citrus. Over half of this acreage was in four counties bordering on Lake Okeechobee—Highlands with 100,000 acres, Hendry with 88,000, Palm Beach with 60,000, and Okeechobee with 40,000.[13] This region of large cattle ranches and dairies had been transformed by the flood control works. Even before these were built, there had been an extensive livestock industry, but the cattle had usually grazed on natural range. The animals had adapted themselves to the climate and the terrain, feeding on the higher ground during the wet season and venturing down into the marshlands during the dry season. But the digging of canals and drainage ditches had brought drastic changes. Not only were thousands of acres reclaimed for ranching but heavy investments were made in artificial grasses to provide better forage. In the Kissimmee Basin alone improved pasture increased 370 percent between 1958 and 1972—from 122,000 acres to 576,000 acres.[14]

This expansion of improved pasture had serious implications for water resources. To thrive, the artificial grasses had to have plenty of moisture, yet the drainage program had resulted in a rapid runoff of rainwater and a lower water table—hence the need for more and more irrigation. Even more serious were the pollution problems from cattle wastes draining off into the streams and lakes. Environmental scientists argued that the number of cattle needed to be reduced, that better management should be required to prevent the discharge of wastes, and that more water should be retained in the uplands. Since the maintenance of improved pasture required heavy expenditures for ditching, fertilizing, and pumping water, the environmentalists argued that the ranchers would make more money by returning to a greater use of natural pasture, limiting the percentage of improved pasture to an average of 25 percent.[15]

Much of the water withdrawn for irrigation soaked into the soil or ran off into neighboring streams and canals. Only the portion utilized by the vegetation or evaporated was actually consumed. Experts estimated that for the state as a whole, irrigation consumed 1.331 billion gallons a day, about 46 percent of the 2.867 billion gallons withdrawn. In the hot southern counties the consumption rate was higher, about 65 percent in Palm Beach County and about 58 percent in Hendry.[16]

Throughout the state urban development was eating away at agriculture. The Institute of Food and Agricultural Sciences at the University of Florida estimated the annual reduction of farmland at 57,000 acres. Because of freezes and urban expansion there were 100,000 fewer acres in orange groves in 1975 than in 1969. Yet through better management the growers were actually growing more oranges. Agricultural experts hoped that more intensive methods and greater diversification would permit a continued growth of Florida agriculture. But heavier irrigation and greater use of fertilizers and pesticides meant more potential water problems.[17]

During 1975 Florida industry withdrew about 2.738 billion gallons of fresh water a day. The heaviest use was for generating electricity. Steam and nuclear power plants used 13.137 billion gallons a day, mostly for their cooling processes. Of this, 11.439 billion gallons were saline water and 1.698 billion gallons fresh. Although electric power generation was increasing rapidly, growing by 42 percent between 1970 and 1975, the industry's water use increased by only 18 percent during the same period. Much of the fresh water was now recycled through cooling ponds and cooling towers. Because most of the water was returned to streams and lakes, the actual consumption was small, estimated at about 36 million gallons a day or 2 percent of the total withdrawals, in contrast with other industrial uses, estimated to consume about 28 percent of the water withdrawn.[18]

The second heaviest industrial use of water was in phosphate mining. In 1976 Florida mines extracted more than 395 million tons

Phosphate mining on the Peace River. Producing a major share of the world's supply, the phosphate industry was so powerful in Florida politics that it long escaped effective regulation despite its damage to the environment. Environmental Information Center.

of phosphate—not only more than that of any other state but more than that of any other country. The few companies dominating the field exerted such power in Florida politics that the legislature did not even impose a severance tax until 1971.[19] Environmentalists disliked phosphate mining because of its heavy water demands, its polluting discharges, and the ugly pit holes and waste piles that followed its operations.

In 1975 the Florida phosphate industry withdrew about 270 million gallons of water a day. Almost 90 percent of this was used in Polk County. Combined with the heavy demands of electric power plants and citrus groves, these withdrawals made Polk County the heaviest water user in the state, 713 million gallons a day. (Palm Beach County, with almost twice the population of Polk, withdrew 660 million gallons a day).[20] Long careless in its disposal of wastes, the phosphate industry had four times since 1960 caused major fish kills in the Peace River. Responding to public criticism and pressure from the new environmental agencies, the mining companies were making a strong effort to clean up their act. They took measures to conserve and reuse as much water as possible and planted timber on their reserve lands and spoil piles to reduce erosion.[21]

There were also phosphate mines in Hamilton County in the upper Suwannee River basin. In 1967 when Congress was considering protection of the Suwannee as one of the nation's "wild and scenic rivers," Senator Holland succeeded in having the proposal deferred for further study. But even this prospect disturbed the chemical companies. A Monsanto executive warned Holland that his company might have to reconsider its plans to expand operations, and a spokesman for the Occidental Agricultural Chemical Company urged that the proposed study be limited to the lower part of the river where there were no mines. Governor Kirk, the Florida cabinet, and the Florida legislature all went on record as opposed to any inclusion of the Suwannee. As finally passed, the bill limited the study to the lower reaches of the river.[22]

In 1973 Occidental asked state permission to expand its operations along a thirty-mile stretch of the Suwannee. Environmentalists charged that this would mar the natural beauty of the area, pollute streams used by sportsmen, and impair the purity of springs and sinkholes that were connected with the aquifer. But the Bureau of Land Planning recommended against declaring the upper Suwannee an area of critical state concern. Instead it praised the phosphate company's plan to refrain from mining along a 1,000-foot buffer zone on either side of the river and in other sensitive areas. "Occidental," the report said, "has shown a relatively high degree of environmental awareness in their existing Hamilton County operation. In their general willingness to cooperate with environmental agencies and their initiative in experimenting with techniques in reclamation and pollution control, the firm provides a fine example to the extractive industry."[23]

Three other industries resembled phosphate mining in that they were both heavy water users and heavy dischargers of polluting wastes. The pulp-and-paper mills of northern Florida withdrew more than 225 million gallons a day; the chemical industry located mostly in the Panhandle withdrew about 100 million gallons a day; and citrus processing in central Florida withdrew 70 million gallons a day.[24]

Limerock mining, which used 88 million gallons a day, was another industry that created water problems. Limerock was the principal ingredient in the cement that Florida contractors used for almost everything they built—office buildings, condominiums, houses, highways, and airport runways. In 1968, the Coastal Petroleum Company, partly owned by Sen. James Buckley of New York and William Buckley, the columnist, sought permission to dig for limerock under the surface of Lake Okeechobee. The company claimed a legal right under an earlier lease from the state permitting it to drill for oil. The Flood Control District strongly objected to mining operations that would not only pollute the lake but might even knock a hole through the rock barrier separating the lake from the saltwater aquifer beneath it. Governor Kirk also strongly opposed the request. In the end, the Army Corps of Engineers denied permission to dredge, and a federal judge upheld the state and the corps. But elsewhere, especially in Hernando County north of Tampa, limerock mining boomed. Gouging out huge pits, sometimes fifty feet deep, the mines marred the landscape and created ponds lacking the pure water needed for healthy plant growth and fish and wildlife.[25]

Although city dwellers required less water than farmers, ranchers, and industrialists, their needs increased rapidly with the burgeoning population. Between 1950 and 1970 Florida's population grew by 145 percent, a faster rate than that of any other state expect Nevada. In 1950 the population had been 2.8 million; in 1970 it was 6.8 million. And the growth continued: in 1978 the population was 8.9 million, and the state's rate of growth was almost four times that of the United States as a whole.[26] Providing these millions of new residents with places to live brought big returns to landowners,

Melaleuca trees. Among the exotic species introduced by Florida foresters and nurserymen was the Melaleuca from Australia. With their dense, white, paperlike bark, these hardy trees spread rapidly, displacing native species, especially in overdrained areas of South Florida. Environmental Information Center.

promoters, contractors, and construction workers. It also provided rich opportunities for lending institutions — banks, insurance companies, and pension funds. Continued growth was therefore of vital interest to many powerful groups.

Strong though this alliance was, the environmentalists were able to convince key public officials that not all construction was good. Experts could now present scientific data to expose the hidden costs involved in unplanned growth. In Dade County there was rising opposition to building projects that would add to the pollution of Biscayne Bay, drain too many of the western wetlands, or create water supply and sewage problems. All of the other urban areas — Tampa, St. Petersburg, Jacksonville, Orlando, West Palm Beach, Fort Lauderdale — were going through parallel experiences. Because of the high price of building lots and the popularity of suburban living, developers preferred to leapfrog over the nearby districts to open up more distant tracts where they could buy cheap swampland or moderately priced farms. By draining lands that might have remained wet, the promoters seriously disrupted the ecology of whole regions. They destroyed the habitats of fish and wildlife; they polluted streams; they converted land better suited for pasturage or wetland crops into home lots. Draining these lowlands reduced aquifer levels, not only endangering water supplies but parching out healthy vegetation and promoting the growth of Melaleuca trees and other undesirable plants.

Many purchasers in these new developments assumed that the drainage ditches and flood control works gave them good protection. But experts predicted that any hurricane like those of 1926, 1928, 1947, or 1948 would inundate thousands of acres of low-lying land. According to Nat Reed, now a member of the South Florida WMD governing board, "tens of thousands" of owners would have their homes flooded for forty to sixty days. "The pain and suffering which our citizens will face is beyond comprehension," Reed said. "They will be the lucky ones for thousands of mobile home owners will have lost their lives and all their personal property."[27]

Who was responsible for this dangerous situation? Reed blamed city and county governments, which had "abdicated their legal responsibilities to the ever present land developers who overbuilt on marginal and submarginal land throughout coastal Florida." From the land planning viewpoint, Reed said, it was a tragedy that the state had not had a major wet hurricane in the last eighteen years of uncontrolled growth. He predicted that when more normal weather conditions again bring hurricanes every three to five years, the elected officials who have been so lax in administering the zoning laws will have passed from the scene, and the water management districts will reap the bitter crop of public wrath. And then what? If history repeats itself, Florida officials will besiege Congress with appeals for expensive new flood control projects. But Reed warned that Washington politicians, fearing taxpayer resentment, will be much less ready to come to the state's rescue. It would be much wiser, Reed said, for the state to learn the lesson that "marginal lands cannot be heavily developed."[28]

Waterfront property commanded such a high price that developers hacked down mangrove swamps near the ocean and the intracoastal canals and dug finger canals. In interior Florida they used similar means to develop the lake fronts—cutting down the bordering cypress, dredging out the lake bottoms, and digging finger canals. Belated state efforts to halt this damage ran into a legal stonewall because the courts ruled that most Florida lakes were private property. The only publicly owned lakes were those that had been "meandered" as navigable waters by federal surveyors during the nineteenth century.[29] The passion for lakefront even extended to the excavation of artificial lakes despite the fact that cutting into the limestone might damage the aquifer and that these man-made lakes were difficult to keep clean of weeds and refuse.

The promoters who most damaged the environment were those who drained and cleared the land before it was needed. Attempting to add plausibility to their sales compaigns, they built roads and canals that completely disrupted the natural flow of the water and thereby disrupted the ecology. Golden Gate Estates in Collier County was the most notorious example of this, but there were many others. Under the pressure of the environmental movement, developers proceeded somewhat more cautiously during the 1970s, choosing their sites more carefully, preserving natural features, and making better provision for water supply and sewage disposal.

But the conscience of the developers was not so highly sensitized that it obviated the need for public regulation, and government at all levels played an increasingly active role. The Army Corps of Engineers gave more serious study to the environmental impact of its projects and blocked the digging of certain private canals. The Environmental Protection Agency took steps to protect the purity of drinking water and prevent pollution. The state legislature passed laws dealing with land and water use and gave important powers to the Department of Environmental Regulation. Municipal officers, county commissions, and regional agencies prepared land use plans to guide them in issuing building permits and authorizing water and sewer hookups.

Developers and their allies continued to fight against what they regarded as interference with the rights of private property. The struggle was particularly bitter in Dade County, where a master plan had carefully mapped areas where development would be permitted, areas that would be reserved for farming, and areas that would be preserved in their natural state. At a hearing of the Metro Planning Advisory Board in 1977, developers blamed the rigidity of the plan for the soaring costs of land and homes and for unemployment in the construction industry. A real estate sales executive said that he was "sick and tired" of this "no growth" policy. Another businessman said: "You and your plan are not the sole contributing cause to Dade County's demise—but you and your plan are one of the causes."[30] To ask a Florida politician to vote against growth was almost like asking him to vote against God and motherhood. How then were the environmentalists able to stiffen so many backbones? One reason was their broadening base. No longer could they be dismissed as bird-watching eccentrics; their ranks now contained thousands of staid newcomers from the North, convinced that helter-skelter development might ruin the state they now called home.

A state water plan was important to both the development lobby and the environmentalists. If growth was to continue at the same pace, it was necessary to make provision for future water needs; if growth was to be restrained or guided, it was vital to identify the regions that could and could not tolerate development. Because of earlier work by the Central and Southern Florida Flood Control District and the Army Corps of Engineers, the South Florida Water Management District had gone farther toward developing its water use plan than any other district. As we have seen, however, the early drafts encountered strong criticism because of their emphasis on technological answers to projected water needs. To meet objections voiced in public hearings and by state agencies, the district began to modify its plans to place more stress on storage and conservation.

Meanwhile, the Southwest Florida Water Management District had also been drafting its plans. Several warning signals had been observed during the 1960s and 1970s. Rainfall in the region had been less than normal during eleven of the thirteen years from 1961 through 1974. In southwestern Polk County and eastern Hillsborough County the groundwater level had dropped sometimes as much as 60 feet. Municipal wells in St. Petersburg were suffering from saltwater intrusion. The level of the Hillsborough River, from which Tampa drew its water supply, was dropping.

Garald Parker, chief hydrologist for the district, made some gloomy predictions. In 1970 the district was withdrawing 467 billion gallons of water a year, about 70 percent of the normal recharge. By 1984 the annual withdrawals would equal the recharge. It was necessary to utilize all the available water crop, but this was difficult to do because residents in the interior were unwilling to allow their water to be moved to the coastal cities where it was needed. Moreover, it was not easy to locate new sources of supply. The Tampa Bay cities could not look south because water was already scarce in Sarasota and Charlotte counties; they could not look east to the Green Swamp because of rapid urbanization along the cross-state highway leading to Disney World and Orlando. The most promising areas to develop were located to the north, in Pasco, Hernando, Citrus, and Levy counties. In the more distant future, Parker said, it might be possible to go out of the district completely and bring in water by aqueduct from the Suwannee and Apalachicola rivers, but there would be strong political opposition to this. "It can only be achieved," said Parker, "when a regional water supply system is established which is incorporated into a workable and acceptable State Water Plan that will guarantee to supply and protect the water resources of this entire rapidly growing region."[31]

In the 1977 draft of the district plan, there was a somewhat more optimistic view. It was estimated that the population of the district would more than double, rising from 2.2 million in 1976 to 4.9 million in 2020. If present consumption patterns continued, demand for water would almost double in the same period, rising from 1.2 billion

Miami Beach. Dredging for landfill. July 1925. By dredging up sand from the bay bottom and spreading it on the oceanfront, developers created high-priced land. SPA.

gallons a day to 2.118 billion. Supplying these needs from sources within the district would require careful management, but it could be done. The Tampa Bay cities would have to develop new wellfields in a region to the north in Pasco and Hernando counties; the "Sun Belt" around Lakeland and Winter Haven would develop sources in the Green Swamp; Sarasota and the other Gulf cities south of Tampa would have to supplement local wellfields with desalination; the interior counties would need to use the Peace River. The future would be more secure, however, if rigorous conservation measures could be taken. The planners particularly recommended experiments in the reuse of wastewater. Industries could either recycle their own or municipal wastewater; farmers could reuse industrial or municipal wastewater for irrigation in addition to cutting down their water needs in other ways; municipalities could reuse wastewater for sprinkling parks, road medians, and lawns, perhaps developing a dual system of mains for drinking water and water for other purposes. By combining such conservation measures, the planners believed that total water use for the year 2020 could be cut from 2.118 billion gallons to 1.494 billion—almost 30 percent.[32] Environmentalists preferred the Southwest Florida WMD approach with its strong emphasis on conservation to that of the South Florida WMD with its continued reliance on more engineering works requiring the use of fossil fuels.

The three new water management districts were not as far advanced in their planning. Northwest and Suwannee were regions of abundant rainfall and brimming lakes, rivers, and springs. A few Panhandle cities like Panama City, Fort Walton Beach, and Quincy were troubled either by saltwater intrusion or dropping water tables, but the more serious problems involved industrial pollution. Chemical plants near Pensacola discharged wastes into Escambia Bay; pulp-and-paper mills in the eastern Panhandle and northern Gulf coast region injured several rivers; phosphate mining in the upper Suwannee Basin was a threat to a beautiful and historic stream.[33]

In contrast to Northwest and Suwannee, the St. Johns Water Management District was in a region of rapidly growing cities—Jacksonville, St. Augustine, Daytona Beach, Titusville, Melbourne, and northern Orlando. The population of the district was expected to more than double in a 45-year period, from 2 million in 1975 to 4.3 million in 2020.[34] In 1975 the district was withdrawing 1.655 billions gallons of fresh water a day.[35] In 2020, according to an estimate made by the Department of Natural Resources in 1970, it would require over 2.6 billion gallons a day. The total available supply in the St. Johns River Basin had been estimated at 4.5 billion gallons a day, about 2.5 billion in groundwater and 2 billion in surface water.[36] This might seem to assure a safe margin, but the situation was complicated by many factors. Not all water was available for all purposes. Many lakes and rivers were magnificent for boating and fishing but too polluted for drinking. Drainage from pastures and croplands conveyed animal wastes, fertilizers, and pesticides into the surface water and threatened to seep into the aquifers. There were serious saltwater intrusion problems in Jacksonville and other coastal cities. In the interior, excessive drainage, poorly planned highways, overdevelopment, and huge parking lots interfered with the recharge of the aquifers and reduced local supplies. Even the much praised Floridan Aquifer did not always provide high quality water. In Indian River County and other eastern regions, the Floridan Aquifer water was too highly mineralized for municipal use although usually good enough for irrigation.

In 1970 DNR experts had recommended careful management to protect the water resources. They advised Jacksonville and Cocoa Beach to develop wellfields farther to the west in areas where the recharge of the aquifers was adequate. These recharge areas should be protected from development. Pumping from the wells should not be permitted to exceed the recharge of the aquifers. To prevent overpumping and saltwater intrusion, standby wells should be provided. The downpour from storms should not be allowed to flow into the ocean but should be impounded for future use. Provision should be made for transferring water from areas of surplus supply to areas of shortage. Minimum levels should be established for the lakes. Control structures should be built on the drainage canals to reduce the need for irrigation.[37]

Further planning for the region was the responsibility of the new water management district. In a draft released in 1977 the district engineers explained their basic problem in a simplified water budget. Out of an average annual rainfall of 53 inches, roughly 73 percent or 39 inches was lost through evapotranspiration. The remaining 14 inches ran out to the ocean through either surface or underground flow. The only water resources available for use came from capturing this 14 inches of runoff or withdrawing water stored in the aquifers. Even these sources had to be carefully used. If the discharge of the rivers into the estuaries was reduced too much, marine life would suffer. If too much groundwater was withdrawn, saltwater would intrude into the wellfields, and changes of vegetation would occur in the overdrained areas.[38]

The 1977 draft plan emphasized environmentalism and conservation of fuels. In a list of management policies, the district committed itself to utilizing water near points of need before seeking more distant sources; considering aspects of quality as well as quantity; giving significant consideration to environmental impact; favoring nonstructural water management that utilized functional aspects of natural systems over structural alternatives; and considering economic impacts and regional and state implications of proposed projects.[39]

While the new water management district was demonstrating

sensitivity to the new environmentalism, the International Tele-phone and Telegraph Company was providing a case study in the old boosterism in its plans for a huge development in Flagler County, midway between St. Augustine and Daytona Beach. The company announced that this new resort city, called Palm Coast, would have a population of 750,000 by the year 2010 and would need 50 million gallons of water a day. (Actually, a place that large would probably require twice that amount, judging from the experience of other Florida cities.) "You can't remove that amount of water from that area," warned Brice Auth, executive director of the St. Johns WMD. A more immediate threat was the honeycomb of canals—28 miles of them—that ITT had dug to provide waterfront lots, some of them priced at $20,000 apiece. Environmentalists warned that these canals with their poor water quality would be plagued with algae blooms and would in turn contaminate the Atlantic Intracoastal Waterway. The Army Corps of Engineers granted permission to connect only 13 miles of the new canals with the waterway.[40] In drawing its grandiose plans, ITT had relied on earlier, more lenient, government policies; now it would have to reshape its project to conform with the more stringent requirements of the new environ-mental agencies.

While the five water management districts were gradually work-ing out their water use plans, other building blocks in the state water plan were also being prepared. The Division of State Planning had provided one such block in the water section of the State Com-prehensive Plan, and the Department of Environmental Regulation was putting together another in the water quality plan that would include state standards and the procedures for enforcing them.

To provide for Florida's future needs, the improvement of water quality was all-important. From all parts of the state came news of rivers and lakes no longer safe for either drinking or swimming. Poisonous discharges from paper mills and cellulose factories had ruined the Amelia River north of Jacksonville and the Fenholloway on the northern Gulf coast; overenrichment from agricultural wastes and sewage had devastated Lake Apopka, once famous for its good fishing; suburban development was threatening Lake Jackson near Tallahassee; pasture runoff was polluting the Kissimmee River and Taylor Creek; discharges from these sources and from the sugar fields were injuring Lake Okeechobee.

If the natural streams and lakes were in poor condition, the artifi-cial ones were in much worse condition. Weeds and trash choked the canals and drainage ditches; oil spillage and sewage fouled the intracoastal waterways. The more heavily populated the areas through which the canals ran, the more they were polluted. According to state standards, water safe for recreational purposes should contain no more than 1,000 coliform bacteria per 100 milliliters. Yet the Miami Canal had a coliform count of 15,000 and ten other Gold Coast canals had 2,000 or more. An environmentalist commented bitterly: "Perhaps if people knew something about the water quality of our canals, they would hesitate before buying a waterfront home. A child can pick up less bacteria playing in a toilet bowl than in many canals."[41]

Miami, fill for Bayfront Park, ca. 1925. Construction of high-rise buildings completed the rapid transformation of the coastal area.

But bacteria were not the only hidden enemies in the waterways. In 1975 inspectors discovered the highest concentration of PCB chemicals ever recorded—1.3 million parts per billion—in Broward County's South New River Canal and lesser concentrations in several other canals. Since PCBs were highly toxic industrial chemicals similar to DDT, they constituted a threat to wildlife in the Everglades, to fish and marine life along the shore, and to the local population. They were suspected, among other things, of causing cancer. But how did the PCBs get into the water? They were used in the manufacture of inks, plastics, paints, lubricants, and electrical equipment, but there was very little of this kind of industry in South

Florida. Puzzled authorities asked a marina to install a screen to help prevent particles of paint and fiber glass from being washed into the New River Canal.[42]

In a state relying so heavily on well-water drawn from relatively shallow aquifers, the proper disposal of sewage was particularly important. Yet Florida cities seemed never to catch up with their needs. New tracts would be opened before there were sewers available. Each household would make do with a cesspool or septic tank. Overflow from these threatened to pollute first the individual's well and then those of his neighbors. In 1948 there were so few sewers in Fort Lauderdale that the county health director said the city was "floating on top of a vast cesspool."[43] In this and other cities sewer systems were gradually extended, but the individual septic tanks were never completely replaced. The systems, moreover, were no better than the treatment provided for the effluents, and these arrangements were rarely thorough and efficient. In the Miami region there were a large number of small, cheaply built systems. Raw or inadequately treated sewage frequently discharged into the ocean or the canals. In 1953 Helen Muir wrote: "Out of sight, out of mind would be Miami's treatment of sewage through the years until the day would come when she had fouled up her clear, sweet river and her blue shining bay to such an extent that it was no longer out of sight and fish would die and sea gardens would disappear and the beautiful Biscayne Bay would lie, a pollution between man and God."[44]

During the 1960s and 1970s belated efforts were made to stop the pollution of the Miami River and Biscayne Bay. The establishment of a metropolitan government was followed by the organization of a Miami-Dade Water and Sewer Authority intended to consolidate the local units. But getting an effective handle on the problem was a slow and expensive process. From time to time an epidemic would remind the community of the continuing danger from the careless disposal of human wastes. In 1971 there was a rise in viral hepatitis both in Dade County and in other parts of Florida; and in 1973 there was an epidemic of typhoid fever among the migrant workers.[45]

Florida public health officials tested the drinking water regularly, and the local authorities chlorinated and otherwise treated the water to maintain it at a safe standard. Episodes of turbidity and high bacteria count nevertheless led to occasional scares and orders to boil water. It was difficult to safeguard the water quality because in many cities the supply was decentralized, with many local water districts and small private water companies in operation. In testing the water of 79 cities throughout the nation, the Environmental Protection Agency found that of Miami to contain the most chloroform—311 parts per billion. Two other chemicals, vinyl chloride and carbon tetrachloride, were also discovered in the Miami water. All three chemicals were suspected of causing cancer. The presence of vinyl chloride and carbon tetrachloride was not easily explained, but the heavy concentration of chloroform was believed to result from the water treatment itself. Because rainwater soaking through the Everglades muck into the aquifer took on an unsightly, though harmless, brown color, the Miami plant had been bleaching it with unusually high doses of chlorine, more than would be necessary to kill the bacteria. Further tests found chloroform and other suspect chemicals in other Dade County waters. EPA officials suggested that carbon filters might be necessary to remove these substances, but local authorities feared that this expensive process would increase water rates by 50 percent. They took no action, awaiting additional evidence on the dangers involved and further mandates from the EPA and other agencies.[46]

As early as 1913 the state legislature had directed the state board of health to prosecute anyone discharging harmful materials into the public waters. But for many decades Florida papermills, chemical factories, phosphate mines, and citrus processors continued to dump disagreeable wastes into the rivers and streams without serious challenge. Indeed, during the 1940s the legislature granted specific exemptions for the benefit of the paper and cellulose manufacturers of Nassau and Taylor counties. It was not until 1969 that a new Pollution Control Board under the leadership of Nat Reed began a more energetic program to protect water quality through a system of requiring waste discharge permits and enforcing compliance with state standards.[47] Subsequent legislation and reorganizations finally deposited these functions in the Department of Environmental Regulation. In addition to safeguarding the quantity and quality of water, the DER was to maintain air quality, control noise, supervise solid waste disposal, protect coastal zones, and approve the location of new power plants.

Over the next few years the DER, headed by Jay Landers, set up a far-reaching program for establishing state standards for water quality, issuing permits, and forcing compliance. In an effort to decentralize these functions, field offices were established for regions roughly paralleling the water management districts. In fixing standards the DER sought to bring the state regulations into harmony with those established by its federal counterpart, the Environmental

Protection Agency. Indeed, one of the DER's most important functions was to help local governments qualify for federal dollars in planning and building sewage treatment plants and other projects for restoring water quality.[48]

The DER established a system under which waters of the state were placed in seven classifications ranging from Class I-A "Potable Water Supplies: Surface Waters" to Class V-B "Freshwater Storage: Utility and Industrial Use: Saline Ground Waters." Cutting across all the classifications was a special designation "Outstanding Florida Waters" (OFWs), which were to receive the highest protection. The OFWs included waters in the national and state parks, the scenic and

Dead lake. Florida's lakes were particularly vulnerable to overenrichment from sewage, pasture runoff, and fertilizer from croplands. They became choked with weeds, and the sport fish, deprived of oxygen, died off. SPA.

wild rivers, the wilderness areas, the Big Cypress National Freshwater Preserve, and state-owned environmentally endangered lands.[49] So far as other waters were concerned, the DER undertook to bring the state into compliance with a federal law specifying that by 1983 all public waters should be pure enough to support aquatic plant and fish life and to permit swimming (Class III, according to Florida standards). By 1977 some 90 percent of industrial and municipal wastewater treatment plants were in compliance with DER regulations or had projects underway to bring them into compliance. A few notorious streams—the Miami River, the Fenholloway on the Gulf coast, Rice Creek near Palatka, and Eleven Mile Creek near

Pensacola—were expected to be still below Class III standards in 1983, but even on these the offending industries, mostly pulp-and-paper or cellulose mills, had installed better facilities for treating their wastewaters.[50] Difficult though it was to curb the discharge of industries and sewage treatment plants, the DER faced a still more challenging problem for the future in dealing with so-called non-point sources, such as agricultural wastes and forestry, mining, and stormwater runoff.

In 1977 the legislature extended the powers of the DER. By the Florida Safe Drinking Water Act the agency was directed to adopt and enforce drinking water standards no less stringent than those specified by the federal government. By the Water Resources Restoration and Preservation Act the DER was authorized to take measures to rehabilitate the state's ailing lakes.[51] Funded half by the federal government and half by the state, the agency concentrated its early efforts on eliminating the sources of pollution that had ruined Lake Apopka and damaged Lake Jackson.[52]

In these efforts to restore the clarity of Florida's lakes and rivers and the purity of her drinking water, we may detect an unconscious yearning to reverse history and return to those Edenic conditions that had existed when Americans first visited the territory. Naturalists like William Bartram and soldiers like George McCall had exulted in the clear blue skies, the balmy weather, and the lush vegetation. They had marveled particularly at the extraordinary transparency of the water—lakes and rivers alive with darting fish, and springs in which one could watch a tiny button sink slowly to the bottom. Even the rainwater seemed to taste better in Florida. In 1853 an early booster urged California-bound ships to fill their casks at Key West: "There is no sweeter water carried to sea than that afforded by our large cisterns. Rainwater never becomes sour, nor does it acquire an unpleasant bilgy taste, but it improves with age and remains pure for years." Another resident boasted that South Florida rainwater was "the healthiest and sweetest water in the world."[53]

Nature had bestowed lavish gifts on Florida, but the early settlers were not happy with all of nature's arrangements. The peninsula had a very long coastline, made doubly dangerous by reefs and by the region's violent storms. Within a few years of American settlement, inhabitants began to agitate for a cross-Florida canal and other waterways that would prevent shipwrecks. The call for these improvements persisted for 150 years, long after the age of sailing vessels when the need had seemed acute.

The Everglades. The "sea of grass" with its tree islands once stretched over much of South Florida. Although reduced by drainage to half their original size, the Everglades survived in the national park and the conservation areas. SPA.

Nature's second alleged mistake in Florida was to dump too much rain on a flat terrain with inadequate runoff. To repair that defect early dreamers concocted schemes for draining the Everglades and other wetlands. To aid in reclamation a generous federal government turned over to the state some 22 million acres of loosely defined swampland. Much of this endowment was diverted to aid the construction of railroads; other large portions fell into the hands of timber lords and land speculators. Not until 1881 when the state made its contract with Hamilton Disston was any large amount of swampland used to promote reclamation. Disston's drainage program had only minimal success, but the state itself went into the reclamation business under Governor Broward and his successors. This effort broke down completely during the Great Depression, but terrible floods brought assistance from the federal government. First around Lake Okeechobee, next in a wide area of South Florida, and finally in the Tampa Bay region, the Army Corps of Engineers carried on a massive campaign to bring errant nature under control. Their works provided flood protection to millions of residents, opened up thousands of acres to crop production and ranching, and stored water for various uses. But in calculating costs and benefits, there was never any adequate accounting for environmental damages—for vegetation destroyed, wildlife disrupted, rivers polluted, lakes killed, and marshes dried up.

The water shortages of the 1960s and 1970s provided a dramatic warning that man's interference with nature had gone too far. For most of its history Florida's problem had been too much water; now residents worried that there would not be enough water of adequate purity to meet future needs. How could a dependable supply be assured? Occasionally someone would suggest a giant aqueduct to transport water from the rivers and springs of northwestern Florida to the heavily populated cities of the central and southern sections. But most planners dismissed such dreams as too expensive and too controversial to win support in Florida's regionally jealous legislature. Rejecting grandiose California-type solutions, the planners sought to have each city and district continue to provide its own supply from nearby wellfields, rivers, and lakes. Instead of radical new departures, they relied for the most part on traditional Florida sources. The only really new element was the strong recognition that water was a treasure to be guarded, not something to be squandered or taken for granted. Instead of treating the rainwater that poured down during summer afternoons as a nuisance to be gotten rid of as speedily as possible, it was to be cherished as a blessing. Open lots where the rainwater might stand for hours should serve to recharge the aquifers; crowded buildings, paved roads, and parking lots would impede such recharge. Good urban planning, therefore, required provision for more open space, better designed highways, and parking lots so constructed that the rainwater would run off onto open land. Individual homeowners could help by installing water-saving faucets, shower heads, and toilet bowls and by landscaping with Bermuda grass and native vegetation rather than varieties that required heavy sprinkling. Farmers and industrialists could save large quantities of water by recycling it for further use. Engineers could devise better means of storing storm water, treating and reusing sewage water, and desalinating saltwater from the ocean and the deep aquifers.

It all added up to a renewed cooperation between man and nature. Nature did its part by dropping more annual rainfall on Florida than

Water into land — nature's way. A mangrove tree forms a new island off Bamboo Key in 1916. A John Small photograph. SPA.

on any other state and by providing extraordinary underground reservoirs. Nature's arrangements, however, did not always suit man's convenience; some years nature flooded the state with more water than people could handle; other years it dispensed rain so grudgingly that wells ran dry, crops were parched, and animals died of thirst. Promethean man could sometimes improve on nature, but painful experience was teaching him humility. He was learning to study more carefully the ecological consequences of his levees and drainage ditches, to understand the importance of preserving swamplands and mangroves, and to restrain the excesses of his developers and land speculators. In a word, man was learning to treat water with due reverence.

# Notes

## 1. The Watery Eden

1. Maj. Gen. George A. McCall, *Letters from the Frontier*. A Facsimile Reproduction of the 1868 Edition (Gainesville: University Presses of Florida, 1974), p. 77.

2. Ibid., p. 169.

3. *The Travels of William Bartram*, Naturalists Edition, ed. Francis Harper (New Haven: Yale University Press, 1958), p. 69.

4. Ibid., pp. 141–42, 145.

5. *Niles Weekly Register*, 26 February 1825.

6. *Notices of East Florida, With an Account of the Seminole Nation of Indians, by a Recent Traveller in the Province*. A Facsimile Reproduction of the 1822 Edition (Gainesville: University of Florida Press, 1973), pp. 38–39.

7. Ibid., p. 40.

8. *Travels of William Bartram*, pp. 104–5.

9. Ibid., pp. 145–46.

10. McCall, *Letters from the Frontier*, pp. 150–51.

11. Ibid., p. 197.

12. *Niles Weekly Register*, 20 November, 1830.

13. Ellen Call Long, *Florida Breezes; or, Florida New and Old*. A Facsimile Reproduction of the 1883 Edition (Gainesville: University of Florida Press, 1962), p. 144.

14. *Niles Weekly Register*, 14 December 1822.

15. Robert F. Marx, *Shipwrecks in Florida Waters* (Eau Gallie, Fla.: Scott Publishing Co., 1969), pp. 61–66.

16. *Niles Weekly Register*, 14 November 1835.

17. Ibid., 12 November 1825.

18. LeRoy Collins, *Forerunners Courageous: Stories of Frontier Florida* (Tallahassee: Colcade Publishers, 1971), pp. 59–60; Walter C. Mallory, *A Sketch of the History of Key West, Florida*. A Facsimile Reproduction of the 1876 Edition (Gainesville: University of Florida Press, 1968), pp. 71–75; Helen Muir, *Miami, U.S.A.* (New York: Henry Holt & Co., 1953), pp. 24–25.

19. *American Quarterly Review* 2 (September 1827): 215.

20. Harriet Beecher Stowe, *Palmetto-Leaves*. A Facsimile Reproduction of the 1873 Edition (Gainesville: University of Florida Press, 1968), p. 117.

21. *Travels of William Bartram*, p. 78.

22. Ibid., p. 76.

23. *Niles Weekly Register,* 18 March 1826.

24. Charles Vignoles, *Observations upon the Floridas* (New York: E. Bliss and E. White, 1823), p. 50.

25. *Notices of East Florida,* pp. 24–25.

26. John Lee Williams, *The Territory of Florida . . . . A Facsimile Reproduction of the 1837 Edition* (Gainesville: University of Florida Press, 1962), p. 151.

27. *North American Review* 54 (January 1842): 7.

28. Ibid., p. 14.

29. Maj. Henry Whiting, "Cursory Remarks upon East Florida in 1838," *American Journal of Science* 35 (January 1839): 57.

30. *North American Review* 54 (January 1842): 14–15.

31. Patricia Caulfield, *Everglades* (San Francisco: Sierra Club, 1970), p. 42.

32. McCall, *Letters from the Frontier,* pp. 397–98.

33. Whiting, "Cursory Remarks upon East Florida," p. 64.

## 2. EARLY BOOSTERS

1. *Niles Weekly Register,* 29 October 1825.

2. Long, *Florida Breezes,* p. 109.

3. James Grant Forbes, *Sketches, Historical and Topographical of the Floridas, More Particularly of East Florida.* A Facsimile Reproduction of the 1821 Edition (Gainesville: University of Florida Press, 1964), p. 101.

4. *Notices of East Florida,* p. 26.

5. Vignoles, *Observations upon the Floridas,* p. 80.

6. U.S. National Archives, *The Territorial Papers of the United States,* comp. and ed. Clarence Edwin Carter (Washington: National Archives, 1934–  ), 23:136.

7. *Niles Weekly Register,* 9 April 1825.

8. Ibid., 22 April 1825.

9. Ibid., 8 October 1825.

10. U.S. Congress, Senate, *Report from Select Committee on Roads and Canals, to Which Was Referred a Bill for the Survey of a Route for a Canal between the Atlantic and the Gulf of Mexico, January 19, 1826,* 19th Cong., 1st sess., 1826, Senate Doc. 21, pp. 6–14.

11. *Gales and Seaton's Register of Debates in Congress* 2 (19 December 1825): 821–22.

12. *Territorial Papers,* 23:379.

13. U.S. Congress, Senate, *Memorial of James Gadsden and E. R. Gibson, Commissioners Appointed by the Legislative Council of Florida, to Examine into the Expediency of Opening a Canal through the Peninsula of Florida,* 19th Cong., 1st sess., 1826, Senate Doc. 15, pp. 3–4.

14. *Register of Debates in Congress* 2 (5 January 1826): 29; (11 January 1826): 31–32; (14 February 1826): 89–108; (21 February 1826): 1421–22.

15. Ibid., 2 (14 February 1826): 99.

16. U.S. Congress, House, *Message from the President of the United States, Transmitting a Report of the Board of Engineers of a Survey with a View to Ascertain the Most Eligible Route for a Canal to Connect the Atlantic with the Gulf of Mexico, February 25, 1829,* 20th Cong., 2d sess., 1829, House Executive Doc. 147, p. 1; *Niles Weekly Register,* 19 August 1826.

17. *Niles Weekly Register,* 20 January 1827.

18. *Territorial Papers,* 23:707–8, 835–36; *Memoirs of John Quincy Adams, Comprising Portions of His Diary from 1795 to 1848.* ed. Charles Francis Adams (Philadelphia: J. B. Lippincott & Co., 1874–77), 7:353.

19. *Territorial Papers,* 24:33–34.

20. U.S. Congress, House, *Letter from the Secretary of War Transmitting a Report of Lieutenant John Pickell Respecting the Practicability of a Canal across the Peninsula of Florida, March 26, 1832,* 22d Cong., 1st sess., 1832, House Doc. 185, pp. 20–52.

21. Ibid., pp. 1–2.

22. *Territorial Papers,* 24:976.

23. Williams, *Territory of Florida,* p. 146.

24. U. S. National Archives, "The Establishment of Lighthouses in Florida, 1823–1828," ed. Henry P. Beers, typescript, P. K. Yonge Library, University of Florida, Gainesville.

25. *Niles Weekly Register,* 5 April 1828.

26. Federal Writers Project, Miami, Florida, "Florida Lighthouses," typescript, P. K. Yonge Library, University of Florida, Gainesville.

27. Ibid.; *Niles Weekly Register,* 19 November 1836.

28. *Niles National Register,* 18 October 1838.

29. Ibid., 17 July 1830, 7 February 1835.

30. *Acts of the Legislative Council of the Territory of Florida, 1832,* pp. 76–81 (10 February 1833).

31. Williams, *Territory of Florida,* p. 146.

32. *Niles Weekly Register,* 19 January 1828, 17 July 1830.

33. Williams, *Territory of Florida,* p. 145.

34. *Niles National Register,* 5 August 1843.

35. *Notices of East Florida,* p. 10.

36. *Niles National Register,* 5 August 1843.

37. *Acts of the Legislative Council, 1833,* p. 95 (15 February 1833).

38. *Territorial Papers,* 23:303.

39. *Acts of the Legislative Council, 1837,* pp. 26–31 (12 February 1837).

40. Whiting, "Cursory Remarks upon East Florida in 1838," p. 54.

41. *Territorial Papers,* 26:802.

42. Ibid., pp. 851–52.

43. *Niles National Register,* 26 November 1842.

44. Ibid., 8 July 1843.

45. Ibid., 17 October 1846.

46. *De Bow's Southern and Western Review* 10 (April 1851):405.

47. *Acts and Resolutions of the First General Assembly of the State of Florida, 1845,* p. 20.

48. Ibid., *Adjourned Session, 1845,* pp. 150–51.

49. Williams, *Territory of Florida,* p. 151.

50. *Niles National Register,* 13 September 1845.

51. U.S. Congress, Senate, *Everglades of Florida, Acts, Reports and Other Papers State and National, Relating to the Everglades of the State of Florida and Their Reclamation,* 62d Cong., 1st sess., 1911, Senate Doc. 89, p. 51.

52. Ibid., p. 52.

53. Ibid., p. 54.

54. Ibid.

55. Ibid., pp. 55–57.

56. Ibid., p. 63.

57. *De Bow's Commercial Review of the South and West*, 7 (October 1848):298.

58. Ibid.; *Niles National Register*, 18 October 1848.

59. Lamar Johnson, *Beyond the Fourth Generation* (Gainesville: University Presses of Florida, 1974), p. 70.

60. *Minutes of the Proceedings of the Board of Trustees of the Internal Improvement Fund of the State of Florida*, 1:vii–viii. Hereafter cited as *Minutes, IIF*.

61. *Acts of the Florida Legislature, 1850–1851*, pp. 93–94 (24 January 1851).

62. *Florida House Journal, 1852–1853*, App., p. 10.

63. Ibid., p. 12.

64. Ibid., p. 10.

65. Ibid., pp. 10–11.

66. *Acts of Florida Legislature, 1852–1853*, pp. 75–77 (10 January 1853).

67. U. S. Congress, House, "Report of 1st Lieutenant M. L. Smith, Topographical Engineers, to Colonel J. J. Abert, October 30, 1852," Appendix F to *Report of Secretary of War*, 34th Cong., 1st sess., 1854, House Exec. Doc. 1, Part 2, pp. 434–65.

68. *Florida House Journal, 1854–1855*, pp. 18–19.

69. John Melvin DeGrove, "The Administration of Internal Improvement Problems in Florida, 1845–1869" (Master's thesis, Emory University, 1954), p. 60.

70. *Minutes, IIF*, 1:xv–xxv.

71. DeGrove, "The Administration of Internal Improvement Problems in Florida," pp. 119–20.

72. Ibid., pp. 121–22.

73. Ibid., pp. 124–25.

74. *Acts of the Florida Legislature, 1856–1857*, pp. 36–39 (1 January 1857).

75. DeGrove, pp. 131–34.

76. *Acts of the Florida Legislature, 1860–1861*, p. 165 (14 February 1861).

77. DeGrove, pp. 154–55.

78. *Minutes, IIF*, 1:251–52.

79. Ibid., p. 254.

80. Ibid., pp. 255–56.

## 3. The Big Dealers

1. *Florida Union* (Jacksonville), 17 December 1868.

2. William Watson Davis, *The Civil War and Reconstruction in Florida*. A Facsimile Reproduction of the 1913 Edition (Gainesville: University of Florida Press, 1964), pp. 451–52.

3. *Minutes, IIF*, 1:270–71. See Johnson, *Beyond the Fourth Generation*, pp. 72–73.

4. *Minutes, IIF*, 1:298–99.

5. Ibid., pp. 308–9.

6. *St. Augustine Examiner*, 29 February 1868.

7. *Florida Union* (Jacksonville), 21 January 1869.

8. *Laws of Florida, 1868*, pp. 137–40 (28 July 1868).

9. Davis, *Civil War and Reconstruction in Florida*, pp. 546–48, 553–55;

Richard Current, *Three Carpetbag Governors* (Baton Rouge: Louisiana State University Press, 1967), pp. 21–22.

10. *Florida Union* (Jacksonville), 14 January 1869; *The Sentinel* (Tallahassee), 30 January 1869.

11. *Minutes, IIF*, 1:351.

12. *Laws of Florida, 1869*, p. 38 (1 February 1869).

13. *Minutes, IIF*, 1:352–58.

14. Ibid., pp. 365–69.

15. Davis, *Civil War and Reconstruction in Florida*, pp. 651–53.

16. Accounts of W. H. Gleason with Southern Inland Navigation Co., 1870 and 1871, William H. Gleason Papers, Box 1, P. K. Yonge Library, University of Florida, Gainesville.

17. *Minutes, IIF*, 1:337–38.

18. Ibid., pp. 403–4.

19. Ibid., pp. 422–23.

20. Ibid., p. 458.

21. Harrison Reed and others to Willis Gaylord, 25 August 1870, Gleason Papers, Box 1.

22. *Minutes, IIF*, 1:365–69.

23. Ibid., p. 441.

24. *Laws of Florida, 1870*, pp. 96–98 (18 February 1870).

25. Jerrell H. Shofner, *Nor Is It Yet Over: Florida in the Era of Reconstruction* (Gainesville: University Presses of Florida, 1974), p. 115.

26. Draft petition to IIF trustees [n.d.], Gleason Papers, Box 5.

27. C. L. Mather to W. H. Gleason, 22 January 1871, ibid., Box 1.

28. Copy of Bill of Complaint, filed in 4th Judicial Court of Florida, W. H. Gleason vs. So. Inland Navigation & I. Co., 12 October 1883, ibid.

29. N. H. Moragne to S. B. Conover, 7 February 1871, ibid.

30. N. H. Moragne to W. H. Gleason, 10 February 1871, ibid.

31. W. Gaylord to W. H. Gleason, 28 March 1871, ibid.

32. Various receipts, ibid., Box 1.

33. Draft petition to IIF trustees [n.d.], ibid., Box 5.

34. Certificate signed by J. S. Adams, 31 October 1871, ibid., Box 6.

35. *Minutes, IIF*, 1:506–12.

36. John Wallace, *Carpet Bag Rule in Florida*. A Facsimile Reproduction of the 1888 Edition (Gainesville: University of Florida Press, 1964), p. 154.

37. *Minutes, IIF*, 1:476, 478–79.

38. Wallace, *Carpet Bag Rule in Florida*, pp. 155, 158.

39. *Minutes, IIF*, 2:8.

40. Resolution passed by Directors of So. Nav. Co., 16 May 1873, Gleason Papers, Box 1.

41. Draft petition to IIF trustees [n.d.], ibid., Box 5.

42. Gulf and Atlantic Transit Canal Co., Articles of Incorporation, 23 February 1874, ibid., Box 6.

43. U.S. Congress, Senate, *Report of Lieut. Col. Q. A. Gillmore, Corps of Engineers on a Waterline of Transportation from the Mouth of Saint Mary's River to the Gulf of Mexico, January 19, 1877*, 44th Cong., 2d sess., 1877, Senate Ex. Doc. 22, p. 23, hereafter cited as *First Gillmore Report*.

44. U.S. Congress, House, *Joint Memorial of the Legislature of Alabama Relating to Ship Communication between the Waters of the Gulf of Mexico and the*

*Atlantic Ocean by Ship Canal through the Florida Peninsula*, 42d Cong., 2d sess., 1872, House Misc. Doc. 110, pp. 1–3; U.S. Congress, House, *Resolution of the Legislature of Texas Instructing and Requesting the Congressional Delegation of Said State to Urge upon Congress the Survey and Construction of a Ship-canal across the Peninsula of Florida*, 43d Cong., 1st sess., 1874, House Misc. Doc. 118, p. 1.

45.  U.S. Congress, Senate, *Report of the Results of an Examination Made of the Peninsula of Florida, with a View to the Construction of a Ship Canal from Saint Mary's River to the Gulf of Mexico, April 2, 1880*, 46th Cong., 2d sess., 1880, Senate Ex. Doc. 154, p. 2. Hereafter cited as *Second Gillmore Report*.

46.  Gulf Coast and Florida Peninsula Canal Company, *Statement and Copy of Charter* (Fernandina: Observer Office, 1875), p. 1.

47.  *First Gillmore Report*, pp. 7–15.

48.  *Second Gillmore Report*, pp. 6, 23–24.

49.  W. H. Gleason to J. H. Fry, 12 July 1874, Gleason Papers, Box 1; Contract: So. Inland Navigation Co. and J. H. Fry, 15 July 1874, ibid., Box 6.

50.  *Minutes*, IIF, 2:62–63.

51.  Power of Attorney: So. Inland Navigation Co. to J. H. Fry, 1 August 1874, Gleason Papers, Box 6.

52.  Articles of Agreement: So. Inland Navigation Co. and J. H. Fry, 13 May 1876, ibid., Box 6.

53.  J. H. Fry to W. H. Gleason, 20 November 1876, ibid., Box 1.

54.  *Minutes*, IIF, 2:93–94.

55.  Ibid., p. 98.

56.  Ibid., pp. 104–7.

57.  Ibid., pp. 131, 193–94.

58.  S. A. Swann to Philip, Thos. Blyth, 13 June 1877, Samuel A. Swann Papers, Box 23, P. K. Yonge Library, University of Florida, Gainesville.

59.  S. A. Swann to Hugh Corley, 11 August 1877, ibid.

60.  *Minutes*, IIF, 2:212–21.

61.  Ibid., p. 222.

62.  Ibid., pp. 236–37.

63.  Hugh Corley to S. A. Swann, 27 January 1879, Swann Papers, Box 23.

64.  *Minutes*, IIF, 2:349.

65.  Ibid., p. 360.

66.  R. Hazard to C. D. Willard, 6 September 1877, Gleason Papers, Box 1.

67.  Frank Sherwin to W. H. Gleason, 4 November 1877, ibid.

68.  Ledger sheets, ibid., Box 6; W. H. Gleason to E. J. Reed, 26 July 1878, ibid., Box 1.

69.  W. H. Gleason to Frank Sherwin, 25 June 1878, ibid., Box 1.

70.  *Second Gillmore Report*, pp. 1–2.

71.  E. J. Reed to W. H. Gleason, 12 August 1879, Gleason Papers, Box 1.

## 4. THE FLOW OF NORTHERN DOLLARS

1.  J. P. Little, "Florida," *Lippincott's Magazine* 5 (April 1870): 420.

2.  Ibid., p. 423.

3.  J. P. Little, "Florida: How to Go and Where to Stay," *Lippincott's Magazine* 6 (December 1870): 606.

4. J. P. Little, "More About Florida," *Lippincott's Magazine* 8 (November 1871): 487.

5. Mary B. Graff, *Mandarin on the St. Johns* (Gainesville: University of Florida Press, 1953), pp. 44–48, 92.

6. Charles E. Stowe, *Life of Harriet Beecher Stowe, Compiled from Her Letters and Journal* (Boston: Houghton Mifflin, 1889), p. 403.

7. Ibid., p. 463.

8. Ibid., p. 407.

9. Harriet Beecher Stowe, *Palmetto-Leaves*. A Facsimile Reproduction of the 1873 Edition with Introductory Matter by Mary B. Graff and Edith Cowles (Gainesville: University of Florida Press, 1968), p. 155.

10. Stowe, *Life of Harriet Beecher Stowe*, p. 404.

11. Jerrell H. Shofner, "Introduction," in Sidney Lanier, *Florida: Its Scenery, Climate, and History*. A Facsimile of the 1875 Edition (Gainesville: University of Florida Press, 1973), p. xii.

12. Lanier, *Florida*, pp. 263–66.

13. "Rambler," *Guide to Florida*. A Facsimile of the 1875 Edition (Gainesville: University of Florida Press, 1964), pp. 67–68, 81, 83.

14. Stowe, *Palmetto-Leaves*, p. 166.

15. George M. Barbour, *Florida for Tourists, Invalids, and Settlers*. A Facsimile Reproduction of the 1882 Edition (Gainesville: University of Florida Press, 1964), p. 108.

16. Rambler, *Guide to Florida*, p. 93; Barbour, *Florida*, pp. 111–12.

17. Barbour, *Florida*, p. 121.

18. Ibid., p. 117.

19. S. C. Clarke, "Among the Alligators," *Lippincott's Magazine* 13 (February 1874): 223.

20. Barbour, *Florida*, pp. 32–33, 122.

21. Little, "More About Florida," p. 488.

22. Lanier, *Florida*, p. 18.

23. Barbour, *Florida*, p. 129.

24. Lanier, *Florida*, p. 20.

25. Barbour, *Florida*, p. 131.

26. Lanier, *Florida*, p. 29.

27. Little, "More About Florida," p. 490.

28. Barbour, *Florida*, pp. 46–47, 125.

29. Lanier, *Florida*, pp. 97–102.

30. Barbour, *Florida*, pp. 148–49.

31. Rambler, *Guide to Florida*, p. 145.

32. Lanier, *Florida*, p. 155.

33. Clarke, "Among the Alligators," p. 220.

34. *New York Times*, 1 May 1896, 1:2.

35. *Minutes*, iif, 2:432, 437, 463–69.

36. *New York Times*, 18 February 1881, 2:7

37. *Minutes*, iif, 3:33, 43.

38. Ibid., pp. 79–80, 94.

39. Barbour, *Florida*, pp. 143–44.

40. *New York Times*, 17 June 1881, 5:4; 21 December 1881, 1:6.

41. *Minutes*, iif, 2:506–7.

42. Ibid., 2:501, 3:52–57.

43. Ibid., 2:506–7.

44. *New York Times,* 17 June 1881, 5:4.

45. Florida Land and Improvement Co., *Disston's Purchase.* Sale Brochure and Map, P. K. Yonge Library, University of Florida, Gainesville.

46. *New York Times,* 21 December 1881, 1:6.

47. *Minutes,* IIF, 3:196; Alfred J. Hanna and Kathryn A. Hanna, *Lake Okeechobee: Well Spring of the Everglades* (Indianapolis: Bobbs-Merrill Co., 1948), pp. 98–99.

48. Report of Special Committee to Investigate the Books and Records of the Internal Improvement Fund of Florida, *House Journal,* 26 May 1893, p. 971.

49. William Bloxham, "The Disston Sale and the State Finances." A Speech Delivered at the Park Theater, Jacksonville, Fla., 26 August 1884, pp. 7–8. P. K. Yonge Library, University of Florida, Gainesville.

50. *Minutes,* IIF, 3:242–45, 332–35.

51. *New York Times,* 22 April 1883, 3:1.

52. Ibid.

53. *Report of the Committee Appointed by the Governor . . . on the Work of the Atlantic and Gulf Coast Canal and Okeechobee Land Company,* 28 January 1887, pp. 6–9.

54. *Laws of Florida, 1885,* pp. 72–73 (16 February 1885).

55. *Report of the Committee Appointed by the Governor under Chapter 369, Laws of Florida, on the Work of the Atlantic and Gulf Coast Canal and Okeechobee Land Company,* 28 Jan. 1887, pp. 6–9. P. K. Yonge Library, University of Florida, Gainesville.

56. *Minutes,* IIF, 5:272–73.

57. Disston Land Co., *Where Farming Pays.* Sales Brochure, P. K. Yonge Library, University of Florida, Gainesville.

58. *Disston's Purchase.*

59. Charles E. Harner, *Florida's Promoters: The Men Who Made It Big* (Tampa: Trend House, 1973), pp. 16–17.

60. Charlton W. Tebeau, *A History of Florida* (Coral Gables, Florida: University of Miami Press, 1971), p. 281.

61. *Where Farming Pays.*

62. Harner, *Florida's Promoters,* p. 17.

63. *Disston's Purchase.*

64. *Minutes,* IIF, 2:298–99.

65. Ibid., pp. 163–64.

66. Letter and telegram, Gleason to Reed, 22 June 1882, Gleason Papers, Box 1.

67. For example, M. G. Webb to W. H. Gleason, 20 December 1883, ibid.

68. *Minutes,* IIF, 2:482, 484–86.

69. Ibid., 3:18–21.

70. *New York Times,* 13 January 1883, 2:6; *Laws of Florida, 1883,* pp. 127–29; *Laws of Florida, 1885,* p. 82.

71. R. R. Peeler to W. H. Gleason, 25 October 1883, Gleason Papers, Box 1.

72. *Minutes,* IIF, 1:416–17, 2:136.

73. Ibid., 3:29, 157; *Prospectus of Florida Coast Line Canal and Transportation Company* (1882), P. K. Yonge Library, University of Florida, Gainesville.

74. *Minutes,* IIF, 3:234–35.

75. Ibid., p. 249.

76. Ibid., pp. 358–59, 404, 424: *Laws of Florida, 1889*, pp. 297–99; *Laws of Florida, 1893*, pp. 274–75; *Laws of Florida, 1897*, pp. 173–74.

77. *National Cyclopaedia of American Biography* (Ann Arbor: University Microfilms, 1967), 14:440–41.

78. *New York Times*, 18 March 1896, 6:7.

79. *Minutes, IIF*, 9:585.


## 5. THE PROGRESSIVE CHALLENGE

1. Tebeau, *History of Florida*, pp. 282–87.

2. Ibid., pp. 297, 302–3.

3. *Minutes, IIF*, 3:507.

4. Trustees of Internal Improvement Fund, *Florida Swamp Lands: Defense of the State against Charges of Fraud: Letter from Governor Fleming to Secretary Noble* (Tallahassee, 1890), p. 21.

5. Hanna and Hanna, *Lake Okeechobee, Well Spring of the Everglades*, pp. 108–16.

6. *Minutes, IIF*, 4:198, 207.

7. *New York Times*, 18 March 1896, 6:7.

8. *Minutes, IIF*, 4:432–33.

9. Ibid., pp. 437–42.

10. Ibid., pp. 446–47.

11. Ibid., 5:32.

12. *National Cyclopaedia of American Biography*, 11:383.

13. *Minutes, IIF*, 5:73.

14. Ibid., pp. 31, 81.

15. Ibid., 7:530.

16. Ibid., 5:62–67.

17. Ibid., p. 121.

18. *Senate Journal: 1905*, pp. 391–92.

19. *Minutes, IIF*, 5:118–19.

20. *Senate Journal: 1905*, pp. 391–94.

21. *Minutes, IIF*, 5:267.

22. Ibid., p. 129.

23. Ibid., p. 137.

24. Message of Gov. W. S. Jennings to the Legislature of Florida Relative to Reclamation of Everglades, in *The Everglades of Florida: Acts, Reports, and Other Papers Relating to the Everglades of the State of Florida and Their Reclamation*, 62d Cong., 1st sess., 1911, Senate Doc. 89, p. 90, hereafter cited as *Sen. Doc. 89*.

25. Ibid., pp. 91–93.

26. Samuel Proctor, *Napoleon Bonaparte Broward, Florida's Fighting Democrat* (Gainesville: University of Florida Press, 1950), pp. 31–177.

27. Napoleon B. Broward Papers, Box 9, P. K. Yonge Library, University of Florida, Gainesville.

28. Ibid.

29. Proctor, *Broward*, pp. 204–7.

30. Ibid., p. 219.

31. *Senate Journal: 1905*, p. 397.

32. Ibid., p. 411.

33. Ibid., p. 413.

34. *Laws of Florida: 1913*, pp. 435–37.

35. Ibid., pp. 22–23.

36. *Minutes, IIF*, 6:57–58, 62.

37. Ibid., pp. 52–53, 96.

38. Proctor, *Broward*, p. 243; Philip J. Weidling and August Burghard, *Checkered Sunshine: The Story of Fort Lauderdale, 1793–1955* (Gainesville: University of Florida Press, 1966), p. 27.

39. *House Journal: 1907*, p. 84.

40. Ibid., pp. 86, 101; Hanna and Hanna, *Lake Okeechobee*, p. 136.

41. Proctor, *Broward*, p. 241.

42. *Senate Journal: 1907*, App., pp. 66–68.

43. *St. Petersburg Independent*, 26 October 1906.

44. *A Plain Answer to Governor Broward's Open Letter to the People of Florida* (n.p., n.d.), p. 7, Broward Papers.

45. Ibid., p. 9.

46. Proctor, *Broward*, p. 250.

47. *House Journal: 1907*, p. 83.

48. *Laws of Florida, 1907*, pp. 220–22.

49. Hanna and Hanna, *Lake Okeechobee*, p. 130.

50. *House Journal: 1907*, pp. 1099–1105.

51. *Minutes, IIF*, 6:185–90.

52. Ibid., pp. 42–43.

53. Ibid., 7:49–50.

54. Ibid., pp. 129–30.

55. Ibid., pp. 144–45.

56. Ibid., pp. 149–53.

57. Ibid., p. 408.

58. Ibid., p. 462.

59. Ibid., 9:610, 616.

60. *House Journal: 1909*, App., pp. 45–46.

61. *Minutes, IIF*, 7:204–5.

62. Ibid., pp. 246–51.

63. Ibid., pp. 261–62.

64. Ibid., 6:338–40, 447–51.

65. Ibid., 7:282–83.

66. Ibid., pp. 412, 436–37.

67. Ibid., pp. 440–41.

68. Ibid., pp. 486–90, 502–13.

69. *What Has Broward Done for the People?* pamphlet in Broward Papers, Box 9.

70. *Absolute Facts Regarding Duncan U. Fletcher*, pamphlet, ibid.

71. Proctor, *Broward*, p. 293.

72. Hanna and Hanna, *Lake Okeechobee*, p. 128.

73. *Senate Journal: 1909*, pp. 1605–23.

74. Ibid., p. 1617.

75. Ibid., pp. 1623–24.

76. Ibid., p. 1597.

77. *House Journal: 1909*, App., pp. 14–15.

78. *House Journal: 1911*, pp. 61–62.
79. Hanna and Hanna, *Lake Okeechobee*, p. 132.
80. *Minutes*, IIF, 8:428–45.
81. Ibid., 9:313–17.
82. Ibid., pp. 61–63.
83. Ibid., pp. 462–69.
84. Ibid., p. 40.
85. Ibid., pp. 131–33.
86. Ibid., pp. 318–28.
87. Ibid., pp. 374–76, 632–33, 648–57.
88. Ibid., 10:324–34.
89. Everglades Drainage District, *Biennial Report: 1927–1928* (Tallahassee, 1929), p. 16.

## 6. Time of Troubles

1. Hanna and Hanna, *Lake Okeechobee*, p. 43.
2. *The Everglades of Florida, the Richest Land in the World.* Brochure of the Florida Everglades Land Company, Chicago, Broward Papers, Box 9.
3. *Everglades of Florida*, Sen. Doc. 89, passim.
4. Hanna and Hanna, *Lake Okeechobee*, pp. 157–58.
5. *Minutes*, IIF, 9:248.
6. *Sen. Doc.* 89, pp. 94–97.
7. U.S. Congress, House, *Hearings before the Committee on Expenditures in the Department of Agriculture, Everglades of Florida, February 3 to August 2, 1912*, 62d Cong., 2d sess., 1912, pp. 140–41.
8. U.S. Congress, House, *Expenditures in the Department of Agriculture*, 62d Cong., 2d sess., 1912, Report No. 1207, p. 3; Hanna and Hanna, *Lake Okeechobee*, pp. 153–58.
9. Weidling and Burghard, *Checkered Sunshine: The Story of Fort Lauderdale, 1793–1955*, p. 40.
10. M. A. Hortt, *Gold Coast Pioneer* (New York: Exposition Press, 1953), pp. 101–3.
11. Hanna and Hanna, *Lake Okeechobee*, pp. 152–54.
12. *New York Times*, 7 February 1912, 5:2; 9 February 1912, 5:3.
13. Ibid., 11 February 1912, 6:3.
14. Ibid., 6 June 1912, 13:1.
15. *Expenditures in the Department of Agriculture*, pp. 1–5, 11.
16. *New York Times*, 31 August 1912, 7:5.
17. Hanna and Hanna, *Lake Okeechobee*, p. 159.
18. *Minutes*, IIF, 9:390–95.
19. Hanna and Hanna, *Lake Okeechobee*, p. 160; Weidling and Burghard, *Checkered Sunshine*, p. 43.
20. Hanna and Hanna, p. 161.
21. *Minutes*, IIF, 9:504–5.
22. *New York Times*, 11 December 1913, sec. 4, 16:5, Hanna and Hanna, pp. 143–44.
23. *New York Times*, 14 April 1914, 16:3.
24. Ibid., 27 March 1917, 11:5.

25. Ibid., 21 November 1914, 9:3; 27 November 1914, 12:4.

26. 241 U.S. 72.

27. *Florida House Journal: 1913*, p. 1156.

28. *Minutes*, IIF, 9:421–22.

29. Ibid., pp. 647–48, 659.

30. Ibid., pp. 667–68.

31. Ibid., p. 484; Hanna and Hanna, *Lake Okeechobee*, pp. 165–66.

32. *Minutes*, IIF, 9:518; Hanna and Hanna, p. 164.

33. U.S. Congress, Senate, *Report of the Florida Everglades Commission to the Board of Commissioners of the Everglades Drainage District and the Trustees of Internal Improvement Fund, State of Florida, 1913*, 63d Cong., 2d sess., 1914, Senate Doc. 379, pp. 4, 8, hereafter cited as *Randolph Report*.

34. *Florida House Journal: 1913*, pp. 1149–50.

35. *Laws of Florida: 1913*, pp. 129–77.

36. Ibid., pp. 177–227.

37. *Randolph Report*, p. 12.

38. Ibid., p. 8.

39. Ibid., p. 67.

40. Ibid., p. 66.

41. Ibid., p. 15.

42. Ibid., p. 7.

43. *House Journal: 1913*, pp. 51–52; *Minutes*, IIF, 11:39–54.

44. Hanna and Hanna, *Lake Okeechobee*, pp. 169–70.

45. *Senate Journal: 1917*, p. 40.

46. *Minutes*, IIF, p. 39; Hanna and Hanna, *Lake Okeechobee*, pp. 171–72.

47. Everglades Drainage District, *Biennial Report: 1927–1928*, p. 73; *Laws of Florida: 1915*, 1:362–403.

48. R. E. Rose, *The Swamp and Overflowed Lands of Florida: The Disston Drainage Company and the Disston Purchase* (Tallahassee: T. Appleyard, 1916), p. 22.

49. Nevin Winter, *Florida: Land of Enchantment* (Boston: The Page Co., 1918), pp. 294–95.

50. Lawrence Will, *Cracker History of Okeechobee* ([St. Petersburg]: Great Outdoors Association, 1964), pp. 184–99, 218–22, 239–48; Hanna and Hanna, *Lake Okeechobee*, pp. 236–53.

51. Everglades Drainage District, *Biennial Report: 1927–1928*, p. 76.

52. Will, *Cracker History of Okeechobee*, pp. 125, 192, 220, 276; Hanna and Hanna, p. 267.

53. Hanna and Hanna, pp. 222–25.

54. Ibid., pp. 168, 292.

55. *Laws of Florida: 1921*, pp. 154–57.

56. *Laws of Florida: 1919*, pp. 327–28.

57. *Laws of Florida: 1925*, p. 191.

58. Everglades Drainage District, *Biennial Report: 1927–1928*, p. 76.

59. Hanna and Hanna, *Lake Okeechobee*, pp. 304–6.

60. Ibid., pp. 306–10; Will, *Cracker History of Okeechobee*, pp. 193–94, 221–22.

61. Muir, *Miami, U.S.A.*, pp. 113–14.

62. Ibid., p. 149.

63. Weidling and Burghard, *Checkered Sunshine*, p. 101.

64. *New York Times*, 11 March 1926, 7:2; Stephen J. Flynn, *Florida, Land of Fortune* (Washington: Luce, 1962), p. 289.

65. *New York Times*, 17 October 1926, sec. 9, 5; Weidling and Burghard, *Checkered Sunshine*, p. 133.

66. *New York Times*, 27 September 1926, 7:1.

67. Ibid., 2 October 1926, 1:7, 15 October 1926, 10:3.

68. U.S. Congress, House, *Hearings before the Committee on Flood Control in Florida and Elsewhere, January 10 to February 1, 1929*, 70th Cong., 2d sess., 1929, p. 247.

69. U.S. Congress, Senate, *A Report to the United States District Engineer, Jacksonville Florida ... Relative to the Caloosahatchee River and Lake Okeechobee Drainage Areas, with Special Reference to Navigation and Flood Control, December 3, 1930*, 71st Cong., 3d sess., 1930, Senate Doc. 225, p. 248, hereafter cited as *Report to U.S. District Engineer.*

70. Will, *Cracker History of Okeechobee*, pp. 296– 97.

71. Lawrence E. Will, *Okeechobee Hurricane and the Hoover Dike*, 2d ed. rev. (St. Petersburg: Great Outdoors Association, 1967), pp. 47– 86, 153– 56.

72. *Address of John W. Martin, Governor of Florida, on the Everglades Drainage Problem, West Palm Beach, October 28, 1926* (West Palm Beach, 1926), pp. 8– 11. P. K. Yonge Library, University of Florida, Gainesville.

73. Ibid., p. 11.

74. Ibid., p. 26.

75. President of Pennsylvania Sugar Company to Governor Martin, 15, November 1926, unsigned carbon copy in Ernest R. Graham Papers, Box 32, P. K. Yonge Library, University of Florida, Gainesville.

76. Gov. John W. Martin, *Financing Everglades Drainage, Discussed before Miami Chamber of Commerce, January 10, 1927*, p. 8.

77. Everglades Drainage District, *Biennial Report, 1925– 1926* (Tallahassee, 1927), pp. 73– 74.

78. *New York Times*, 4 April 1927, 9:6.

79. Ibid., 16 April 1927, 25:6.

80. *Laws of Florida, 1927*, pp. 588– 93 (28 April 1927); pp. 593– 612 (4 June 1927).

81. *Report of Engineering Board of Review to Board of Commission of Everglades Drainage District* (Tallahassee, 1927), p. 71.

82. Ibid., pp. 20– 23.

83. *New York Times*, 12 May 1927, 39:1.

84. Ibid., 12 July 1928, 14:4.

85. Ibid., 14 July 1928, 21:3; Rorick et al. v. Board of Commissioners of Everglades Drainage District, 27 *Federal Reporter*, 2d ser., pp. 377– 83 (7 July 1928).

86. *Minutes, IIF*, 18:163.

## 7. TAPPING THE FEDERAL TREASURY

1. U.S. Congress, House, *Hearings before the Committee on Flood Control, House of Representatives, 70th Cong., 2d sess., on Flood Control in Florida and*

*Elsewhere, January 10 to February 1, 1929*, pp. 247–48, hereafter cited as *Hearings on Flood Control*.

2. U.S. Congress, House, *Report from the Secretary of War Transmitting Report from the Chief of Engineers on Survey of Caloosahatchee River and Lake Okeechobee Drainage Areas, Florida, with a View to Improvement for Navigation and the Control of Floods, April 9, 1928*, 70th Cong., 1st sess., 1928, House Doc. 215, p. 50, hereafter cited as *Drainage Areas, Florida*.

3. Ibid., p. 52.

4. Johnson, *Beyond the Fourth Generation*, pp. 150–51.

5. *Hearings on Flood Control*, p. 253.

6. Ibid., p. 145.

7. U.S. Congress, Senate, *Letter from the Chief of Engineers, United States Army, Transmitting to the Chairman of the Committee on Commerce, United States Senate, in Response to a Letter Dated December 6, 1928, a Report on the Caloosahatchee River and Lake Okeechobee Drainage Areas, Florida*, 70th Cong., 2d sess., 1929, Senate Doc. 213, pp. 2–3, 7.

8. *New York Times*, 17 February 1929, 1:5.

9. *The Memoirs of Herbert Hoover: The Cabinet and the Presidency, 1920–1933* (New York: Macmillan, 1952), pp. 119, 124.

10. *Florida House Journal: 1929*, pp. 7–8.

11. *Laws of Florida: 1929*, pp. 386–406 (10 June 1929).

12. Ibid., pp. 146–63 (10 June 1929).

13. *Report to United States District Engineer*, pp. 5–6.

14. U.S. Congress, Senate, *Letter from the Chief of Engineers, United States Army, to the Chairman of the Committee on Commerce, United States Senate, Submitting a Review of the Report on the Caloosahatchee River and Lake Okeechobee Drainage Areas . . .*, 71st Cong., 2d sess., 1930, Senate Doc. 115, pp. 4–5.

15. Johnson, *Beyond the Fourth Generation*, p. 151.

16. *A Report of the Board of Commissioners of Okeechobee Flood Control District on the Activities of the District and on Lake Okeechobee, 1929–1943*, p. 22, hereafter cited as *OFCD Report*.

17. Will, *Okeechobee Hurricane and the Hoover Dike*, p. 191.

18. *OFCD Report*, pp. 11, 21; Johnson, *Beyond the Fourth Generation*, pp. 152–53.

19. U.S. Congress, Senate, *Report of the Florida Inland and Coastal Waterways Association Relative to the Waterways in Florida Improved by the United States; Waterways Improved by Nonfederal Agencies; Waterways Unimproved and Potential Artificial Waterways Connecting Natural Waterway Systems, May 16, 1929*, 71st Cong., 1st sess., 1929, Senate Doc. 14, pp. 9–50, hereafter cited as *Inland and Coastal Waterways*.

20. Ibid., pp. 36–41; *Florida Senate Journal: 1931*, pp. 885–86.

21. *Commissioners of Florida Inland Navigation District Announce Completion of Florida Intracoastal Waterway* (1935), p. 1, hereafter cited as *Florida Intracoastal Waterway*.

22. *Florida House Journal: 1913*, p. 63.

23. *Inland and Coastal Waterways*, pp. 13–14.

24. *Laws of Florida: 1927*, pp. 625–38 (25 May 1927).

25. *Laws of Florida: 1931*, pp. 625–40 (6 June 1927).

26. *New York Times*, 29 October 1933, 9:1.
27. *Florida Intracoastal Waterway*, p. 1.
28. "Platform of Principles," flyer in Broward Papers, Box 9.
29. "Mississippi to Atlantic Inland Waterway Association," flyer in Broward Papers, Box 10.
30. *Inland and Coastal Waterways*, pp. 79–80.
31. *Laws of Florida: 1921*, pp. 389–91, 431–32.
32. *Inland and Coastal Waterways*, pp. 79–80.
33. Ibid., p. 86.
34. U.S. Congress, Senate, *Documentary History of the Florida Canal: Ten Year Period January 1927 to June 1936*, 74th Cong., 2d sess., 1936, Senate Doc. 275, pp. 95–97, hereafter cited as *Doc. Hist.*
35. *Ocala Evening Star*, 3 September 1935.
36. *Doc. Hist.*, pp. 8–24.
37. Ibid., pp. 27–28.
38. Ibid., pp. 28–30, 34, 80–81.
39. Ibid., pp. 32–35.
40. R. A. Green to B. Dosh, 22 March 1933, Bert Dosh Papers, Box 2, P. K. Yonge Library, University of Florida, Gainesville.
41. *Laws of Florida: 1933*, pp. 712–20.
42. *Doc. Hist.*, p. 82.
43. *Laws of Florida: 1933*, pp. 876–77.
44. *Doc. Hist.*, p. 94.
45. Ibid., pp. 100–101.
46. Ibid., pp. 104–5.
47. Ibid., p. 105.
48. Ibid., pp. 112–13, 119.
49. Ibid., p. 125.
50. Ibid., pp. 125, 137–39.
51. *New York Times*, 1 June 1935, 9:4.
52. *Laws of Florida: General Laws, 1935*, pp. 562–76 (chap. 17023, approved 1 June 1935).
53. *Doc. Hist.*, p. 143.
54. Ibid., pp. 70–80.
55. Ibid., p. 74.
56. Ibid., pp. 85, 149.
57. Ibid., p. 144.
58. Ibid., pp. 141–43.
59. *Ocala Evening Star*, 25, 26, 27 July 1935.
60. Ibid., 2 August, 3, 4, 5 September 1935.
61. *Doc. Hist.*, p. 154; *New York Times*, 27 August 1935, 37:5.
62. *Ocala Evening Star*, 31 August 1935.
63. *Doc. Hist.*, pp. 155–56.
64. *Ocala Evening Star*, 3, 5 September 1935.
65. Ibid., 7 September 1935.
66. Ibid., 20 September 1935; *New York Times*, 20 September 1935, 2:1.
67. *New York Times*, 24 November 1935, sec. 4,10:4.
68. Ibid., 9 November 1935, 5:1.
69. Ibid., 24 October 1935, 34:2.
70. Ibid., 24 January 1936, 30:2.

71. Ibid., 20 October 1935, sec. 4, 10:1.

72. U.S. Congress, House, *Hearings before the Committee on Rivers and Harbors, House of Representatives, 75th Cong., 1st sess., on H.R. 6150, A Bill for the Completion of the Atlantic-Gulf Ship Canal across Florida, April 1937*, p. 226.

73. *Doc. Hist.*, pp. 159–60.

74. *New York Times*, 5 January 1936, sec. 4, 7:6.

75. Ibid., 18 December 1935, 1:1.

76. *Doc. Hist.*, pp. 163, 193–97.

77. *New York Times*, 11 February 1936, 1:6; 13 February 1936, 4:4.

78. Ibid., 7 March 1936, 1:4.

79. *Doc. Hist.*, pp. 296–311.

80. Ibid., p. 315.

81. Ibid., p. 312.

82. Ibid., pp. 337–38.

83. Ibid., p. 358.

84. *New York Times*, 11 April 1936, 2:2; 16 April 1936, 1:7.

85. *Doc. Hist.*, p. 400.

86. *New York Times*, 30 May 1936, 15:1.

87. *Doc. Hist.*, pp. 435, 457–58.

88. *New York Times*, 18 June 1936, 1:8.

89. U.S. Congress, House, *Letter from the Secretary of War Transmitting to the House of Representatives a Letter from the Chief of Engineers, United States Army, Dated April 1, 1937, Submitting a Report Together with Accompanying Papers and Illustrations on a Preliminary Examination and Survey of Various Routes for a Waterway across Southern Georgia or Northern Florida to Connect the Atlantic Ocean with the Gulf of Mexico . . .*, 75th Cong., 1st sess., 1937, House Doc. 194, p. 9, hereafter cited as *Atlantic-Gulf Ship Canal*.

90. *New York Times*, 20 July 1936, 22:3.

91. *Atlantic-Gulf Ship Canal*, p. 148.

92. Ibid., p. 29.

93. Ibid., p. 6.

94. Ibid., p. 5.

95. *New York Times*, 17 June 1937, 5:2.

96. Ibid., 18 January 1939, 1:7.

97. Ibid., 18 May 1939, 1:3.

98. Telegram W. F. Coachman, Jr., to B. Dosh, Bert Dosh Papers, Box 2.

99. *New York Times*, 9 August 1941, 1:7.

100. Confidential memorandum in Bert Dosh Papers, Box 2.

101. Walter F. Coachman, Jr., to Members of Executive Committee of Canal Counties, 29 January 1942, ibid.

102. Coachman to Members of Executive Committee of Canal Counties, 2 February 1942, ibid.

103. Coachman to Rush H. Todd, 13 February 1942, ibid.

104. *New York Times*, 18 June 1942, 1:1.

105. Florida Defenders of the Environment, *Environmental Impact of the Cross-Florida Barge Canal with Special Emphasis on the Oklawaha River Ecosystem* (Gainesville, 1970), p. 53.

106. *New York Times*, 17 July 1942, 9:1.

107. Ibid., 18 July 1942, 7:1.

108. C. P. Sumerall to Governors of Eastern States, 16 January 1943, Bert Dosh Papers, Box 2.

## 8. STRUGGLE FOR CONSERVATION

1. Charlton W. Tebeau, *Man in the Everglades: 2000 Years of Human History in the Everglades National Park* (Coral Gables: University of Miami Press, 1968), pp. 169–70.

2. Ibid., pp. 167–72.

3. Ibid., pp. 173–81.

4. John M. DeGrove, *Approaches to Water Resources Development in Central and Southern Florida, 1845–1847* (Gainesville: Public Administration Clearing House of the University of Florida, 1958), pp. 45–47.

5. Ibid., pp. 31–32.

6. Johnson, *Beyond the Fourth Generation*, pp. 85–86.

7. *Laws of Florida: 1941*, pp. 1443–79 (3 June 1941).

8. *New York Times*, 11 June 1941, 31:4.

9. *Minutes*, IIF, 24:291.

10. Johnson, *Beyond the Fourth Generation*, pp. 174–75.

11. Ibid., p. 175.

12. *Minutes*, IIF, 24:128–31.

13. Ibid., 24:281–83.

14. Typescript in Graham Papers, Box 32.

15. *Laws of Florida: 1947, General Acts*, pp. 1494–95; *Special Acts*, pp. 329–33, 581–84, 2225–29.

16. James A. Franklin to Sam Collier, 19 August 1947, Graham Papers, Box 32.

17. Johnson, *Beyond the Fourth Generation*, pp. 135–39; Weidling and Burghard, *Checkered Sunshine*, pp. 235–36; Nixon Smiley, *Yesterday's Miami* (Miami: E. A. Seaman Publishing, Inc., 1973), p. 151.

18. Johnson, *Beyond the Fourth Generation*, pp. 139–45, 180.

19. Holland to Hiram Faver, 25 November 1947, Spessard L. Holland Papers, Box 287.61–Flood Control, P. K. Yonge Library, University of Florida, Gainesville. Unless otherwise specified, references to the Holland Papers are to this box.

20. See notations on telegram, Irlo Brownson to Holland, Holland Papers.

21. Thad H. Carlton to Holland, 12 February 1948; Holland to Maj. Gen. R. C. Crawford, Acting Chief of Engineers, 17 February 1948; Millard Caldwell to Holland, 17 February 1948, Holland Papers.

22. U.S. Congress, House of Representatives, *Comprehensive Report on Central and Southern Florida for Flood Control and Other Purposes*, 80th Cong., 2d sess., 1948, House Doc. 643, pp. 1–5.

23. Sam Collier to Holland, 24 February 1948, Holland Papers.

24. E. A. Menninger to Holland, 5 March 1948, ibid.

25. Holland to L. B. Eurit, 23 February 1948, ibid.

26. Menninger to Holland, 16 March 1948, ibid.

27. Johnson, *Beyond the Fourth Generation*, p. 160.

28. C. C. Spades to Holland, 5 March 1948; telegram R. Y. Patterson to Holland, 14 June 1948, Holland Papers.

29. Holland to Harold Collee, 22 June 1948, ibid.

30. Holland to H. M. Forman, 21 June 1948, ibid.

31. *Minutes, IIF*, 27:28, 55–56.

32. Holland to Lamar Johnson, 30 September 1948, Holland Papers.

33. *Laws of Florida: 1949*, pp. 476–99 (2 June 1949).

34. Ibid., pp. 629–36 (10 June 1949).

35. Johnson, *Beyond the Fourth Generation*, pp. 160–63.

36. John DeGrove, *The Florida Flood Control District: Inter-University Case Program #58* (Indianapolis: Bobbs Merrill, 1960), pp. 3–4.

37. Ibid., p. 22.

38. Ibid., p. 12.

39. *Miami Herald*, 9–10 August 1951, clippings in Holland Papers, Box 374–4c.

40. DeGrove, *The Florida Flood Control District*, pp. 12–20, 23–24.

41. *Miami Herald*, 9 December 1976, 6B:1.

42. Central and Southern Florida Flood Control District, *Fifteen Years of Progress, 1949–1964* (West Palm Beach, n.d.), p. 21.

43. Ibid., pp. 10–11.

44. Ibid., pp. 8–9, 21–22.

45. Lester J. Carter, *The Florida Experience: Land and Water Policy in a Growth State* (Baltimore: Johns Hopkins University Press, 1974), pp. 97–98.

46. Johnson, *Beyond the Fourth Generation*, p. 82.

47. *New York Times*, 7 August 1966, sec. 4, 8:1.

48. *Water Management Bulletin*, 2 (August–September 1968): 3 (published by Central and Southern Florida Flood Control District).

49. *Miami Herald*, 20 March 1970, 6A:3.

50. *New York Times*, 30 November 1969, 122:5.

51. Johnson, *Beyond the Fourth Generation*, pp. 184–85.

52. *New York Times*, 6 May 1962, 131:3.

53. U.S. Congress, House of Representatives, *Public Works Appropriations for 1965, Hearings before a Subcommittee of the Committee on Appropriations*, 88th Cong., 2d sess., 1964, Pt. 4, p. 11.

54. *New York Times*, 30 January 1966, sec. 5, 12:2.

55. U.S. Congress, House of Representatives, *Public Works Appropriations for 1967, Hearings before a Subcommittee of the Committee on Appropriations*, 89th Cong., 2d sess., 1966, Pt. 3, p. 1370.

56. *New York Times*, 9 May 1967, 40:1.

57. Ibid., 8 May 1967, 1:1, 14 May 1967, sec. 4, 10:2.

58. *Water Management Bulletin* 4 (August–September 1970): 1; 1 (December–January 1967–68): 2.

59. U.S. Congress, House of Representatives, *Water Resources for Central and Southern Florida, July 30, 1968, Letter from the Secretary of the Army Transmitting a Letter from the Chief of Engineers, Department of the Army, Dated June 3, 1968, Submitting a Report . . .*, 90th Cong., 2d sess., 1968, House Doc. 369, p. 248.

60. Ibid., pp. 257–59.

61. Ibid., p. 53.

62. Ibid., p. 9.

63. Ibid., pp. x–xi.
64. Ibid., pp. xiv–xvi.
65. *New York Times*, 16 March 1969, 37:1.
66. *Water Management Bulletin* 2 (June–July 1970): 1.
67. Carter, *The Florida Experience*, pp. 123–24.
68. Johnson, *Beyond the Fourth Generation*, pp. 211, 214.

9. ENVIRONMENTALISTS TO THE RESCUE

1. Cambridge Survey Research, *Environment and Florida Voters: Their Concerns on Growth, Energy, Pollution, Land Use Controls, In-Migration Taxes, Politics and the Future of the State* (Gainesville: Urban and Regional Development Center, University of Florida, 1974), p.iii.
2. Carter, *The Florida Experience*, p. 50.
3. Ibid., pp. 53–54.
4. Speech by the Honorable Nathaniel P. Reed at the 14th American Water Resources Conference on 6 November 1978, at the Dutch Inn, Disneyworld Village, Lake Buena Vista, Florida, copy in author's possession, pp. 3–4.
5. Ibid., p. 6.
6. William R. McCluney, *The Environmental Destruction of South Florida: Handbook for Citizens* (Coral Gables: University of Miami Press, 1969), pp. 123–24; interview with Loring Lovell, 28 November 1978.
7. Bob Dow to Bert Dosh, 3 January 1951, Dosh Papers, Box 2.
8. John H. Perry to Dosh, 8 January 1951, ibid.
9. Henry Buchman to J. H. Perry, 1 February 1951, ibid.
10. Memoranda, 8, 14 February 1951, Holland Papers, Box 374–4c.
11. Robert A. Lovett to President Truman, 29 May 1951, Dosh Papers, Box 2.
12. U.S. Army Engineer District, Jacksonville, *Economic Restudy of Cross-Florida Barge Canal, January 10, 1958* (Jacksonville, 1958), p. i.
13. Collins to Chairman, House Appropriations Subcommittee, Cross-Florida Barge Canal Hearings, 1 May 1958; S. L. Holland to Chief of Army Corps of Engineers, 24 November 1958, Dosh Papers, Box 2.
14. R. N. Dosh to Holland, 19 June 1959, A. J. Ellender to Holland, 25 June 1959, Dosh Papers, Box 2.
15. Clipping, ibid.
16. J. W. Wakefield to Holland, 21 June 1961, ibid.
17. *New York Times*, 21 September 1963, 48:6.
18. Bryant to Dosh, 26 February 1962, Dosh Papers, Box 2.
19. Giles Evans, Jr., to Dosh, 16 March 1962, ibid.
20. Memorandum in Robert Henry Davis Papers, Box 1, P. K. Yonge Library, University of Florida, Gainesville.
21. Carter, *The Florida Experience*, pp. 277–78.
22. Buchman to Dosh, 1 March 1963, Dosh Papers, Box 2.
23. Dosh to Bailey, 5 March 1963, ibid.
24. Dosh to Bailey, 28 December 1963, ibid.
25. U.S. Congress, House of Representatives, *Public Works Appropriations for 1966, Hearings before a Subcommittee of the Committee on Appropriations*, 89th Cong., 1st sess., 1965, Pt. 4, p. 949.
26. *New York Times*, 24 November 1963, sec. 5, 15:4.

27. Dosh to John Bailey, 28 December 1963, Dosh Papers, Box 2.

28. *New York Times*, 28 February 1964, 1:3.

29. Paul E. Rogers, "The Oldest (Permanent) Floating Boondoggle in American Politics," *Miami Interaction* 5 (Spring 1974):7.

30. Chronology in R. H. Davis Papers.

31. Mimeographed letter, 10 March 1965, and brochure, Miscellaneous Material on Cross-Florida Barge Canal, P. K. Yonge Library, University of Florida, Gainesville.

32. *Public Works Appropriations for 1966*, Pt. 4, pp. 1329–34.

33. Ibid., pp. 946–47.

34. Carter, *The Florida Experience*, p. 282.

35. *Life Magazine* 55 (16 August 1963): 26–27, 55; *New York Times*, 21 July 1965, 36:2.

36. *New York Times*, 6 November 1965, 28:4.

37. Raymond F. Dassman, *No Further Retreat: The Fight to Save Florida* (New York: Macmillan, 1971), p. 152.

38. *New York Times*, 23 October 1966, sec. 5, 27:5.

39. Ibid., 18 December 1966, sec. 10, 3:1.

40. Memorandum in R. H. Davis Papers.

41. *New York Times*, 11 August 1965, 34:4.

42. Florida Game and Fresh Water Fish Commission, "A Brief Assessment of the Ecological Impact of the Cross-Florida Barge Canal," November 1969, copy in R. H. Davis Papers.

43. Carter, *The Florida Experience*, p. 287.

44. James Nathan Miller, "Rape on the Oklawaha," *Reader's Digest* 96 (January 1970): 54–60.

45. Florida Defenders of the Environment, *Environmental Impact of the Cross-Florida Barge Canal, with Special Emphasis on the Oklawaha River Ecosystem*, pp. 1–5.

46. U.S. Congress, House of Representatives, *Public Works Appropriations for 1969, Hearings before a Subcommittee of the Committee on Appropriations*, 90th Cong., 2d sess., 1969, Pt. 4, p. 1085.

47. *New York Times*, 4 March 1968, 73:5.

48. Ibid., 27 April 1969, 94:6.

49. Carter, *The Florida Experience*, p. 294; *New York Times*, 24 March 1970, 20:8.

50. U.S. Congress, House, *Public Works Appropriations for 1971, Hearings before a Subcommittee of the Committee on Appropriations*, 91st Cong., 2d sess., 1970, Pt. 5, pp. 567, 581.

51. *New York Times*, 19 June 1970, 12:5.

52. Ibid., 9 June 1970, 21:1.

53. Carter, *The Florida Experience*, p. 295.

54. C. E. Bennett to Randolph Hodges, 12 February 1971, copy in Davis Papers; chronology, ibid.

55. *New York Times*, 16 January 1971, 57:1.

56. Ibid., 22 January 1971, 38:1.

57. Ibid.

58. Carter, *The Florida Experience*, pp. 303–4.

59. *New York Times*, 14 February 1971, 61:5.

60. *Miami Herald*, 15 July 1973, clipping in Davis Papers.

61. *Daytona Beach News*, 21 August 1972; *Jacksonville Journal*, 16 January 1973, clippings in Davis Papers.

62. *Canal Authority of the State of Florida* v. *Harold H. Callaway, Secretary of the Army*, copy of decision in Davis Papers.

63. *Miami Herald*, 18 August 1976, 19A:1.

64. Florida Department of Administration, Division of State Planning, *The Cross Florida Barge Canal: A Review and Analysis* (Tallahassee, 1976), p. 13.

65. *Florida Water Management Activities*, newsletter of Division of Environmental Programs, October 1976, p. 3.

66. *Cross Florida Barge Canal*, pp. v, 5–11.

67. *Miami Herald*, 18 December 1976, 1A:2; *Florida Conservation News* 12 (January 1977): 1, 12.

68. *Miami Herald*, 9 February 1978, 1A:4; 27 July 1978, 15A:1, 23 October 1978, 7A:7.

69. Carter, *The Florida Experience*, pp. 156–62.

70. Ibid., pp. 162–72.

71. Gene Marine, "Algae and Aerojet," in McCluney, *The Environmental Destruction of South Florida*, pp. 32–33.

72. *New York Times*, 19 March 1967, 46:4.

73. Arthur R. Marshall, "Can the Everglades Be Saved?" *Florida Naturalist* 44 (October 1971): 105–6.

74. *Miami Herald*, 3 November 1967, 1B:6.

75. *New York Times*, 4 February 1968, sec. 10, 5:1; *Florida Naturalist* 43 (April 1970): 45.

76. Carter, *The Florida Experience*, p. 193.

77. *Miami Herald*, 19 September 1968, 1A:1.

78. *Water Management Bulletin* 2 (December–January 1968–69): 8.

79. Carter, *The Florida Experience*, pp. 194–96.

80. *National Parks and Conservation Magazine* 43 (January 1969): 2; 49 (April 1975): 2, 31; Carter, *The Florida Experience*, p. 196.

81. Carter, pp. 197–98.

82. *New York Times*, 4 June 1969, 94:4; *Miami Herald*, 4 June 1969, 1A:1; 12 June 1969, 1C:5.

83. *New York Times*, 12 July 1969, 26:3; 11 August 1969, 37:1.

84. Ibid., 30 August 1969, 44:1; 5 September 1969, 14:7; 17 September 1969, sec. 4, 14:1; 11 September 1969, 93:2.

85. *Miami Herald*, 18 September 1969, 1A:1, 12A:1.

86. Ibid., 19 September 1969, 1A:1.

87. Carter, *The Florida Experience*, p. 207.

88. Ibid., pp. 106, 200.

89. *New York Times*, 26 November 1969, 90:4.

90. *Florida Naturalist* 43 (April 1970): 45.

91. *New York Times*, 31 December 1969, 48:1; 1 February 1970, sec. 10, 1.

92. *Miami Herald*, 29 August 1975, 1B:5.

93. Ibid., 29 November 1976, 1A:1; 30 November 1976, 1B:5.

94. Ibid., 12 July 1977, 1B:6.

## 10. FLORIDA TAKES THE LEAD

1. Governor Askew's Message, 3 April 1973, p. 14, copy in Office of the Governor, Tallahassee.

2. *New York Times*, 30 April 1967, 86:1.

3. Robert B. Rackleff, *Close to Crisis: Florida's Environmental Problems* (Tallahassee: New Issues Press, 1972), p. 4.

4. *New York Times*, 24 November 1973, 17:1.

5. Hillsborough County Planning Commission, *Foundations for Future Growth, Hillsborough County* (Tampa, 1973), p. 8.

6. South Florida Water Management District, *Water Use and Supply Development Plan: Executive Summary: Draft* (West Palm Beach, 1977), 2:1.

7. *New York Times*, 16 May 1971, 74:1.

8. Rackleff, *Close to Crisis*, p. 18.

9. D. Robert Graham, "A Quiet Revolution, Florida's Future on Trial," *Florida Naturalist* 45 (October 1972): 146–51.

10. Arthur R. Marshall, "Are the Everglades Nearing Extinction?" *Florida Naturalist* 44 (July 1971): 80–81, 87.

11. Interviews with Joel Kuperberg, 28 November 1978, and John DeGrove, 12 December 1978.

12. *Water Management Bulletin* 5 (December–January 1971–72): 1–2, 4.

13. Ibid., p. 4.

14. Carter, *The Florida Experience*, pp. 126–28.

15. *Journal of the House of Representatives, Regular Session*, 1972, p. 6.

16. Carter, *The Florida Experience*, pp. 135–37.

17. *Miami Herald*, 8 April 1972, 1A:1.

18. *Laws of Florida: General Acts, 1972*, pp. 1082–1126 (Chap. 72–299, approved 24 April 1972).

19. Ibid., pp. 1162–81 (Chap. 72–317, approved 24 April 1972); *New York Times*, 19 November 1973, 41:3.

20. *Laws of Florida: General Acts, 1972*, pp. 1072–77 (Chap. 72–295, approved 24 April 1972); pp. 1126–30 (Chap. 72–300, approved 24 April 1972).

21. *Miami Herald*, Brevard ed., 8 November 1972, 1A:2.

22. Ibid., 29 May 1973, 16A:1.

23. Ibid., 20 May 1975, 14A:1.

24. *Laws of Florida: General Acts, 1975*, pp. 42–54 (Chap. 75–22, approved 22 May 1975).

25. *Laws of Florida: General Acts, 1976*, pp. 586–608 (Chap. 76–243, approved 23 June 1976).

26. John DeGrove, "Administrative Systems for Water Management in Florida," paper prepared for presentation at the Southeast Conference on Legal and Administrative Systems for Water Allocations, 19–20 April 1978, at Virginia Polytechnic Institute and State University, Blacksburg, pp. 10–11.

27. Anthony W. Smith, "Progress in the Everglades," *National Parks and Conservation Magazine* 46 (January 1972): 4.

28. Carter, *The Florida Experience*, p. 244.

29. *Miami Herald*, 24 November 1971, 14:5.

30. *Florida Statutes*, 1973, vol. 1, pp. 1958–59 (Chap. 280.055).

31. U.S. Congress, Senate, *Miscellaneous Reports*, 93d Cong., 2d sess., 1974, Report 93–1128 (22 August 1974), pp. 1–2.

32.  U.S., *Statutes at Large*, 88:1258–61 (Approved 11 October 1974).

33.  *Miami Herald*, 2 October 1974, 2A:2.

34.  Florida, Bureau of Land Planning, *Final Report and Recommendations for the Big Cypress Area of Critical State Concern, October 1973* (Tallahassee, 1973), pp. 25–41; Robert M. Rhodes, "Areas of Critical State Concern: Fact and Fiction," *Florida Naturalist* 48 (April 1975): 19.

35.  *Miami Herald*, 31 March 1975, 1A:1.

36.  Division of State Planning, *Public Works Program FY 80, Project Review* (Tallahassee, 1978), pp. 166–67.

37.  Luther J. Carter, "Wetlands: Denial of Marco Permits Fails to Resolve the Dilemma," *Science* 192 (14 May 1976): 641–44.

38.  *Miami Herald*, 13 March 1976, 24A:1.

39.  Ibid., 17 April 1976, 1A:6.

40.  National Audubon Society, *Corkscrew Swamp Sanctuary: A Self-Guided Tour of the Boardwalk* (n.p., n.d.), pp. 1–2; *Miami Herald*, Gulf ed., 20 April 1977, 1B:2.

41.  Joel Kuperberg, "The Trust for Public Land: Toward a Land Ethic," *Florida Environmental & Urban Issues* 2 (June 1975): 1–3, 13.

42.  *New York Times*, 28 March 1978, 18:3.

43.  Ibid., 17 July 1974, 14A:1.

44.  *Miami Herald*, Gulf ed., 18 April 1977, 1B:1.

45.  *Laws of Florida: General Laws*, 1961, pp. 230–41 (Chap. 61–691, approved 22 June 1961).

46.  U.S. Army Engineer District, Jacksonville, *Comprehensive Report on Four River Basins, Florida, November 30, 1961*, p. 11.

47.  Rackleff, *Close to Crisis*, pp. 9–10; *Tampa Tribune*, 19 May 1970, clipping in R. H. Davis Papers.

48.  *Florida Water Management Activities*, newsletter of Bureau of Water Resources Management, January 1977, p. 6.

49.  Rackleff, *Close to Crisis*, pp. 10–11.

50.  Florida, Bureau of Land Planning, *Final Report and Recommendations for the Proposed Green Swamp Area of Critical State Concern, June 1974* (Tallahassee, 1974), pp. 15–17, 22.

51.  *Miami Herald*, 17 July 1974, 14A:1.

52.  *New York Times*, 11 August 1974, 33:1.

53.  *Rules of the Department of Administration, Administrative Commission*, Chaps. 22F5–22F7, Land Planning Parts 5–7.

54.  *New York Times*, 23 February 1975, sec. 1, 41:1.

55.  Ibid., 21 July 1967, 1:7.

56.  Ibid., 12 March 1969, 94:7, 20 November 1972, 13:1.

57.  *Miami Herald*, 10 May 1975, 25A:4, 28 July 1976, 4B:2.

58.  Ibid., 20 February 1975, 1A:1.

59.  Ibid., 12 July 1975, 5A:6.

60.  Ibid., 8 June 1974, 6A:1, 14 October 1974, 6A:1.

61.  Ibid., 7 May 1975, 24A:1, 26 June 1975, 5C:1.

62.  Ibid., 8 February 1975, 1B:1, 10 July 1975, 1B:1; *New York Times*, 22 February 1975, sec. 1, 41:1.

63.  *Miami Herald*, 18 February 1976, 1A:2.

64.  Ibid., 17 July 1974, 14A:1.

65.  Ibid., 16 April 1975, 1A:5.

66. *Rules of the Department of Administration, Administrative Commission,* Chaps. 22F8–22F13, Land Use.

67. *Miami Herald,* 11 August 1977, 1A:2, 23 November 1978, 1B:1, 7 December 1978, 1A:5.

68. *Laws of Florida, 1972: General Acts,* pp. 1172–74; *Laws of Florida, 1976: General Acts,* pp. 117–19 (Chap. 76–69, approved 8 June 1976).

69. *Laws of Florida, 1975: General Acts,* p. 794 (Chap. 75–257, approved 29 June 1975).

70. Florida Department of Administration, Division of State Planning, *An Evaluation of the Environmental Impact Statement Process* (Tallahassee, 1975), pp. 1–5.

## 11. Rival Prescriptions for South Florida

1. U.S. Department of the Army, Jacksonville District, Corps of Engineers, *Water Resources for Central and Southern Florida* (Jacksonville, 1968), pp. 1–2, 12, 37–38.

2. William V. Storch, "A 'Rough Cut' Model of a South Florida Water Supply Plan," *In Depth Report* (Central and Southern Florida Flood Control District) 1 (December–January 1972–73): 12.

3. South Florida Water Management District, *Water Use and Supply Development Plan: Draft 3A* (West Palm Beach, 1977), 3:3–3:9.

4. Ibid., Executive Summary, 4:5–4:8.

5. Ibid., 4:11.

6. Ibid., 4:21–4:22; *Florida Water Management Activities* 4 (August–September 1977):2–3.

7. *Water Use and Development Plan,* Executive Summary, 4:17–4:18.

8. Ibid., 4:14–4:16.

9. Storch, *In Depth Report* 1:8.

10. *Bulletin from Your Water Managers* (South Florida Water Management District) 3 (July 1977): 4.

11. *Miami Herald,* 19 April 1977, 6A:1.

12. *Findings and Recommendations of the Governing Board, Central and Southern Florida Flood Control District, as the Result of Public Hearings Concerning Environmental Damage Resulting from Channelization of the Kissimmee River, November 15, 1972,* p. 2; hereafter cited as *Channelization of the Kissimmee River.*

13. *Miami Herald,* 3 October 1965, 7F:1.

14. Arthur Marshall et al., *The Kissimmee-Okeechobee Basin: A Report to the Cabinet of Florida,* 12 December 1972 (Miami, 1972), p. 22.

15. *Water Management Bulletin* 4 (October–November 1970): 5.

16. *Channelization of the Kissimmee River,* p. 2.

17. Marshall, *Kissimmee-Okeechobee Basin,* pp. 48–49.

18. Governor Askew's Message, 3 April 1973, copy in Office of the Governor, Tallahassee, p. 15.

19. Paul Roberts, Donald Patton, and Curry Hutchinson, "An Analysis of the Economic & Ecological Relationships of Water Management in South Florida,"

copy in Bureau of Comprehensive Planning, Tallahassee [c. 1976], pp. viii, 19, 30, 55–56.

20. *Miami Herald*, 19 December 1975, 5A:1.

21. Curry Hutchinson, "Review of Nelson M. Blake's Manuscript 'Man and Water in Florida History,' 6 October 1978, in author's possession, p. 29; hereafter cited as Hutchinson, "Review."

22. *Final Report on the Special Project to Prevent Eutrophication of Lake Okeechobee*, prepared by the Special Project Staff of the Division of State Planning (Tallahassee, November 1976), pp. 24, 47–79, 85–101.

23. Ibid., pp. 129–35, 154–60.

24. Ibid., pp. 102–6.

25. Ibid., pp. 80–84.

26. Curry Hutchinson et al., "Final Report on the Management Plans of the Special Project to Prevent Eutrophication of Lake Okeechobee," copy in Bureau of Comprehensive Planning, Tallahassee [c. 1976], pp. 14, 50.

27. Hutchinson, "Review," pp. 15–16.

28. *Laws of Florida: 1976, General Acts*, 1:194–96 (Chap. 76–113, approved 14 June 1976).

29. Coordinating Council on the Restoration of Kissimmee River Valley and Taylor Creek–Nubbin Slough Basin, *First Annual Report to the Florida Legislature, April 1977*, pp. 7–10.

30. *Miami Herald*, 25 May 1977, 11A:1.

31. *Bulletin from Your Water Managers* (South Florida Water Management District) 3 (July 1977):3–4.

32. Center for Wetlands, University of Florida, and Bureau of Comprehensive Planning, *South Florida: Seeking a Balance of Man and Nature* (1976), pp. 94–95.

33. Ibid., pp. 99–103.

34. Division of State Planning, *Water Element: The Florida Comprehensive Plan, Draft, April 1977*, p. 3.

35. *Miami Herald*, 18 January 1978, 8A:1.

36. Hutchinson, "Review," pp. 32–33.

37. Governor Reubin O'D. Askew, *The Florida State Comprehensive Plan* (Tallahassee, 1978), p. 176.

38. Ibid., pp. 174–88.

39. "Adoption of the State Comprehensive Plan," manuscript in Bureau of Comprehensive Planning, Tallahassee, pp. 1–4.

40. Division of State Planning, *Public Works Program FY80, Project Reviews* (Tallahassee, 1978), pp. 90, 188.

41. Divison of State Planning, "Public Works Program FY79, Project Reviews," copy in Bureau of Comprehensive Planning, Tallahassee [1977], pp. 29–33.

42. *Miami Herald*, 18 March 1977, 22A:1.

43. South Florida Water Management District, News Release, 17 November 1978, pp. 1–2; "SFWMD TOP for Lake Okeechobee Pumping and Control Structures, Draft of 11/13/78," copy in Department of Environmental Regulation, Tallahassee.

44. *Clewiston News*, 15 November 1978.

## 12. WATER FOR THE FUTURE

1. Florida Geological Survey, *Your Water Resources* (Tallahassee, 1963), pp. 9–10, 30.
2. *Laws of Florida: 1972, General Acts,* p. 1089 (Chap. 72–299, approved 24 April 1972).
3. S. D. Leach, *Source, Use, and Disposition of Water in Florida, 1975,* U.S. Geological Survey Water Resources Investigation (Tallahassee, 1978), p. 1.
4. *World Almanac: 1978,* p. 138.
5. *Florida Statistical Abstract 1978,* ed. Ralph B. Thompson (Gainesville: University Presses of Florida, 1978), pp. 215, 216, 239.
6. Rackleff, *Close to Crisis,* p. 57.
7. Leach, *Source, Use, and Disposition of Water,* pp. 25–26.
8. Carter, *The Florida Experience,* pp. 35–38.
9. Leach, *Source, Use, and Disposition of Water,* pp. 25–26.
10. *Miami Herald,* 29 March 1976, 1A:2.
11. Leach, pp. 25–26.
12. Hutchinson et al., "Final Report on the Management Plans of the Special Project to Prevent Eutrophication of Lake Okeechobee," p. 78.
13. Leach, pp. 25–28.
14. Hutchinson et al., "Final Report on the Management Plans," pp. 131–32.
15. Ibid., p. 132.
16. Leach, pp. 24, 27–28.
17. *Miami Herald,* 12 February 1975, 1A:4.
18. Leach, pp. 19, 30–33.
19. *Miami Herald,* 18 April 1977, 1B:1.
20. Ibid., pp. 41, 75–78.
21. John W. Sweeney, *Land Use Conflicts and Phosphate Mining in Florida* (Tallahassee: Department of Natural Resources, 1971), p. 22.
22. Statement by Mrs. Carl E. Shifflette, April 1967; Robert Rumer to S. L. Holland, 15 May 1967; Maywood Chasson to Holland, 16 May 1967; Holland to Tom Adams, 12 June 1967, Holland Papers, 1967, 61–Rivers and Harbors, Box 924.
23. Bureau of Land Planning, *Upper Suwannee River: Evaluation of a Proposed DRI as an Area of Critical State Concern, March 1974* (Tallahassee, 1974), pp. 4–5.
24. Leach, *Source, Use, and Disposition of Water,* p. 78.
25. *Water Management Bulletin* 2 (October–November 1968): 4; 2 (June–July 1969): 8; 4 (February–March 1971): 2; *Miami Herald,* 14 October 1974, 1B:5.
26. *Miami Herald,* 4 January 1979, 2B:1; 18 January 1979, 20A:1.
27. Speech by Reed at 14th American Water Resources Conference, 6 November 1978, p. 12.
28. Ibid.
29. Carter, *The Florida Experience,* p. 59.
30. *World Almanac: 1978,* p. 191; *Miami Herald,* 26 May 1977, 2C:1.
31. Gay D. Lynne and Clyde F. Kiker, *Water Use in Southwest Florida: An Economic Perspective* (Gainesville: Food and Resource Economics Department, University of Florida, 1976), pp. 1, 48.
32. Southwest Florida Water Management District, *District Water Management Plan 78, Preliminary Draft* (1977), pp. 28, 139–43.

33. Northwest Florida Water Management District, *Water Resources Assessment* (April 1976), pp. 51, 81; Carter, *The Florida Experience*, p. 38.

34. St. Johns Water Management District, *Water Resource Management Plan: Phase 1*, H3–H6.

35. Leach, *Source, Use, and Disposition of Water*, pp. 47–64.

36. Florida Department of Natural Resources, *St. Johns River Basin: Report on Water and Related Land Resources, Availability and Use in the St. Johns River Basin and Adjoining Coastal Area* (Tallahassee, 1970), pp. 94, 173.

37. Ibid., p. 175.

38. St. Johns River Water Management District, *Water Resource Management Plan: Phase 1*, p. 67.

39. Ibid., pp. 70–71.

40. *Miami Herald*, 3 February 1975, 10A:1.

41. Chris G. Pflum, "Canals of South Florida," *Florida Naturalist* 48 (October 1975): 10–11.

42. *Miami Herald*, 29 January 1976, 1A:5.

43. Weidling and Burghard, *Checkered Sunshine*, p. 240.

44. Muir, *Miami, U.S.A.*, p. 67.

45. Rackleff, *Close to Crisis*, p. 68; Carter, *The Florida Experience*, p. 148.

46. *Miami Herald*, 17 April 1975, 1A:3; 19 April 1975, 16A:1; 30 December 1977, 1A:2; 25 January 1978, 1C:4.

47. Carter, *The Florida Experience*, pp. 46, 53.

48. Florida Department of Environmental Regulation, *Water Quality*, DER Information Series No. 102, pp. 1–13.

49. *Environmental Regulation News* (September 1978): 1, 3.

50. Florida Department of Environmental Regulation, *1977 Water Quality Inventory for the State of Florida* (Tallahassee, 1977), pp. 53–56.

51. *Laws of Florida: 1977, General Acts*, pp. 1426–40 (Chap. 77–337, approved 24 June 1977); pp. 1599–1600 (Chap. 77–369, approved 27 June 1977).

52. Department of Environmental Regulation, *Newsletter* (September 1977).

53. *DeBow's Southern and Western Review* 14 (April 1853): 336; 12 (January 1852):105.

# Index

# 30 Years Later, and Still Powerful

CHRISTOPHER F. MEINDL

I remember my first encounter with Nelson Manfred Blake's book *Land into Water—Water into Land* as a graduate student in the early 1990s: I was captivated with Blake's discussions of the century-long attempt to manage the Everglades, the many ill-fated efforts to create a Cross Florida Barge Canal, and the evolution of Florida water management over the past century or so. I enjoyed the book so much that I wanted to buy a copy, but this book, originally published by the University Presses of Florida in 1980, was either impossible to find or very expensive if I could find it, so I gave up.

You can imagine my delight when Tom Swihart, a Florida water policy analyst, contacted me in early summer 2007. As a long-time employee of the Florida Department of Environmental Protection's Office of Water Policy, Tom is a careful observer of water management in Florida and he sought help in resurrecting Blake's book. I had previously published some historical geographic work on the Everglades, and we agreed that Blake's view of Florida water management over the past 150 years was spot on; but so much has happened since Blake wrote three decades ago (like a near doubling of the state's population!) that the book could stand some updating.

Tom eventually hooked up with historians Steve Noll and David Tegeder (who have recently written their own book on the Cross Florida Barge Canal, *Ditch of Dreams*, published by University Press of Florida in 2009), and we met in Fall 2007 to discuss how we might resurrect Blake's book. We decided that it would be best to maintain Nelson Blake's original text without alteration—and then to add a few chapters that update an otherwise brilliant discussion of Florida's emerging water management. This way, readers would have access to Blake's original text *and* a few additional chapters that comment on selected aspects of the rapidly changing Florida water management landscape since the late 1970s.

Our work has been complicated by several issues. To begin with, Blake and his wife have long since passed away. Tom eventually tracked down Nelson's son James Blake (a retired professor living on the Pacific coast), and James thought his father would be flattered to learn we were interested in reissuing *Land into Water—Water into Land,* so he endorsed our proposal. Next, since the book had been out of print since the late 1980s, the University Press of Florida had a thin file of documents related to the original project—and no electronic or even hard copy of the book. We contacted Dr. Mark Greenberg, director of the Florida Studies Center at the University of South Florida (in Tampa), about obtaining one of the several university-owned copies of the original book. Mark suggested he and his staff (including Barbara Lewis) could scan the book to provide an electronic copy of the original for us to work with. Meanwhile, Tom Swihart began writing his own book-length review of Florida water management, and it became impossible for him to continue with our enterprise. Tom agonized over this decision for a few weeks, and only after Steve Noll, David Tegeder, and I assured him that we would indeed resurrect Blake's book according to the plan we had established at our fall 2007 meeting did Tom eventually withdraw from the project. Although we are saddened that Tom was not able to actively participate in the project he helped initiate, fortunately for us he provided many suggestions and critiques of our proposed updated chapters. Finally, I thank Bill Belleville and Gary Mormino for reading prior drafts of the concluding chapter and offering their constructive questions and comments. That said, the interpretation of events since the late 1970s (and any remaining errors) in this updated version of Blake's book remain our responsibility.

\*    \*    \*

Nelson Manfred Blake was born in Island Pond, Vermont, in 1908 and earned degrees from Dartmouth College, and Brown and Clark Universities. He had a long and productive career at Syracuse University where he taught from 1936 until his retirement as Maxwell Distinguished Professor of History in 1973. He wrote several innovative books on American social history such as *The Road to Reno: A History of Divorce in the United States* (1962) and *Novelist's America: Fiction as History, 1910–1940* (1969). Moreover, Blake foreshadowed his interest in Florida water policy when in 1956 he published a book on the development of water resources in the northeastern United States (a fact Blake alludes to in the original preface to this book). Indeed, as late as 2001, environmental historian Joel Tarr—in reviewing another author's book about water resources in New York City opined: "Few historians, however, have written about how such an impressive record of [water] service provision evolved—with Nelson Blake, *Water for the Cities: A History of the Urban Water Supply Problem in the United States* (1956), still setting the standard."[1] After retiring to South Florida in the 1970s, Blake set his sights on the evolution of Florida land and water management, with special attention to the Everglades and the Cross Florida Barge Canal. After completing *Land into Water—Water into Land* in 1980, Blake worked on a few less intense projects before passing away in November 1996.

The original edition of this book attracted immediate notice in scholarly circles, where it was reviewed in no less than seven academic journals.[2] Almost all of these reviews deeply admired Blake's work and, although Blake was born more than a century ago, his writing is virtually timeless. One reviewer contended that Blake's discussion of water management "is a component of a larger problem: whether human beings can analyze situations, make choices, and persist in the politics that these choices render necessary."[3] Two others complimented Blake for successfully using the past to help us understand pressing contemporary problems—an infrequent and admirable accomplishment.[4] Yet another reviewer lauded Blake for revealing "the extremes to which people may go to further their own interests, no matter what the cost."[5] In spite of these accolades, however, other reviewers suggested that Blake neglected some important issues. For example, Thomas Dunlap was perhaps most critical of the book, complaining that Blake ignored the development of water law, administrative agencies, and hydrological science in Florida. Furthermore, Dunlap wished Blake had added more of his own opinion on land and water management in the Sunshine State, concluding that there was "too much narrative, generally political narrative, and far too little analysis. Anyone who knows as much about his subject as Blake does has opinions and judgments that are worth sharing, but he avoids even the most obvious comments."[6] In addition, Abraham Hoffman took Blake to task for failing to comment on the explosive growth of southeast Florida that both led to, and was stimulated by, excessive manipulation of the region's water. George Buker agreed, contending that Blake spent so much time detailing the "evils of overdeveloped engineering" that he ignored grappling with why Floridians demanded flood control in the first place: "Floridians must decide how much of their floodplain, which is a good percentage of the state, should be inhabited or used for agricultural purposes, for the question of levees and canals versus swamp and marshland hinges upon that point."[7]

These critiques notwithstanding, the current edition of the book contains every single word of Nelson Blake's original text without modification of any kind. Each of our new chapters has its own reference list. We include a brand new chapter featuring a review of the barge canal controversy since the late 1970s by Steve Noll and David Tegeder. Blake reported the decommissioning of the barge canal by the Nixon administration in the early 1970s, but it took nearly two more decades of political wrangling for Congress to permanently terminate the project. Moreover, although the Cross Florida Barge Canal will not be completed, the fate of the surviving structures (dams, portions of canals, and man-made lakes) and property along the proposed canal route quickly became a political hot potato. Rodman Reservoir, in particular, has attracted many contemporary champions, especially among Central Florida anglers (including politically powerful people) who want to maintain their fishing hole. Noll and Tegeder artfully review the barge canal's death, the struggle to create a Central Florida greenway named for the canal's leading opponent, Marjory Harris Carr, and the failed efforts to liberate the Ocklawaha River from the shackles of Kirkpatrick Dam.

The next chapter in this updated volume is my own analysis of the continuing effort to manage the South Florida environment, especially the Everglades. Blake demonstrated a firm grasp of the connection between people and the Everglades even as south Floridians were just beginning to sense their dependence on a "healthy" collection of ecosystems for water resources, natural amenities, open space, and tourism. Over the past three decades, however, there have been enormous efforts by state and federal governments, as well as a range of private interests, to mold a course of action that allows extensive agriculture and millions of urbanites to thrive alongside a somewhat more naturally functioning series of South Florida ecosystems.

Finally, in the last section, I review the substantive issues associated with Florida's evolving efforts to manage water resources since the late 1970s. Blake saw the ground beginning to shift with the state legislature's passing of several pieces of important environmental and resource protection legislation in the early 1970s, including the creation of water management districts. Yet he was not in a position to comment on the successes and failures of water management since 1980. Although Florida has made much progress in water resources management over the past few decades—and the public seems to take these matters seriously—water management districts are still reluctant to more fully integrate land use planning into water resources planning. Indeed, the development community has prevented any serious discussion of limits to population growth that is capable of being supported by inexpensive local water resources, using property rights rhetoric to justify their desire to provide an unending supply of housing to new Floridians, regardless of the cost of new water sources.

Central and South Florida's inexpensive groundwater resources have now been almost entirely developed. Additional population growth will require more expensive water sources such as ocean water subjected to costly desalination processes, or more significant use of reclaimed wastewater, which will require hundreds of millions of dollars of additional investment in distribution infrastructure. Blake may be accused of not taking a stand on water management issues; but in the conclusion to this volume I contend that population growth (particularly in new, sprawling subdivisions) ought to pay the *full* cost of providing the more expensive water resources necessary to accommodate such growth—rather than spreading the costs of expensive water on to people who did not create the demand. If people have to pay the full cost of the resources they consume, they will have a powerful incentive to build in places where these costs can be minimized. This would reduce suburban sprawl and population growth in peninsular Florida to more sustainable levels, and provide the revenue to develop water resources without burdening established residents, particularly those of more modest means who benefit little from additional population growth. Some might argue that such a policy shift would be "unfair" for newcomers, but I believe it is equally unfair to distribute the hefty costs of growth on to people who do not ask for it and who cannot afford it. Water management districts are inching toward a time when they "just say no" to development that imposes significant monetary and environmental costs on Floridians to meet constantly increasing demands for progressively more expensive water resources; only time will tell if they reach this point while Florida remains a terrific place to live.

## Notes

1. Joel A. Tarr, book review in *Enterprise and Society* 2 (2001): 398.

2. The only review of the seven not specifically referred to here is by Phil Vaughn in *History* 9 (6) (1981): 134.

3. E. F. Abbott, review of Blake's book in *Professional Geographer* 33 (1981): 498.

4. F. J. Dobney, review of Blake's book in *American Historical Review* 86 (1981): 954–55; D. G. McComb, review of Blake's book in *Journal of Southern History* 47 (1981): 468–69.

5. A. Hoffman, review of Blake's book in *Technology and Culture* 25 (1984): 161.

6. T. R. Dunlap, review of Blake's book in *Journal of American History* 68 (1981): 160.

7. G. E. Buker, review of Blake's book in *Florida Historical Quarterly* 59 (1981): 478.

# Cross Florida Barge Canal

STEVEN NOLL AND DAVID TEGEDER

With the 1980 publication of *Land into Water—Water into Land*, Nelson Blake concluded his discussion of the Cross Florida Barge Canal on an ambivalent note. Most observers, including Blake, understood the canal project was virtually dead, yet he cautiously concluded that "the 150-year old canal scheme clung to life by a narrow thread." Now nearly thirty years later, the future of the canal is no longer in question. Instead, the story of the Cross Florida Barge Canal has largely been subsumed by the controversy surrounding one of its legacies: Kirkpatrick Dam and its accompanying Rodman Reservoir. Though Marjorie Carr and the Florida Defenders of the Environment achieved success in stopping canal construction, Rodman Reservoir has remained intact for over forty years. Thus, their victory remains incomplete because the Ocklawaha River does not flow freely. For many observers, the years since Richard Nixon's 1971 announcement stopping the canal have been much like Hollywood's *Groundhog Day:* an endless cycle of repetitious actions that never seemed to resolve anything. Disputes over river restoration, reservoir drawdowns, and the ultimate removal of the dam itself have taken center stage in the ongoing battles. However, by focusing solely on the Rodman controversy, one can lose sight of the incredible accomplishments of Carr and her allies. For out of the ruins of the failed canal project, Florida has developed a thriving 107-mile linear park. The aptly named Marjorie Harris Carr Cross Florida Greenway is a ribbon of relatively pristine land and water that cuts across the middle of the state. In a state marked by rapid development and suburban sprawl, the establishment of the Greenway marks a significant achievement for those who wanted to preserve a piece of natural Florida. The transition from canal to greenspace was, like everything involving the Cross Florida Barge Canal, difficult, ambivalent, and time consuming. At the time of Blake's publication, the State of Florida's December 1976 Cabinet meeting appeared as an important turning point.

State officials, who had for so long demanded canal construction, voted with near unanimity to stop backing the project. In retrospect, however, the meeting looks less crucial and seems like just another of the many controversies that invoked much heat and little resolution of the issues surrounding the Cross Florida Barge Canal.

Marjorie Carr and the Florida Defenders of the Environment (FDE) viewed that December 1976 State Cabinet decision to withdraw support from the canal as "exhilarating and historic." Recognizing that this was only part of a larger struggle, most activists restrained themselves and remained relatively low key. The lone exception was Florida Audubon's Hal Scott, who gleefully proclaimed, "we are planning an Irish wake. . . . A wake for an old devil whose demise we have been looking for a long time, and thank heavens it is finally here." Conversely, canal boosters considered the political setback "disappointing" and "hard to understand," but they were hardly making funeral arrangements. Putnam County's George Linville called the Cabinet meeting a "travesty. It was the most stacked deck I ever appeared before. They won one today but we are definitely not dead." Canal Authority Chairman Lewis Smith concurred, announcing that canal supporters needed to "do what we can to see this project through to a successful conclusion. Not only for the people of today, but I think we're talking about 20, 30, or 40 years down the road. All these jobs may not be for us but will be for our children and their children." Marjory Stoneman Douglas, the other grande dame of Florida environmentalism, was all too familiar with the intractability of opponents like Linville and Smith. In a congratulatory holiday message to Marjorie Carr, she cautioned that "I know you will not rest easy until the final word is said . . . but surely all the preliminaries for success are in your hand." Understanding the difficulties of the continuing conflict, she concluded her letter by noting, though "your fine work is almost complete, we will keep up what pressure we can bring until it is over."[1]

Signs that Carr's long struggle may have been nearing completion appeared almost immediately. On January 6, 1977, General Ernest Graves, Director of Civil Works of the Army Corps of Engineers, submitted a disposition form that laid out his agency's position in light of the upcoming filing of the final environmental impact statement (EIS) in February. Through all of Graves' bureaucratic verbiage, one thing stood out. He concluded with finality that the Corps "should not recommend resumption of construction under the current authorization." Five days later, a federal interagency taskforce concurred. Underscoring the importance of the December Cabinet decision, it released a document which stated that the position of Florida officials "will make it difficult, if not impossible, to fulfill the elements of local cooperation required by the current Congressional authorization for the project." Sounding like Marjorie Carr, the group recommended the "Oklawaha River should be restored to a free-flowing river condition. This would involve elimination of Rodman Pool." Following Federal Appeals Judge Harvey M. Johnsen's earlier demand for a restudy, this was the clearest indication yet that FDE's vision would soon be realized.[2]

On February 24, 1977, the Army Corps formally submitted its long-awaited environmental impact statement to Judge Louis Bechtle, who had replaced Johnsen following his death in late 1975. A tersely worded press release categorically recommended termination of the project. Though the Chief of Engineers conceded construction was still feasible, he asserted the project's "economic justification is presently marginal and, when combined with the potential adverse environmental impacts, [the Corps] does not favor completion." Twenty-four volumes of dense scientific text accompanied the announcement that in many respects reinforced anti-canal claims made seven years earlier. FDE's David Anthony gleefully announced he was "certainly gratified after over a dozen years of work that finally even the Corps of Engineers has come to the same conclusion we did, that it's [the canal] no good economically, and it's environmentally damaging. We have known for some time that it's a turkey, and now the Corps admits it." While it appeared the Corps had done a complete turn-around, other long-time activists took issue with Anthony's optimistic assessment. They felt, with good reason, that Army engineers could not be trusted to halt the project. Such a radical shift in the Corps' position, especially considering its long history of environmentally destructive projects, justifiably engendered a great deal of skepticism. Unable to believe its engineers could actually terminate the project, Nathaniel Reed fulminated that the "spectacle of the Corps groping for new benefits as the EIS is 'completed' reinforces my opinion that the Corps is incapable of an honest evaluation of a project which it has promoted and supported for so many years."[3]

Reed's sense of frustration and mistrust was not unwarranted. By the mid-1970s, the Corps remained profoundly divided over its mission and how that related to the emerging environmental movement. Its response to the canal controversy reflected the schism. While many officials viewed environmental activists like FDE as nothing more than a bunch of troublemakers, some, particularly junior officers and civilian employees, actually sympathized with the concerns of Anthony and Carr. Little of this bureaucratic infighting left the Corps' offices, but the institution was ever so slowly moving away from the "dredge and fill" mentality of the early 1960s. Indeed, by 1975 the Army had created a new level of Corps' management—a civilian Assistant Secretary for Civil Works, ostensibly established to keep a watch over expensive public works projects. It tabbed Victor Veysey, a stalwart Republican and a former congressman from California, for the position. As General Ernest Graves, deputy chief of the Corps, remembered, Veysey "was determined to turn the image of the Corps around to an agency that was among the most, if not the most, responsive to environmental concerns." Almost immediately, he clashed with Major General Frank Koisch, the Corps' district engineer for the Lower Mississippi Valley. Koisch represented the traditional vision of the Corps—let's finish this project and the environmentalists be damned. "At breakfast one morning Veysey and Koisch got into the most incredible argument about the Cross-Florida Barge Canal," Graves continued. "As far as Koisch was concerned, get the shovels and start digging, which, of course, was the very image of the Corps that Veysey deplored." Though Veysey would eventually win the argument, Reed certainly was correct in remaining cautious about the Corps' ability to objectively evaluate one of its own projects.[4]

Amid these bureaucratic shifts, the election of Jimmy Carter in 1976 marked a significant departure in presidential leadership concerning environmental issues. Campaigning as an outsider far removed from the corrupting influence of traditional power, the Georgia peanut farmer appeared supportive of causes like the one championed by Marjorie Carr. Sensing a potential ally in the White House, FDE seized the initiative to lobby the new president, who was already working on an ambitious environmental policy within the first few months of his administration. On May 20, 1977, drawing on a time-worn strategy, more than 180 scientists signed a letter addressed to Carter seeking the president's assistance in the removal of Rodman Dam, which would allow the Ocklawaha to once again flow freely. Safely presuming the canal would never be built, the message instead focused on the restoration of what had been destroyed. Three days later, the president went before Congress and issued a sweeping thirty-six page message that laid out an agenda to strengthen environmental policy on several fronts. Within a statement calling for clean air, clean water, and the protection of endangered species, Carter strongly encouraged Congress to finally deauthorize Florida's canal. Following FDE's recommendations, he also called for the designation of the Ocklawaha as a wild and scenic river. Though he did not address the controversy directly, Carter's statement implicitly supported eliminating Rodman Dam. Marjorie Carr announced that she was "just delighted" with the announcement, especially with Carter's emphasis on "the restoration of the Oklawaha River. The river," she recalled, "is where it all began . . . where the public outrage began."[5]

A sense of outrage remained, yet this time it was expressed among canal proponents. Some were completely dejected. The president of the Putnam County Chamber of Commerce mournfully declared his county had "been dealt a mortal blow." In Ocala, vice-chairman of the Canal Authority Bill Rodgers confessed with more than a hint of understatement that Carter's announcement "certainly is not very encouraging." However, he blamed the boosters themselves for their predicament, since "we have not really fought hard enough for the canal—[we] did not exert enough pressure." The implication seemed clear: with more lobbying, there would be greater support for the canal, and thus the project could continue. A gloomy Putnam County commissioner saw promise in the growing distinction between canal construction and the removal of Rodman Dam. "If the canal project is scrapped," he plaintively suggested, "we hope to save Lake Ocklawaha." The most truculent response came from Canal Authority Director Giles Evans. Emphasizing the limits of executive authority, Evans minimized the threat of Carter's announcement. "The canal is a project begun and controlled by the Congress," he snarled. "Nixon tried the same thing before and the canal is still here, so far." Warning that he and other proponents were going to fight until the bitter end, he boldly predicted that the canal is "going to be built one of these days. It will just cost more money." Evans, however, was simply whistling past the graveyard. Even the pro-canal *Ocala Star Banner* grasped the significance of

Carter's speech. "President Carter," it announced, "prescribed the death sentence Monday for the Cross-Florida Barge Canal."[6]

As any observer of the American legal system can attest, death sentences often take torturous paths and innumerable years to reach their conclusion. Such was the case for the canal. Although Florida's Senators Lawton Chiles and Richard Stone immediately sponsored a Senate bill to deauthorize the canal, prompting the *Ocala Star Banner* to label them as Carter's "volunteer executioners," the legislation failed to pass. For the next decade, despite an overwhelming consensus for deauthorization in both Tallahassee and Washington, recalcitrant House members—diehards like Charles Bennett, Bob Sikes, and particularly Ocala's Bill Chappell—blocked any measure to kill the project in Congress. The struggle became so protracted and so arcane that newspaper editors had to resort to metaphors—often awkwardly mixed—to convey the growing sense of frustration with a controversy seemingly without end. The *Orlando Sentinel* chimed in early, presciently suggesting in February 1977 that "the reason the Cross-Florida Barge Canal seems to have more lives than a cat is, it can't be declared dead by anyone but Congress and Congress has a way of keeping boondoggles attached to life machines." Most newspapers clung to this imagery of death: from the cute, "This wicked ditch is dead;" to the maudlin, "Barge Canal May Face Watery Grave;" to the utterly morbid, "Environmentalist Wants Cemetery to Mean Death for Canal." The latter stemmed from Marjorie Carr's 1983 proposal to locate a burial ground for 250,000 veterans along the path of the canal. No matter how one looked at it, the controversy was becoming absurdly intractable. As Florida Attorney General Jim Smith noted after the problem had dragged on into early 1983, any "delay in resolving the fate of the canal will further complicate an already complex situation."[7]

In April 1979, Florida's legislature waded into the controversy by passing a bill that disbanded the Canal Authority and developed a repayment plan for the six counties that contributed land for canal construction. The law seemed rational enough, but it offered no firm solutions, since it could only take effect when Congress deauthorized the project. The impatient House sponsor, Frank Mann of Fort Myers, confidently proclaimed the law would finally "kill the cotton-picken [sic] canal . . . by sending one more message to Congress that we want the barge canal gone." Others mistakenly thought the end was near. Jacksonville Representative Tommy

Hazouri conceded defeat, announcing despondently, "we recognize the fact that when the canal is dead, it's dead." The legislation may have struck a bold blow against the project but that was only in Tallahassee. Canal opponents still had to reckon with Congress. Thus even Mann had to admit some doubt. The canal, he said, was "a snake with a lot of heads. We keep chopping them off and it keeps coming back."[8]

While the death of the canal may have been a foregone conclusion for most Floridians, a few members of Florida's Congressional delegation begged to differ. For the rest of the 1970s and 1980s, Charles Bennett and Bill Chappell stubbornly kept the canal alive, if barely. With their years of seniority, which led to influential positions on such important Congressional Committees as Appropriations, Armed Services, and Water Resources, they commanded considerable influence. As fellow Florida Congressman Clay Shaw explained with a touch of awe, "they are tough adversaries. They know how to twist arms and get votes." Few could rival Bill Chappell for his knowledge of legislative protocol and willingness to use it to support the canal. Anyone seeking legislation eventually had to horse-trade with him. And Chappell almost always got his way. His very presence seemed to stop the anti-canal movement in its tracks. "During one committee vote on the canal last year," reported the *Miami Herald* in 1985, "he stood in the back of the room, arms folded, trademark cigar in his mouth. The canal survived the vote."[9]

Chappell's command of the legislative process allowed for nothing more than a series of obstructive rear-guard actions. Savvy enough to understand that Congress would never fully fund canal construction, he instead focused his energies on forestalling deauthorization, for he believed that at some point in the future "if it is not deauthorized, it *will* be built [emphasis added]." Twice the Senate, prodded by Lawton Chiles, voted favorably on such legislation, only to be rebuffed in the House by Chappell's willingness to play hardball and manipulate parliamentary procedures. For Chappell, deauthorization represented not only the death of a dream, but the admission of defeat to those whom he considered unworthy adversaries. Moreover, he realized the legislation would hardly signal the final act of an ongoing drama. Deauthorization would simply create a whole new set of problems concerning the disposition of canal lands and the ultimate fate of Rodman Dam, all of which centered on the "restoration of the land to its original state." It would mean the destruction of Lake

Ocklawaha, which Chappell saw as having developed "a unique ecology ...abound[ing] with waterfowl, egrets, eagles, fish and the changes brought about [that] have resulted in a national recreational treasure enjoyed by thousands of families annually." The ensuing economic costs—ranging from compensation to the threat of never-ending lawsuits—would also result "in an unconscionable taxpayer burden: one beyond calculable projection." This was ironic talk for someone who, as late as 1982, fervently demanded nearly half a million dollars for yet another Corps feasibility study. And canal opponents saw the idea for what it was—"an attempt on the part of the proponents to keep the canal alive."[10]

Chappell's political maneuvering appeared even more contradictory as support for his cause increasingly dwindled. Even Ronald Reagan's notoriously prodevelopment Secretary of the Interior, James Watt, declared the canal should not be completed. By 1983, the overwhelming majority of Florida's political establishment, including Governor Bob Graham and former Governor LeRoy Collins, firmly supported Congressional deauthorization. At the same time, public approval for the project had dramatically waned in areas that were once the very center of procanal boosterism. Even Chappell's once personal bailiwick of Marion County deserted him. On April 7, 1983, the Ocala Board of Realtors—never noted for their radical environmental views—issued a resolution urging Congress to finally pull the plug. Claiming the project would "be of no economic benefit to Marion County . . . and provide an economic threat to the Florida Aquifer," the realtors suggested the canal dream must come to an end. To add insult to injury, a recent Congressional redistricting plan pushed Chappell out of the central Florida county and into a new district along Florida's east coast. Now representing Marion County, freshman Congressman Kenneth "Buddy" MacKay vividly demonstrated just how much the situation had changed by immediately joining with Senator Lawton Chiles to sponsor deauthorization legislation.[11]

Jacksonville's business community provided the nucleus for what little support remained for the canal. Strongly backing Chappell's fight in Congress, they found an ally in Andy Johnson, a young, strident, and vociferous state representative who enthusiastically assumed the mantle of canal boosterism once held by the likes of Duncan Fletcher and Gilbert Youngberg. In 1981, he helped organize the Coalition for Rational Energy and Economic Development (CREED) and pushed, against imposing political odds, for canal completion with an entirely new rationale. Johnson focused almost exclusively on the project's assumed importance in delivering cheap energy to Florida, a major consideration in the early 1980s as the continuing oil crisis and problems associated with nuclear power bedeviled the nation. Johnson and other members of CREED claimed the canal presented an opportunity to move coal inexpensively to Jacksonville's new electric power plants. While extolling the economic benefits of the project, Johnson sounded much like former Lieutenant Governor Tom Adams, perhaps the canal's most vociferous proponent, as he blasted Marjorie Carr and her allies as "crazy phony environmentalists." He combatively offered "to go to any city in Florida to debate her and show her for the liar she is." Appealing for a broader constituency, he enlisted "Dr. X.," a Jacksonville radio talk show host, to spread the message and distribute procanal bumper stickers. All of Johnson's frenetic activity energized even the aging Claude Pepper, who had wavered in his support for the canal nearly a decade earlier. By 1985, the octogenarian seemed once again as devoted to the canal as he was to Social Security. "Why should we throw it all away," Pepper asked rhetorically, "with a resolution to deauthorize it? The dream of centuries will be done away with by the precipitous action of the people of this generation." Despite all the posturing, Johnson's boosterism provided few tangible results. Even CREED's membership realized they were significantly outgunned. One charter member, according to a political observer, had "never attended a meeting, thinking it is a waste of time. He has told Johnson a number of times that the canal project is dead." More than anything, the basic mathematics that lay behind political calculation suggested Johnson's last-ditch efforts had little chance of success. "A procanal vote is worth about 20,000 votes," the observer asserted, "whereas a vote for the deauthorization is worth an easy 250,000 state-wide." With those numbers, the question surrounding deauthorization became not "if" but "how."[12]

By the mid-1980s, the stars finally began to align for Congressional deauthorization. From 1983 to 1986, state legislators held a series of hearings around the state to determine the ultimate disposition of the canal and Rodman Dam, as well as the future use of lands previously allocated for canal construction. The usual cast of characters appeared and made their case. On one side, Marjorie Carr and David Anthony called for a measure that would end the canal controversy once and for all. For them, deauthorization had only one meaning; the removal of Rodman so the river could finally begin the long process toward restoration. On the other side, the few remaining canal supporters tried to convince Floridians the waterway would yield untold economic benefits for the state. However, if the canal was no longer possible—which was becoming increasingly obvious—they argued Rodman Dam should at least remain to preserve the vibrant recreational playground of Lake Ocklawaha. While a forest had indeed been lost under the tracks of a wantonly destructive crusher nearly twenty years beforehand, a new environment had taken its place. They now extolled the virtues of the reservoir as a thriving ecosystem where wildlife was abundant. In many respects, arguments from both sides were simply old news: a rehashing of time-worn and seemingly intractable positions. Yet the hearings provided frustrated state officials the chance to publicly push the canal controversy toward resolution. At the Palatka meeting of June 1985, Governor Bob Graham made clear the state's unequivocal position. "We do not want this canal, period," he asserted. "We have many, many needs—we need new schools, more teachers, roads, bridges, mass transit, water and sewer lines—but there is one thing we don't need, and that's the Cross Florida Barge Canal." Furthermore, he complained that years of Congressional inaction had exacerbated the problem. Understanding that the lack of resolution allowed for a continuing victory, albeit one with little reward, for procanal forces, he called on Washington for an ultimate solution. "Congressmen, how many times do we have to say no? How many ways are there to say no? Please—take no for an answer."[13]

In the Senate, Lawton Chiles remained a staunch advocate of deauthorization. And Paula Hawkins, who spent most of her term vacillating on the issue, finally came down firmly for the project's termination. Her stance came at a price, however, which profoundly troubled FDE. She supported eliminating the canal but "on the condition that the locks, dams, and other canal structures now in place will be permanently maintained for the benefit of boaters, fishermen, and other sportsmen who utilize the structures." This left open the very real possibility that Rodman Dam would remain standing. On the other side of Capitol Hill, an overwhelming majority of Florida's representatives signaled support for deauthorization. Democrat Buddy MacKay and Republican Clay Shaw of Fort Lauderdale fought hardest for the issue, authoring bills to finally end the project. Of course, Bennett, Chappell, and Pepper stood firmly as the lone exceptions to the growing House unanimity. Here, too, though, things were changing. Claude Pepper continued his opposition, but his primary legislative interests related to health care and Social Security. Moreover, his increasing age (by the summer of 1986 he was eighty-five) and his weakening physical condition made him significantly less effective on the House floor. Bill Chappell could also no longer give the fight his undivided attention as rumors of kickbacks from defense contractors swirled around the congressman. That left Charles Bennett as the solitary stalwart, and even he began wavering in his defense of the canal. Never simply a shill for local business interests, Bennett slowly recognized the futility of continually pushing for the project in the face of significant opposition from fellow Floridians. By 1986, he began to see deauthorization as an acceptable compromise, under the condition that the property allocated for canal construction remain in public hands. Bennett's position was gradually moving toward Marjorie Carr's—if the waterway was no longer possible, canal lands could best serve as the basis for a unique linear greenspace across Florida. Under the auspices of either the state or federal government, this swath of land would both protect a unique part of natural Florida from rampant development and provide a suitable return for the millions of tax dollars expended on the project. Even as Bennett came on board, contentious questions remained, especially concerning compensation for lands taken for the canal. Would deauthorization mean that hundreds of parcels of land automatically reverted to their previous owners? Could the state use the land for other purposes, such as the park proposed by Carr and Bennett? Were former owners due reimbursement for lands no longer dedicated for canal construction? Would counties that had spent millions in taxpayer dollars purchasing property for the canal right-of-way similarly expect reimbursement? And if they were due some form of repayment, who would assume responsibility for the compensation, Washington or Tallahassee?[14]

By the fall of 1986, Congress finally addressed these issues head-on when it passed a deauthorization measure as part of a huge $16.3 billion omnibus water resources act. Signed by President Reagan on November 17th, Section 1114 of Public Law 99-662 established the "Cross Florida National Conservation Area" and declared "that portion of the barge canal project located between the Eureka Lock and Dam and the Inglis Lock and Dam (exclusive of such structures) is not authorized." As the

*Miami Herald* simply put it, the act "drove a stake through the heart of the monster known as the Cross Florida Barge Canal." The law answered many of the questions that had dogged the project for decades. Besides the obvious death of the canal, it allocated the return of $32 million to the six counties (Duval, Clay, Putnam, Marion, Levy, and Citrus) associated with land purchases. It mandated an interagency management plan for former canal lands, under the auspices of the Corps of Engineers, stressing the "enhancement of the environment" and the "conservation and development of natural resources." It demanded a federal presence in the new conservation area and maintained that Washington, not Tallahassee, should "operate, maintain, and manage the lands and facilities." All this sounded wonderful to Marjorie Carr and FDE. And yet, victory was not complete. The law granted the Corps of Engineers, the bane of environmental activists, a significant voice in the disposition of the canal. Worse yet, "the Secretary [of the Army] shall operate the Rodman Dam, authorized by the Act of July 23, 1942 . . . in a manner which will assure the continuation of the reservoir known as Lake Ocklawaha." The canal was finally, irrevocably dead, but the continued operation of Rodman assured the Ocklawaha River would not yet flow freely.[15]

Major questions persisted over the relationship of the state and federal governments and their role in the new conservation area. State officials adamantly asserted that Florida, not Washington, should manage and operate the conservation area. As late as 1989, the state legislature had even issued a memorial calling for an amendment to the bill that would ensure greater state latitude in disposing of canal lands. Charles Bennett was just as convinced that federal control, through some sort of national park designation, would best provide protection for the land. At the same time, private citizens prepared for legal battles over the taking of their lands for a project that had now been terminated without their consent or input. Not surprisingly, the Corps had yet to finalize its management plan within the stipulated one-year period. And, most important, the contentious issue of Rodman Dam remained unsettled.

Finally, in 1990, everything came into place as Congress took up the canal question once again. In the four years since deauthorization, both Claude Pepper and Bill Chappell had died, stilling the most vigorous and long-lasting voices favoring canal completion. In an ironic twist, Charles Bennett himself introduced a new deauthorization proposal in January.

Under pressure from Tallahassee officials who sought state control of canal lands, the Jacksonville congressman now maintained, "the most acceptable solution is to create a state park or state conservation area [that] would be like a Phoenix bird arising from the ashes of yesterday's idea." A month later, Senator Bob Graham and Republican Congressman Cliff Stearns of Ocala, who had filled MacKay's seat, offered an alternative bill that closely resembled Bennett's. "I am very hopeful something will come out of this Congress," Bennett announced, "to put this behind us and create something valuable for future generations." FDE gladly supported these measures more than the 1986 legislation because Congress had now placed the future of Rodman Dam in the hands of the state of Florida, where environmental activists thought they could exert more influence. An FDE press release applauded the bills as "a constructive and surprisingly happy solution to a problem that has been plaguing Floridians for 20 years." Carr herself was positively ebullient. "The people of Florida," she announced, "will have a beautiful greenbelt now, instead of this albatross hanging around their necks." Florida state officials joined the love fest. Republican Governor Bob Martinez remarked that the "passage of this legislation would make a fitting end of the misguided era of 'ditch and drain.'" Looking forward to a future without the same tireless annual debates about the fate of the Cross Florida Barge Canal, Fred Ayer, assistant director of the Canal Authority, announced, "now it's up to the state to go ahead and finish it off. . . . The idea of a linear park from coast to coast is pretty exciting."[16]

With Bennett's agreement to the compromise measure, the entire Florida congressional delegation threw its support behind the bill. In May 1990, the Florida legislature passed its own measure that agreed to the terms of the federal legislation, assuming it passed through Congress and was signed by the president. Submitted that same month, the compromise proposal was folded into another large omnibus water resources act. Enduring a summer of obligatory hearings, Congress finally passed the measure on October 27 and sent the bill to President George H. W. Bush. One month later, Bush signed the comprehensive act, ending once and for all the Cross Florida Barge Canal. The legislation immediately deauthorized the canal and transferred all project lands to the state of Florida. The state, in accordance with its own statute, received the lands to "create a State park or conservation/recreation area" and preserve and manage them "for the benefit and enjoyment of present and future generations of people and the development of outdoor recreation." Like the 1986 act, the 1990 statute stipulated a reimbursement of $32 million to the six counties involved in the project. This time, however, Florida assumed responsibility for the payment, with funds originating from the assets of the state's Canal Authority and the Navigation District. Finally, the law prescribed a two-year turnover for the Corps to transfer land and management responsibilities to the state. As the *Miami Herald* explained, the law "is akin to a team of doctors deciding to cut off life support to a comatose patient." Conspicuously absent from the legislation was any mention of the disposition of Rodman Dam and the pool/lake/reservoir/impoundment that lay behind it.[17]

With the January 22, 1991, passage of a resolution signed by new Governor Lawton Chiles and the Cabinet agreeing to the terms of the federal deauthorization bill, the era of the Cross Florida Canal was finally, mercifully, over. Though Marjorie Carr and FDE could justifiably feel proud of their efforts in that victory, they also understood that the fight was far from over. Profound questions remained over the shape of the 77,000-acre park that was to take the place of the canal. Legal issues concerning the control of former canal lands threatened to keep Florida in a state of continuous litigation for years to come. The rancorous debate over the fate of the Ocklawaha River loomed largest of all. If that was not solved to the satisfaction of Marjorie Carr, if the dam still remained blocking the river, would the years of hard work be in vain? After all, this had started as a campaign to save the river itself. Yet divergent groups offered differing visions of recreation in the space that was to be the canal. The decisions made by Florida politicians on these concerns would determine the very nature of the entity that would replace the Cross Florida Barge Canal.

In the summer of 1991, the Florida legislature began the process of preparing to decide how to use and develop the swath of land now bureaucratically designated as the Cross Florida Greenbelt State Recreation and Conservation Area. To do so, it established the twenty-one-member Canal Lands Advisory Committee (CLAC), an advisory board composed of politicians and interested citizens from the surrounding area. In recognition of her involvement and influence, the legislature appointed Marjorie Carr as the committee's representative of "the public at large." CLAC's primary responsibility lay in creating a master plan for the best use of the land. That meant balancing a variety of competing interests, articulated during more than a year of local public meetings. For Carr and many in FDE there was not much to debate. They felt such passive recreational pursuits as hiking, nature trails, and canoeing should stand alone at the center of the greenway experience. As Manley Fuller of the Florida Wildlife Federation explained at a CLAC hearing, "we get sort of nervous about building and paving within the greenbelt." Yet as early as September, the *St. Petersburg Times* pointed to radically different visions of recreational use. "Environmentalists envision picnic tables and horse trails. Developers dream of a marina and motel complex. And home owners hope to restore the original flow of the Withlacoochee River." There were even disputes within those large constituent groups. Many people from Marion County's horse country yearned for a world class equestrian and agricultural center that seemed more like a tourist trap than an escape from the hustle and bustle of modern living. On the western boundary of the proposed park, Jim Eyster, a Crystal River developer, formulated plans for a mammoth 367-slip marina near Inglis Lock while others were more content with primitive fish camps. And to the east, many of Putnam County's residents remained steadfast in their demand for the retention of Rodman Reservoir as a bass fishing paradise. Spending the weekend trolling on a bass boat, they saw "something magic about the shout of the adult female when she realizes she has caught her first fish. Take them to Rodman Reservoir and enjoy life." All of this was rather alien to Marjorie Carr and her allies. For them, fishing was something better experienced on the free-flowing, densely canopied Ocklawaha with a "canoe or johnboat, . . . not a noisy two-cycle smoke-belching gasoline guzzling outboard engine" powering an expensive rig on the flat and unappealing waters of the stagnant Rodman Reservoir.[18]

On September 17, 1992, following more than a year of deliberation, CLAC met in Ocala to issue its final report on the future of the greenbelt, now called the Cross Florida Greenway. As an advisory board, its recommendations held considerable weight, but the ultimate fate of the land rested in the hands of state officials. During a two-day meeting, the committee settled a host of difficult issues pertaining to park boundaries, governance, funding, and local land use. With regard to the heavy imprint of canal construction, especially the 1930s excavations and bridge stanchions, CLAC recommended leaving most of the Corps' work intact.

In many respects, CLAC validated much of Carr's environmental vision. Expressing a belief in passive recreation, it rejected the Inglis marina outright and looked cautiously at other relatively invasive forms of outdoor activities. Yet it abdicated its most important responsibility by refusing to address the contentious issue concerning the ultimate disposition of Rodman Dam and the Ocklawaha River. Instead, it voted fourteen to seven for yet another study, this time a three-year review under the auspices of the St. Johns River Water Management District. This new demand that once again examined the usual technical, environmental, and economic cost-benefits of the reservoir left many members of FDE howling in protest at what they saw as just another round of delays. With Marjorie Carr now weak with emphysema at the age of 77, FDE officials plaintively conceded their leader would not live to see her dream fulfilled. "The river will not be restored in her lifetime," announced David Godfrey, FDE's Ocklawaha restoration project director. "This decision today means that action may not even begin in her lifetime."[19]

The September committee meeting represented an important transitional moment. Besides wrestling with the issues associated with deauthorization, it also introduced a new player to the debate: state senator George Kirkpatrick of Gainesville. A member of the state legislature since 1980, the 53-year-old Democrat quickly became the face of the movement to retain Rodman Reservoir. Contentious and prickly, he reveled in his well-earned reputation as a political street fighter. "I'm someone who comes on the scene asking the questions that these frustrated rednecks have always wanted to ask," he remarked in a 1995 interview. "I keep refusing to take no for an answer. I pound and I pound. . . . I'm perceived as arrogant. But if someone manages to turn me on their side, and I know they're right, then they've got their own personal Rottweiler." Dogged, vitriolic, and politically astute, Kirkpatrick was more than just another loud-mouthed politician. As a result of senatorial seniority, he would become the chairman of the powerful Senate Rules Committee in 1993 and remain a bitter adversary of Marjorie Carr and other environmentalists who wanted to see the Ocklawaha flowing freely.[20]

Even before the final CLAC meeting, Kirkpatrick was instrumental in organizing a coalition of interests bent on preserving Rodman Reservoir, which had become a haven for recreational and sports fishing, even considered by some experts as one of the best bass lakes in America. In

July, the senator encouraged Dan Canfield, a professor at the University of Florida's Department of Fisheries and Aquatic Sciences, to conduct yet another study—this time designed to refute FDE's claim that the reservoir was nothing more than a weed-congested ecological disaster. Funded in part by the Putnam County Chamber of Commerce, Canfield's forty-six-page report added to the furor over the disposition of Rodman. Pro-Rodman forces now went beyond traditional assaults upon FDE's research as they used Canfield's research to buttress their position to protect the lake. Canfield conceded as much when he wrote that "proponents of restoration have written extensively and eloquently about their concerns," but his study was designed "to determine if a case could be made for Rodman Reservoir." Asserting that Lake Ocklawaha was "not a 'dying' water body that is destined for 'biological senility' in our lifetime," he added the lake "would continue to serve as a refuge for not only fish and wildlife, but also anglers." With consideration of the reservoir's economic benefits for the local Putnam County economy, Canfield reached a simple conclusion: "we recommend that Rodman Reservoir be retained for now. . . . There is no compelling biological/ecological reason to rush restoration at this time." The scientific rationale behind the Canfield report soon became the basis of support for keeping the reservoir intact.[21]

Canfield's research was remarkably effective, especially as he delivered the report on the first day of CLAC's September meeting. Kirkpatrick praised the study as a significant improvement over FDE's examination of the lake, which he claimed had "numbers . . . quoted from a study done in 1988 whose numbers were collected from a report done in 1978 which had been taken straight from biased studies done . . . in the early 1970s." Not surprisingly, FDE dismissed Canfield's conclusions as "garbage." Faced with evidence that had only appeared in the final hours of more than a year of difficult meetings, and with a whirlwind of competing claims circling the room as a result of the study, CLAC played it safe and, almost by default, concluded that further scientific investigation was necessary. Another round of delays led many FDE members to see another, more sinister reason for the decision in the very person of Senator Kirkpatrick himself. Marjorie Carr blasted him for his strong-arm bullying tactics. "Senator Kirkpatrick has clobbered them [CLAC members]," she fumed. "He has carried out the most intensive campaign of intimidation that I have ever seen. God knows he has clout, but I'd call that a misuse of power." FDE, recognizing Kirkpatrick's power as the incoming chairman of both the Rules Committee and next session's Appropriations Committee, accused the senator of threatening various state agencies with budget cuts if they blocked any effort to study the lake and dam once again. Kirkpatrick downplayed his influence. "My effort," he averred, "has been to make sure that the recommendation is based on accurate information." When asked about his alleged threats, Kirkpatrick played coy. "I didn't do any of that," he said. "I talked to DNR [Department of Natural Resources] and asked how we could come up with a compromise. There's been no threats by me." With the cockiness that became part of his persona, he loudly proclaimed FDE's complaints were "just sour grapes."[22]

In December 1992, the governor and Cabinet met in Tallahassee to review CLAC's recommendations on turning the former canal into a linear park. Though the public meeting dealt with many of the broader concerns related to the transitional process, debate centered on the fate of Rodman. Once again, adversaries descended on the capital and staked out their positions in the hope of swaying government officials their way. This time, however, Marjorie Carr's illness made her too weak to appear in person. Instead her supporters brought along an emotional videotaped appeal from their leader. In it, Carr called the Ocklawaha "a natural work of art" and asked the Cabinet to "restore it and care for it as if it was a Pieta by Michelangelo." She summarily dismissed the economic and recreational concerns of those who pleaded for retaining Rodman Reservoir. "I realize bass fishermen will be inconvenienced," she said. "I trust they will find good fishing in nearby lakes." Heeding Carr's words, Commissioner of Education Betty Castor offered an amendment to the CLAC proposals that overrode their call for another study of the Rodman area. Directing the Department of Natural Resources to "immediately take steps" to "complete the restoration of the free flowing Ocklawaha River," she called for the drawdown of Rodman Reservoir. Backed by Governor Chiles, who expressed frustration with the glacial pace of resolving the controversy, the amendment passed unanimously. This policy statement placed the executive branch and its agencies firmly on the side of Marjorie Carr and river restoration. FDE and fellow environmentalists were elated. Calling the amendment a "wise decision," Timothy Keyser of the Florida Wildlife Federation agreed that "restoration of the wildlife habitat is more important than maintaining a degrading [sic] system." From Gainesville, Carr concurred, "It is a giant step forward for Floridians."[23]

Not all Floridians were as excited as Carr. In Putnam County, local fishermen expressed disbelief as the Cabinet pulled the plug on Lake Ocklawaha. "I can't imagine how anybody can go to Rodman," announced fishing guide Billy Peoples, "and see what's there and make that kind of decision." Wes Larson of the Putnam County Chamber of Commerce bemoaned the loss of 110 jobs and $7.2 million in annual fishing revenue if the dam was removed. Putnam County Administrator Gary Adams concluded, "I think it is a terrible economic blow to Putnam County. I think it is the wrong thing to do for a multitude of reasons." He also assailed Carr's growing influence in Tallahassee. "It appears to me that the Florida Defenders of the Environment had enough clout that they could get their position through." In Gainesville, George Kirkpatrick seconded Adams's assessment. Embittered with the Cabinet meeting's result, he took on the very nature by which the decision was reached. Claiming the Cabinet's vote was "based on strong emotions that had very little relationships to the facts," the senator concluded that the Cabinet "bypass[ed] an appointed task force and completely rejected all their recommendations. . . . I realize that this is a very well orchestrated political decision," he said with no hint of irony. "I realize the people I represent will probably lose." In a moment of self-deprecating sarcasm, he took a personal swipe at Marjorie Carr herself. "I'm not a scientist, I'm not an eloquent speaker," he intoned, "and I don't have a T.V. video to show you."[24]

At first glance the Cabinet decision seemed to finally resolve the issue in FDE's favor. However, buried in the language of Castor's amendment was the phrase, "upon favorable legislative action," which took the controversy out of the governor's hands and placed it in the state house. Even FDE recognized the tentative nature of their victory. We are "fully aware that only half the task is done," David Godfrey admitted. "The unanimous vote gives us momentum going to the legislature, and that's a whole other ball game. But it sends a strong message." That message would be countered by George Kirkpatrick, who warned "the Cabinet decision Tuesday is far from the final say on the future of the Rodman Dam and the lower Ocklawaha River." On the other side of the Capitol, Ocala Representative George Albright concurred: "By no means is this cast in stone." For the next few months, Kirkpatrick and his allies prepared for battle over the fate of Rodman.[25]

By the next legislative session, George Kirkpatrick dominated the debate surrounding Rodman Dam. Beating back numerous efforts to comply with the Cabinet's decision, Kirkpatrick instead offered a plan to fulfill CLAC's demand for further study. By the summer of 1993, the legislature passed a measure allocating $900,000 for an eighteen-month examination of Rodman Reservoir. The law called for four possible scenarios for future action—full or partial retention of the reservoir, or full or partial restoration of the river. In many respects, the study—managed by the newly established Department of Environmental Protection (DEP), which then subcontracted most of the research to the St. Johns River Water Management District—was the summation of a generation of scientific research. And given the contentious nature of much of that work, the resulting twenty-volume report, submitted in January 1995, offered no final resolution of the issue. Though it concluded that "no further studies are necessary to answer the question" concerning Rodman, the report was often so ambiguous and technically arcane that both sides saw it as confirming their position. George Kirkpatrick most certainly thought so. After combing the report for the slightest bit of evidence that would favor his cause, he announced he was "elated by the findings included in the DEP report," which "gave us even greater evidence of the positive environmental impact of the [Rodman] ecosystem." Though small parts of the study may have supported his position, the thrust of the report clearly warmed Marjorie Carr's heart. Hidden in the volumes of dense prose was the simple statement—"efforts should be directed instead at restoration of the Ocklawaha River."[26]

Following the report's recommendation, Governor Lawton Chiles ordered the Department of Environmental Protection to begin an immediate drawdown of the reservoir in anticipation of restoration. Kirkpatrick lashed back, informing DEP Secretary Virginia Wetherell that he, representing the legislature, and not the governor, was in charge. "Any movement towards restoration on the part of the Department," he asserted, "would be highly presumptive. . . . Any movement towards restoration would presume that the Department has already determined that the legislature will eventually decide against keeping the structure [Rodman Dam]." He added presciently, "This would be highly premature." Thus began what became an annual ritual of Florida politics. With the emergence of spring, the governor and executive agencies, in addition to a majority of the state legislature, would call for the removal of Rodman Dam. And George Kirkpartrick, much like his Congressional predecessors who had blocked deauthorization, stood in the way.[27]

When first examined, George Kirkpatrick's commitment to Rodman Dam appeared rather unusual. Representing a university town that stood at the center of the anticanal movement, he seemed out of sync with its environmentally conscious constituency. However, his district stretched far beyond the city limits and embraced rural areas of north central Florida, particularly Putnam County. An avid angler, Kirkpatrick had an affinity for the lake and the good ol' boys who spent whatever free time they had fishing in it. As he once noted, I "represent the interests of the folks who love, use and depend on the Reservoir for their livelihood." He had to, for he recognized more than anyone that his political fate rested in their hands. Left-leaning Gainesville rarely granted its own senator a majority of votes. Thus Kirkpatrick's base of support came from those rural residents who saw him as the lone defender of their way of life. And with the governor and Cabinet consistently calling for restoration, both he and the people of Putnam County would join forces to fight what they considered an elitist alliance between government bureaucrats and scientific experts, who either at best ignored them or at worst dismissed them as ignorant rednecks.[28]

Things were ironically coming full circle. In the summer of 1995, a group of Putnam County residents and recreational fishermen organized a group called Save Rodman Reservoir, Inc., to "fight off the wishes of 'those who know better.'" Working within the neo-populist legacy of Ronald Reagan and the conservative revolution, they were determined to protect "their" lake from outsiders, those they considered "paid 'enviro-wonks' [who] pontificated at public hearings about the evil that is Rodman." Relying on strategies strangely similar to the nascent anticanal movement thirty years earlier, they sought the preservation of Lake Ocklawaha and its new "ecosystem with abundant flora and fauna." "Our band of ragtag supporters had grown into a throng," Kirkpatrick reminisced, "with folks calling and writing from every place imaginable. Weary travelers made the trip to Tallahassee for committee meetings on a weekly basis, sometimes without any plan to speak, but just to be there to make their presence felt.

... Like a modern day barn raising, they rallied the troops with newsletters, phone calls and faxes. . . . Meanwhile paid consultants and strangers to Rodman pushed the anti-retention agenda." Those very same words could well have described Marjorie Carr's earlier efforts against the Canal Authority and the Army Corps of Engineers. Kirkpatrick's chief legislative aide, Mike Murtha, certainly thought so. "They [FDE] had something they loved back in the Sixties and some bastards came and took it away from them," he exclaimed. "Well, now we have something that we love and some bastards are trying to take it away from us."[29]

Over the next three legislative sessions, Kirkpatrick and his allies did their job well, as they blocked any effort toward restoration by Governor Chiles and the Department of Environmental Protection. For Marjorie Carr, 82 years old and now terminally ill with emphysema, these setbacks must have seemed like all her work was for nought. Rodman Dam—"that obscenity, that ridiculous mistake, that hideous monstrosity"—remained. By the summer of 1997, "feeling lousy," tethered to an oxygen bottle, and forced to move from her cherished Micanopy homestead to a patio home in the middle of Gainesville, Carr plaintively asked, "will I live to see it [the Ocklawaha] run free or not? I don't know." What she did know, was that George Kirkpatrick was now the source of all her frustration. Characterizing his defense of Rodman as "an obsession," she added that the senator's success stemmed from the fact that "he is feared and I don't think he cares." Though no longer able to lead the battle for restoration, she still showed signs of her legendary feistiness. She railed against those who failed to see the wisdom of Rodman's removal. She complained that bass fishermen "ought to be ashamed of themselves" for their unyielding support for the reservoir. At the same time, Carr reaffirmed her sentimental attachment to the river, sounding more like Sidney Lanier than a research scientist with a stubborn commitment to the facts. "Once the dam is gone," she reflected, "the manatees will be able to come up there during the winter. What a sight that will be. How lovely that will be."[30]

On October 10, 1997, Marjorie Harris Carr finally succumbed to her illness. Almost immediately, accolades began pouring in for the woman now beatified as "Our Lady of the Rivers." Lawton Chiles commended her as "a true giant in the environmental community. Our state is a truly better place because of her work." Carol Browner, native Floridian and director of the Environmental Protection Agency, called her "one of the true pioneers of the movement to preserve what is best about Florida." Bob Graham, who had met with Carr only weeks before her death, said her "name will always be synonymous with conservation." She "served as the environmental conscience for Florida's leaders." Closer to home, her friends and allies within the movement she had created sorrowfully lamented their loss. Her longtime colleague David Anthony reflected on her commitment to the river. Considering she had dedicated nearly forty years of her life to the struggle, he lamented, "it's sad to realize that Marjorie has died without the Ocklawaha running free. It was our dream to have a celebration on its banks." Joe Little, University of Florida law professor and a veteran of FDE since the 1970s, expressed his "deepest disappointment" in Carr's inability to see the dam removed. It was "a bitter pill that Marjorie's death leaves us to swallow." Alyson Flournoy, current president of FDE, took Carr's death as a call to action. "Just as she was an inspiration in life ... [in death] she can only inspire us to continue to work to see that restoration happens. It's the best tribute we can pay to her."[31]

FDE members hoped Carr's demise would signal a change of heart in Tallahassee. Their expectations were buoyed in late May of 1998, when the legislature commemorated Carr with the passage of a law that named the Cross Florida Greenway after her. In many respects it marked the crowning achievement for a woman who had dedicated her life to environmental protection. However, if FDE's membership thought this could provide the political momentum to finally restore the Ocklawaha, they were sadly mistaken. Indeed, the day after the legislature honored Carr with the name change, it also saw fit to memorialize her leading adversary by renaming Rodman Dam after Senator George Kirkpatrick. Calling the senator "an avid bass fisherman, naturalist, and outdoorsman" with a "keen interest in the final disposition of Rodman Dam," the legislature complimented him for leading "the opposition to the removal of the dam throughout his Senate career." It was the worst form of tit-for-tat in an already rancorous debate.[32]

With the turn of a new century, the future of the Ocklawaha still remained unresolved. Even with such federal agencies as the U.S. Forest Service pushing for Rodman's removal, nothing changed. Even with a popular new Republican governor, Jeb Bush, publicly committed to restoring the river, nothing changed. Even with Kirkpatrick's forced retirement in 2000, nothing changed. With their nemesis now removed by state-mandated term limits, FDE mistakenly thought they had a chance for success. "Especially with George Kirkpatrick gone," one member asked, "who else is going to be there to champion the dam?" The answer was a bipartisan coalition of north Florida politicians led by Republicans Jim Pickens of Palatka and Jim King of Jacksonville, and Democrat Rod Smith of Gainesville. Smith had not only taken Kirkpatrick's seat, but his passion for the reservoir. Following the death of Kirkpatrick in 2003, he would even introduce legislation protecting the reservoir as the "George Kirkpatrick State Reserve." If such a measure became law, it would make it nearly impossible to remove the dam. Though the legislation was vetoed by Governor Bush, it remained a legislative perennial, introduced session after session, that demanded FDE's constant vigilance. Even seemingly insignificant issues placed environmental activists on the defensive. Every tax dollar spent on the reservoir's recreational facilities—be they boat ramps, campsites, or bathrooms—reinforced Rodman's permanence. Reservoir supporters argued that after nearly forty years of existence, the artificial lake had become part of the natural environment itself. As one explained, "it's got its own ecology. It's got its own value." The reservoir remained alive, with newspaper headlines as late as the spring of 2007 observing, "Year after Year, it's the Same Dam Debate," and "Ocklawaha Restoration Remains in Limbo."[33]

Despite the ongoing controversy over the fate of Rodman Dam and the Ocklawaha River, the establishment of the Marjorie Harris Carr Cross Florida Greenway turned the century-old boondoggle of a canal into a model conservation project. As Florida Representative Bill Grant explained immediately following federal deauthorization, the state now had the chance to "convert an environmental lemon into lemonade for the citizens of Florida." Over the next two decades, Florida's legislature took advantage of an unprecedented opportunity and established a 107-mile greenway dedicated to recreation and natural preservation in a region undergoing rampant growth and economic development. In 1990, one Marion County resident, excited over the promise of a new future, wrote a letter filled with anticipation to the *Ocala Star Banner*, once the unrivaled voice of procanal boosterism. Recalling the words of Sidney Lanier and William Bartram, Dee Cirino praised "the fruition of our linear park [which] can begin with a system of leisure lanes that lead to a wide oasis of canopied hardwoods, scrub habitat covers, carpets of leaves, and a variety of grasses. We can arrive by car, foot, bicycle, and horseback, until we reach the rivers called Ocklawaha, to the east, and Withlacoochee, to the west. To paddle along shaded waters is to feel the past, understand the present, and be consoled that the future brings hope for 'natural' adventure. For those who think these kind of dreams, this can be a tribute to the future as well."[34]

This vision reached fruition by the first decade of the twenty-first century. In 2000, the Office of Greenways and Trails spent $3.1 million to construct a 200-foot-long "land bridge" to connect the two parts of the Greenway bisected by Interstate 75. Hikers, mountain bikers, equestrians, and even wildlife shared this connector which linked the east and west sides of the Greenway. With the development of campgrounds, trails, and boat ramps, thousands of visitors flocked to the variety of recreational opportunities afforded by the Greenway. According to the Greenway's 2007 management plan, "The Cross Florida Greenway probably supports a wider variety of outdoor public recreation uses than any other park and recreation land in Florida." In 2005 (the last year total annual statistics were available) over 1,100,000 people used the facilities of the 79,000-acre Marjorie Harris Carr Greenway. By all accounts, the Greenway has been a resounding success and provided a lasting legacy for Marjorie Carr.[35]

Yet contentious echoes of past issues continue to plague the Greenway. On its eastern side, the controversies over the fate of Kirkpatrick Dam and Rodman Reservoir continue to swirl in new and different ways. In June 2008, the St Johns River Water Management District received a permit application to build a 400-slip marina at an existing RV park on the shores of Rodman Reservoir. Supporters of river restoration saw the plan as just another attempt to keep the reservoir intact. Karen Ahlers of the Putnam County Environmental Council concluded that "if you've been on the natural parts of the Ocklawaha, you know that the river is simply not big enough anywhere in its reach to accommodate 400 boats." Conversely, Ed Taylor, a founder of "Save Rodman Reservoir" and a Putnam County commissioner, favored the proposal simply because "we'd like to see anything and everything that keeps that dam in place." Public opinion ran heavily toward denying the permit. As of March 2009, the water management district had received over 500 letters and e-mails opposing the project. Charles Lee of the Florida Audubon Society expressed the views of many when he wrote, "this is a highly controversial application, and we have a strong interest in making sure this application is denied. . . . There are obviously extraordinary implications regarding the restoration of the Ocklawaha River, and even the management of the existing reservoir." In spite of this groundswell of concern and the stance of myriad state and federal agencies opposing construction, no decision has yet been reached—either concerning the approval of the marina permit or the broader issue of the restoration of the Ocklawaha River itself.[36]

On the usually quiet western side of the Greenway, the application by Progress Energy Corporation to build a twin reactor nuclear power plant in Levy County near Inglis Lock has raised problems as well. If the significant bureaucratic hurdles are cleared, the facility is projected for completion by 2016–2017 and will generate 2,200 megawatts of electricity at an estimated construction cost of $17 billion. Proximity to the completed sections of the canal has provided significant rationale for the location of the plant. Water for cooling the reactors would be "taken from the unfinished Cross Florida barge canal and pip[ed] several miles to the plant, and then several miles back out the Gulf of Mexico." In addition, the completed portion of the canal west of Inglis Lock will serve as the major access point for shipping materials to the plant itself. Similar to the Rodman marina controversy, little has been resolved as to the ultimate disposition of this issue.[37]

The legacy of the Cross Florida Barge Canal therefore remains profoundly ambivalent. The unintended consequences of canal development and the unfulfilled dreams of canal boosters have created the Marjorie Harris Carr Greenway out of the lands designated for canal construction. The dogged activism of Carr and her cohorts proved that citizen involvement can achieve positive results by changing the course of seemingly inexorable government projects. Yet canal supporters have their monuments as well. Kirkpatrick Dam and Rodman Reservoir on the eastern end of the Greenway and Inglis Lock on its western side represent the continuing effort to fundamentally tame Florida's waterways. The remnants of the canal project contain elements of both nature and human endeavor, which points to the strained relationship between people and Florida's environment. The issues and concerns surrounding the Cross

Florida Barge Canal still resonate thirty years after Nelson Blake first published this book and raise profound questions about how future Floridians will grapple with similar questions.

## Notes

1. Marjorie Carr to John Bustered, 30 December 1976, RG 1, Series 1, Box 5, Folder 1976 (2), FDE, PKY; "Cabinet Votes 6-1 Against Completion of Barge Canal," *St Petersburg Times*, 18 December 1976; "Cabinet Votes Against Canal," *Florida Times Union*, 18 December 1976; "Cabinet Minutes of the Canal Authority," 31 January 1977, OGT; Marjory Stoneman Douglas to Marjorie Carr, 30 December 1976, RG 1, Series 1, Box 5, Folder 1976 (1), FDE, PKY.

2. Lieutenant General John W. Morris, Memorandum for Washington Policy Group, 11 January 1977, Box 20, Folder 5, ACE, Office of History, Humphreys Engineer Center, Fort Belvoir, Alexandria, Va.; Nathaniel Reed et al., Memorandum for Lieutenant General John W. Morris, 12 January 1977, Box 20, Folder 4, ACE, Office of History, Humphreys Engineer Center, Fort Belvoir, Alexandria, Va.

3. Edward Greene, News Release, "Chief of Army Engineers Recommends Cross-Florida Barge Canal Project be Terminated," 24 February 1977, Box 20, Folder 6; "Terminate Canal, Army Engineers Say," *Ocala Star Banner*, 25 February 1977; Nathaniel Reed to John Bustered, 9 December 1976, Box 20, Folder 4, ACE, Office of History, Humphreys Engineer Center, Fort Belvoir, Alexandria, Va.

4. Ernest Graves, "Engineer Memoirs," 168, *http://www.usace.army.mil/publications/ eng-pamphlets/ep870-1-52/part1.pdf*.

5. "End Florida Canal Project Carter Urges Congress," *St Petersburg Times*, 24 May 1977.

6. "End Florida Barge Canal: President," *Florida Times Union*, 24 May 1977; "Marion Commissioners' Canal Reaction Mixed," *Ocala Star Banner*, 24 May 1977; "Congress Asked to Put 'RIP' on Barge Canal," *Orlando Sentinel*, 24 May 1977; "Carter Urges Death for Canal," *Ocala Star Banner*, 24 May 1977.

7. "Carter Urges Death for Canal," *OSB*, 24 May 1977; "Close Ledger on Useless Project," *Orlando Sentinel*, 19 February 1977; "Florida House Votes to Kill Barge Canal," *Palatka Daily News*, 5 April 1979; "Barge Canal May Face Watery Grave," *Independent Florida Alligator*, 20 April 1983; "Environmentalist Wants Cemetery to Mean Death for Canal," *Independent Florida Alligator*, 25 January 1983; Jim Smith to Paula Hawkins, 3 May 1983, Series VI, Box 3, Folder Cross Florida Barge Canal, Paula Hawkins Papers, Winter Park Public Library, Winter Park, Fla.

8. "Florida House Votes to Kill Barge Canal," *Palatka Daily News*, 5 April 1979.

9. "Feud over Florida Barge Canal Reheats," *Miami Herald*, 10 June 1985.

10. "Why Cross Florida Barge Canal Refuses to Die," *St Petersburg Times*, 26 May 1985; Bill Chappell to Marsha Chance, 18 April 1983, RG 1, Series 1, Box 7, Folder 1983 (1), FDE,

PKY; "Cross-Florida Barge Canal Shows Signs of Life," *Independent Florida Alligator*, 21 September 1982.

11. LeRoy Collins to Claude Pepper, 14 July 1983, Series 301, Box 472A, Folder 3, CPP; Resolution, Ocala Board of Realtors, Inc., 7 April 1983, RG 2, Box 4, Folder CFBC Easy Reference, FDE, PKY.

12. Andy Johnson to Friends of the Cross Florida Barge Canal, 19 October 1981, Box 9, Folder 3, Bill Chappell Papers, PKY; "Barge Canal Opponents and Proponents Line Up on Either Side of Project," *Daytona Beach Morning Journal*, 9 February 1983; "Feud over Florida Barge Canal Reheats," *Miami Herald*, 10 June 1985; David Gencarelli, Memorandum to Senator Hawkins, 21 April 1983, Series VI, Box 3, Folder Cross Florida Barge Canal, Paula Hawkins Papers, Winter Park Public Library, Winter Park, Fla.

13. "Barge Canal Is Still Hotly Debated," *Gainesville Sun*, 17 June 1985.

14. Paula Hawkins Press Release, undated, Series VI, Box 3, Folder Cross Florida Barge Canal, Paula Hawkins Papers, Winter Park Public Library, Winter Park, Fla.

15. Water Resources Development Act of 1986, PL 99-662, 7 November 1986, *http://www.fws.gov/habitatconservation/Omnibus/WRDA1986.pdf*; "A Monster Slain, *Miami Herald*, 20 November 1986; Section 1114, PL 99-662, *http://www.fws.gov/habitatconservation/Omnibus/WRDA1986.pdf*.

16. Charles Bennett press release, 29 January 1990, RG 1, Series 1, box 7, Folder 1990s (2), FDE, PKY; "Bill Would Kill Canal, Return Land to State," *Ocala Star Banner*, 9 March 1990; ibid.; "Land for Florida Barge Canal May Become a Ribbon of Parks," *Miami Herald*, 10 May 1990; "Graham, Stearns: Give Canal to State," *Gainesville Sun*, 9 March 1990; "Land for Florida Barge Canal May Become a Ribbon of Parks," *Miami Herald*, 10 May 1990.

17. "Land for Florida Barge Canal May Become a Ribbon of Parks," *Miami Herald*, 10 May 1990; Water Resources Development Act of 1990, PL 101-640, 28 November 1990, *http://www.nab.usace.army.mil/whatwedo/civwks/wrda90.pdf*.

18. For a listing of CLAC members, see "Minutes of Meeting of Canal Lands Advisory Committee, April 9, 1992," Accession II, Box 19, Cross Florida Greenbelt Plan Folder, FDE, PK; "Barge Canal's Fate in Dispute," *St. Petersburg Times*, 29 October 1992; "One Strip of Land Is the Focus of Many Different Desires," *St. Petersburg Times*, 4 September 1991; Richard Coleman, "The Joys of Fishing," Letter to the Editor, *Gainesville Sun*, 24 May 1998; David Bruderly, "Fishing Would Be Great," Op-Ed, *Gainesville Sun*, 1 June 1998.

19. "Panel: Study Rodman 3 Years," *Gainesville Sun*, 18 September 1982.

20. "Ex-Senator Kirkpatrick Dead at 64," *Gainesville Sun*, 6 February 2003; "Kirkpatrick Created Legacy of Action, Controversy," *Gainesville Sun*, 6 February 2003.

21. Daniel Canfield, Eric Schulz, Mark Hoyer, "'To Be or Not to Be'—The Rodman Reservoir Controversy, A Review of Available Data, February 1993," v, viii, St. Johns Water Management District Library, Palatka, Fla.

22. George Kirkpatrick, "Musings on Rodman," n.d., 3, George Kirkpatrick Papers,

Mike Murtha Collection, Gainesville, Florida; "Rodman Decision Relayed," *Palatka Daily News*, 18 September 1992; "Rodman's Fate Put on Hold, *Ocala Star-Banner*, 18 September 1992; "Panel: Study Rodman 3 Years," *Gainesville Sun*, 18 September 1982.

23. "Cabinet: Pull Rodman Plug," *Florida Times Union*, 16 December 1992; "Cabinet Urges End to Dam," *Gainesville Sun*, 16 December 1992; motion by Commissioner Betty Castor, 15 December 1992, Historic Documents Pertaining to Ocklawaha River Restoration, FDE, 2000 (blue folder), FDE Headquarters, Gainesville, Fla.; "Cabinet: Pull Rodman Plug," *Florida Times Union*, 16 December 1992.

24. "Fishermen Worried About Another One Getting Away," *Florida Times Union*, 16 December 1992; "Cabinet: Pull Rodman Plug," *Florida Times Union*, 16 December 1992; "Cabinet Votes to Restore River," *Ocala Star Banner*, 16 December 1992; "Cabinet Urges End to Dam," *Gainesville Sun*, 16 December 1992.

25. "Cabinet Urges End to Dam," *Gainesville Sun*, 16 December 1992; "Cabinet Votes to Restore River," *Ocala Star Banner*, 16 December 1992.

26. Environmental Studies Concerning Four Alternatives for Rodman Reservoir and the Lower Ocklawaha River, Volume 1, Executive Summary, St. Johns River Water Management District, 22, St. Johns Water Management District Library, Palatka, Florida; George Kirkpatrick, "Musings on Rodman," n.d., 5, George Kirkpatrick Papers, Mike Murtha Collection, Gainesville, Fla.

27. George Kirkpatrick to Virginia Wetherell, 4 April 1995, George Kirkpatrick Papers, Mike Murtha Collection, Gainesville, Fla.

28. George Kirkpatrick, Memorandum to Members of the Board of Trustees of the Internal Improvement Trust Fund, n.d., 11, George Kirkpatrick Papers, Mike Murtha Collection, Gainesville, Fla.

29. George Kirkpatrick, "Musings on Rodman," n.d., 3, 4, 6, George Kirkpatrick Papers, Mike Murtha Collection, Gainesville, Fla.; "The Battle of the Dams," *Smithsonian*, 28, November 1998, 52.

30. "Barge Canal's Nemesis Takes on the Dam," *Miami Herald*, 4 February 1990; "Activist Recalls Fight to Let the River Run," *Gainesville Sun*, 13 June 1997.

31. "Gainesville's Marjorie Carr, Environmentalist, Dies at 82," *Gainesville Sun*, 11 October 1997; "'Steward of God's Garden' Laid to Rest," *Gainesville Sun*, 17 October 1997.

32. *http://election.dos.state.fl.us/laws/981aws/ch_98-398.pdf.*

33. "Should the River Run Free?," *Florida Times Union*, 13 March 2000; "Ocklawaha Restoration Remains in Limbo," *Gainesville Sun*, 26 April 2007; "Year after Year, It's the Same Dam Debate," *Ocala Star Banner*, 26 April 2007.

34. "Bill Would Kill Canal, Return Land to State," *Ocala Star Banner*, 9 March 1990; Dee Cirino, "Conserving Land Where Bridge Was to Cross Canal," letter to editor, *Ocala Star Banner*, 8 March 1990.

35. Marjorie Harris Carr Cross Florida Greenway Management Plan, prepared by Muller and Associates, Inc. with the Office of Greenways and Trails, June 2007, 35, *http://www.dep.state.fl.us/gwt/cfg/Plan_PDF/CFG_LMP_Final.pdf*; visitor numbers from OGT

2005 figures, attachment in e-mail to Steven Noll from Patricia Root, OGT, DEP, 16 March 2009. Over 2,000 more acres have been added to the Greenway since its original configuration of 77,000 acres.

36. "Rodman Dam Removal Faces New Twist: A Proposed Marina," *St. Petersburg Times*, 9 February 2009; Charles Lee e-mail objector letter *OL_26668_6_701507.tif* at *https://permitting.sjrwmd.com/epermitting/jsp/Search.do?theAction=searchDetail&theIndex=10*

37. "Progress Energy Florida Signs Contract for New, Advanced-Design Nuclear Plant," 5 January 2009, *http://www.progress-energy.com/aboutus/news/article.asp?id=20482*; "Florida Nuke Plant Avoids Drought Woes with Saltwater," *St. Petersburg Times*, 24 January 2008.

# Repairing the Damage or Making It Worse? The Everglades since 1980

CHRISTOPHER F. MEINDL

As Nelson Blake finished writing the original edition of this book, he had access to a handful of significant works that treated selected aspects of human and natural history in the Everglades including Marjory Stoneman Douglas's 1947 classic *The Everglades: River of Grass*.[1] Blake made generous use of primary sources, but he could not have imagined how easily many of these documents are now accessed. For example, Florida International University's Everglades Digital Library features an on-line assembly of nearly 10,000 pages of primary documents and images in a collection entitled *Reclaiming the Everglades: South Florida Natural History, 1884–1934*.[2] Nor could Blake have imagined the avalanche of literature generated on the Everglades since he completed his book in 1980.[3]

Above and beyond the huge volume of primary source material on the Everglades since 1980, including government documents and reports, collections of personal papers and oral histories from a range of influential Everglades personalities, and extensive newspaper coverage of events regarding Everglades management, there are now a large number of scholarly books and articles on virtually every aspect of the history, natural science, and social science of the Everglades since 1980. In this chapter, I will use some primary sources but I will rely even more on the enormous volume of relatively recent books and articles, and attempt to synthesize the various scientific and management issues in the greater Everglades ecosystem over the past three decades using the same (but probably less eloquent) narrative form Blake used.

Blake recognized the interconnectedness of the Kissimmee River, Lake Okeechobee, and Everglades systems, but it is not entirely clear that he comprehended the enormous diversity of land and waterscapes across South Florida—and how closely they are connected by slowly moving water. Indeed, what most people refer to as "the Everglades" consists of a wide variety of ecosystems, including extensive sawgrass marshes on thick beds of peat and muck soils; marl prairies featuring thin, dried algae-based soils, outcropping limestone and sparse sawgrass; the somewhat deeper water Shark River Slough (in the heart of the Glades) with its myriad tree islands just a foot or so above the surrounding landscape; Taylor Slough and the estuarine environment along the southern edge of mainland Florida; the dwarf cypress–dominated Big Cypress Swamp; the higher pine "keys" (such as Paradise Key or Long Pine Key)—large "inland tree islands" far from the ocean but surrounded by marsh; the mangrove-dominated south and southwest coasts and the shallow flats of Florida Bay; and even the extensive littoral (shoreline) marshes along the southern and western shores of Lake Okeechobee. Yet Blake was certainly beginning to appreciate the growing human footprint in the region.[4] As population growth continued unabated in South Florida, ecological problems appeared to spread beyond the Everglades. When Congress authorized the Central and Southern Florida Project for Flood Control and Other Purposes (C&SF Project) in 1948, the population of South Florida[*] had not yet reached 750,000, and planners estimated that the region would have just 2 million people by the year 2000. As Blake's book went to press in 1980, however, South Florida had nearly 3.8 million people; by 2008, the U.S. Census estimated there were nearly 7 million people in the region—and before the national economic meltdown that began in late 2007, some observers believed that as many as 11 million people might have called South Florida home by 2030.[5]

The increasing intensity of urban and agricultural land use in the region ultimately led to a host of water quantity and quality problems that Blake began to see. For example, he noted that Lake Okeechobee had begun to suffer noticeable water quality problems by the early 1970s. Total phosphorus in the big lake nearly doubled between 1974 and 1984, and this important plant nutrient contributed to a series of algal blooms during the 1980s and early 1990s (the largest covering some 42 percent of the lake in 1987). Although the lake continues to support significant sport and

---

[*] Since 1948, defined here as the following counties: Monroe, Collier, Lee, Miami-Dade, Broward, Palm Beach, Martin, St. Lucie, Okeechobee, Glades and Hendry.

# Population of South Florida since 1900

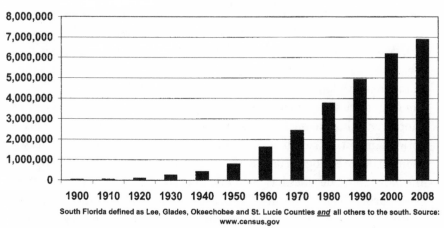

South Florida defined as Lee, Glades, Okeechobee and St. Lucie Counties *and* all others to the south. Source: www.census.gov

Figure 3.1

commercial fisheries, algal blooms are often blown into and do damage to the extensive littoral marshes along the southern and western portions of the lake. Environmentalists initially suspected that channelization of the Kissimmee River, and consequent destruction of roughly 30,000 acres of flood plain wetlands during the 1950s and 1960s, was primarily responsible for rushing excessive nutrients from expanding cattle ranches into Lake Okeechobee. Yet careful scientific research ultimately demonstrated that although the Kissimmee was contributing some additional phosphorus to the big lake, the lion's share of excess phosphorus made its way into the lake compliments of dairy farms in the Taylor Creek/Nubbin Slough area (just northeast of Lake Okeechobee)—while back-pumped water from the Everglades Agricultural Area (EAA) also contributed some phosphorus and particularly nitrogen to the lake. It does not help that Lake Okeechobee is relatively shallow (less than 20 feet deep at flood stage, but more often between 10 and 15 feet deep) and that periodic strong winds produce waves capable of re-suspending nutrients that otherwise sink to the lake bottom.[6]

Water managers decided to reduce back-pumping from the EAA into Lake Okeechobee in 1979, sending nutrient-laden water from the agricultural area into the water conservation areas (WCAs) farther south. Unfortunately, they inadvertently altered the vegetation in the WCAs. Sawgrass has long dominated much of the Everglades because it can survive in environments with low concentrations of nutrients, especially phosphorus. When water managers directed the EAA's nutrient laden runoff away from the lake and into the WCAs, dense stands of cattails began to appear in the conservation areas. Cattails are native to Florida but they usually do not form thick stands that crowd out other species of plants and animals. Moreover, although much is made about the Everglades not receiving historical amounts of runoff after construction of the C&SF project, at least as much of the ecological damage in Everglades National Park (ENP) over the past several decades has been due to dumping excess water into the park during the dry season (November to May), and especially during unusually wet months that can occasionally occur during the dry season. Over several millennia, plants and animals in the region developed biological communities adapted to the annual dry season. The wood stork, for example, depends upon the natural annual drawdown of water to concentrate fish in progressively smaller pools so they are easy to catch—and then feed to their young who are hatched at this time. Yet in an attempt to provide the park its fair share of water, managers began providing ENP an equal allotment of water each month (and flooding it during extremely wet months).[7]

Continuing the chain of problems, the general reduction of water passing though the WCAs and into Everglades National Park throughout the year (compared to historic flows) meant less water oozed from the Park into Florida Bay; and a series of ecological problems became manifest in Florida Bay by the 1980s.[8] Of course, the once pristine Biscayne Bay also suffers from water quality and related ecological problems stemming from water manipulation and significant development in Southeast Florida.[9] Furthermore, it eventually became clear that flushing excess fresh (and nutrient laden) water from Lake Okeechobee down the Caloosahatchee River (to the Gulf) and St. Lucie Canal (to the Atlantic Ocean) created water quality crises in the Caloosahatchee and St. Lucie estuaries. Blake noted human impacts to the Kissimmee River, Lake Okeechobee, and Everglades proper; but continuing population growth, increasingly intensive land use, and progressively more complex water manipulations ultimately began to cause ecological problems throughout the greater South Florida ecosystem, including coastal waters. Indeed, in the years after Blake's book was published, the federal government worked closely with the state of Florida and the South Florida Water Management District to create Biscayne National Park (1980), the Florida Keys National Marine Sanctuary (1990), and Dry Tortugas National Park (1992)—and add over 100,000 acres to Big Cypress National Preserve in 1988 and over 100,000 acres to Everglades National Park in 1989. Although he did not realize it at the time, Blake's coverage of initial attempts to cope with water quality problems in the Kissimmee River and Lake Okeechobee were the beginnings of the movement to "restore" the Everglades.[10]

Blake commented on the failure of Florida's Kissimmee River Restoration Act (passed in 1976) to accomplish what its supporters originally intended. Recall that Florida officials begged Congress and the U.S. Army Corps of Engineers (COE or Corps) to do something after the peninsula's incredibly destructive floods of the late 1940s. The Corps responded, in part, by digging a straight, wide canal (C-38) through the lazily meandering river during the 1950s and 1960s. Such action provoked almost immediate reaction from Florida's environmental community, which lobbied hard to get the legislature to restore the Kissimmee River in 1976. Passage of this bill set off nearly two years of argument among South Florida's farmers, ranchers, and environmentalists, but just five years after completing the big ditch, the state legislature asked Congress to have the Corps of Engineers restudy the Kissimmee River/C-38 canal with an eye toward restoring the river. The COE was still adjusting to its "new environmental mission," so it was in no rush to restore even a small part of the river. In 1984, the Corps finally issued a report in which they found that restoring the Kissimmee would yield no net economic benefit, and since federally funded projects at that time had to generate net economic benefits, the COE temporarily dashed hopes of federal participation in Kissimmee River restoration.[11]

It is no secret that President Ronald Reagan and his administration took a dim view of virtually all environmental preservation and restoration efforts throughout the 1980s. Reagan certainly had little use for federal government sponsored environmental protection and he wanted to shift responsibility for this activity to the states. Such a stance left Flor-

ida's Governor Bob Graham (1979–1987) to tackle environmental problems without much in the way of federal support. Indeed, the governor
cemented ties with environmentalists after *Sports Illustrated* ran a story
in their popular swimsuit issue in February 1981 entitled "There's Trouble
in Paradise," an expose that lambasted Graham's mediocre record on the
environment. Between the *Sports Illustrated* article, the drought of 1980–
1981, and El Nino–induced flooding in early 1982 (in which Everglades
National Park was used as a dumping ground for huge amounts of excess
water from urban and agricultural areas), Graham was moved to launch
his Save Our Everglades program in 1983.[12]

In early 1983, the governor insisted that his top environmental administrators produce a plan to improve ecological conditions in the Everglades. Indeed, Nelson Blake was among the experts consulted by the
governor as his staff tried to determine how to best revive the Glades.[13] By
August of that year, Graham proclaimed "Save Our Everglades" as a plan
intended to rejuvenate much of the South Florida ecosystem. He called for
Kissimmee River restoration, strategic land acquisition in South Florida,
wetland restoration on state-owned lands within the EAA, more effective
wildlife management and modifying the east-west Tamiami Trail and Alligator Alley highways to enable more natural sheet flow of water from
north to south. Although far short of more recent efforts to "restore the
Everglades," Graham's initiative represented a crucial change of focus: it
succeeded in raising the profile of the Everglades and in highlighting the
importance of restoring the environment of much of South Florida (not
just Everglades National Park). Graham's vision for the region can be put
into context another way: as an academic area of study, ecological *restoration* was in its infancy in the early 1980s.[14]

Bob Graham's appointees to the governing board of the South Florida
Water Management District (SFWMD) initiated the Kissimmee River
Demonstration Project in 1984. The SFWMD eventually decided to buy
some 50,000 acres in the Kissimmee Valley in an effort to restore a section
of the old meandering river channel. By 1986, a demonstration project
was in place and the preliminary results were very encouraging. The small
portions of revived river channel soon behaved as they had for centuries
before modification, with point or sand bars developing along the inside
bends of the stream and wetland plants and animals returning to adjacent floodplains. Of course, any hoped-for river restoration would have to

prevent flood damage, and this would not be easy given the expansion of settlement and ranching in the Kissimmee Valley since the completion of C-38 in 1971. Meanwhile, the Corps' lack of enthusiasm for the SFWMD's demonstration project was palpable, and in July 1987, the COE reported to Congress that they ought not participate in project modifications of the Kissimmee River. Despite this, Congress included $2 million in its 1988 fiscal year budget for the Corps to conduct its own Kissimmee River demonstration project, but the Reagan Administration refused to authorize the Corps to use funds for this purpose.[15]

Meanwhile, in an effort to better cope with apparent water quality problems in Lake Okeechobee, Governor Graham assembled the Lake Okeechobee Technical Advisory Committee (LOTAC) in 1985. This committee of experts was charged with preparing a course of action to help improve the big lake's water quality. A year later, LOTAC made several recommendations including the development of best management practices intended to reduce the nutrient-laden effluent emanating from the dairy farms north and east of the lake; moving surface water from Okeechobee dairies into neighboring Martin and St. Lucie Counties for agricultural use; and developing long-term monitoring, research, and management capability for the lake. Indeed, thirty of the region's forty-eight dairy operations chose to participate in the state's Dairy Rule Program, a series of actions intended to reduce phosphorus runoff from dairies. These actions were paid for with a combination of taxpayer and dairy farm money. The state ultimately bought the remaining eighteen dairies.[16] Not long after this, the Florida legislature passed the Surface Water Improvement and Management Act (SWIM Act) in 1987, and Governor Bob Martinez (1987–1991) reconvened the LOTAC (often referred to as LOTAC II) to help the water management district develop a SWIM plan for Lake Okeechobee. Recognizing that it would be difficult to significantly reduce the production of nutrients in the Taylor Creek/Nubbin Slough dairy district, or to prevent the movement of nutrient-laden water into the lake, LOTAC II recommended the construction of a long-term, large-scale water treatment project using wetlands. Wetland scientists at the University of Florida had published studies on the ability of wetland plants to extract nutrients from wastewater back in the 1970s. The idea is relatively simple: create a gently sloped wetland environment packed with nutrient-loving marsh plants that consume a large percentage of the nutrients (particularly phosphorus and nitrogen), so that by the time water leaves the system, it contains far fewer nutrients. In a move foreshadowing a significant portion of the Comprehensive Everglades Restoration Plan more than a decade later, in 1989 SFWMD devoted more than $14 million toward construction of the Everglades Nutrient Removal Project adjacent to Water Conservation Area I. Flow through operations finally began on the 1,544-acre treatment wetland in 1994.[17] Still, the State of Florida continued to allow water polluted with excessive nutrients (especially phosphorus) to pass into federal properties in the region. This despite the fact that the state's own narrative standard for class III waters states: "in no case shall nutrient concentrations of a body of water be altered so as to cause an imbalance in natural populations of aquatic flora and fauna." To be sure, interpreting this water quality standard consistently in the field is almost impossible, but from the perspective of federal land managers in South Florida, the water management district's 1987 SWIM plan appeared to be too little, too late. Accordingly, the U.S. Attorney in Miami—Dexter Lehtinen—decided in his first year on the job (without consulting his bosses in Washington) to sue the State of Florida and the state-supervised South Florida Water Management District for failing to enforce Florida's own water quality standards. Lehtinen filed suit in Federal Court on 11 October 1988.[18]

It turns out that the Everglades is a very oligotrophic system: its plants and animals have adapted over millennia to an environment with very low concentrations of essential plant nutrients, especially phosphorus. How low? Nobody knows for certain, but many scientists and others have followed the lead of Professor Ron Jones, who has long argued that water in the Everglades generally had no more than 10 parts phosphorus per one billion parts water (10 ppb). Water with just a couple dozen ppb of phosphorus is enough to create dramatic ecological changes in the Everglades. Specifically, phosphorus-loving cattails can out-compete and crowd out other plant species to the detriment of both native flora and fauna adapted to a low nutrient environment. Large swaths of all three Water Conservation Areas have become choked with cattails, and little else. This is because total phosphorus levels now routinely average more than 100 ppb in Lake Okeechobee and often average around 147 ppb in the EAA before treatment. EAA farmers continue to be blamed for excess nutrients. The region's farmers object, claiming to use fertilizers that contain relatively little phosphorus, but they do use water from Lake Okeechobee and some observers suggest that phosphorus emanating from the EAA may be a result of this nutrient's mineralization as peat soils oxidize. The fact remains that phosphorus-laden water leaves the EAA and is pushed into the WCAs.[19]

The Federal government's lawsuit against the State and SFWMD charges that the district's 1987 SWIM plan for the Everglades simply would not reduce phosphorus levels quickly enough to prevent significant ecological damage to Everglades National Park and nearby Water Conservation Area 1, also known as the Arthur R. Marshall Loxahatchee National Wildlife Refuge. Although the Reagan Administration probably was not happy about the lawsuit, Dexter Lehtinen apparently counted on support (or at least no interference) from Vice President George H.W. Bush as he campaigned for President in October 1988, denouncing Massachusetts Governor Michael S. Dukakis for his failure to clean up Boston Harbor. Because Florida's own water quality rules state that water quality should not cause an imbalance of plant species, and because there appeared to be scientific consensus that nutrient laden water caused cattails to replace sawgrass in South Florida, the State's lawyers had very little wiggle room. Conceding defeat, however, was not the preferred option for South Florida sugar farmers. Admitting guilt would lead to a solution that would come out of their pockets, probably in the form of retired agricultural land that would be used to create artificial wetlands to remove excess phosphorus (an option sugar farmers did not believe would work). Although some members of the SFWMD governing board suggested that the district ought to do more to reduce excess nutrients in the region's water, a majority of board members agreed with the farmers and preferred to duke it out in court, ultimately spending several million dollars of the public's tax money challenging the lawsuit.[20]

Lehtinen's action may have been necessary in order to bring about more significant environmental protection in South Florida, but it shredded relationships between many state and federal officials and it created a toxic atmosphere for bureaucrats, environmentalists, farmers, and politicians throughout South Florida and beyond. During the 1990 Florida gubernatorial campaign, former U.S. Senator Lawton Chiles denounced Governor Bob Martinez for wasting tax money in an attempt to defend against a hopeless lawsuit. Floridians elected Chiles governor (1991–1998) and several months later, he stunned many observers by appearing in federal court to ask for a truce. On 20 May 1991, Chiles told the judge: "I am here and brought my sword. I want to find out who I can give that sword to and I want to be able to give that sword up and have our troops start the reparation, the clean up. . . . We want to surrender. We want to plead that the water is dirty. We want the water to be clean. . . ." The settlement agreement (itself the subject of intense negotiations between state and federal authorities) eventually conceded that excess nutrients were causing ecosystem change, and that phosphorus concentrations should meet an interim limit of 50 ppb by July 1997, and long-term limits (to be determined by additional research) by July 2002. The State ultimately developed a complex water quality monitoring system throughout the Water Conservation Areas and Everglades National Park featuring several dozen data collection sites. Although the annual average amount of phosphorus detected at a particular site in the Everglades may be as high as 15 ppb, the average amount of phosphorus throughout the network of sampling stations in the park and in each WCA, over rolling five-year periods, should be no more than 10 ppb. Recognizing that it was not likely to reach these long-term goals immediately, the State later pushed back the date this standard must be achieved until the end of 2006, and then again to 2016. In any event, storm water treatment areas (STAs or carefully engineered wetlands) were to become the primary means of extracting nutrients from slowly moving farm runoff. The federal government's lawsuit against Florida prompted the legislature to pass the Marjory Stoneman Douglas Everglades Protection Act in May 1991. This act called for a more aggressive Everglades SWIM plan and served to codify the settlement with the U.S. government. Although the lawsuit succeeded in placing water quality in South Florida near the top of the environmental agenda, the acrimony and bitterness it spawned among public officials probably delayed Everglades rehabilitation by several years.[21]

At the same time, large and small sugar growers in the EAA (often collectively referred to as Big Sugar even if they occasionally disagree among themselves) were furious with the State's settlement. They played no role in negotiating the agreement between the state and federal governments—even though they would be heavily affected by it. Within a year of Chiles's "surrender," Big Sugar initiated a series of legal actions in an effort to delay and sabotage the court order approving the settlement (and cleanup of nutrient-laden water). Meanwhile, throughout the 1990s and beyond, Big Sugar came under increasing attack as the chief source of ecological problems in the Everglades. In 1996, environmentalists attempted to force Big Sugar to contribute more money toward Everglades cleanup by proposing a two-cents-per-pound tax on refined sugar. Florida voters narrowly defeated this proposal in November, but only after Big Sugar retaliated with a vigorous public relations campaign in which they challenged existing science (especially the very small limits for phosphorus), defended their right to continue farming in the region, and claimed (with some justification) that they were the backbone of the EAA's economy; they flooded Tallahassee with high-priced lobbyists and contributions to state and federal politicians' reelection campaigns. Indeed, it became increasingly easy for environmentalists and their sympathizers to blame Big Sugar for all ecological problems in the region. Between historic mistreatment of migrant farm workers and using a portion of what used to be the Everglades to reap handsome profits, EAA sugar growers made an easy target, and excessive phosphorus became a handy weapon. What some of the region's environmentalists conveniently ignore is the fact that their own demand for water and products grown in the EAA, and even flood control, contributes to the impetus for water manipulation in South Florida. This does not mean that Big Sugar is blameless; but it does mean that urban demands for sugar, water, and flood control have contributed to the ecological mess that South Florida has become.

By 1993, the planned cleanup of the Everglades was still tied up in court, but there was a new occupant of the White House (President Bill Clinton), and his entourage included the likes of environmentally friendly leaders such as Vice President Al Gore (of global warming fame); Attorney General Janet Reno (who grew up in what used to be the wilds west of Miami); Environmental Protection Agency chief Carol Browner (another native Floridian who used to run the state's Department of Environmental Regulation); and Secretary of the Interior Bruce Babbitt (who embraced Everglades restoration almost immediately). Indeed, Babbitt worked hard to broker a compromise that farmers and environmentalists could live with, but many environmentalists objected to Babbitt's deal because it did not guarantee clean water for the Everglades or flog the region's farmers, nor did it force agriculturalists to pay most of the cost of the cleanup. Disgusted, Babbitt dropped his proposed settlement idea and left the Florida legislature to work out an agreement; the legislature, however, had long been an institution beholden to Big Sugar, its campaign contributions, and its army of lobbyists.[22]

Indeed, in early 1994, sugar lobbyists wrote the first draft of the Marjory Stoneman Douglas Everglades Forever Act (not to be confused with the moribund 1991 Marjory Stoneman Douglas Everglades *Protection* Act), which postponed enforcement of final phosphorus standards until 2006, provided $700 million for creating 40,000 acres of filtering marshes designed to reduce phosphorus to 50 ppb (with less than one-third of the funding coming from farmers)—and no apparent plan (or funding) to reduce phosphorus any further than 50 ppb. Environmentalists howled in protest and the 103-year-old Douglas demanded that her name be taken off the 1994 legislation because she believed it marked a retreat from the original settlement agreement; but the law passed anyway, renamed the Everglades Protection Act. In fact, a federal judge continues to oversee this lawsuit and settlement more than twenty years later because even though phosphorus levels have been significantly reduced, water entering the WCAs still has more phosphorus than allowed by law.[23]

Clearly, a settlement crafted by lawmakers alone would not be able to deliver a plan for the Everglades that did not also produce protests from one quarter or another. Well-entrenched economic and political interests built fortunes on the degraded South Florida ecosystem—both in the EAA and along the coast. Furthermore, the region's natural resource agency managers often viewed responsibilities to their own institutions as more significant than those of other agencies. For example, the Corps of Engineers was more interested in providing flood control than environmental enhancement, while officials at Everglades National Park were more interested in the relative health of the park than in water supply for nearby urbanites. By the late 1980s, a handful of scientists from a variety of governmental bodies and universities recognized that much of their work remained buried in technical reports that were difficult or impossible to access. Moreover, despite the growing volume of individual scientific effort, the compartmentalization of scientists (like compartmentalization of the remaining Everglades) reduced the likelihood that a synthesis and deeper understanding of the South Florida ecosystem might emerge. Because of this, several dozen researchers from different agencies and institutions assembled at Key Largo in 1989 for a symposium intended to share scientific information. Over the next couple of years, as a series of workshops sustained the interaction of scientists, it eventually became clear to the scientific community that South Florida featured a range of interconnected and human-dominated ecosystems whose degradation could be reversed; in fact, they resolved that the Everglades and its related ecosystems could and must be rehabilitated if South Florida was to continue to sustain millions of people at a reasonable quality of life.[24]

At the same time, the U.S. State Department's Human Dominated Systems Directorate of its Man and Biosphere Program (MAB HDS) developed a five-year project on ecosystem management for ecological sustainability. MAB HDS assembled more than 150 government and academic scientists to engage in a South Florida case study examining sustainability goals for the region, estimating water resource needs, and forming generic principles for ecosystem management—and then developing land use scenarios to judge the potential for socio-ecological sustainability. The ecosystem management concept dates back to Aldo Leopold (1949) and emphasizes environmental protection, a position very different from that of the past century in South Florida where the focus has been on satisfying anthropocentric desires for water-based agriculture and urban development. The project identified regional boundaries, ecological endpoints for assessing the relative well-being of different South Florida ecosystems, as well as natural and anthropogenic stresses on these ecosystems, and analyzed the policy, legal, economic, and institutional framework of South Florida. Scientists also developed a series of conceptual models that helped specify the numerous interactions between people and environment throughout the region. These models are often working hypotheses that attempt to explain the chain reaction between *driving forces* (such as water management or development), *stressors* (such as altered hydrology or degraded water quality), and *ecological effects* (such as chemical responses) that lead to *attributes* or somewhat easily measured *indicators* that have important values (such as the population of endangered or other important species). For example, water management practices (driver) have reduced the sheet flow of water through the Glades (stressor); this, in turn, has not only increased salinities in Florida Bay but also resulted in the loss of submerged aquatic vegetation. These two ecological effects are thought to be largely responsible for the measurable decline in the region's waterfowl populations since the 1930s. This otherwise academic exercise demonstrated that a large interdisciplinary group of social and natural scientists could cooperate and produce meaningful assessments of current conditions, that they could generate and assess a series of working hypotheses regarding the region's human-environment interaction, and that they could suggest alternative land use scenarios to policymakers.[25]

As the 1990s progressed, scientists began to assemble impressive bodies of published, accessible work. For example, 1994 marked the appearance of a trio of books in which authors synthesized a tremendous amount of scientific information on the Everglades. Perhaps the most significant of the three is the massive *Everglades: The Ecosystem and Its Restoration*, an 826-page compendium edited by Steven Davis and John Ogden (at the time, ecosystem scientists with the SFWMD and Everglades National Park, respectively). This volume features thirty-one mostly technical chapters that outline what has happened to the Everglades over the past century and how it might be restored. Of course, "restoration" is a loaded term. Although some activists think outright restoration is possible, most scientists argue that the Everglades can never be fully restored because half of the original system is now urban or agricultural land. Rather, scientists contend that it might be possible to rehabilitate what's left of the system so that it functions more like it did a century ago than it does today. Indeed, for many scientists, Everglades "restoration" is really about restoring selected *functions* in the system rather than restoring the Glades to their early twentieth-century condition. Accordingly, the Davis and Ogden volume proposes a large-scale effort based on restoring ecosystem-driving forces (such as regional scale hydrology) rather than merely attempting to re-create a patchwork of restored wetlands. This is more difficult than it appears because we do not have enough hydrological data from the predrainage era to say with certainty what the region's hydrology was like in 1900. Meanwhile, A. B. (Del) Bottcher (president of a soil and water engineering firm) and Forest Izuno (a professor of agricultural engineering) edited *Everglades Agricultural Area: Water, Soil, Crop and Environmental Management*. Their book features a series of technical discussions regarding soils, crops, and nutrients limited to the EAA. This volume is helpful because it highlights the economic significance of the EAA, and it confronts, in a straightforward and nonpartisan way, the problems of soil loss and nutrient export. Finally, in *The Everglades Handbook: Understanding the Ecosystem*, Thomas Lodge (a biologist) reviews the range of ecosystems, biota, and human impacts to the region. In Lodge's own words, he wanted to prepare a book that would help cope with this central question: "What would one need to know about the Everglades and related ecosystems in order to have a good understanding of what they are and how they work?" His work is not technical but is an excellent summary of scientific investigations in the region (and his third edition was published in 2010). Whatever else they may have accomplished, these three volumes bring together an enormous volume of Everglades science in reasonably accessible formats.[26]

Meanwhile, in the Water Resources Development Act (WRDA) of 1992, Congress authorized the Corps of Engineers and the SFWMD to engage in a comprehensive review study (or Re-study) of the 1948 Central and Southern Florida Project for Flood Control and Other Purposes (C&SF Project). The C&SF system made possible an explosion of population growth and development in southeast Florida such that by the early 1990s, more than four million people were relying on a water system originally designed for just two million people. The practical implication of this fact is simple: South Florida's periodic minor droughts became progressively more painful. Water use restrictions are becoming routine. Major droughts (not to mention possible climate change) might cause drastic reductions in water availability. Moreover, as we have seen, not only was the Everglades being denied an appropriate quantity of water distributed when plants and animals expected it—the remnant Glades received poor *quality* water to boot. Politicians ballyhooed the Re-study as an opportunity to "restore" the Everglades, even as engineers focused on the water supply aspects of the study. But unlike COE project planning of the past, the Re-study would be informed by a pair of ad hoc institutions that brought together "voices" of many different interests at both the state and federal level. First, the South Florida Ecosystem Restoration Task Force (SFERTF), originally created by the Clinton Administration in 1993 and expanded by Congress in the 1996 WRDA, consists of 14 members, mostly representatives of several federal agencies including the Secretaries of the Interior, Commerce, Army, Agriculture, and Transportation. Their mission is to coordinate federal agency activity related to water and environment in South Florida. Much of the work of the SFERTF is accomplished by a couple of subunits: the Science Coordination Group and the Working Group, whose members have significant policy and technical expertise. Second, and perhaps even more important, Florida Governor Lawton

Chiles created the Governor's Commission for a Sustainable South Florida (GCSSF) in March 1994. Chiles hand-picked nearly 50 commissioners and intended for them to represent virtually all significant state and local interests in the region. The Corps and the SFWMD completed their initial reconnaissance phase of the Re-study in 1995 and recommended a thorough six-year study to examine the region's hydrology and economics, engage in computer modeling of South Florida's many systems, and produce a comprehensive plan for water in the area. Yet the GCSSF suggested a quicker pace, so in the WRDA of 1996, Congress not only demanded that the planned six-year Re-study be complete by 1999, they insisted that it follow the contours of a plan suggested by the GCSSF.[27]

Governor Chiles was careful to select a broad range of people to sit on the GCSSF, which included mostly Democrats but also some Republican state and local government representatives, business leaders (including a banker, a developer, and a vice president from U.S. Sugar Corporation among others), Dexter Lehtinen (who had resigned from the Justice Department and now worked for South Florida's Miccosukee Indian Tribe), leaders of mainstream environmental organizations (such as the National and Florida Audubon Societies and the Florida Wildlife Federation) and others. Aside from the leader of the Florida Keys National Marine Sanctuary, the only other federal government representative was the colonel who led the Corps of Engineers district office in Jacksonville (which has jurisdiction in South Florida). Significantly, the GCSSF was instructed to reach consensus among sectional interests. At first, this appeared to be an impossible task because many of these interests distrusted and disliked each other. Yet monthly two-day meetings to listen to expert presentations and participation in evening social events ultimately allowed the group to engage in frank discussions of their positions with a minimum of political posturing. Ultimately, the GCSSF produced five reports, including a 1996 conceptual plan for water allocation and storage in South Florida that Congress directed Re-study team members to consider. Indeed, according to Col. Terry Rice (leader of the Corps' Jacksonville District and Re-study team from 1994–1997, and participant in both the SFERTF and GCSSF during this time), Re-study team members adopted virtually all of the conceptual plan put forward by the GCSSF. Their reasoning was that since it represented a consensus product of many diverse interests, it was the only chance to avoid another lawsuit by disaffected parties, and ultimately be capable of attracting congressional appropriations. The GCSSF made generous use of sustainability and restoration rhetoric, and they struggled mightily to develop a plan of action that would prevent the loss of water to agricultural and urban interests while restoring important functions in the remaining Everglades. After the commission laid important groundwork for a restoration/water supply plan, Republican Governor Jeb Bush (1999–2007) quietly terminated the commission on 30 June 1999, several months after he assumed office.[28]

In October 1999, the Corps of Engineers and the South Florida Water Management District released the Central and Southern Florida Comprehensive Review Study, or Re-Study.[29] Acknowledging that the original C&SF Project was immensely successful in protecting people from floods and in making water available to a growing population, the report's authors do not seem troubled by unsustainable population growth and declining environmental quality unleashed by the mid-twentieth-century project. For them, the problem is simple: in order to provide adequate flood protection, the current system flushes an average of 1.7 billion gallons of fresh water out to sea each day (from Lake Okeechobee through the Caloosahatchee River to the Gulf of Mexico, and through the St. Lucie Canal to the Atlantic Ocean). If this water could be stored and redirected, there should be no more water shortages for farmers, urbanites, or the environment. One alternative, using Lake Okeechobee as a reservoir, would not only further degrade the big lake's water quality and littoral environments, it would place unacceptable pressure on the aging Herbert Hoover Dike, which badly needs decades and millions of dollars of repair work.[30] The Re-study (slightly revised and renamed the Comprehensive Everglades Restoration Plan, or CERP) originally called for the construction of 68 major projects related to the region's water resources to take place over several decades and at an initial projected cost of $7.8 billion. (Several projects have since been combined, reducing the total number of CERP projects to 60). CERP projects would be added to the region's many ongoing environmental efforts (such as the construction of treatment marshes). Although CERP would level and fill in more than 200 miles of existing canals and levees in South Florida (and reintroduce more natural sheet flow of water in parts of the region), the centerpiece of CERP is water storage. Specifically, the project envisions some 300 aquifer storage and recovery wells (ASRs), most around Lake Okeechobee; a series of deep lakes created from trashing wetlands and gouging limestone rock out of the eastern Everglades; and building a small number of surface reservoirs.

ASR technology has been used with some success on a much smaller scale in a handful of places in Florida over the past 25 years. Essentially, ASR wells inject large quantities of freshwater into the ground each day for subsequent withdrawal when needed.* The two major benefits of this technology are (1) its potential to store large quantities of water without having to buy much property at the surface, and (2) such storage would not be subject to evaporation losses typical of surface reservoirs. Both of these benefits greatly reduce the cost of storing water. Yet such a scheme is not without risks or problems. To begin with, this technology has never been attempted on such a large scale anywhere in the world. Nobody can say with certainty (or even near certainty) that it will work. Worse still, when authorities pump fresh water containing normal amounts of dissolved oxygen into a subsurface environment with very low oxygen levels it often causes arsenic to be liberated from rocks and introduced into the groundwater that is later retrieved.[31] It remains to be seen if ASR wells in the Glades will perform as hoped.

In addition to aquifer storage and recovery, CERP calls for digging many limestone rock pits just west of the urbanized area in southeast Florida that will become a lake belt capable of storing hundreds of millions of gallons of water. The limestone pits would be created by the lime rock mining industry that happily feeds the state's insatiable demand for new roadbed material. Critics have pointed out that not only will these mines destroy several thousand acres of wetlands, they may quickly introduce pollutants from surface water runoff into the Biscayne aquifer—the major source of drinking water for most south Floridians.[32]

Vigorous opposition to CERP appeared almost immediately. The consensus forged by the GCSSF did not include the perspective of officials from Everglades National Park (ENP), nor did it include many members of the Everglades Coalition, an assembly of nearly fifty environmental groups (such as the Sierra Club, Florida Defenders of the Environment,

---

* ASR is not to be confused with deep well injection of treated wastewater, which is often injected in much deeper levels of the aquifer, and is not intended for recovery.

and Earthjustice), all committed to Everglades protection and restoration. They observed that the plan provided very little additional water for Everglades National Park, and not until the year 2036. Meanwhile, there would be plenty of water available to keep the South Florida growth machine humming. All of this negative feedback from ENP staff and elements of the environmental community greatly concerned local, state, and federal politicians, who wondered how they would convince Congress to approve a $7.8 billion plan (costs to be split evenly between Florida and the federal government) that generated so much disagreement. Was not the proverbial half loaf for the Everglades better than none at all? Regardless of the water supply elements in CERP, virtually all politicians peddled the plan as an effort to "restore" the Everglades—and almost nobody in Congress wanted to appear *against* restoring the Glades. Objections to CERP by several environmental groups were ultimately brushed aside, and by December 2000, Congress passed and President Bill Clinton signed CERP into law.[33]

Much has been written about the Comprehensive Everglades Restoration Plan; some people are happy with it and others much less so. Although CERP is not exactly "comprehensive," it is a large chunk of a bewildering number of environmental rehabilitation and water supply projects sponsored by local (SFWMD), state, and federal agencies in South Florida. Although the collection of projects that form CERP were projected to cost $7.8 billion in 2000, there are several more ongoing projects (such as the Kissimmee River restoration, the C-111 canal project near Taylor Slough in the southeastern Glades, the Modified Water Deliveries to ENP Project, the Everglades Construction Project featuring thousands of acres of filtering marshes, planned state and federal land acquisitions in the region, and several other projects) whose total non-CERP costs initially exceeded *another* $7 billion. From the vantage point of the twenty-first century, it is easy to damn the Corps of Engineers for building the C&SF Project in the first place; but it must be recalled that Floridians called for the Corps' "help" with flood control in the late 1940s, and from the perspective of the middle twentieth century, promoting growth in South Florida seemed like a good idea.[34]

When Congress passed CERP in late 2000, it included a provision for periodic scientific review of the project's progress. Even before CERP was signed into law, the U.S. Department of the Interior asked the National

Research Council of the National Academy of Science to create a Committee on the Restoration of the Greater Everglades Ecosystem to comment on various technical issues associated with Everglades restoration activities. This panel of esteemed scientists (mostly leading university professors) published seven reports between 2001 and 2005 in which they commented on their findings and made recommendations.[35] Many members of this initial review committee now sit on the National Research Council's Committee on Independent Scientific Review of Everglades Restoration Progress, a group that is legally responsible for providing biennial reviews of CERP for the life of the project (several decades into the future), beginning with their first review in 2006. Committee members expressed concern that up to 2006, no CERP projects had been completed, "and anticipated restoration progress in the Water Conservation Areas (WCAs) and Everglades National Park appears to be lagging behind the production of natural system restoration benefits in other portions of the South Florida ecosystem." This is particularly disconcerting considering that ten CERP components scheduled for completion in 2005 have been delayed, and that six more pilot projects scheduled for completion in 2004 are likely to be delayed an average of eight years. The committee cited (among other issues) a significant lack of funding by the federal government. In authorizing CERP, Congress merely expressed conditional support for the Everglades, and most observers argue that it was quite an accomplishment for Congress even to tentatively commit to a host of projects that were—at that time—more conceptual and likely to be revised substantially over time. Through 2007, however, Congress had appropriated less money than originally planned for CERP. This is problematic at least in part because the region's constantly increasing land values have already added measurably to the cost of CERP.[36]

Yet a lack of federal funding for CERP is only one source of delay in implementing this complex series of projects. Some delay is inevitable as scientists cope with much uncertainty by continually collecting and assessing data on how natural systems respond to human manipulation. Indeed, the authors of CERP have embraced a concept called adaptive management, a principle first advanced in the late 1970s. Adherents of adaptive management accept uncertainty as a fact of scientific life, yet they believe that sound decisions can be made on complex projects (such as Everglades restoration) by "learning as you go" rather than studying phenomena for decades before deciding to take any action. Major disagreement remains among agencies that have a stake in South Florida, and the complex project planning and approval process is such that unresolved scientific uncertainties, especially for complex or contentious projects associated with ecosystem restoration, have also delayed the work. This is not to say that there is no ecosystem restoration progress in South Florida. In fact, there has been very encouraging progress on the Kissimmee River restoration project (begun before CERP). Moreover, storm water treatment areas and best management practices within the EAA have taken water that averaged 147 ppb phosphorus and reduced it to 41 ppb. More research needs to be done to determine how many more acres of STAs are needed to reduce phosphorus loading to 10 ppb and to evaluate their long-term sustainability, but clearly there has been some progress.[37]

Frustrated by the relative lack of progress on CERP, and anxious to leave his own mark on the South Florida ecosystem restoration initiative, Florida Governor Jeb Bush launched *Acceler8* in October 2004—a state-funded program designed to jump start a handful of CERP projects that Congress authorized in 2000, and on which the SFWMD could begin work immediately. This move demonstrated Florida's commitment to CERP by contributing funds now and completing seven CERP projects ahead of schedule, plus one non-CERP expansion of a storm water treatment area. With *Acceler8* the state has proposed investing an additional $1.5 billion of its CERP cost sharing over the next several years in an effort to complete selected projects by 2011. Completing these projects ahead of schedule should save money, and it is anticipated that the work will provide about half of the planned surface water storage components, which should help improve the distribution and timing of water deliveries in South Florida's ecosystems. Moreover, several of the project components should improve water quality. Yet the National Academy of Science review committee contends that most of the benefits of these projects will accrue to the northern part of the system, especially Lake Okeechobee, the St. Lucie and Caloosahatchee estuaries, 10,000 Islands, and Biscayne Bay—and relatively little benefit to the WCAs and Everglades National Park. Indeed, some members of the environmental community have assailed *Acceler8* for its emphasis on projects that do not directly benefit the Everglades. Some people fear that CERP and other related projects are being sold as "Everglades restoration" when they may provide far less restoration, but plenty of water to accommodate economic and population growth in South Florida.[38]

In September 2007, the Government Accountability Office (GAO) provided testimony to a U.S. Senate Subcommittee on progress toward ecosystem restoration in South Florida between 1999 and 2006. This testimony was based on a GAO report published in May 2007 on the same subject. The GAO cited a total of 222 planned restoration related projects in South Florida since 1999, only 60 of which are part of CERP. The scope of environmental and water supply projects in the region is truly breathtaking and undoubtedly worthy of the label "largest environmental rehabilitation project in the world." These projects include land acquisition, wetland construction, levee removal, and a range of water storage and ecosystem restoration projects. The GAO classified these projects as CERP, CERP-related, or non-CERP; and they further classified them as completed, in implementation, in planning or design, or not yet started. According to the GAO, although 43 of the 222 projects were complete, this number is far fewer than the 91 projects that should have been completed by the end of 2006. Moreover, in spite of its original authorization in 2000, not a single CERP project was completed by New Year's Day 2007, and more than half were not even on the drawing board. In fact, of the seven CERP projects under construction at the end of 2006, five were initiated by the State of Florida (*Acceler8*). Although nearly one-third of all CERP projects are finally in the planning/design stage, 90 of 107 projects being implemented at the end of 2006 were non-CERP projects. "Consequently," according to the GAO, "the full environmental benefits for the South Florida ecosystem restoration that CERP projects were intended to provide will not be realized for several decades."[39]

The GAO attributes the delay to several issues. For starters, it took longer than expected to develop the policy, guidance, and regulations that WRDA 2000 requires of CERP. Moreover, some delays were caused by the requirement to modify the design of some projects so that they comply with the WRDA 2000's savings clause. In addition, many projects encountered delays associated with a cumbersome review process that includes stakeholder comment and dispute resolution. Finally, there has been a lack of federal funding and dearth of required congressional authorization for several specific projects above and beyond the ten initially cleared by Congress in 2000. The funding issue requires further discussion.[40]

According to the GAO, in 1999, the total estimated cost for ecosystem restoration projects in South Florida was $15.4 billion: this includes CERP, as well as on-going and planned CERP-related and non-CERP projects. CERP projects originally accounted for just over half of this total ($7.8 billion). By the end of 2006, the total cost figure for all projects ballooned to $19.7 billion due to changes in project scope, increased construction costs, and higher land costs. Worse yet, even these cost estimates do not reflect the fact that several projects are still in their conceptual phase and their full cost is not yet known. From 1999 to 2006, federal government agencies devoted $2.3 billion to South Florida water supply and ecosystem restoration projects, a truly significant sum. Yet by its own admission, the federal government's funding during this time period was about $1.4 billion less than the funding originally projected for this time period. During the same time, however, the State of Florida committed $4.8 billion. Although Congress took some steps toward the end of 2007 to authorize specific CERP projects, appropriations of federal money to fund this authorized construction were not immediately forthcoming.[41]

As we have seen, despite CERP's passage as part of the 2000 Water Resources Development Act, congressional appropriations for ecosystem restoration have fallen behind schedule. It is important to remember that WRDAs are part political pork and part useful water infrastructure legislation normally passed every two years—but Congress did not pass a single WRDA between 2000 and 2007. As the 2007 legislative session wound down, leaders in the U.S. Senate and House of Representatives began to negotiate the differences between their respective WRDA bills. The Senate proposed a $15 billion version and the House a $14 billion version, both of which contained nearly $2 billion of CERP projects. By the time the conference committee completed its negotiations, the new WRDA had ballooned to more than $23 billion. President George W. Bush lobbied against, and ultimately vetoed, the bill on the grounds that it cost too much and contained too many additional pork barrel projects. Yet political pork often pays dividends in the form of satisfied constituents, and most of the Florida legislative delegation desperately wanted to score points at home by funding work in the Everglades. Less than a week after Bush vetoed this bill, Congress rebuked him, overriding his veto with far more than the two-thirds vote necessary in both the House and Senate. The Everglades appeared to have authorization for roughly $1.8 billion worth of projects, but appropriations continue to lag far behind authorization for the work.[42]

By early 2008, work toward Everglades restoration appeared to be out of "intensive care" and inching closer toward "recovery" thanks to some success in restoring parts of the Kissimmee River, the creation and partial success of storm water treatment (filter) marshes, Florida's *Acceler8* program, and the recently passed WRDA 2007. Yet the optimism of early 2008 soon faded. In September, the National Research Council's CERP review committee completed its second biennial review of restoration activities in South Florida—and they expressed clear concerns with the lack of progress to date.[43] The committee concluded that restoration activities are mired in budgeting, planning, and procedural issues, and that there has been only scant progress toward meeting restoration goals. Both CERP and many non-CERP projects in South Florida are closely related, but the federal government's project approval bureaucracy treats each component separately, causing what appears to be endless delay and frustration. The committee found that not only are almost all CERP and non-CERP projects far behind schedule but also many scientists in South Florida complain: "it appears that planning rather than doing, reporting rather than constructing, and administering rather than restoring are consuming their talents and time."[44]

Worse yet, the committee found that the natural system is deteriorating and that if such degradation is not arrested and reversed soon, it may become impossible to recover important ecosystem functions. To be sure, the task of restoration is growing more difficult over time as more people take up residence in South Florida's sprawling neighborhoods. Continued population growth is adding to the cost of land acquisition, the materials needed for the restoration, and the water needed to support them. Finally, the committee observed that the fragile coalition of interests that once supported the restoration effort is beginning to show cracks as delays and lack of funding suggest that some parts of the project may never come to fruition. The committee fears that if demonstrable progress is not made soon, the restoration effort may begin to lose public support, and such an outcome might spell disaster for South Florida.

Yet just a few months before the committee's report came out in late 2008, a virtual environmental bombshell exploded in Tallahassee: Governor Charlie Crist (2007–) announced in late June 2008 that the state planned to buy practically all of U.S. Sugar's 187,858 acres of agricultural land in South Florida, much of it in the EAA. This deal had its genesis more than a year earlier when environmentalists sued to block sugar farmers from back-pumping agricultural runoff into Lake Okeechobee, and the South Florida Water Management District's governing board voted to outlaw back-pumping into the big lake in August 2007.[45] This led U.S. Sugar to approach Governor Crist for help. Yet the perceptual transformation of the Everglades from useless swamp to wetland worthy of restoration is nearly complete, and Big Sugar has become increasingly difficult for politicians to defend.[46] Accordingly, Crist offered to buy them out, quietly negotiating a deal with U.S. Sugar Corporation in the following months. Crist's bold move would cost Floridians $1.75 billion, although a small fraction of this cost (some $50 million) would be offset because the plan allows U.S. Sugar to lease this land back from the state for continued agricultural use over the next five years. This deal came at a time when the state's taxpayers expressed widespread dissatisfaction with property taxes, and when the state legislature decided to cope with a broadening economic downturn (first detected in middle 2007) by slashing the budget and initially avoiding any attempts to increase revenue. This is not an insignificant issue because the governor was basically negotiating on behalf of residents of the South Florida Water Management District, who would be taxed to pay for the property.[47]

Environmentalists were initially flabbergasted at the governor's announcement and SFWMD's governing board chairman Eric Buermann referred to the buyout as "Florida's Louisiana's Purchase."[48] But not everybody is happy. For one thing, many of the thousands of people who live along Lake Okeechobee's southern shore and who depend either directly or indirectly upon the well-being of the region's agriculture, are terrified that they will lose their jobs or suffer significant loss in home value. Furthermore, several members of the Florida legislature, ticked off that they were not consulted prior to Crist's negotiations, have expressed concern over the consequences of such a secret deal—such as the fate of southern Lake Okeechobee residents, possible impacts on future federal funding for the restoration effort, what to do with the planned aquifer storage and recovery wells slated for the big lake's southern shore, and so forth. Indeed, the Miccosukee Indians' legal representative (Dexter Lehtinen) wondered aloud if the planned buyout is "nothing but a publicity stunt."

He worries that so much restoration money will be needed for the buyout that little will be left for other important restoration projects.[49]

Ironically, although lobbyists for both U.S. Sugar and the region's other major sugar producer, Florida Crystals, generally take the same side on most issues—Florida Crystals does NOT want its chief competitor to receive what amounts to a bailout, remaining in business under very favorable terms for several more years. Florida Crystals claims that the proposed deal would act like a bailout partly because U.S. Sugar has serious debt problems and partly because a recent appraisal claims that U.S. Sugar ought to be paying closer to $200 an acre to lease the land back from the state after the sale (not $50 per acre, as suggested in the preliminary agreement with the governor). State officials want Florida Crystals to approve the deal because restoration officials would probably want to swap selected parcels of U.S. Sugar land for some Florida Crystals land in order to create a "flow way" through the Everglades Agricultural Area.[50]

The state's worsening economy eventually forced Governor Crist to negotiate a less costly deal, which was announced in November 2008. The scaled-back purchase called for the state to buy 181,000 acres for $1.34 billion, allowing U.S. Sugar to retain more than 6,000 acres and virtually its entire infrastructure—including an extensive railroad as well as citrus and sugar processing plants. Hanging on to these facilities would allow the company to continue to employ many workers who could process raw material from elsewhere. The November agreement would allow U.S. Sugar to continue leasing the land for seven years, with the company supplying $21 million for soil pollution cleanup. All of these changes were intended to deflect attacks on the initial deal. Such criticism included the fact that the first appraisal of the property suggested it was worth only $930 million.[51]

Both the U.S. Sugar board of directors and the governing board of the South Florida Water Management District voted to accept the 181,000-acre ($1.34 billion) purchase in December 2008, yet the state's tanking economy led the governor to renegotiate the land buyout a third time. In April 2009, Crist announced important changes to the settlement. First, the state agreed to buy just 72,500 acres for $533 million, with an option to buy the remaining 108,000 acres over the next 10 years. The acquisition of 72,500 acres seems far less bold, but it would still qualify as the state's largest conservation purchase ever. Furthermore, environmentalists claim that only 120,000 acres are needed for reservoirs and treatment marshes (not 181,000 acres). Second, U.S. Sugar would pay $150 per acre to lease land back from the state in order to remain in business. Nonetheless, Florida Crystals and the Miccosukee Indian Tribe challenged the scaled-down land purchase in court, claiming that property owners in the South Florida Water Management District should not be burdened with the district's proposal to borrow up to $2.2 billion, because aside from buying land, the district does not yet have a plan for how to incorporate that property into ongoing restoration activities. Furthermore, they argue that buying out U.S. Sugar will ultimately cost so much that the district will not have any additional revenue for other restoration work. Regardless of the outcome, Palm Beach County Circuit Court Judge Donald Hafele's ruling on the legality of the state's proposed land purchase is expected to be appealed.[52]

Creating a "flow way" through the EAA featuring treatment marshes and reservoirs is certainly appealing, but it will be virtually impossible to simply re-create the sheet flow of shallow water in a River of Grass between southern Lake Okeechobee and Everglades National Park. Because the EAA was historically the most desirable land for agriculture (it had the deepest and most productive soils), and it has been drained and farmed the longest, this means it has long been subjected to the invisible but relentless physical and biological processes leading to soil subsidence. Nearly six feet of soil just south of the big lake has disappeared since 1900 due to shrinkage, compaction, burning, wind erosion—and mostly—microbial oxidation of now generally dry organic soils that formed under flooded conditions. In other words, ground elevations immediately south of the lake are now so low that any attempt to reinitiate sheet flow from the lakeshore to Florida Bay would likely produce a huge southern extension of Lake Okeechobee. Water would simply pond on old U.S. Sugar land and not ooze south because this property is now lower than land at the southern (more recently drained) end of the EAA. Even if this obstacle could be overcome (perhaps with pumps?), scientists point out that allowing nutrient rich water from Lake Okeechobee to move south over old U.S. Sugar land, and then into what are now the WCAs, would yield an ecological disaster because lake water contains excessive nutrients. At the same time, some argue that U.S. Sugar's land is so loaded with decades of residual fertilizer that water passing over it would also cause major problems for the low-nutrient Glades further south. Of course, the Everglades can never be fully restored for millions of other reasons, such as the nearly seven million people who call South Florida home, most of whom now live on Florida's lower east coast in suburban communities that used to be the eastern Everglades.[53]

It is not yet clear how U.S. Sugar's land would be used in the attempted ecosystem rehabilitation. Since the 72,500 acres the water management district wants to acquire in several more years is scattered in a variety of parcels south of Lake Okeechobee, it is likely that the state will try to swap some of this land for land from Florida Crystals and other farmers in the region so that some sort of contiguous flow way (featuring several treatment marshes) might ultimately be created through the EAA. With U.S. Sugar on its way out, however, it does appear that Everglades rehabilitation will lurch forward, even if it takes a very different shape than CERP planners envisioned in 2000. Some CERP projects (such as water supply for agriculture) will not be necessary if the state takes control of thousands of acres of farmland. Of course, all eyes are on the remaining sugar and vegetable farmers farther south in the EAA, for they occupy land whose soil is becoming thinner each year. One of the more frightening prospects for restoration supporters is that remaining EAA farmers may eventually give up and sell their land to developers, who would love to fill the remainder of the region with all species of urban development.

Finally, in perhaps the cruelest irony of all, some critics of Everglades restoration suggest that if global warming leads to significant sea level rise, the billions of dollars being poured into the Everglades would be wasted. While future sea level rise is likely to cause serious problems in the southern Everglades (particularly in Everglades National Park, not to mention consequences for the rest of the state), it would be disastrous public policy to allow the complete collapse of South Florida's ecosystems because decision makers thought pouring money into the region's environmental rehabilitation was a waste. The National Research Council acknowledges that climate change cannot be ignored and they call for more detailed analyses of climate change impacts on CERP. Indeed, the SFWMD is determining the research necessary to cope with potential impacts of climate change.[54]

Both current and future residents of South Florida need a healthy Everglades if the region is to maintain a reasonable quality of life. How will we know if the restoration has been a success? Scientists have developed several performance measures such as reduced salinity in Florida Bay, increased sheetflow of water in large portions of the WCAs and ENP, reducing phosphorus in water moving as sheetflow to 10 ppb, the expansion of sea grasses and oyster beds in coastal waters, and an increase in wading bird nesting. Although we may see evidence of success in several years, significant progress is likely to take several decades.

Despite all of the problems highlighted above, the Corps of Engineers and the South Florida Water Management District are aggressively attempting to rehabilitate South Florida's beleaguered ecosystems. For example, the district has plans to back-fill more than one third (22 of 56 miles) of C-38 that runs through the Kissimmee River Valley; this will restore over 40 miles (more than one-third) of the old river channel and reestablish more than 12,000 acres of floodplain wetlands. As of September 2007, almost half of this work has been completed and the other half is projected to be finished in late 2013, with environmental monitoring continuing until at least 2018.[55]

Furthermore, total phosphorus levels in the Everglades Protection Area (the three water conservation areas and Everglades National Park) are approaching the state's intended targets. The 2008 water year (1 May 2007 to 30 April 2008) annual geometric mean of phosphorus in water flowing into several points along the northern end of the Everglades Protection Area was just under 47 ppb; and levels of phosphorus generally declined at points farther south in the protection area until water flowing into Everglades National Park during this time averaged just 11.2 ppb of phosphorus (just above the state's target limit of 10 ppb for the Park). Authorities with the SFWMD contend that phosphorus levels were lower in water year 2008 than in previous years due to ecosystem recovery from the 2004 and 2005 hurricanes, subsequent drought, and the work of storm water treatment areas. Yet they caution that natural events will always cause variability in the amount of phosphorus detected in the system, and that it will take decades to restore phosphorus levels in soils to historical levels.[56]

Progress in rehabilitating Lake Okeechobee has been less impressive, but not for lack of effort. For one thing, the lake's littoral zone continues to experience the rapid spread of exotic and nuisance plants. For another, the big lake endures unnaturally high and low water levels. For example, in the midst of a recent drought, the lake reached a record low of 8.82

feet above NGVD (National Geodetic Vertical Datum, very near current mean sea level) in early July 2007. Two years later, the lake level reached 13.82 feet, prompting the Corps of Engineers to drain water from the lake into the ocean in order to maintain storage capacity for the remainder of the 2009 hurricane season.[57] Meanwhile, in April 2008, the Corps of Engineers approved a revised water level regulation schedule for the big lake that calls for maintenance of lake levels between 12.5 and 15.5 feet. The new target elevations are a foot lower than in previous years because the Corps is trying to ensure public safety as it repairs the 143-mile long dike around the big lake.[58] Finally, like the Everglades, Lake Okeechobee suffers from excessive phosphorus loading with total phosphorus in the lake averaging 191 ppb in 2008, far above the state's lake target of 40 ppb. Recent research suggests that hurricanes in 2004 and 2005 appear to have resuspended phosphorus from lakebed sediments. According to authorities with the SFWMD, "Despite a long history of regulatory and voluntary incentive-based programs to control phosphorus inputs into Lake Okeechobee, no substantial reduction in loading occurred during the 1990s." This prompted both the state legislature and the district to develop an alphabet soup of lake protection programs with acronyms that rival the federal government's famed economic stimulus and relief programs during the Great Depression; the state has spent $137 million on these programs between 2001 and 2008.[59]

Despite problems associated with the potential impacts of global climate change, recent cuts to the state budget, and continuing demographic pressure, there is reason for cautious optimism in South Florida. Work continues (albeit slowly) on a host of water supply and environmental rehabilitation projects in the region, state and federal politicians appear committed to "Everglades restoration" (in one form or another), and Floridians continue to embrace environmental protection. Furthermore, President Barack Obama and Congress joined forces to funnel some $279 million in federal money for Everglades projects in early 2009. This is the largest one-year infusion of federal money into the Everglades work since CERP passed in 2000.[60] Within a year, federal authorities directed even more money (nearly a half billion dollars)—some of it economic stimulus funding for "shovel ready" projects—into Everglades work.[61] As more of South Florida becomes filled with development and choked with traffic, citizens are likely to cling even tighter to the idea of a rehabilitated

Everglades, for as Marjory Stoneman Douglas reminded us more than 60 years ago, "There are no other Everglades in the world. . . . Nothing else is like them: their vast glittering openness, wider than the enormous visible round of the horizon, the racing free saltness and sweetness of their massive winds under the dazzling blue heights of space."[62]

## Notes

1. Marjory Stoneman Douglas, *The Everglades: River of Grass* (New York: Reinhart, 1947); Charlton W. Tebeau, *Man in the Everglades: 2,000 years of Human History in Everglades National Park* (Coral Gables: University of Miami Press, 1968); Archie Carr, *The Everglades* (New York: Time-Life Books, 1973); Patrick J. Gleason (ed.), *Environments of South Florida, Present and Past* (Miami: Miami Geological Society, 1974); Patrick J. Gleason (ed.), *Environments of South Florida, Present and Past II*, 2nd ed. (Coral Gables: Miami Geological Society, 1984); Lamar Johnson, *Beyond the Fourth Generation* (Gainesville: University Presses of Florida, 1974); Lawrence E. Will, *Cracker History of Okeechobee: Custard Apple, Moonvine, Catfish, and Moonshine* (St. Petersburg, Fla.: Great Outdoors Publishing Co., 1964); Lawrence E. Will, *A Pioneer Boatman Tells of Okeechobee Boats and Skippers* (St. Petersburg, Fla.: Great Outdoors Publishing Co., 1965); Lawrence E. Will, *Okeechobee Catfishing* (St. Petersburg, Fla.: Great Outdoors Publishing Co., 1965); Lawrence E. Will, *A Dredgeman of Cape Sable* (St. Petersburg, Fla.: Great Outdoors Publishing Co., 1967); Lawrence E. Will, *Okeechobee Hurricane and the Hoover Dike* (St. Petersburg, Fla.: Great Outdoors Publishing Co., 1967); Lawrence E. Will, *From Swamp to Sugar Bowl: Pioneer Days in Belle Glade* (St. Petersburg, Fla.: Great Outdoors Publishing Co., 1968).

2. Everglades Digital Library, last accessed via the World Wide Web on 19 August 2008 at: http://everglades.fiu.edu/.

3. Among the more significant are Jack E. Davis, *An Everglades Providence: Marjory Stoneman Douglas and the American Environmental Century* (Athens: University of Georgia Press, 2009); David McCally, *The Everglades: An Environmental History* (Gainesville: University Press of Florida, 1999); Michael Grunwald, *The Swamp: The Everglades, Florida and the Politics of Paradise* (New York: Simon and Schuster, 2006); Susan Cerulean (ed.), *The Book of the Everglades* (Minneapolis, Minn.: Milkweed Editions, 2002); Gail M. Hollander, *Raising Cane in the 'Glades: The Global Sugar Trade and the Transformation of Florida* (Chicago: University of Chicago Press, 2008); James W. Porter and Karen W. Porter (eds.), *The Everglades, Florida Bay, and Coral Reefs of the Florida Keys: An Ecosystem Sourcebook* (Boca Raton, Fla.: CRC Press, 2002); Ted Levin, *Liquid Land: A Journey through the Florida Everglades* (Athens: University of Georgia Press, 2003).

4. Bonnie Kranzer, "Everglades restoration: interactions of population and environment," *Population and Environment* 24 (July 2003): 455–84.

5. Richard Weisskoff, *The Economics of Everglades Restoration*, (Northampton, Mass.: Edward Elgar, 2005).

6. Nicholas G. Aumen, "The history of human impacts, lake management, and limnological research on Lake Okeechobee, Florida," *Arch. Hydrobiol. Spec. Issues Advanced Limnology* 45 (May 1995): 1–16; Karl E. Havens, Nicholas G. Aumen, R. Thomas James, and Val H. Smith, "Rapid ecological change in a large subtropical lake undergoing cultural eutrophication," *Ambio* 25 (May 1996): 150–55.

7. Thomas E. Lodge, *The Everglades Handbook: Understanding the Ecosystem* (Boca Raton, Fla.: CRC Press, 2005, 39 and 189–90).

8. Carl Hiaasen, "The Last Days of Florida Bay," in Susan Cerulean (ed.), *The Book of the Everglades* (Minneapolis, Minn.: Milkweed Editions, 2002), 208–19).

9. Mahadev Bhat and Athena Stamatiades, "Institutions, incentives, and resource use conflicts: the case of Biscayne Bay, Florida," *Population and Environment* 24 (July 2003): 485–509.

10. Matthew C. Godfrey, *River of Interests: Water Management in South Florida and the Everglades, 1948-2000* (written for the U.S. Army Corps of Engineers, 2006). Last accessed via the World Wide Web on 19 August 2008 at: http://www.evergladesplan.org/about/river_interest_history.aspx.

11. Ibid, 187–210.

12. C. Brant Short, *Ronald Reagan and the Public Lands: America's Conservation Debate, 1979–1984* (College Station: Texas A&M University Press, 1989); Norman J. Vig and Michael E. Kraft, (eds.), *Environmental Policy in the 1980s: Reagan's New Agenda* (Washington, D.C.: Congressional Quarterly Press, 1984); Robert H. Boyle and Rose Mary Mechem, "There's Trouble in Paradise," *Sports Illustrated* 54 (9 February 1981): 82–93; Lance H. Gunderson, Stephen S. Light and C. S. Holling, "Lessons From the Everglades," *BioScience* Supplement (1995): S66–S73.

13. Jack E. Davis, *An Everglades Providence: Marjory Stoneman Douglas and the American Environmental Century* (Athens: University of Georgia Press, 2009), 546.

14. Godfrey, *River of Interests*, 163–86; the academic journal *Ecological Management and Restoration* commenced publication in 2000, *Restoration Ecology* began in 1993, and *Ecological Restoration* produced its first issue in 1981.

15. Godfrey, *River of Interests*, 203–4; Joeseph W. Koebel, "An historical perspective on the Kissimmee River restoration project," *Restoration Ecology* 3 (September 1995): 149–59; Louis A. Toth, *Environmental Responses to the Kissimmee River Demonstration Project* (West Palm Beach: Environmental Resources Division, Research and Evaluation Department, South Florida Water Management District, 1991); Louis A. Toth, "The ecological basis of the Kissimmee River restoration plan," *Florida Scientist* 56 (1993): 25–51.

16. Karl. E. Havens, Eric C. Flaig, R. Thomas James, Sergio Lostal, and Dera Muszick, "Environmental auditing: results from a program to control phosphorus discharges from dairy operations in south-central Florida, USA," *Environmental Management* 21 (1996): 585–93.

17. Godfrey, *River of Interests*, 211–32; F. T. Izuno and A. B. Bottcher, "Introduction" in A. B. Bottcher and F. T. Izuno (eds.), *Everglades Agricultural Area (EAA): Water, Soil, Crop*

*and Environmental Management* (Gainesville: University Press of Florida, 1994), 1–12; F. T. Izuno and A. B. Bottcher, "The History of Water Management in South Florida," in A. B. Bottcher and F. T. Izuno (eds.), *Everglades Agricultural Area (EAA): Water, Soil, Crop and Environmental Management* (Gainesville: University Press of Florida), 13–26); Michael J. Chimney and Gary Goforth, "History and description of the Everglades nutrient removal project, a subtropical constructed wetland in south Florida (USA)," *Ecological Engineering* 27 (2006): 268–78.

18. Godfrey, *River of Interests*, 281.

19. Grunwald, *The Swamp*, 284–90; Nicholas Aumen, "The history of human impacts," 4–8; Michael Chimney and Gary Goforth, "History and description of the Everglades Nutrient Removal Project," 272; National Research Council, *Progress Toward Restoring the Everglades: The First Biennial Review—2006* (Washington, D.C.: National Academies Press), 6; Naomi Lubick, "Revisiting phosphorus in the Everglades," *Environmental Science and Technology* 41 (December 2007): 7954–55.

20. Grunwald, *The Swamp*, 285–91; Godfrey, *River of Interests*, 279–92.

21. Grunwald, *The Swamp*, 358–61; Lawton Chiles, as quoted in Godfrey, *River of Interests*, 284; Grover G. Payne, Shi Kui Xue and Kenneth C. Weaver, "Chapter 3A: Status of Water Quality in the Everglades Protection Area," in Volume 1: The South Florida Environment, (draft) *2009 South Florida Environmental Report* (West Palm Beach: South Florida Water Management District, 2008): 3A-20.

22. Grunwald, *The Swamp*, 297–301.

23. Ibid.

24. Steven Davis and John Ogden, "Introduction," in Steven Davis and John Ogden (eds.), *Everglades: The Ecosystem and Its Restoration* (Delray Beach, Fla.: St. Lucie Press, 1994): 3–6.

25. Aldo Leopold, *A Sand County Almanac, and Sketches Here and There* (New York: Oxford University Press, 1949); Mark A. Harwell, John F. Long, Ann M. Bartuska, John H. Gentile, Christine C. Harwell, Victoria Myers, and John C. Ogden, "Ecosystem management to achieve ecological sustainability: the case of south Florida," *Environmental Management* 20 (1996): 497–521; Mark A. Harwell, "Ecosystem management of south Florida," *BioScience* 47 (September 1997): 499–512; Mark A. Harwell, "Science and environmental decision making in south Florida," *Ecological Applications* 8 (1998): 580–90; J. H. Gentile, M. A. Harwell, W. Cropper, C. C. Harwell, D. DeAngelis, S. Davis, J. C. Ogden, and D. Lirman, "Ecological conceptual models: a framework and case study on ecosystem management for south Florida sustainability," *The Science of the total Environment* 274 (2001): 231–53; John C. Ogden, Steve M. Davis, Kimberly J. Jacobs, Tomma Barnes, and Holly Fling, "The use of conceptual ecological models to guide ecosystem restoration in south Florida," *Wetlands* 25 (December 2005): 795–809.

26. Steven Davis and John Ogden (eds.), *Everglades: The Ecosystem and its Restoration* (Delray Beach, Fla.: St. Lucie Press, 1994); A. B. Bottcher and F. T. Izuno (eds.), *Everglades Agricultural Area (EAA): Water, Soil, Crop and Environmental Management* (Gainesville: University Press of Florida, 1994); Thomas E. Lodge, *The Everglades Handbook: Understanding the Ecosystem* (Delray Beach, Fla.: St. Lucie Press, 1994); Thomas E. Lodge,

*The Everglades Handbook: Understanding the Ecosystem, 3rd ed.* (Boca Raton, Fla.: CRC Press, 2010).

27. Mary Dengler, "Spaces of power for action: governance of the Everglades Restudy process, 1992–2000," *Political Geography* 26 (2007): 423–54; Mary Dengler, "Finding the political 'sweet spot': sectional interests, consensus, power and the Everglades Restudy, 1992–2000," *Environment and Planning A* 40 (2008): 766–84.

28. Dengler, "Finding the political 'sweet spot,'" 774.

29. U.S. Army Corps of Engineers and South Florida Water Management District, *The Central and Southern Florida Project Comprehensive Review Study, Final Integrated Feasibility Report and Programmatic Environmental Impact Assessment* (West Palm Beach: U.S. Army Corps of Engineers [Jacksonville District] and South Florida Water Management District, 1999).

30. Andy Reid, "Lake Okeechobee Dike is bolstered" *South Florida Sun-Sentinel*, 18 June 2009.

31. R. David G. Pyne, *Groundwater Recharge and Wells: A Guide to Aquifer Storage and Recovery* (Boca Raton, Fla.: Lewis Publishers, 1995); Eberhard Roeder, "Aquifer Storage and Recovery: Technology and Public Learning" in John T. Scholz and Bruce Stiftel (eds.) *Adaptive Governance and Water Conflict* (Washington, D.C.: Resources for the Future, 2005), 106–16.

32. National Research Council, *Re-engineering Water Storage in the Everglades: Risks and Opportunities* (Washington, D.C.: National Academies Press, 2005).

33. Grunwald, *The Swamp*, 320–55.

34. National Research Council, *Science and the Greater Everglades Ecosystem Restoration: An Assessment of the Critical Ecosystem Initiative* (Washington, D.C.: National Academies Press, 2003); National Research Council, *Progress Toward Restoring the Everglades: The First Biennial Review—2006* (Washington, D.C.: National Academies Press, 2007); Godfrey, *River of Interests*; Grunwald, *The Swamp*.

35. National Research Council, *Aquifer Storage and Recovery in the Comprehensive Everglades Restoration Plan: A Critique of the Pilot Projects and Related Plans for ASR in the Lake Okeechobee and Western Hillsboro Areas* (Washington, D.C.: National Academies Press, 2001); National Research Council, *Regional Issues in Aquifer Storage and Recovery for Everglades Restoration* (Washington, D.C.: National Academies Press, 2002); National Research Council, *Florida Bay Research Programs and Their Relation to the Comprehensive Everglades Restoration Plan* (Washington, D.C.: National Academies Press, 2002); National Research Council, *Adaptive Monitoring and Assessment for the Comprehensive Everglades Restoration Plan* (Washington, D.C.: National Academies Press, 2003); National Research Council, *Does Water Flow Influence Everglades Landscape Patterns?* (Washington, D.C.: National Academies Press, 2003); National Research Council, *Science and the Greater Everglades Ecosystem Restoration: An Assessment of the Critical Ecosystem Initiative* (Washington, D.C.: National Academies Press, 2003); National Research Council, *Re-engineering Water Storage in the Everglades: Risks and Opportunities* (Washington, D.C.: National Academies Press, 2005).

36. National Research Council, *Progress 2006*, 2.

37. National Research Council, *Progress 2006*, 1–13; Crawford S. Holling (ed.), *Adaptive Environmental Assessment and Management* (New York: Wiley, 1978); Lance H. Gunderson, "Managing surprising ecosystems in southern Florida," *Ecological Economics* 37 (2001): 371–78; Clyde F. Kiker, J. Walter Milon and Alan W. Hodges, "Adaptive learning for science-based policy: the Everglades restoration," *Ecological Economics* 37 (2001): 403–16.

38. National Research Council, *Progress*, 136–41.

39. U.S. Government Accountability Office, *South Florida Ecosystem: Some Restoration Progress has been Made, but the Effort Faces Significant Delays, Implementation Challenges, and Rising Costs*, Testimony Before the Subcommittee on International Operations and Organizations, Democracy and Human Rights, Committee on Foreign Relations, U.S. Senate (19 September 2007): 8.

40. U.S. Government Accountability Office, *South Florida Ecosystem*, 8–9.

41. Ibid., 13–14.

42. Craig Pittman and Wes Allison, "Bush vetoes water bill," *St. Petersburg Times*, 3 November 2007, 1A; Asjylyn Loder and Craig Pittman, "Water worries," *St. Petersburg Times*, 9 November 2008, 1A.

43. National Research Council, *Progress Toward Restoring the Everglades: The Second Biennial Review—2008* (Washington, D.C.: National Academies Press, 2008).

44. Ibid., p. 229.

45. Jeff Harrington and Craig Pittman, "2nd suitor woos U.S. Sugar," *St. Petersburg Times*, 21 November 2008, 1B.

46. Gail M. Hollander, *Raising Cane in the Glades: The Global Sugar Trade and the Transformation of Florida* (Chicago: University of Chicago Press, 2008).

47. Alex Leary and Jennifer Liberto, "Everglades deal shocks, delights," *St. Petersburg Times*, 24 June 2008, 1A; Kris Hundley, "Deal would be the end for Florida sugar giant," *St. Petersburg Times*, 24 June 2008, 1A; Craig Pittman, Jennifer Liberto, and Alex Leary, "Crist offered buyout as U.S. Sugar hit wall," *St. Petersburg Times*, 25 June 2008, 1A; Craig Pittman, "Everglades of past now out of reach?" *St. Petersburg Times*, 28 June 2008, 1A; Wes Allison, "Lawmakers blast sugar deal," *St. Petersburg Times*, 31 July 2008, 12A.

48. Eric Beurmann, "Florida's Louisiana Purchase," *St. Petersburg Times*, 20 May 2009, 11A.

49. Craig Pittman, "Everglades of past now out of reach?" *St. Petersburg Times*, 28 June 2008, 7A.

50. Craig Pittman, "Sugar giant decries rival's deal," *St. Petersburg Times*, 13 December 2008, 3B.

51. Craig Pittman, "State, U.S. Sugar lay out sale details," *St. Petersburg Times*, 26 November 2008, 8B.

52. Mary Ellen Klas and Curtis Morgan, "Governor halves U.S. Sugar Glades deal," *St. Petersburg Times*, 2 April 2009, 1A; Andy Reid, "Closing arguments end in lawsuit against Everglades land deal," *South Florida Sun Sentinel*, 7 August 2009; Andy Reid, "Sides argue pros and cons of U.S. Sugar deal," *South Florida Sun Sentinel*, 15 July 2009.

53. Craig Pittman, "Everglades of past now out of reach?" *St. Petersburg Times*, 28

June 2008, 1A; S. F. Shih, B. Glaz, and R. E. Barnes, "Subsidence of organic soils in the Everglades Agricultural Area during the past 19 years," *Soil and Crop Science Society of Florida, Proceedings* 57 (1998): 20–29; G. H. Snyder, "Everglades Agricultural Area soil subsidence and land use projections," *Soil and Crop Science Society of Florida, Proceedings* 64 (2005): 44–51.

54. Beth Williams, Agnes Ramsey, and Larry Gerry, "Chapter 7A: Everglades Restoration Update," in Volume 1: The South Florida Environment, *2009 South Florida Environmental Report* (West Palm Beach: South Florida Water Management District, 2008).

55. Stephen G. Bousquin, David H. Anderson, Michael D. Cheek, David J. Colangelo, Lynda Dirk, J. Lawrence Glenn, Bradley L. Jones, Joseph W. Koebel Jr., Jo Ann Mossa, and Jose Valdes, "Chapter 11: Kissimmee Basin," in Volume 1: The South Florida Environment, *2009 South Florida Environmental Report* (West Palm Beach: South Florida Water Management District, 2008).

56. Grover G. Payne, Shi Kui Xue and Kenneth C. Weaver, "Chapter 3A: Status of Water Quality in the Everglades Protection Area," in Volume 1: The South Florida Environment, *2009 South Florida Environmental Report* (West Palm Beach: South Florida Water Management District, 2008).

57. Paul Quinlan, "Army Corps of Engineers halts dumping from Lake Okeechobee," *Palm Beach Post*, 11 August 2009.

58. U.S. Army Corps of Engineers, "Corps approves 2008 Lake Okeechobee regulation schedule," news release #0831, 30 April 2008. Available at: http://www.saj.usace.army.mil/Documents/NewsReleases/archive/2008/NR0831.pdf (last accessed on 19 July 2009).

59. Joyce Zhang, R. Thomas James, and Paul McCormick, "Chapter 10: Lake Okeechobee Protection Program—State of the Lake and Watershed," in Volume 1: The South Florida Environment, *2009 South Florida Environmental Report* (West Palm Beach: South Florida Water Management District, 2008).

60. Curtis Morgan and Lesley Clark, "River of cash: stimulus aid for the Glades," *Miami Herald*, 29 April 2009, 1A.

61. Craig Pittman, "Everglades Restoration gets boost from stimulus," *St. Petersburg Times*, 9 January 2010, 1A.

62. Douglas, *River of Grass*, 1.

# Florida Water Management Since 1980: Challenges in a State Addicted to Population Growth

CHRISTOPHER F. MEINDL

The publication of *Land into Water—Water into Land* in 1980 drew attention to Florida's mounting water management challenges, much as Marjory Stoneman Douglas focused public attention on the plight of the Glades with *Everglades: River of Grass* in 1947. Because of Nelson Blake's seminal study, we learn much about the spasmodic efforts to construct a cross-state barge canal, the well-intentioned but misguided efforts to thoroughly re-plumb the Everglades, and the development of water policy in Florida from the early nineteenth century to 1980. Indeed, Blake traces the evolution of water policy from its initial emphasis on navigation improvement (beginning in the 1820s) and drainage (beginning in the 1880s) to an emphasis on flood control (beginning in the late 1920s) and ultimately water supply and management (beginning in the 1970s). Blake concludes his analysis in the late 1970s, immediately after "Florida's environmental revolution," a period when state lawmakers passed landmark pieces of legislation intended to ameliorate the impacts of massive economic and population growth. Blake argued that Floridians finally began to treat water as a valuable resource, not just a nuisance to be eliminated.

The decade of the 1970s witnessed extraordinary efforts to preserve and manage the environment in Florida, among them the creation of five water management districts (WMDs) with boundaries closely matching surface watershed boundaries rather than county or other political boundaries (see map on p. 278). All five WMDs are overseen by the Florida Department of Environmental Protection, and each district is governed by a board of district residents appointed by the governor and approved by the state senate, while day to day operations of the districts are handled by an executive director hired by the district board (subject to gubernatorial and senate approval). As Blake originally reported, the WMDs had responsibility for providing flood protection and water resources management. Today, their responsibilities are even broader. Of course, the story of Florida's water management did not end in 1980.

When Blake's book was first published in 1980, Florida had just over 9.7 million permanent residents; in 2009, the U.S. Census Bureau estimated that more than 18.5 million people called Florida home—most of whom live in Central and South Florida—and they predicted in 2000 that Florida would have more than 28 million people in the year 2030.[1] Although the national economic crisis that erupted in 2008 dramatically reduced migration into Florida, the retirement of millions of baby boomers over the next couple of decades will almost certainly impact what historian Gary Mormino calls the *Land of Sunshine, State of Dreams*.[2] Moreover, population figures do not include the more than 80 million additional people who visit the state each year as tourists, most of whom arrive during the dry winter and spring seasons.[3] As much of the state confronts the reality of massive population growth and overuse of its relatively inexpensive groundwater sources, water supply has become an increasingly contentious issue and arguably the greatest challenge confronting Florida today. Important water resources (particularly well fields, groundwater recharge areas, and floodplains) are now the subject of preservation and even restoration activities, significant features of the WMDs almost since their creation in the 1970s. Drainage and even flood control are now less prominent issues, due in part to the operation of many engineering projects built over the last several decades.

Despite significant quantities of precipitation and large quantities of surface and ground water, the geographic scope and conceptual range of Florida's water challenges is breathtaking. To be sure, some regions of Florida experience more serious water-related problems than others. Yet none of the five water management districts has been immune from the stress and strain on water resources caused by the stampede of people into Florida since 1980. The U.S. Geological Survey reports that each Floridian uses about 158 gallons of water each day (although about half of this is poured on grass).[4] Meanwhile, the concept of sustainability, which began to take root in the early 1980s, has become increasingly important in terms of managing Florida's water resources. Sustainability remains an

# Population Growth in Florida Since 1980

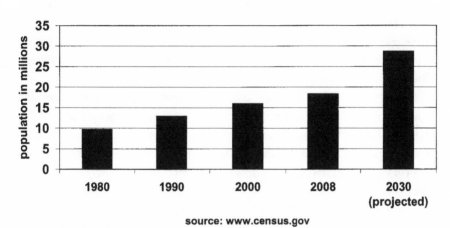

source: www.census.gov

Figure 4.1

# Estimated Annual Visitors to Florida since 1980

source: www.visitflorida.com

Figure 4.2

elusive concept, having evolved over the past two centuries or so from quaint notions of carrying capacity.[5] Originally, carrying capacity referred to the limits of cargo that could be transported by sailing ships. Over time, scholars attempted (with only modest success) to apply the idea of carrying capacity to a landscape's ability to support wildlife and livestock. Some have tried to apply it directly to humans—suggesting that the earth has a limited capacity to support people and that we are fast approaching those limits.[6]

Clearly, the idea of carrying capacity connotes limits but it is almost impossible to directly and concretely apply this idea to people and their relationship with the landscape.[7] Carrying capacity eventually morphed into the phrase "sustainable development," famously touted in 1987 by the World Commission on Environment and Development.[8] Academics and others frequently quote the commission's simple but attractive definition of sustainable development: "development which meets the needs of the present without compromising the ability of future generations to meet their own needs."[9] Of course such a protean definition allowed the term to be interpreted in many different ways, including a business-friendly interpretation that essentially views sustainable development as a "light green" form of business as usual.[10] Indeed, so quickly and significantly had the business community promoted its own version of sustainable development that environmentalists and others began speaking in terms of "sustainability" as a way of countering the emphasis on "development." Like its predecessors carrying capacity and sustainable development, sustainability is difficult to define with precision, but most definitions imply a devotion to three ideals: economic development, environmental protection, and social equity—all to be achieved simultaneously over the long term.

Early conceptualizations of sustainability often emphasized economic development, both in wealthy nations as well as in impoverished countries. Yet environmentalists promoted an emphasis on protecting the planet's resources. Indeed, several writers have employed the concept of sustainability in the analysis of water resources.[11] One of those writers, Leonard Shabman, argues that applying notions of sustainability to water resources requires questioning the twentieth-century drive to control water with engineering structures.[12] Shabman suggests a couple of sustainability principles that can be applied to water resources. One such principle calls for maintaining and restoring the flow and variability of water levels in rivers so that the natural hydrograph is minimally disturbed. It may be difficult to know what natural flows were prior to human manipulations and impacts because virtually all Florida rivers have been altered by changes in land use, but that does not preclude scientists from developing close approximations of natural flow. Another principle, very significant in Florida, advocates restricting groundwater pumping to minimize adverse effects on surface water bodies, including lakes, rivers, and wetlands. Defining "adverse impacts" remains difficult (much like defining sustainability), but it is not impossible.

The one aspect of sustainability that often receives short shrift in discussions of sustainable water use is *social equity*.[13] Equity, like sustainability, can be defined in a number of ways. Some people might argue that an equitable distribution of the cost of providing water would mean charging all of a utility's customers the same per unit price for water they consume. Yet I submit that concern for social equity requires that we manage water resources so that established residents, particularly less fortunate citizens of a place or region, are not harmed by rising water costs caused by the action of others. This is especially salient in Florida where significant population increase in recent decades has forced water managers to pursue more expensive infrastructure and alternative sources of water to meet these new demands. Over time (given the current paradigm), all residents end up paying additional costs for water—whether they can easily afford it or not. Social equity as it applies to water resources should be redefined to mean those who create the need for expensive alternative water sources ought to be the ones who pay the full cost of developing and using them.

The significant costs associated with providing water include capital costs of extraction, treatment, and delivery facilities (and related debt service payments); electricity for pumping and treatment; chemicals used in treatment; salaries of workers and administrators; maintenance; and other costs.[14] Yet calculating the cost of water is a complicated affair because of its naturally occurring variability and other factors. For example, although a water provider's legal fees associated with defending its more controversial decisions (such as excessive groundwater pumping) are calculable—what are the costs of possible environmental degradation and community aggravation associated with such decisions? Moreover, similar sources of water may have very different costs in different locations due to variable energy costs or varying water quality (requiring more or less treatment). Using estimates obtained from Tampa Bay Water, the regional water wholesaler for much of Pinellas, Pasco and Hillsborough Counties, and the St. Johns River Water Management District (SJRWMD) helps illustrate these issues.

Most of Florida is fortunate to have a huge quantity of continually replaced, high quality groundwater that requires far less treatment than most other sources. Ignoring for the moment fixed costs such as debt service on infrastructure and salaries, officials at Tampa Bay Water contend that it costs a bit more than 21 cents to produce 1,000 gallons of groundwater; almost 88 cents to produce 1,000 gallons of surface water; and about $2.72 for 1,000 gallons of potable water from seawater at their relatively new desalination plant south of Tampa.[15] If we factor in fixed costs, both SJRWMD and Tampa Bay Water officials claim that groundwater costs about $1 per 1,000 gallons.[16] Furthermore, Tampa Bay Water estimates that expanding its use of purified seawater in the region will cost between $5.66 and $8.20 per 1,000 gallons,* depending on the specific project, and that additional drinking water from the Alafia River may be produced at a cost of between nearly $4 and up to $10 per 1,000 gallons.[17] The SJRWMD estimates that it can turn seawater into potable water at a cost of between $5.71 and $7.08 per 1,000 gallons, and additional surface water may be obtained at a cost of $3 to $4 per 1,000 gallons.[18] Yet it is not clear if even these costs reflect subsidies, such as those provided by the state to encourage alternative water supply development. Regardless, alternative sources such as surface water and particularly seawater desalination are substantially more expensive than fresh groundwater. Florida is not running out of water; rather, the peninsula can no longer support unchecked growth with cheap groundwater.[19]

Concerns for the social equity dimension of sustainability, particularly with regard to the increasing cost of water in Florida, informs the rest of this chapter. South Florida's water problems are well chronicled in this book, and so is the story of the Cross-Florida Barge Canal. No less serious, however, are a range of water conflicts in many other parts of the state.

---

* The low unit cost of water from Tampa Bay Water's existing desalination facility near Apollo Beach at the mouth of Tampa Bay is largely a function of the fact that the plant takes in bay water that is not as salty as average seawater, and therefore requires somewhat less purification.

Like the "cattle wars" that defined southern Florida more than a century ago, Tampa Bay's "water wars" were a struggle beginning in the late 1980s between the region's local governments and the Southwest Florida Water Management District (SWFWMD or Swiftmud; map on p. 278) over how to provide adequate water supplies to rapidly growing communities whose populations have long since exceeded the capacity of local groundwater resources.[20] For example, Pinellas County—a peninsula bracketing the west side of Tampa Bay—began to experience saltwater intrusion as early as the 1920s.[21] Yet the county and the city of St. Petersburg bought land in neighboring counties during the early twentieth century (including Weeki Wachee Springs) in order to pump relatively inexpensive groundwater into Pinellas so that the local population and economic growth machine could be kept humming. Pinellas County is now virtually built out, a densely populated area with nearly a million people. When several lakes and wetlands in neighboring Pasco County began to dry up in the 1980s, affected landowners pointed to excessive groundwater pumping; Pinellas officials claimed they were pumping what Swiftmud permitted them to extract, and in any case, they blamed drought for the disappearing surface water. In 1997, after Swiftmud and the West Coast Regional Water Supply Authority (West Coast, the regional water wholesaler run by local government leaders) spent much of the 1990s and $10 million of the public's money arguing with each other in court, Swiftmud offered to help West Coast (which reorganized in 1998, becoming Tampa Bay Water) pay for more expensive alternative water sources in order to meet the demands of continuing population growth *and* reduce the pumping of cheap (but environmentally damaging) groundwater from outside Pinellas County.[22]

Accordingly, there is now a large desalination plant at the southern edge of Tampa Bay. This complex, the largest in the western hemisphere, stands as a monument to prodevelopment politics and is designed to produce a maximum of 25 million gallons of fresh water per day (25 mgd). To put this in perspective, the three Tampa Bay area counties of Pinellas, Hillsborough, and Pasco withdrew more than 432 mgd of fresh water during 2005.[23] Unfortunately, the plant did not begin peak production until late 2007, after four years of delay caused by technical problems, which led to $40 million in cost overruns that boosted the plant's final price tag to $158 million. Mechanical difficulties appeared again in March 2009, and the plant reduced its production by several million gallons per day for a few months while technicians made additional costly repairs.[24] On top of the price tag for building the desalination plant is the cost of the water it produces, which is far more expensive than fresh groundwater.

One of the region's other expensive engineering solutions to water supply is a huge, 15-billion-gallon surface water reservoir southeast of Tampa (opened in 2005) that can store water taken from the Alafia and Hillsborough Rivers and the Tampa Bypass Canal for later use. Yet the $146 million facility soon developed unexplained cracks, which dramatically reduced its capacity, and then a severe drought virtually drained what was left in the 1,100-acre reservoir by March 2009.[25] Engineers later discovered that the cracks occurred due to a design flaw that will necessitate keeping the reservoir dry for at least two years; the repairs are now scheduled to begin in June 2012.[26] While it is not clear precisely how much it will cost to fix the reservoir and prevent future cracking, some have suggested a price tag as high as $125 million. Such a repair bill will almost certainly be paid by Tampa Bay Water users in the form of higher rates for water unless the utility successfully sues the reservoir's builder.[27]

Finally, in order to treat surface water coming directly from the Alafia and Hillsborough Rivers and Tampa Bypass Canal as well as the huge reservoir, Tampa Bay Water spent $144 million to build a water treatment plant. Opened in 2002, the surface water treatment facility—which was originally designed to treat more than 60 million gallons of surface water per day—soon encountered clogged filters, greatly reducing its capacity. Although the technical problems have been resolved, reservoir problems and drought reduced available surface water so much by early 2009 that Tampa Bay Water had little choice but to temporarily shut down the plant.[28]

The conundrum of water management in the Tampa Bay area since 1980 remains simple: expensive water supply structures have been built in an effort to reduce environmental impacts and accommodate continued population growth, but these engineering "solutions" have cost the region's taxpayers several hundred million dollars, have raised the price of water for all of the region's residents, and because they have not worked out as intended, the region is now even more vulnerable to drought. Most people are tempted to view technology as a fix for many problems, including water resource development. Yet water supply technology is usually expensive and often fails to work exactly as planned. Indeed, as of April 2009 (in the midst of a three-year drought), Tampa Bay Water was in the uncomfortable position of having to resume excessive groundwater pumping in order to supply water to the region's residents who number one million *more* than they did in 1980.[29] Furthermore, now that so many more people live and work in the Tampa Bay area, Swiftmud was initially reluctant to enact significant water use restrictions in early 2009 because such limitations would effectively close many businesses and put people out of work during a deepening recession.[30] By the end of March 2009, however, the WMD had no choice but to enact severe water restrictions.[31] Such limitations, supported by modest local enforcement efforts, encouraged some people to reduce water use—particularly lawn watering. Yet many others refused to comply, perhaps wondering what is the point of living in paradise if you cannot wash your car or water your lawn in April?

Much of northeast and east central Florida lies in the St. Johns River Water Management District (SJRWMD; see map on p. 278), a region that has also experienced recent, significant population growth. Here as elsewhere on the peninsula, water challenges abound, extending well beyond the barge canal and Rodman Reservoir controversies. Perhaps the most significant problem has been the environmental tragedy involving Lake Apopka, just northwest of Orlando.[32] In the early twentieth century, Lake Apopka boasted a resort economy featuring outstanding fishing, but discharges of inadequately treated wastewater from surrounding communities and especially agricultural runoff overwhelmed the lake's assimilative capacity during the middle twentieth century, severely degrading one of the largest lakes in the state. Well-intentioned and expensive lake restoration efforts led by the SJRWMD initially backfired in 1998 and 1999 when several hundred birds died after former agricultural lands were reflooded (agitating and recirculating deposits of toxic chemicals); but the district's persistence is finally paying off with slow improvement in water quality. Still, in early 2009, the Lake County Water Authority opened a $7.3 million facility to treat millions of gallons of tainted water that flow each day from Lake Apopka down the Apopka-Beauclair canal into a chain of lakes to the north.[33]

Less well known are the efforts of the SJRWMD to manage water resources along its namesake—the St. Johns River. During the early 1900s, just as others were attempting to drain and reclaim the Everglades for agricultural activity, pioneers and investors dug many miles of ditches and canals in an effort to drain much of the marshy headwaters of the St. Johns River, southwest of Melbourne.[34] As part of the original Central and Southern Florida Flood Control Project primarily intended to control water in the Everglades, the U.S. Army Corps of Engineers worked to eliminate persistent flooding in the upper St. Johns region by digging canals capable of dumping large quantities of agricultural runoff into the east coast's Indian River Lagoon. After water quality in the lagoon plummeted, this Corps project—like the Cross-Florida Barge Canal—was halted in the 1970s. In an effort foreshadowing Everglades restoration, the SJRWMD began work in 1988, eventually restoring some 150,000 acres of wetlands that constitute part of the headwaters of the St. Johns River. Meanwhile, the lower St. Johns River (in and around Jacksonville) suffers from significant pollution associated with urban, suburban and agricultural development in northeast Florida. Sadly, the river is being "loved to death" by people and farms.[35]

Efforts to organize some of the district's communities in order to plan and invest in more expensive water resource development so as to avoid a repeat of the Tampa Bay water wars appear to be treading water at best.[36] Leaders in east central Florida rightly want to avoid paying more for water—but they want to accommodate continued population growth as well. Accordingly, the middle St. Johns River is being eyed as a significant source of relatively inexpensive water to help sustain Central Florida's population growth. Although Seminole County recently received permission to withdraw just 5.5 million gallons per day from the St. Johns, Central Florida utilities would ultimately like to divert much more water from the St. Johns and Ocklawaha rivers. Seminole County's action sparked public protest from the City of Jacksonville, St. Johns County, and the watchdog group St. Johns Riverkeeper. The St. Johns River WMD claims that up to 155 million gallons a day can safely be withdrawn from the St. Johns near DeLand (north of Orlando), but the WMD continues to study the matter.[37] Meanwhile, despite much protest, the governing board of the SJRWMD voted 5-4 in April 2009 to accept the WMD staff's recommendation to allow Seminole County to withdraw 5.5 mgd from the St. Johns River.[38]

At first glance, North Florida's thinly populated Suwannee River Water

Management District (SRWMD; see map on p. 278) would appear less likely to have significant water challenges, but first glances can be deceiving. To be sure, water supply is generally not an issue in this sparsely populated part of the state, at least as long as interbasin water transfers are prohibited. Yet it is precisely because the district supports less than a half million people—and much agricultural activity including many animal feedlots and row crop farms—that it has its own water challenges, especially in water quality.[39] Nitrogen-laden water is moving from farms into the groundwater system via porous sandy soils and numerous sinkholes, and then reappearing in undesirable concentrations in springs and streams, including the iconic Suwannee River. The district originally tried to avoid harsh remedial measures to improve water quality by the U.S. Environmental Protection Agency (EPA) by offering farmers financial and technical assistance in establishing best management practices that are intended to reduce nitrogen runoff. The district's efforts were complicated by vocal environmentalists who claim they did not have a significant voice in the policy-making conversation, and that all farmers should reduce their polluted runoff at their own (not taxpayer) expense—but this criticism now appears moot.[40]

Since 1998, the EPA has encouraged all 50 states to develop specific numeric criteria for total maximum daily loads of pollutants (such as phosphorus and nitrogen) that can be present in public waters.[41] As we saw in the Everglades, vague narrative standards are difficult to enforce. The Florida Department of Environmental Protection (FDEP) studied the issue for a decade, but several environmental groups grew tired of waiting and sued the EPA in 2008 for not enforcing the Clean Water Act in Florida.[42] Accordingly, in January 2009, the federal environmental agency formally declared that it would take the lead in developing numeric criteria for the state, using some of FDEP's data and methodology. Meanwhile, a host of interests—particularly those associated with Florida industry, agriculture, and water treatment works—argue that the EPA water quality standards are likely to be stringent and expensive to comply with.[43] Federal authorities concede that it might cost Florida polluters collectively more than a billion dollars to clean their water—and this would be on top of the cost to upgrade local storm water systems. Yet an apoplectic president of Associated Industries of Florida contended that the new federal standards would cost more than $50 billion: "it's onerous, stupid, ridiculous and idiotic."[44] Given that Florida's waters are vital for tourism, seafood, and other businesses, one might argue that it is stupid, ridiculous, and idiotic that so many Florida waters remain polluted. After studying half the state's rivers and streams and most of its estuaries and other coastal waters, the FDEP reported in 2008 that more than of a quarter of the river miles and lake acreage examined—and some 59 percent of Florida's estuaries—have poor water quality.[45]

Meanwhile, the small southern town of Perry (in Taylor County) sits squarely within the SRWMD. Buckeye Technologies Inc., a Memphis-based spinoff from Procter and Gamble, which built a pulp mill in the 1950s, is both neighbor and bully.[46] The pulp mill turns one of the county's most plentiful resources, pine trees, into fibers that are used in a host of products that many people consume on a regular basis such as diapers, feminine hygiene products, casings for hot dogs and sausage, pharmaceuticals, tire and hose reinforcement, and many more. The mill is located near the swampy headwaters of the Fenholloway River, a small stream that wriggles some twenty miles or so before emptying into the northeastern Gulf of Mexico. Like most old pulp mills, the Buckeye mill is a voracious water consumer and disposes of huge amounts of effluent: the mill withdraws some 40 million gallons of groundwater per day (significantly reducing stream flows) and then dumps partially treated effluent back into the river as it passes the mill. Despite Buckeye's significant investment in water treatment over the years, water quality remains a contentious issue in the region. Buckeye has offered to pipe its effluent directly into the Gulf of Mexico (by-passing the Fenholloway), but environmentalists claim that this merely moves the dirty water to the same location by different means; they insist that Buckeye should invest even more in pollution control technology. Furthermore, the Fenholloway River water quality problem is complicated by other issues. For example, when Procter and Gamble first received permission to build the mill in 1947, the Florida legislature granted the company authority to use the Fenholloway River as a virtual "industrial sewer." The mill has no such permission today, and as the nation began to take pollution control seriously, the company invested many millions of dollars in altered production processes and water treatment, which improved effluent quality—but not by as much as critics believe is necessary. On top of all this is the fact that Buckeye is the largest provider of reasonably well-paid jobs in one of Florida's poorest counties.

If environmentalists and the Florida Department of Environmental Protection push Buckeye to invest "too much" in water quality improvement, the company may ultimately decide to establish operations elsewhere—and this would devastate Taylor County's economy.

Nor is the Northwest Florida Water Management District (NWF-WMD, map on p. 278) immune to water challenges. For example, rapid population growth along spectacular panhandle beaches in the state's four westernmost counties has begun to strain the near surface sand and gravel aquifer, particularly during drought.[47] Yet this water management district's most significant headache involves the state of Georgia. Florida's largest river in terms of discharge (water volume)—the Apalachicola River—forms along the Florida-Georgia border at the confluence of the Flint and Chattahoochee rivers (often collectively referred to as the ACF basin).[48] Both the Flint and the Chattahoochee trace their headwaters to north Georgia. The Flint begins at the southern edge of metropolitan Atlanta and drains a large chunk of central Georgia. The Chattahoochee originates in the northeast Georgia mountains, flows through the Atlanta metro area, and then forms more than 100 miles of the southwestern Georgia border with Alabama and Florida.

Georgia developers and politicians naturally claim the Chattahoochee and Flint rivers as Georgia streams, and demand more of this water to help fuel continued population and economic growth. Development interests believe continued growth in northern Georgia is tied to the ability to draw more water from the Chattahoochee River because there are no other inexpensive sources of water in the region. Yet homeowners living along the shores of Lake Lanier, a large body of water created by a U.S. Army Corps of Engineers dam (Buford Dam) on the Chattahoochee River some 16 miles northeast of Atlanta, resist lower lake levels. Finally, communities downstream of Atlanta (such as Columbus) express concern about relatively low flows and poor water quality caused by major users such as Atlanta, which discharges millions of gallons of partially treated wastewater back into the river each day. Meanwhile, Alabama depends on large quantities of Chattahoochee River water to operate the Joseph M. Farley nuclear power plant—and Alabama politicians would prefer to be able to use the river's water to support future growth in eastern Alabama. Florida's interest in the Apalachicola River is primarily related to maintaining diverse habitats along the extensive river floodplain, and sustaining the rich oyster grounds in Apalachicola Bay. Apalachicola supplies 90 percent of Florida's oysters and more than 10 percent of those consumed in the United States, and its oyster beds are extremely sensitive to the volume of fresh water flowing from the river into Apalachicola Bay.[49] Alabama, Florida, and Georgia have spent two decades attempting to develop a mutually acceptable water allocation formula, but to no avail. Although some legal scholars suggested this ongoing disagreement would likely be settled by the U.S. Supreme Court, that now appears less likely.[50]

In July 2009, U.S. District Court judge Paul A. Magnuson ruled that the Corps of Engineers may not unilaterally grant Georgia authorities more water from Lake Lanier. Congress authorized and paid for Buford Dam,* so only Congress can grant Georgia a larger water supply from this dam. The judge also ruled that all water withdrawals from the lake are to be frozen at current levels for the next three years, or until such time as Florida, Georgia, and Alabama agree otherwise. If the states, and then Congress, fail to act within three years, water allocation from Lake Lanier will revert to baseline rules from the 1970s. This means that only the small north Georgia communities of Buford and Gainesville (not the rest of rapidly growing metro Atlanta) will be allowed to continue drawing water from Lake Lanier. This decision must have come as welcome news to Florida and Alabama leaders, who now have the upper hand in negotiating a deal with Georgia. As of this writing, it remains to be seen what sort of water use agreement may emerge.[51]

Everyone agrees that Florida faces significant water challenges, both now and particularly in the future. Nevertheless, the benefits of continued population and economic growth remain an article of faith among most policymakers and business leaders. Indeed, as economists often remind us: "Economic growth is the tide that floats everyone's boat." Yet growth-induced competition for water produces winners and losers. Alas, the grim truth may be that yacht owners, as well as nursery owners, construction workers, and lifeguards will all suffer the consequences of too little water. Furthermore, population and economic growth often produce side effects such as pollution, stress on water supplies, and overcrowding, but these are often viewed as less significant impacts of capitalism that can

---

* Indeed, Judge Magnuson discovered that in the 1940s, Georgia authorities were offered an opportunity to help pay for the dam, but they declined—claiming it was not necessary for water supply.

be easily ameliorated with a few common-sense regulations and proper planning. According to Cynthia Barnett, however, the problem is not a lack of rules and regulations to cope with growth's side effects, "It's the way local elected officials make exceptions to them, the way savvy land-use lawyers and others get around them."[52] Unfortunately, growth-related problems are likely to become more pronounced as powerful people remain convinced that more population growth is the answer to all that ails the state.[53]

Frank Matthews, a lobbyist for the building and development industry, asks a self-fulfilling question: "You know what the Florida economy is based on?"[54] Indeed we do. In Florida, population growth is the primary engine of the economy—an economy built mostly on low-wage jobs related to tourism, retail, and agriculture as well as a steady stream of newcomers who support construction and real estate activity. David Reed, an investment banker, puts it this way: "The Florida economy has been based on the selling of Florida. . . . Our growth is all about population growth. When you take that away, what have you got?"[55] The answer is, not very much. Leading economists such as David Denslow of the University of Florida have called for a reorientation of the state's economy toward higher wage innovative industries and professional work, but this would require significant investment in higher education, something the state legislature refuses to do because it is more interested in keeping taxes low.[56]

Meanwhile, politicians and business people never tire of repeating the phrase "you can't stop people from moving to Florida." What they don't add is that they are addicted to the ideology of growth, an ideology that resembles a Ponzi scheme, especially in Florida. As essayist George Packer reminds us, "A Ponzi scheme succeeds only when enough people are willing to put aside common sense."[57] For over half a century, the Florida economy has run on the principle of a thousand new people moving to the Sunshine State each day. Remarkably, the principle served as a self-fulfilling prophecy and richly rewarded those who bought into the Florida dream. Ominously, few state or county officials dared think about the consequences of that moment when senior citizens, barefoot Toledo lawyers, and displaced autoworkers stopped coming to Florida. The confidence game—today's investments depend on tomorrow's thousand new residents—worked efficiently if not always fairly until 2008. When population growth in Florida sputters, as it did beginning in late 2007, the state's economy is devastated. Between 1970 and 2007, Florida attracted roughly 300,000 new residents every single year. Yet between July 2007 and July 2008, Florida actually lost more than 9,000 domestic residents, and the decline would have been worse were it not for attracting more than 77,000 international immigrants.[58] And between April 2008 and April 2009, the University of Florida's Bureau of Business and Economic Research estimated that the state experienced a net loss of more than 58,000 people—the first time since 1946 that Florida had a year in which more residents left than arrived.[59] Florida's lack of population growth spilled over into significantly reduced tax revenue and appropriations by the state legislature. In May 2006, the Florida legislature approved a budget totaling $73.9 billion; three years later the legislature budgeted only $66.5 billion and more spending cuts are expected.[60]

What many business leaders and policymakers refuse to acknowledge is that economic and population growth has also led to a deterioration in the quality of life for many Floridians.[61] At the same time, those in a position to profit the most from population growth are also in a position to avoid many of growth's side effects. For example, many of economic growth's most significant beneficiaries can afford more expensive water sources and private schools for their children; everybody else simply has to endure the problems: brutal traffic, overcrowded and underfunded public schools and universities, rapidly escalating energy costs, and increasing costs for water as progressively more expensive sources must be tapped. Moreover, what many people used to think were reasonable uses of water are now branded a "waste" because population growth has made Florida's water resources progressively more expensive. For example, turning the faucet on and letting kids play with water coming out of a hose in the front yard during hot summer days used to be a "normal" part of life in Florida; but now, such activity is shunned as a "waste" for all but those who can afford to "let the water run." Even wealthy landowners who use huge quantities of water to maintain large, manicured lawns have been affected. In the midst of a serious drought in early 2009, the *St. Petersburg Times* published an article holding up for ridicule the 35 largest water users in the Tampa Bay area.[62]

Given the fact that continued economic and population growth continues to subtly erode many Floridians' quality of life, some business people have backed away from advocating growth and simply brand growth as "inevitable." Of course, population growth only appears inevitable if the state continues to send market signals to prospective newcomers that they are welcome to add to the state's challenges without a corresponding obligation to pay more to cope with these problems. In other words, some Florida policymakers and business leaders are working overtime to keep the state's Ponzi scheme afloat: they brand growth as inevitable, pretend we can maintain an outstanding quality of life, and attempt to conceal the real costs of growth by spreading these costs over the entire population. Evidence of this perspective is not hard to find.

In September 2003, a group of Florida business leaders called the Florida Council of 100 published a report entitled *Improving Florida's Water Supply Management Structure.*[63] They acknowledge that we must take action to maintain the remaining quality of our environment. Yet predictably, they treat population growth as inevitable, arguing, "It is obvious that Florida will need to increase its supply of fresh water in order to meet future demand."[64] They simply dismiss critics as angry malcontents.

The council blames a decentralized and fragmented governance structure for not being able to resolve regional water shortages, ignoring the state's habit of spreading the costs of growth across large regions. They suggest that the state should create a Water Supply Commission, which would play a leading role in coordinating Florida's water resources.[65] Apparently the council was moved by California's experience of transferring water long distances (from the northern part of the state) in order to continue supporting otherwise unsustainable population growth in the south—and believes Florida ought to do the same.[66] They take aim at the legislature's 1998 "Local Sources First" policy, a policy wisely promulgated in an effort to force local governments to develop water resources within their boundaries—a first step intended to force rapidly growing regions to develop in more sustainable ways. The council insists that North Florida's water would not be "stolen," adding that north Floridians mistakenly view water in their region as their property—when in fact the state's waters belong to all Floridians. Alas, the council cannot avoid the suggestion that water in sparsely populated North Florida maybe should be moved south where it is in high demand. Of course, the reason for this line of argument is to help reduce the costs of otherwise unsustainable growth in Central and South Florida. Although they profess concern for environments across the state, they express no interest in allowing water to become expensive enough in Central and South Florida's *new* developments (the source of water stress) as a way of sending a market signal that future population growth ought to occur elsewhere. Meanwhile, the economic shock of 2007–2010 powerfully reinforces the point that if Florida's population stagnates, the state experiences severe economic problems. Essentially, slow growth or no growth means the death of the Florida dream, 1950–2007.[67]

The council invokes "sustainability" on the cover of its report, yet it appears that what they are most interested in sustaining is population growth in places where it probably should not occur. Not content to view unsustainable population growth in Central and South Florida as merely a mismatch between supply and demand that can be fixed by engineers, the council contends that the private sector ought to be invited to profit from "developing, treating, distributing and creating alternative water supplies."[68] Indeed, they suggest providing the private sector incentives to help "solve" Florida's water challenges. What they don't say is that water provided by private entities would undoubtedly cost more for long-time and low-income residents. Perhaps more expensive water is fine for people who can afford to pay more, but it is not so good for large numbers of poorly paid service workers. Evidently the council prefers a market mechanism that disproportionately impacts less fortunate people rather than trouble those who have been led to believe they can add to Florida's water problems on the cheap.

The council articulates that there is a "clear, inherent conflict to have the [water management] districts responsible for water supply planning and the regulation of consumptive use of water."[69] Perhaps, but the council tips its hand when it expresses dissatisfaction with the WMDs' planning efforts because they did not "lay out time-phased, specific plans with funding sources" and that "the decentralized structure has not solved the uncertainty of meeting our future water needs."[70] Because their view of sustainability is limited to accommodating forecast population growth, it does not occur to them that continuing to provide relatively inexpensive water to hordes of recent arrivals in places where water supplies are stressed is the source of the problem. Their path to sustainability ignores the impacts of population growth and instead focuses on initiating a combination of water transfers from North Florida AND on privatizing alternative water resource development. Of course, profit-motivated companies developing and selling water from alternative sources would mean more expensive water for everybody, not just those responsible for creating the need for more water. Regardless, the council's proposal to create a state authority which presumably would have the power to send water from North Florida to water-stressed portions of the state set off a public uproar that forced Governor Jeb Bush to drop the idea.[71] Yet far from representing a death knell in the battle for state control of water resources, the governor's retreat merely signaled a temporary truce.

More recently, despite Florida's recession-induced glut of 300,000 unoccupied houses in early 2009, state legislator Rep. Trudi Williams (R-Fort Myers) contended, "We've got to get [building] permits going and flowing."[72] She and her supporters such as state Sen. Mike Bennett (R-Bradenton), the Florida Homebuilders Association, Associated Industries, and the Association of Florida Community Developers, argue that impact fees and excessive and duplicative environmental protection regulations at the federal, state, and county level have stifled Florida's population growth—and are therefore the root of Florida's economic problems.[73] Moreover, Sen. Bennett and Rep. Chris Dorworth (R-Lake Mary) want to abolish the Florida Department of Community Affairs, the state's growth management agency. In June 2009, Gov. Charlie Crist (2007–) signed Senate Bill 360 in private, without public fanfare. Virtually everybody agrees this legislation is intended to spur additional construction in Florida, but that is where agreement ends. Builders celebrated the bill's signing because it reduces regulatory oversight of development and relieves them of the responsibility to pay for roads to support their new neighborhoods. Meanwhile, environmentalists and many others contend that Florida's flawed growth management rules have served as little more than a worn-out speed bump on population growth in Florida since 1980, and that the state does not need fewer rules on development—just better ones.[74] Recall that the state's population has nearly doubled from 9.7 million in 1980 to 18.5 million in 2009. And as one columnist points out, "It may not be entirely irrelevant that Bennett is a contractor and Dorworth is a real estate broker."[75] Indeed, state Sen. Dan Gelber (D-Miami Beach) cautions: "I don't want to use the term Ponzi scheme. . . . [but] Our No.1 industry has been growth and our No.1 policy has been optimism. Well guess what? Growth is not an industry and optimism is not a policy."[76]

Admittedly, it would be unfair to suggest that Florida's business and political leaders are completely unconcerned about the impacts of significant population and economic growth. Indeed, the state continues to grapple with growth-induced water demands, and there have been some successes. For example, since 1980, Floridians have embraced the land preservation and environmental restoration activities going on in many parts of the state. In addition to environmental restoration projects in the Everglades and St. Johns River headwaters marshes, Florida has purchased 3.8 million acres of conservation land through Programs such as Preservation 2000 and Florida Forever.[77] Moreover, thanks to more significant regulation of water pollution, water quality in many of the state's waters is far better today than it was in the 1950s. Finally, the Florida Water Resources Act of 1972 instructed each water management district to determine minimum flows and levels (MFLs) for rivers, lakes, springs, and wetlands so as to avoid causing "significant harm" to these water resources and natural systems. Essentially, the task is to determine how much water can be extracted from the environment without disrupting the natural systems we depend on. In other words, WMDs have to determine the sustainable limit of water use.

Unfortunately, the districts did not devote much attention to MFLs until the courts and the legislature revisited the issue two decades later, essentially demanding that the districts avoid issuing consumptive water use permits that would cause water flows and levels to drop below established minimums.[78] Each district is allowed to develop its own methodology for establishing MFLs and the techniques used are varied. Furthermore, each district is required to submit a revised priority MFL project list every year to the Florida Department of Environmental Protection.[79] MFLs are an important tool to help bring the state much closer to sustainable use of its water resources, but scientists have a hard time saying with certainty how much water can be extracted from the landscape without causing significant harm to natural systems.

Of course, an emphasis on MFLs alone ignores another important element of sustainability and sustainable water use: social equity. Some might define "equity" to mean equal, as in all consumers paying the same price for water. Yet such a view pretends that all water users have the same income, and this is obviously not the case. Real social equity in terms of water in Florida means that established residents would not have to pay

more to develop new (and more expensive) water supplies that recent immigrants to Florida require. As things now stand, rather than force those
who are the impetus for more expensive water sources to pay the full cost
for the privilege of living in Florida, costs are spread out across the entire
population so that, on a day-to-day basis, they are somewhat less noticeable (particularly for new residents). Recent proposals to increase rates
for the top water consumers in the Tampa Bay area is a step in the right
direction,[80] but such action would not send appropriate signals to most
future immigrants, who will likely receive water for far less than it costs
to provide. We are often reminded that growth is inevitable; therefore,
despite otherwise plentiful water resources, we must accept the cost of
more expensive sources of water. Virtually every alternative water source
is more expensive than fresh groundwater, but their real cost is "hidden"
because this expensive water is blended with less expensive sources of
groundwater. Only over longer periods of time do we notice how much
more expensive water has become.[81]

One might assume that in a rapidly growing state like Florida, there
would be a clear link between water resources management and land use
planning, but this has generally not been the case.[82] Water management
districts are responsible for managing water supply, providing flood protection, maintaining water quality, and protecting the environment. In
addition to buying land and working to improve water quality in impaired
waters, WMDs issue consumptive use permits for the withdrawal of water, and environmental resource permits for land use activities that could
impact the quantity or quality of water resources (including wetlands). It
is true that regulating the consumptive use of water is the exclusive pur-
view of WMDs and not within the jurisdiction of local governments. At
the same time, however, WMDs complain that they have nothing to do
with determining the densities or intensities of land use, and they have
no role in guiding the location of new development—all of which determine the demand for water. Those issues remain the function of local
government policymakers and planners. Yet such a stance ignores the influence WMDs could exert if they so chose, for they have broad statutory
authority to reject permit applications that would cause harm to water
resources.[83]

Water use permitting authority became less complicated during the
summer of 2009 when Governor Charlie Crist signed Senate Bill 2080.

Prior to this legislation, wetland destruction permits involving more than an acre of wetlands—and water use permits applications proposing more than 500,000 gallons per day of groundwater pumping—were approved by water management districts only after a district's governing board discussed and voted on permits in monthly public meetings. Such a process was time-consuming and governing boards rarely rejected permit applications, but it provided an opportunity for citizens to voice their opinion. Although Senate Bill 2080's original purpose was to promote water conservation, on the next-to-the-last day of the 2009 legislative session, Sen. J. D. Alexander (R-Lake Wales) quietly slipped an amendment into the bill authorizing executive directors of each WMD to approve permits without a public meeting. Both critics and supporters of the bill widely view this action as a way to reduce the time it takes to issue permits. Skeptics add that eliminating public discussion and votes on permits may allow WMDs to authorize significant projects that an informed public would occasionally have made difficult. Governor Crist lamely added that he hoped WMDs would continue to include permits on board meeting agendas. Only two executive directors claim to be comfortable with the new responsibility, and all WMDs appear to be developing better public notice and participation procedures. Meanwhile, David Still of the Suwannee River Water Management District intends to ignore the law and continue having his governing board publicly discuss and vote on water and wetland permits. "Are you going to sue me for opening up the process to the public?" he asked.[84]

Over the past few decades, the Florida legislature has occasionally attempted to forge a better link between water resources management and land use planning. For example, the legislature has instructed the WMDs to develop twenty-year regional water supply plans. Yet the legislature's stance appears to be that water supply challenges should not limit future population growth. *St. Petersburg Times* journalists reported that Senate leaders told them that they intended to "keep Florida attractive to new residents and companies."[85] Keeping the state attractive to newcomers is one thing, but doing so at great expense to everybody else is another. Perhaps the most significant example of attempts to improve the link between water resources management and land use planning—and an example of the Florida legislature's priorities—is the state's landmark Growth Management Act of 1985.[86] This act endeavored (among many other things) to impose concurrency between economic development and the transportation, solid waste, recreation, and water-related infrastructure needed to support such development. In other words, development should not be approved unless the supporting infrastructure appears concurrent with that development. Of course, infrastructure costs a lot of money the state does not have (even before the economic downturn beginning in 2007). In 1987, the legislature attempted to raise taxes enough to cover almost 40 percent of the cost of concurrent infrastructure, assigning 34 percent of the costs to local governments, and basically pretending economic growth would produce additional tax receipts to cover the other 26 percent.[87] Public schools were not incorporated into the 1985 infrastructure concurrency rules because that would have added an even larger obligation for the state to pay. These facts alone should have been enough to expose the illusion that growth pays for itself.

Unfortunately, paying for growth soon became far more difficult. The antitax backlash was so swift and severe that Governor Bob Martinez called the 1987 legislature back into special session to repeal the objectionable new sales taxes on services that had not been previously taxed—and left local governments to pay for most infrastructure themselves. This action had the effect of severely weakening the 1985 Growth Management Act. Local governments raised their taxes to the extent allowable under law (much to the chagrin of their taxpayers), and they have dumped some of the infrastructure obligation on to developers, but much of the infrastructure that is supposed to accompany development is often not built until long after the construction is complete, if it is built at all. Water infrastructure is usually provided on time, but there is often far less tax revenue left over to cope with the range of other needs such as transportation and schools. Given Florida's copious water resources, and the reliability of water coming out of the tap, it seems hard to imagine that supplying water to new developments has become a significant issue—but it has.

Most of peninsular Florida is situated on top of aquifers that store huge amounts of water, much like a gigantic underground sponge. Yet Florida's population grew by roughly 3 million people between the late 1980s and the late 1990s, much of this in Central and South Florida, and the peninsula's once abundant groundwater resources began to show signs of stress, particularly during the drier spring months and again during drought. As the nation prepared for Y2K, the Florida legislature required water management districts to submit to the Florida Department of Environmental Protection regional water supply plans every five years. These assessments are supposed not only to anticipate demand twenty years into the future but also to outline specific water supply projects that can help meet that goal. Four of Florida's five WMDs prepared such plans in 2001, projecting water needs into 2020, as well as their plans to assist in developing new supplies. The slow-growing Suwannee River WMD has not yet engaged in this exercise because it has readily accessible resources for its projected needs several decades into the future. Updated plans for the other four WMDs (completed in early 2007) project water use and supplies into 2025.[88] The U.S. Geological Survey estimates that Floridians used more than 6.8 billion gallons of fresh water per day (bgd) in 2005,[89] and the state's water management districts believe demand will grow by roughly 2 bgd by 2025.[90] This is a frightening prospect, particularly in Central and South Florida where water resources are already stretched very thin.

In attempting to meet future demands, water authorities must consider not only the quantity of water needed, but also where the resource is wanted, and whether existing resources can meet anticipated demand without harming natural systems. Florida is blessed with tremendous

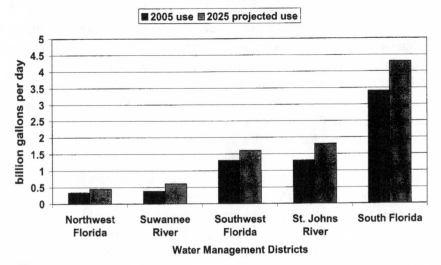

Figure 4.3

quantities of water and some argue that surely we are not approaching limits to what we can use. For example, Florida has over 700 known springs, thirty-three of which are classified as first-magnitude springs—which means they yield at least 64.6 million gallons of water per day.[91] Florida's first magnitude springs collectively spew some six billion gallons of water to the surface each day.[92] Several of these prolific gushers, such as Weeki Wachee, Homosassa, or Wakulla springs, flush hundreds of millions of gallons of high quality water down very short rivers and out to the ocean every day. Although some of this water can undoubtedly be tapped for human consumption, it is important to remember that unique but delicate ecosystems have evolved in concert with this large amount of water and significant withdrawal from springs may cause irreparable ecosystem damage. Such damage would be tragic for both local environments and for tourist-based economies that have developed around springs.

In some parts of the state (such as Tampa Bay and southeast Florida), water managers are engaging in water supply planning at regional, rather than community levels. A regional water supply system can be more responsive to localized shortages than local utilities with fewer source options.[93] Indeed, the South Florida Water Management District forecasts that if growth continues unchecked, it will probably need nearly a billion *more* gallons of water per day in 2025.[94] Given this possibility, it is clear why critics suggest that the Comprehensive Everglades Restoration Plan is more about providing water for endless population growth in South Florida than restoring the Everglades.[95] Where will future Floridians find all this extra water? Historically, growing communities developed new well fields, sometimes from neighboring counties, but inexpensive groundwater will no longer sustain Florida's population growth.[96] Additional water supplies can be developed, but they will be much more expensive.

As we have seen, water supply was already a contentious issue in South Florida as Nelson Blake completed the first edition of this book in 1980. As Blake wrote, some geologists speculated that they might be able to store large quantities of drinking water in deep and relatively confined portions of the aquifer so that it could be retrieved during the dry season or during drought. The theory is that water pumped into the aquifer, with confining layers of rock and other natural materials above and below the injection site would form a virtually stationary bubble of clean fresh water—even in a groundwater zone dominated by salt or brackish water.

As we learned earlier, this process is called aquifer storage and recovery, or ASR. It was first used along the Peace River in Southwest Florida in 1983, and it became more popular during the 1980s.[97]

The U.S. Environmental Protection Agency (EPA) has established rules to ensure that only high quality water can be part of an ASR operation. By the late 1990s, however, three things started to crystallize. First, in some cases much of the ASR water was incapable of being recovered. Second, significant concentrations of arsenic have been discovered in the water recovered from several ASR sites in Florida. Third, evidence emerged suggesting that even deep well–injected wastewater did not always remain in a bubble well below the earth's surface: it sometimes moved.[98] Yet as witnessed in the Everglades, one of the most significant elements of the CERP passed by Congress in 2000 is the more than 300 planned aquifer storage and recovery wells in South Florida that water managers hope can store hundreds of millions of gallons of water per day—water that is currently flushed to sea during the wet season.

In the fall of 2000, as CERP was being debated in Congress, a group of Florida water managers—supported by Governor Jeb Bush and his secretary of the Florida Department of Environmental Protection, David Struhs—asked the Florida legislature to relax the rules governing ASR operations. Specifically, water managers (and adherents of the progrowth ideology) wanted to save money by seeking authority to inject surface water that did not meet drinking quality standards into the ground. They claimed they could institute procedures to ensure the retrieved water would cause no adverse effects on human health.[99] Meanwhile, the National Research Council's Committee on the Restoration of the Greater Everglades Ecosystem, which had been reviewing CERP (and elements of ASR), released a report of their findings immediately prior to the 2001 legislative session—and they expressed reservations about ASR.[100] Among other issues, the committee remained skeptical of claims that partially treated water sent into the ground would be safe to drink once recovered. Opponents of relaxing ASR rules in Florida eventually generated enough public pressure on the legislature to force withdrawal of the proposed rule changes. Pumping partially treated wastewater or even untreated fresh water into ASR wells for later recovery and human consumption is one problem; an even bigger problem in many ASR wells is that authorities inject fresh surface water into the ground and get arsenic-laden water in return. The arsenic in retrieved water can be removed at the surface, but such treatment adds to the expense of the ASR method of storing water. Although some ASR wells in Florida have not revealed arsenic, and geoscientists continue to work on the arsenic problem where it does occur, it appears that ASR is an alternative water star whose luster has been tarnished by technical and economic problems. Perhaps this was a driving force behind Florida's efforts to buy out U.S. Sugar; the reduced demand for agricultural water and the increased surface storage space may help reduce reliance on ASR technology in South Florida.

Projecting demand and identifying future sources of water is important, but harvesting alternative supplies requires money. Accordingly, the 2005 Florida legislature created the Water Protection and Sustainability Program to help local utilities build the alternative water source infrastructure they will need by 2025. In fiscal year 2005–2006, the legislature committed $100 million to the program; in 2006–2007, the state provided $60 million; in 2007–2008 (as the economy worsened), lawmakers barely scraped together $52 million; and in 2008–2009, as the state and national economic downturn deepened further still, this program received just $7.7 million (and $2.16 million of this was later slashed due to Florida's ongoing budget crisis).[101] Water management districts will often use their own revenue to match this state money, but given that the first three years of the program generated 344 alternative water supply projects for the entire state that will cost $3.8 *billion*, the bulk of the expense for these projects clearly rests with local and regional water suppliers and utilities (and the citizens who pay for that water). The funded projects are forecast to produce 842 mgd of "new" water, a lot of water to be sure;[102] but water managers may need to ramp up conservation efforts more than they already have and identify additional (probably expensive) alternatives to produce the additional billion gallons per day that are forecast to be needed in 2025—and then hope that current forecasts do not underestimate future needs.

If ASR is proving to be more of a challenge than initially expected, where will this "new water" come from? Figure 4 details the category of alternative water supply projects during the first three years of the Water Protection and Sustainability Program. Clearly, the state intends to rely more upon reclaimed water (partially treated waste water) to meet its future needs. Given that roughly half of the 2.5 billion gallons of fresh water withdrawn from the environment each day for public supply* is sprayed on lawns to irrigate plants that are often not well suited to the state's climate and soils, there is much potential to use reclaimed water for lawn and golf course irrigation.[103] Florida is already among the nation's leaders in using treated wastewater, currently reusing more than 25 percent (660 mgd) of its roughly 2.4 bgd permitted capacity for domestic wastewater facilities.[104] Moreover, according to the St. Johns River Water Management District, the unit cost of producing 1,000 gallons of reclaimed water from its many proposed projects is often less than $1 and seldom more than $1.50.[105] Of course, reclaimed water systems require significant investment in new distribution systems, an expensive endeavor. Still, rather than flushing much of its wastewater into deep wells or the ocean, as is often the case, this water could serve as a drought resistant source of additional water for irrigating yards and golf courses.[106]

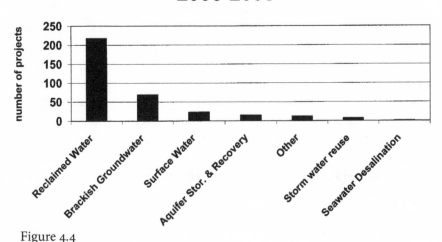

**Alternative Water Supply Projects funded by the**
*Water Protection and Sustainability Program*
**2005-2008**

Figure 4.4

---

* Public supply does NOT include water used for agricultural or recreational (golf course) irrigation, nor does it include freshwater withdrawn for power generation or other industrial/commercial uses.

The next most significant alternative water source is withdrawing and turning brackish groundwater (mostly from coastal areas) into drinking water. This process is similar to desalination (turning sea water into drinking water), but because brackish groundwater often has well under half the salt of sea water, its purification costs much less (although it costs more than treating fresh groundwater). According to the SJRWMD, unit costs for its planned brackish water projects are generally between $1.50 and $3.50 per 1,000 gallons.[107] Because desalination plants generally produce water that costs far more than fresh groundwater, Florida has only three desalination plants (two small emergency backup units in South Florida's Keys and the Big Bend plant just south of Tampa).[108]

A variety of alternative sources will supply a relatively small amount of water in Florida's near future, although this might have to change if Florida insists upon encouraging and subsidizing population growth. Eleven surface water projects exist, mostly in North Florida, although as we saw, Orlando area utilities ignited a firestorm of protest when they first proposed sticking their water resource straws into the St. Johns River a few years ago.[109] In northwest Florida, several coastal utilities are advancing plans to tap inland sources of fresh groundwater. Finally, there are a few projects intended to treat and reuse storm water runoff, and a small number of ASR projects being developed in places where arsenic is not a problem.[110]

Modest investments in water conservation will reduce the stress on natural systems and serve as a source of water for additional population growth. As Audubon Florida's Charles Lee contends, "The most immediate, attainable, economical, low-hanging fruit is conservation."[111] Lee has a point. While Florida's per capita fresh water consumption is 158 gallons per day (and inching very slowly downward each year), Sarasota County has made conservation a major issue and its residents consume just 96 gallons per day.[112] Indeed, Tampa Bay Water officials claim that water conservation projects not only have the potential to save millions of dollars in capital and debt service costs, they are a relatively inexpensive way to meet new demand, costing anywhere from $0.25 to $3.25 per 1,000 gallons.[113] Yet even an idea as benign as conservation has angered some who resent being asked to consume less water so developers can profit by accommodating additional residents.[114] According to one city commissioner from Ormond Beach, if he insisted on requiring water conserving toilets and other fixtures in existing homes or commercial buildings, his constituents would be furious.[115] Perhaps constituents in other Florida communities would be more forgiving. Conservation will certainly have to become part of Florida's water resources future, but it remains to be seen how much more efficiently Floridians will be willing to use water. The state remains dominated by Republican politics, which prizes freedom (including the freedom to consume plenty of water) above almost all else.

Sustainability is an elusive concept, but that did not stop the 2005 Florida legislature from creating the Century Commission for a Sustainable Florida, a body of fifteen civic leaders, five of whom are appointed by the governor, five by the Speaker of the Florida House of Representatives, and five by the president of the Florida Senate (all of whom were Republicans in 2005). The commission's primary task is to "continually consider laws and regulations and make recommendations as to how we can best *accommodate population growth* while maintaining our quality of life" (italics mine).[116] This group meets several times a year in different locations around the state and invites the perspectives of a range of knowledgeable and thoughtful observers, from academics to policymakers to business leaders, each of whom attempts to help the commission understand what changes need to be made to ensure a sustainable Florida. The commission prepares annual reports and recommendations to the governor and legislature, and despite their goal of accommodating future population growth, they appear to be sincerely concerned about the future sustainability of the state.[117] One of their recent recommendations was to host a statewide "Water Congress" in 2008.

The commission invited 120 delegates representing a broad range of interests to Orlando in late September 2008 for two days of discussions about the future of Florida's water resources. The delegates (40 from state and local governments, 40 from business, agriculture, and industry, and 40 from nonprofit groups) were divided into small groups each charged with considering, and ultimately voting on, a series of proposed recommendations generated by the Century Commission. The commission's *3rd Annual Report* lists the top four recommendations as voted on by delegates to the 2008 Florida Water Congress:[118]

1. Reinstate the annual funding for alternative water supply development and water quality improvement.

2. Support regional partnerships, incentives, and cooperative approaches to addressing long-term water sustainability for Florida.

3. Amend, as necessary, any statute, rule, or policy so that quantifiable water conservation best management practices are considered an "alternative water supply" and are equally as eligible for funding as capital facility expansion proposals.

4. Set a per capita target or goal for water use and quantifiable best management water practices and provide a stable funding base for the Conserve Florida program directed by Sect. 373.227, F.S., including the statewide water conservation clearinghouse for public water supply.

The Century Commissioners (some of whom actively participated in the Congress) then added a 5th recommendation to the governor and the legislature in their *3rd Annual Report*:

5. While protecting water quality, maximize the beneficial use of reclaimed water and improve upon the capture and storage of excess water. Recruit and connect large industrial users to reclaimed water systems to reduce demand on existing and future potable systems. . . . The management of wastewater needs to continue to evolve from a disposal problem to a valuable water supply opportunity.[119]

Most of the other thirteen recommendations published in the Century Commission's 2009 annual report focus on increasing storage and reducing water use; none of them says anything about redirecting population growth away from locations where inexpensive water is becoming scarce.[120] The silver lining for North Florida is that delegates easily voted down a proposal to establish a Florida water czar, widely viewed as the first step in seizing water from North Florida for use in the central and southern parts of the state.[121]

Yet dreams die hard. Those who insist that Floridians should continue subsidizing population growth with water and distribution systems at least partially paid for by the state remain undaunted. Just a year after being thoroughly rejected by the Florida Water Congress, staff members of the Florida Senate's Environmental Preservation and Conservation Committee prepared a report suggesting once again that the legislature should create a statewide body to govern Florida's water supply. Indeed, Susan Pareigis—President of the Council of 100—agreed that the Senate staff's 2009 report reads as if it is a second draft of the council's 2003 report, and she views this as a positive sign. It remains to be seen if Florida's

Republican-dominated legislature (which often portrays itself as the en-emy of "big government") will embrace a plan to create state, rather than regional, control of water resources.[122]

Florida is now widely known as the Sunshine State, but it could just as easily be called the Water State. As Blake makes clear, for most of Florida's history the problem has been that of too much water. In addition to be-ing surrounded by the Gulf of Mexico and Atlantic Ocean, and receiving an average of fifty-four inches of precipitation each year (Louisiana is the only state that receives more)—until the early twentieth century much of Florida remained under water: lakes of all sizes covered more than 7 percent of the state and ubiquitous swamps and marshes covered another 54 percent. Furthermore, hordes of mosquitoes and other bugs associ-ated with this water were not only annoying, they were debilitating for many early residents of this impoverished state. For good reason, many nineteenth- and early-twentieth-century Florida policymakers remained fixated on improving navigation and draining wetlands.[123]

Florida may receive an average of 54 inches of rainfall per year, but the critical phrase is "on average." To begin with, even average rainfall is variable across the state (see Table 1). Many northwest Florida locations average more than 62 inches of precipitation per year; and the same may be said for several stations in southeast Florida. But much of the rest of the peninsula is a bit less fortunate. Rapidly growing Fort Myers and Na-ples each receive about 53 inches of rain per year; Jacksonville, Orlando, and Daytona less still; and Tampa averages just over 47 inches of rainfall each year. Of course, every year is different. Although some years wit-ness upwards of 70 or more inches of rainfall, other years are much drier. And because Florida is so warm for most of the year, about 70 percent of the state's annual precipitation (some 39 inches) is lost to a combination of evaporation and transpiration from plants.[124] Furthermore, although drought may not be a constant companion in Florida as it is in the western United States, the Sunshine State is often just that: plenty of sunshine and not much rain.[125] Over the past century, Florida has had eleven years in which statewide precipitation averaged 45 inches or less,[126] and selected stations routinely receive much less. For example, since 1942, Tampa has received less than 40 inches of rainfall no fewer than 21 different years—and just under 30 inches as recently as 2000.[127] Tampa may receive less than 40 inches of annual rainfall 3 years out of every 10, but below average rainfall does not become a serious problem unless decision makers insist upon promoting and subsidizing significant population growth.

Florida's water management system has performed reasonably well during recent droughts. According to a recent report from the Florida Department of Environmental Protection, "Regulatory tools such as water shortage orders, irrigation restrictions, and mandatory use limitations were implemented to stretch limited supplies and protect water resources. Alternative water supplies developed over the last several years supplemented traditional groundwater sources and reduced stress on aquifers. ... Conservation programs and public education helped ensure that water was used efficiently and not wasted."[128] Of course, even these successes cost money. Moreover, how will Florida cope with drought in the future? If current trends continue, Florida's residents will have to use even less water and water managers will have to hustle just to provide enough water to accommodate future population growth and cope with modest (but occasional) drought.

Yet Florida will have to do more to defend itself against serious drought, and it might accomplish this in a number of ways. First, relying upon more diverse sources of water will help. For example, (re)use of wastewater is a drought-resistant source, and the state appears to be moving more in this direction than they already have. Moreover, Florida water managers probably have to continue developing more expensive alternative sources of water, such as brackish groundwater and even sea water. Second, Central and South Floridians will probably be forced to abandon traditional lawns in favor of yards much better able to tolerate the peninsula's annual dry season and periodic droughts. Third, conservation and significant water-use restrictions will probably become more common than they already are.[129] Will these tools be adequate after the state has welcomed several million additional residents, and then severe drought occurs? It simply is not feasible for water officials to build enough water infrastructure to survive *extreme* droughts. Unfettered population growth in Central and South Florida puts water managers in a difficult position. Worse, as residents of the Tampa Bay area have seen, engineered water "solutions" do not always work as intended. Such water resource structures create a false sense of security (like building levees along rivers) that allows otherwise unsustainable populations to accumulate. Yet as populations in Central and South Florida's metropolitan areas grow, they simultaneously grow more vulnerable to drought. On one hand, too many people already reside in peninsular Florida to make coping with severe drought "easy." Yet the state's political leadership could prevent increasing the drought vulnerability of its existing population if it chose to assess new construction (particularly in undeveloped) areas the *full* cost of additional (more expensive) sources of water. This would reduce population growth to more sustainable levels (in terms of water resources), provide the funds to develop and pay for new water sources, and it would be equitable in the sense that it would not pass these costs on to established residents.

If the specter of severe drought frightens an increasingly crowded peninsula, then the possible impacts of global climate change offer potentially devastating consequences for much of Florida.[130] Flat earthers and neoconservatives notwithstanding, there is virtually no debate that the planet is becoming warmer, particularly since 1970.[131] Most scientists believe that increasing concentrations of greenhouse gases such as carbon dioxide (mostly from fossil fuel combustion) will trap progressively more heat in the earth's atmosphere that might otherwise escape to space. Since water is an integral part of all elements of the global climate system, changes in that system impact water in a variety of ways. For example, a warmer atmosphere will probably hold more water vapor. As a result, climatologists are reasonably certain that geographic patterns of precipitation are likely to shift in a warmer world, and although some regions are likely to receive more precipitation, others (such as the subtropical portions of the earth, including Florida) are likely to receive less.[132] Moreover, a warmer atmosphere is likely to produce more *variable* precipitation regimes featuring a larger number of heavy downpours, and droughts of increasing length and intensity. On top of all this are the possibilities of more frequent and more powerful tropical storms, sea level rise, increased cooling costs, and changes to Florida's ecosystems. Indeed, Florida is a state where a few inches of topographic relief result in major ecosystem differences, so even modest sea level rise would probably wreak havoc in low lying coastal areas.

Climate change may not dramatically impact the state's water resources over the next couple of decades, but after that, climate change and associated water resource impacts are a real possibility. If people around the world take immediate and aggressive action to curtail fossil fuel use (on the order of Florida governor Charlie Crist's call to reduce greenhouse gas emissions 80 percent by the year 2050), global average annual temperature would probably rise less than two degrees (F) during this next century, sparing Florida the worst consequences of climate change.[133] Yet as two Massachusetts economists contend, if the world pursues a "business as usual" scenario, rejecting the current monetary and social costs of shifting to more expensive alternative energy sources, the planet's annual average temperature may increase more than eight degrees (F) by the year 2100.[134] Such warming could lead to sea level rise in Florida of three to four feet, and a five-inch (nearly 10 percent) reduction of average annual precipitation across the state within a century.[135]

Such changes would have a dramatic impact on the state's water resources. First, sea level rise would not only damage coastal property (particularly during storms), it would likely render coastal well fields more vulnerable to salt water intrusion. This has the potential to be a huge problem because the vast majority of Floridians live in coastal counties. As we have seen, fresh groundwater is relatively inexpensive to treat and then distribute to homes and businesses, and in 2005, groundwater accounted for 62 percent of all freshwater withdrawals and 88 percent of drinking water in Florida.[136] The net result of sea level rise to Florida's coastal area groundwater resources would probably be a significant increase in the cost of making this water drinkable. Second, most of peninsular Florida is almost entirely dependent upon precipitation for maintenance of its water resources. Precipitation feeds Florida's rivers and recharges the groundwater aquifers Floridians depend on. Most of the peninsula receives no surface or groundwater from outside the state.[137] If average annual precipitation across the peninsula decreases even a few inches, if drought becomes even more common and severe than at present, and if warmer temperatures evaporate even more surface water than is already the case, global climate change could present insurmountable challenges for Florida's water managers given that Florida may have more than thirty million residents a few decades from now.

Unrestricted and heavily subsidized population growth, particularly in Central and South Florida, remains one of the most serious threats to the state's water resources. Yet many policymakers and business leaders appear unwilling to take action to slow population growth in peninsular Florida; namely, they do not want to make future residents pay the full cost associated with the more expensive water that must be obtained to support them. Such action would likely reduce population growth to a (sustainable) fraction of previous growth rates, but it would also reduce Florida's chief source of economic growth. At the same time, Florida already has a model for such a policy. In an effort to prevent population growth from raising local property taxes to the point that established residents can no longer afford annual assessments on their homes, Florida voters passed the "Save our Homes" amendment to the Florida Constitution in 1992 (and implemented it in 1995). This amendment caps increases on local property taxes for a qualified homeowner's Florida residence (if it is their primary residence) at no more than 3 percent per year. When an established Florida homeowner sells their house, the new resident usually pays much more in property taxes because the 3 percent cap is lifted until the new homeowner has lived in the house for a year, and their house is taxed at the current property value. Florida's frenetic population growth (especially in urban and suburban areas) has caused home values to increase significantly in recent decades. Some people argue that "Save our Homes" is unfair because otherwise identical properties across the street from each other may be taxed at very different rates, based only on the homeowner's length of residence. This is true, but it seems fairer than allowing population growth to escalate property values to the point that it taxes long-established or low-income residents out of their homes. I argue that Florida should do the same with water, charging residents of new homes (particularly those sprawling outside urban areas) the full cost of providing additional water. If inexpensive local sources are available, residents of new homes might pay the same as established residents, but if expensive sources must be tapped, many potential buyers of new homes are less likely to be interested in paying the full cost of providing alternative water supplies and would seek homes in places where water costs less. Why should suburban sprawl be subsidized with artificially cheap water?

Another practical example of protecting established residents came to light in early 2010. The groundwater level at a Southwest Florida Water Management District monitoring well 15 miles east of Tampa remained steady throughout December 2009 until 4 January 2010, when a weeklong blast of frigid air threatened the Tampa Bay area's strawberry crop. As overnight temperatures in the region dove below freezing for several consecutive nights in early January, frantic farmers (legally) pumped hundreds of millions of gallons of 70-degree groundwater on their land to help save their crops. Groundwater levels suddenly plunged almost 60 feet at the Swiftmud monitoring well east of Tampa; scientists believe this led to dozens of sinkholes that damaged a handful of homes, shut down an elementary school, and temporarily closed several roads around Plant City. The sudden drop in the water table also led hundreds of nearby household wells to run dry. Although groundwater levels recovered within a few weeks, homeowners who experienced damaged wells, and whose wells were sunk *before* farms appeared in their area, can be compensated for their losses. According to Southwest Florida Water Management District officials, "we can require the farmer to provide water or pay for damages if there have been damages to their well." Homeowners whose dwellings and wells were built *after* area farms began operations have no recourse. This is yet another example of protecting established residents from the problems created by subsequent growth and development, and it supports the contention that recent arrivals should pay the full cost of providing the additional water they need.[138]

As we have seen, proponents of continuing population and economic growth claim they want to "protect the environment." Yet our addiction to accommodating population growth is placing significant stress on natural systems, forcing changes in lifestyles (some of which are surely for the better), and it calls for *everybody* to pay more for increasingly expensive infrastructure and alternative sources of water. Paying more for water is hardly a problem for economic growth's most significant beneficiaries, but it is burdensome and unfair for less fortunate people. Of course, it is easy to overstate this case. For example, Florida is not "running out of water"; but we must face the fact that it is running out of *cheap* water. In most parts of Central and South Florida, "accommodating" population growth essentially means providing new residents a perverse subsidy by spreading the costs for all manner of infrastructure and the cost of producing alternative water resources over entire regions; in this way, population (and associated economic) growth showers a few with many benefits while sticking everybody else with the bill.

Florida has come a long way since the early twentieth century when the state was still mostly under water and most transportation was tied to navigable streams. Nelson Blake shows us how previous generations of Floridians worked hard to improve navigation by digging canals and, essentially, turning land into water. He also illustrates how many others turned water into land by draining many of the state's swamps and marshes. Although many cases exist where wetland loss occurs in Florida, at least some of these wetland losses are supposed to be mitigated with attempts to create or enhance wetlands elsewhere.[139] If anything, Florida's focus on environmental and wetland restoration (in the Everglades and elsewhere) suggests that in some respects we have come full circle—turning land back into water. Blake's original conclusion was mildly optimistic because he noted that by 1980, Floridians had begun to treat water as a resource to be treasured rather than as a curse to be rid of. Florida has experienced many success stories in water management since 1980, particularly in terms of efforts to improve water quality, establishing minimum flows and levels, purchasing land in order to protect water resources, restoring degraded waterscapes, and effective drought management. Yet a virtual doubling of the state's population since 1980, and a business and political culture that believes we must accommodate (subsidize) continued substantial population growth, augers ill for many established Floridians who cannot escape growth's problems and who find it increasingly painful to continue subsidizing population growth.

## Notes

1. U.S. Census Bureau, *Table 1: Annual Estimates for the Population of the United States, Regions, States, and Puerto Rico: April 1, 2000 to July 1, 2009* (available at: http://www.census.gov/popest/states/NST-ann-est.html last accessed on 4 February 2010); U.S. Census Bureau, *Table 1: Ranking of census 2000 and projected 2030 state population and change* (available at: http://www.census.gov/population/www/projections/projection-sagesex.html last accessed on 4 February 2010).

2. Jim Ash, "Expert: Florida economy worsening," *Tallahassee Democrat*, 1 March 2009; Gary Mormino, *Land of Sunshine, State of Dreams: A Social History of Modern Florida* (Gainesville: University Press of Florida, 2005).

3. Florida Department of Transportation Office of Policy Planning Web site: http://www.floridatransportationindicators.org/detail.php?chart=11b (accessed on 18 March 2009).

4. U.S. Geological Survey, Water Use Facts for 2005 and Trends, available at http://fl.water.usgs.gov/infodata/wateruse/waterusefacts2005.html (last accessed on 17 July 2009).

5. Nathan Sayre, "The genesis, history and limits of carrying capacity," *Annals of the Association of American Geographers* 98 (2008): 120–34.

6. Donella Meadows, Dennis Meadows, Jorgen Randers, and William Behrens, *The*

*Limits to Growth; a report for the Club of Rome's project on the predicament of mankind* (New York: Universe Books, 1972); Donella Meadows, Jorgen Randers, and Dennis Meadows, *Limits to Growth: The 30-Year Update* (White River Junction, Vt.: Chelsea Green Publishing, 2004).

7. Sayre, "Carrying capacity," 2008; National Research Council, *A Review of the Florida Keys Carrying Capacity Study* (Washington, D.C.: National Academy Press, 2002).

8. World Commission on Environment and Development, *Our Common Future* (Oxford: Oxford University Press, 1987).

9. Ibid., 8.

10. Simon Dresner, *The Principles of Sustainability*, 2nd ed. (London: Earthscan, 2008); Mark Whitehead, *Spaces of Sustainability: Geographic Perspectives on the Sustainable Society* (New York and London: Routledge, 2007).

11. Peter H. Gleik, "Water in crisis: paths to sustainable water use," *Ecological Applications* 8 (1998): 571–79; Brian D. Richter, Ruth Mathews, David L. Harrison, and Robert Wigington, "Ecologically sustainable water management: managing river flows for ecological integrity," *Ecological Applications* 13 (2003): 206–24; David L. Feldman, *Water Policy for Sustainable Development* (Baltimore: Johns Hopkins University Press and Center for American Places, 2007); Malin Falkenmark, "Water and sustainability: a reappraisal," *Environment* 50 (2008) 5–16; Claudia Pahl-Wostl, David Tabara, Rene Bouwen, Marc Craps, Art Dewulf, Erik Mostert, Dagmar Ridder, and Tharsi Taillieu, "The importance of social learning and culture for sustainable water management," *Ecological Economics* 64 (2008): 484–95.

12. Leonard Shabman, "Water resources management and the challenge of sustainability," in Roger Sedjo (ed.), *Perspectives on Sustainable Resources in America* (Washington, D.C.: Resources for the Future, 2008), 104–32.

13. For an exception to this, see Manuel P. Teodoro, "Measuring fairness: assessing the equity of municipal water rates," *Journal of the American Water Works Association* 97(4) (2005): 111–24.

14. Tampa Bay Water, *Tampa Bay Water Proposed Budget Fiscal Year 2010*, Budget Workshop 20 April 2009 (presentation made before the Tampa Bay Water Board, copy provided to the author by Kristal Karatsanos of Tampa Bay Water).

15. Personal (e-mail) communication with Kristal Karatsanos of Tampa Bay Water on 2 March 2009. According to Karatsanos, the unit cost (without fixed costs) of producing groundwater for Tampa Bay Water in early 2009 is $0.2126 per 1000 gallons; unit cost of surface water costs $0.8759 per 1000 gallons; and the unit cost of water from the desalination plant costs $2.725 per 1000 gallons.

16. Ken Herd, as cited by Cynthia Barnett, *Mirage: Florida and the Vanishing Water of the Eastern U.S.* (Ann Arbor, MI: University of Michigan Press, 2007, p. 177; St. Johns River Water Management District, *District Water Supply Plan 2005—Draft Fourth Addendum*, Technical Publication SJ2006-2D (Palatka, FL: St. Johns River Water Management District, 2009, 17).

17. Tampa Bay Water, *Master Water Plan Development Study Workshop: Demand*

*Management Plan Update*, April 2009 (presentation made before the Tampa Bay Water Board, copy provided to the author by Kristal Karatsanos of Tampa Bay Water).

18. St. Johns River Water Management District, *District Water Supply Plan 2005—Draft Fourth Addendum*, Technical Publication SJ2006-2D (Palatka, Fla.: St. Johns River Water Management District, 2009), 17.

19. Cynthia Barnett, *Mirage*, 5.

20. Honey Rand, *Water Wars: A Story of People, Politics and Power* (Philadelphia: Xlibris, 2003); Ayşin Dedekorkut, "Tampa Bay water wars: from conflict to collaboration?" in John T. Scholz and Bruce Stiftel (eds.), *Adaptive Governance and Water Conflict* (Washington, D.C.: Resources for the Future, 2005), 52–63.

21. Ralph C. Heath and Peter C. Smith, *Water Resource Studies: Ground Water Resources of Pinellas County, Florida* (Tallahassee: Florida Geological Survey, 1954), 31–37.

22. Honey Rand, *Water Wars*, 2003; Ayşin Dedekorkut "Tampa Bay water wars," 2005.

23. Richard R. Marella, *Water Use in Florida, 2005 and Trends 1950–2005* (U.S. Geological Survey, Fact Sheet 2008-5080, 2008), Table 1.

24. Craig Pittman, "More trouble at Desal plant," *St. Petersburg Times,* 17 March 2009, A1.

25. Craig Pittman, "Utility's basin options dry up, reservoir options drying up," *St. Petersburg Times,* 16 December 2008, B1.

26. Craig Pittman, "To mend reservoir, tack on $2 million," *St. Petersburg Times,* 16 October 2009, A1.

27. Ibid.; Craig Pittman, "Water bills will rise to fix reservoir," *St. Petersburg Times,* 5 June 2009, A1; Janet Zink, "Water board okays repair," *St. Petersburg Times,* 16 June 2009, B1.

28. Craig Pittman, "Water projects: money down the drain," *St. Petersburg Times,* 14 June 2009, B1.

29. Craig Pittman, "Tampa Bay Water warned of $1 million fine," *St. Petersburg Times,* 21 April 2009, B1.

30. Craig Pittman, "Harsh water rules averted," *St. Petersburg Times,* 25 February 2009, B1.

31. Southwest Florida Water Management District, *Water Shortage Order No. SWF 09-012*, 31 March 2009 (available on-line at http://www.swfwmd.state.fl.us/rules/files/water_shortage_swf09-012_mod.pdf).

32. Nano Riley, "Lake Apopka: From Natural Wonder to Unnatural Disaster," in Jack E. Davis and Raymond Arsenault (eds.), *Paradise Lost? The Environmental History of Florida* (Gainesville: University Press of Florida, 2005), 280–93.

33. Martin E. Comas, "Can ancient Roman cure save lakes?" *Orlando Sentinel,* 1 February 2009, B1.

34. Gordon Patterson, "Raising cane and refining sugar: Florida Crystals and the fame of Fellsmere," *Florida Historical Quarterly* 74 (1997): 408–28.

35. Bill Belleville, *River of Lakes: A Journey on the St. Johns River* (Athens: University of Georgia Press, 2000).

36. Ramiro Berardo, "The East Central Florida Regional Water Supply Planning Initiative," in John T. Scholz and Bruce Stiftel (eds.), *Adaptive Governance and Water Conflict* (Washington, D.C.: Resources for the Future, 2005), pp. 64–73.

37. St. Johns River Water Management District, *District Water Supply Plan 2005: Technical Publication SJ2006-2* (Palatka, Fla.: St. Johns River Water Management District, 2006), 52–55; Kevin Spear, "Mighty river to flow from Seminole faucets," *Orlando Sentinel*, 14 January 2009, B1; Mary Jane Angelo, Richard C. Hamann and Christine A. Klein, "Where did our water go? Give the law a chance," *Orlando Sentinel*, 23 September 2008, A11; anonymous, "Analysis of Hearing and Judge's Ruling," St. Johns Riverkeeper (http://www.mystjohnsriver.com/river_news.php accessed on 9 February 2009).

38. Ludmilla Lelis, "Seminole gets OK to pump from St. Johns," *Orlando Sentinel*, 14 April 2009, A1.

39. Ayşin Dedekorkut, "Suwannee River Partnership: representation instead of regulation," in John T. Scholz and Bruce Stiftel (eds.), *Adaptive Governance and Water Conflict* (Washington, D.C.: Resources for the Future, 2005), 25–39).

40. Dedekorkut, "Suwannee River Partnership," 2005.

41. Anonymous, "U.S. EPA steps in to set Florida water quality standards," *Environmental News Service*, 21 January 2009 (available on line at http://www.ens-newswire.com/ens/jan2009/2009-01-21-092.asp last accessed on 9 November 2009).

42. John Frank, "EPA steps in on pollution," *St. Petersburg Times*, 16 January 2010, B1.

43. David Guest, "The fight to protect Florida waters," *St. Petersburg Times*, 9 November 2009, A13; Charles Bronson, "The fight to protect Florida waters," *St. Petersburg Times*, 9 November 2009, A13; Fred Hiers, "State wants to set water quality standards," *Ocala Star-Banner*, 6 October 2009.

44. Barney Bishop, as quoted in John Frank, "EPA steps in on pollution," B8.

45. Florida Department of Environmental Protection, *Integrated Water Quality Assessment for Florida: 2008 355(b) report and 303(d) list update* (Tallahassee: FDEP Division of Environmental Assessment and Restoration, Bureau of Watershed Management, October 2008), x.

46. William D. Solecki, "Paternalism. Pollution and protest in a company town," *Political Geography* 15 (1996): 5–20; Simon A. Andrew, "Fenholloway River Evaluation Initiative: collaborative problem-solving within the permit system," in John T. Scholz and Bruce Stiftel (eds.), *Adaptive Governance and Water Conflict* (Washington, D.C.: Resources for the Future, 2005), 40–51.

47. Northwest Florida Water Management District, "Issuance of a water shortage warning within the Northwest Florida Water Management District, Order No. 07-001" (available on line at http://www.nwfwmd.state.fl.us/shortage/order_07-001.pdf last accessed on 9 February 2009).

48. Jeffrey L. Jordan and Aaron T. Wolf (eds.), *Interstate Water Allocation in Alabama, Florida, and Georgia: New Issues, New Methods, New Models* (Gainesville: University Press of Florida, 2006); Steve Leitman, "Apalachicola-Chattahoochee-Flint Basin: tristate negotiations of a water allocation formula," in John T. Scholz and Bruce Stiftel

(eds.), *Adaptive Governance and Water Conflict* (Washington, D.C.: Resources for the Future, 2005), 74–88.

49. K. M. McCarthy, *Apalachicola Bay* (Sarasota, Fla.: Pineapple Press, 2004); Florida Department of Agriculture and Consumer Services (http://www.fl-seafood.com/apalachicola.htm).

50. J. B. Ruhl, "Equitable apportionment of ecosystem services: new water law for a new water age," *Journal of Land Use and Environmental Law* 19 (2003): 47–57; Drew Melville, "'Whiskey is for drinking' . . . recent water law developments in Florida," *Journal of Land Use and Environmental Law* 19 (2003): 1–13; David Lewis Feldman, "Barriers to adaptive management: lessons from the Apalachicola-Chattahoochee-Flint Compact," *Society and Natural Resources* 21 (2008): 512–25.

51. Florida Department of Environmental Protection, "Judge's Ruling Signals End to Tri-State Water Dispute," press release from 17 July 2009. Available at: http://www.dep.state.fl.us/secretary/news/2009/07/0717_03.htm (last accessed on 22 July 2009); United States District Court: Middle District of Florida (Judge Paul A. Magnuson). 17 July 2009. Memorandum and Order in Case No. 3:07-md-01 (PAM/JRK). 97 pages.

52. Cynthia Barnett, *Mirage*, 55.

53. N. Skene, "The growth that ate Florida" *St. Petersburg Times*, 24 April 2005, P1; Herman E. Daly, *Beyond Growth: The Economics of Sustainable Development* (Boston: Beacon Press, 1996); Douglas E. Booth, *Hooked on Growth: Economics, Addictions and the Environment* (Lanham, Md.: Rowman and Littlefield, 2004).

54. Craig Pittman and Matthew Waite, "Is more growth the solution?" *St. Petersburg Times*, 17 February 2009, A1.

55. David Reed, as quoted in George Packer, "The Ponzi state: Florida's foreclosure disaster," *New Yorker* 85 (2009): 83.

56. David A. Denslow, "A shift to high-level jobs is crucial," *Forum, The Magazine of the Florida Humanities Council* 33(1) (2009): 18–20.

57. George Packer, "The Ponzi state," 85; Gary Mormino deserves much credit for suggesting to me the idea of Florida's growth resembling a Ponzi scheme. Indeed, he is cited in George Packer's article, 83.

58. Mike Schneider, "More leave than come from other states," *Lakeland Ledger*, 22 April 2009, A1.

59. James Thorner, "Population drop stops our streak," *St. Petersburg Times*, 11 August 2009, A1; Jeff Ostrowski, "Sunshine State losing luster?" *Palm Beach Post*, 18 August 2009, A1.

60. Janet Zink, "Crist grabs credit for cut," *St. Petersburg Times*, 27 October 2009, B1.

61. Christopher F. Meindl, "Toward a historical geography of Florida: assessing the consequences of massive population growth," *Florida Geographer* 37 (2006): 72–87.

62. Drew Harwell, "Where the grass is always greener," *St. Petersburg Times*, 19 March 2009, A1.

63. The Florida Council of 100, *Improving Florida's Water Supply Management Structure* (Tampa: Florida Council of 100, 2003).

64. Ibid., 10.

65. Ibid., 12–15, 20.

66. Dorothy Green, *Managing Water: Avoiding Crisis in California* (Berkeley: University of California Press, 2007).

67. Gary Mormino, *Land of Sunshine, State of Dreams*.

68. The Florida Council of 100, *Improving Florida's Water*, 17.

69. Ibid., 19.

70. Ibid.

71. Greg C. Bruno, "Key water figure tried to allay fears: emotions remained high at the Florida water congress due to transfer concerns," *Gainesville Sun*, 5 December 2003; Greg C. Bruno, "Water proposal may have dried up: Gov. Bush suggests that water transfers will not be on this year's agenda," *Gainesville Sun*, 23 January 2004.

72. Craig Pittman and Matthew Waite, *St. Petersburg Times*, 17 February 2009.

73. Ibid.

74. Mike Salerno and Catherine Dolinski, "Laws impact on roads yet to be determined," *Tampa Tribune*, 7 June 2009.

75. Diane Roberts, "Develop, bulldoze, fill, pave; repeat," *St. Petersburg Times*, 19 April 2009, P1.

76. Jim Ash, *Tallahassee Democrat*, 1 March 2009.

77. Florida Department of Environmental Protection, available at http://www.dep. state.fl.us/lands/fl_forever.htm last accessed on 9 February 2009.

78. Adam B. Munson, Joseph J. Delfino, and Douglas A. Leeper, "Determining minimum flows and levels: the Florida experience," *Journal of the American Water Resources Association* 41 (2005): 1–10; Florida Department of Environmental Protection, *2005 Statewide MFL Water Body Priority List* (MS Excel Worksheet available at http://www. dep.state.fl.us/water/waterpolicy/mfl.htm last accessed on 9 February 2009.

79. Adam B. Munson and Joseph J. Delfino, "Minimum wet-season flows and levels in southwest Florida rivers," *Journal of the American Water Resources Association* 43 (2007): 522–32; Clifford P. Neubauer, Greeneville B. Hall, Edgar F. Lowe, C. Price Robinson, Richard B. Hupalo, and Lawrence W. Keenan, "Minimum flows and levels method of the St. Johns River Water Management District, Florida, USA," *Environmental Management* 42 (2008); 1101–14.

80. Craig Pittman, "Utilities may add surcharge for big water users," *St. Petersburg Times*, 6 May 2009, B6.

81. Gary R. Mormino, *Land of Sunshine, State of Dreams*.

82. Mary Jane Angelo, "Integrating water management and land use planning: uncovering the missing link in the protection of Florida's water resources?" *University of Florida Journal of Law and Public Policy* 12 (2001): 223–49.

83. Florida Statutes, Chapter 373.219.

84. Craig Pittman, "5 uneasy with clout over water," *St. Petersburg Times*, 7 July 2009, B1.

85. Mary Ellen Klas, Marc Caputo, and Alex Leary, "Senate ready to talk taxes," *St. Petersburg Times*, 26 March 2009, B1.

86. Timothy S. Chapin, Charles E. Connerly, and Harrison T. Higgins (eds.), *Growth Management in Florida: Planning for Paradise* (Burlington, Vt.: Ashgate, 2007).

87. James C. Nicholas and Timothy S. Chapin, "The fiscal theory and reality of growth management in Florida," in Timothy S. Chapin, Charles E. Connerly, and Harrison T. Higgins (eds.), *Growth Management in Florida: Planning for Paradise*, 51–66.

88. Florida Department of Environmental Protection, *Tapping New Sources: Meeting 2025 Water Supply Needs* (Tallahassee: Florida Department of Environmental Protection, 2007).

89. Richard R. Marella, *Water Use in Florida*, 590.

90. Florida Department of Environmental Protection, *Tapping New Sources.*

91. Doug Stamm, *The Springs of Florida*, 2nd ed. (Sarasota, Fla.: Pineapple Press, 2008), 11.

92. Ibid., 16.

93. Florida Department of Environmental Protection, *Learning from the Drought: Annual Status Report on Regional Water Supply Planning* (Tallahassee: Florida Department of Environmental Protection, 2008), 4–5.

94. Florida Department of Environmental Protection, *Tapping New Sources.*

95. Michael Grunwald, *The Swamp* (New York: Simon and Schuster, 2006), 357–70.

96. Don Wilhite, as cited in Cynthia Barnett, *Mirage*, 5.

97. R. David G. Pyne, *Groundwater Recharge and Wells: A Guide to Aquifer Storage and Recovery* (Boca Raton, Fla.: Lewis Publishers, 1995); Eberhard Roeder, "Aquifer Storage and Recovery: Technology and Public Learning," in John T. Scholz and Bruce Stiftel (eds.) *Adaptive Governance and Water Conflict* (Washington, D.C.: Resources for the Future, 2005), 106–16).

98. Roeder, "Aquifer Storage and Recovery," 108–9.

99. Ibid., 115.

100. National Research Council, *Aquifer Storage and Recovery in the Comprehensive Everglades Restoration Plan: A Critique of the Pilot Projects and Related Plans for ASR in the Lake Okeechobee and West Hillsboro Areas* (Washington, D.C.: National Academies Press, 2001).

101. Florida Department of Environmental Protection, *Learning from the Drought*, 12; personal conversation with Tom Swihart, Florida Department of Environmental Protection.

102. Florida Department of Environmental Protection, *Learning from the Drought*, 12.

103. Ibid.

104. Florida Department of Environmental Protection web sites accessed on 12 March 2009: http://www.dep.state.fl.us/water/wastewater/fatcs.com and http://www.dep.state.fl.us/water/reuse/index.htm

105. St. Johns River Water Management District, *District Water Supply Plan 2005 (Draft 4th Addendum)*, 26–28.

106. Richard Marella, *Water Use in Florida.*

107. St. Johns River Water Management District, *District Water Supply Plan 2005 (Draft 4th Addendum)*, 26.

108. South Florida Water Management District, *Water Desalination Overview* (available at https://mysfwmd.gov/portal/page?_pageid=1874,22230182,1874_4167300& _dad=portal&_schema=PORTAL last accessed on 9 February 2009).

109. Craig Pittman, "Counties clash over last cheap Fla. Water," *St. Petersburg Times*, 10 April 2006, A1; Nathan Crabtree, "Rivers to quench a thirsty South," *Gainesville Sun*, 18 September 2007; Kevin Spear, "Whose thirst comes first? Central Florida faces a fight with northeast Florida over St. Johns water," *Orlando Sentinel*, 9 December 2007, A1; Kevin Spear, "Mighty river to flow from Seminole faucets," *Orlando Sentinel*, 14 January 2009, B1.

110. Florida Department of Environmental Protection, *Tapping New Sources*; Florida Department of Environmental Protection, *Learning From the Drought*.

111. Charles Lee, as quoted in Dinah Voyles Pulver, "Where should we go from here? One thing is for sure: we can't waste any more time in search for water solution," *Daytona News-Journal*, 25 December 2008, A9.

112. Mary Jane Angelo, Richard C. Hamann, and Christine A. Klein, *Orlando Sentinel*, 23 September 2008.

113. Tampa Bay Water, *Master Water Plan Development Study Workshop: Demand Management Plan Update*, April 2009 (presentation made before the Tampa Bay Water Board, copy provided to the author by Kristal Karatsanos of Tampa Bay Water).

114. The Florida Council of 100, *Improving Florida's Water Supply*, 11.

115. Steve Patterson, *Florida Times-Union*, 26 September 2008.

116. Century Commission for a Sustainable Florida, *About the Commission* (available at http://www.centurycommission.org/about.asp last accessed on 9 February 2009).

117. Century Commission for a Sustainable Florida, *First Annual Report to the Governor and the Legislature* (Tallahassee: Century Commission for a Sustainable Florida, 2007); Century Commission for a Sustainable Florida, *Second Annual Report to the Governor and the Legislature* (Tallahassee: Century Commission for a Sustainable Florida, 2008); Century Commission for a Sustainable Florida, *Third Annual Report to the Governor and the Legislature* (Tallahassee: Century Commission for a Sustainable Florida, 2009).

118. Century Commission for a Sustainable Florida, *Third Annual Report to the Governor and the Legislature*, 4.

119. Ibid., 5.

120. Ibid., 5–6.

121. Craig Pittman, "Water czar idea returns," *St. Petersburg Times*, 24 September 2008, B1; Craig Pittman, "State water czar idea dismissed," *St. Petersburg Times*, 26 September 2008, B3.

122. The Florida Senate Committee on Environmental Preservation and Conservation, *Chapter 373, F.S., Water Resources* Interim Report 2010-114 (Tallahassee, September 2009); Craig Pittman, "State 'water czar' idea resurfaces," *St. Petersburg Times*, 31 October 2009, A1.

123. Thomas E. Dahl, *Wetlands Losses in the United States 1780s to 1980s* (Washington, D.C.: U.S. Department of the Interior, Fish and Wildlife Service, 1990); Gordon Patterson, *The Mosquito Wars: A History of Mosquito Control in Florida* (Gainesville: University Press of Florida, 2004).

124. James A. Henry, Kenneth M. Porter and Jan Coyne, *The Climate and Weather of Florida* (Sarasota, Fla.: Pineapple Press, 1994, 23).

125. Ibid.; Morton D. Winsberg with the assistance of James J. O'Brien, David. F. Zierden, and Melissa L. Griffin, *Florida Weather,* 2nd ed. (Gainesville: University Press of Florida, 2003).

126. Florida Department of Environmental Protection, *Learning from the Drought,* 2008, 7.

127. Southeast Regional Climate Center, annual precipitation data for Tampa Airport available at http://sercc.com/cgi-bin/sercc/cliMAIN.pl?fi8788 last accessed on 9 February 2009.

128. Florida Department of Environmental Protection, *Learning from the Drought,* 9.

129. Ibid., 16.

130. Asjylyn Loder and Craig Pittman, "Water Worries," *St. Petersburg Times,* 9 November 2008, D1; Elizabeth A. Stanton and Frank Ackerman, *Florida and Climate Change: The Cost of Inaction* (Tufts University, Global Development and Environment Institute and Stockholm Environment Institute—US Center: Medford, Mass., 2007), 92 pp.; B. C. Bates, Z. W. Kundzewicz, S. Wu, and J. P. Palutikof (eds.), *Climate Change and Water,* Technical Paper of the Intergovernmental Panel on Climate Change (Geneva: IPCC Secretariat, 2008), 210 pp.

131. B. C. Bates et al., *Climate Change and Water,* 15.

132. Ibid., 25.

133. Stanton and Ackerman, *Florida and Climate* Change, 7.

134. Ibid., 8.

135. Ibid., 10 and 18.

136. Florida Department of Environmental Protection, *Learning from the Drought,* 11.

137. Elizabeth D. Purdum, *Florida Waters* (Brooksville: Distributed by the Southwest Florida Water Management District, 2002), 37–39.

138. Jessica Vander Velde, Andy Boyle, Robbyn Mitchell, and Kim Wilmath, "Roads sink, close around Plant City," *St. Petersburg Times,* 13 January 2010, B1 (quote from B10); Craig Pittman and Jessica Vander Velde, "30% of crops lost, 22 sinkholes form," *St. Petersburg Times,* 14 January 2010, A1; Kim Wilmath and Tom Marshall, "Sinkhole closes school in Plant City," *St. Petersburg Times,* 20 January 2010, B9; Craig Pittman, " Freeze costly for aquifer," *St. Petersburg Times,* 27 January 2010, B1; Southwest Florida Water Management District, Regional Observation and Monitor-well Program, groundwater well number 18796, ROMP DV-1 Avon Park, near Dover, Florida.

139. Craig Pittman and Matthew Waite, *Paving Paradise: Florida's Vanishing Wetlands and the Failure of No Net Loss* (Gainesville: University Press of Florida, 2009); Thomas E. Dahl, *Florida's Wetlands: An Update on Status and Trends, 1985–1996* (Washington, D.C.: U.S. Fish and Wildlife Service, 2005), 80 pp.

Nelson M. Blake was Maxwell Distinguished Professor of History at Syracuse University and the author of many books including *Water for the Cities: A History of the Urban Water Supply Problem in the United States* and *The Road to Reno: A History of Divorce in the United States*.

Christopher F. Meindl is associate professor of geography at the University of South Florida, St. Petersburg, and a contributor to *Paradise Lost? An Environmental History of Florida*.

Steven Noll is a senior lecturer at the University of Florida's department of history and coauthor of *Ditch of Dreams: The Cross Florida Barge Canal and the Struggle for Florida's Future*.

David Tegeder is associate professor of history at Santa Fe College, Gainesville, Florida, and coauthor of *Ditch of Dreams: The Cross Florida Barge Canal and the Struggle for Florida's Future*.

CPSIA information can be obtained
at www.ICGtesting.com
Printed in the USA
LVHW030908031221
705037LV00001B/5